D0713427

HISTORICAL DICTIONARIES OF RELIGIONS, PHILOSOPHIES, AND MOVEMENTS

Jon Woronoff, Series Editor

1. *Buddhism*, by Charles S. Prebish, 1993
2. *Mormonism*, by Davis Bitton, 1994. *Out of print. See no. 32.*
3. *Ecumenical Christianity*, by Ans Joachim van der Bent, 1994
4. *Terrorism*, by Sean Anderson and Stephen Sloan, 1995. *Out of print. See no. 41.*
5. *Sikhism*, by W. H. McLeod, 1995. *Out of print. See no. 59.*
6. *Feminism*, by Janet K. Boles and Diane Long Hoeveler, 1995. *Out of print. See no. 52.*
7. *Olympic Movement*, by Ian Buchanan and Bill Mallon, 1995. *Out of print. See no. 39.*
8. *Methodism*, by Charles Yrigoyen Jr. and Susan E. Warrick, 1996. *Out of print. See no. 57.*
9. *Orthodox Church*, by Michael Prokurat, Alexander Golitzin, and Michael D. Peterson, 1996
10. *Organized Labor*, by James C. Docherty, 1996. *Out of print. See no. 50.*
11. *Civil Rights Movement*, by Ralph E. Luker, 1997
12. *Catholicism*, by William J. Collinge, 1997
13. *Hinduism*, by Bruce M. Sullivan, 1997
14. *North American Environmentalism*, by Edward R. Wells and Alan M. Schwartz, 1997
15. *Welfare State*, by Bent Greve, 1998. *Out of print. See no. 63.*
16. *Socialism*, by James C. Docherty, 1997. *Out of print. See no. 73.*
17. *Bahá'í Faith*, by Hugh C. Adamson and Philip Hainsworth, 1998. *Out of print. See no. 71.*
18. *Taoism*, by Julian F. Pas in cooperation with Man Kam Leung, 1998
19. *Judaism*, by Norman Solomon, 1998. *Out of print. See no. 69.*
20. *Green Movement*, by Elim Papadakis, 1998. *Out of print. See No. 80.*
21. *Nietzscheanism*, by Carol Diethe, 1999. *Out of print. See No. 75.*
22. *Gay Liberation Movement*, by Ronald J. Hunt, 1999
23. *Islamic Fundamentalist Movements in the Arab World, Iran, and Turkey*, by Ahmad S. Moussalli, 1999

Historical Dictionary
of the Coptic Church

Gawdat Gabra

With contributions by Birger A. Pearson,
Mark N. Swanson, and Youhanna Nessim Youssef

*Historical Dictionaries of Religions,
Philosophies, and Movements, No. 84*

The Scarecrow Press, Inc.
Lanham, Maryland • Toronto • Plymouth, UK
2008

SCARECROW PRESS, INC.

Published in the United States of America
by Scarecrow Press, Inc.
A wholly owned subsidiary of
The Rowman & Littlefield Publishing Group, Inc.
4501 Forbes Boulevard, Suite 200, Lanham, Maryland 20706
www.scarecrowpress.com

Estover Road
Plymouth PL6 7PY
United Kingdom

British Library Cataloguing in Publication Information Available

Library of Congress Cataloging-in-Publication Data

Gabra, Gawdat.
  Historical dictionary of the Coptic Church / Gawdat Gabra ; with contributions
by Birger A. Pearson, Mark N. Swanson, and Youhanna Nessim Youssef.
    p. cm. — (Historical dictionaries of religions, philosophies, and movements ;
no. 84)
  Includes bibliographical references.
  ISBN-13: 978-0-8108-6097-1 (hardcover : alk. paper)
  ISBN-10: 0-8108-6097-X (hardcover : alk. paper)
  eISBN-13: 978-0-8108-6259-3
  eISBN-10: 0-8108-6259-X
  1. Coptic Church—History—Dictionaries. I. Pearson, Birger A. II. Swanson,
Mark N. III. Youssef, Youhanna Nessim. IV. Title.
  BX130.5.G33 2008
  281'.7203—dc22

2008003511

DEDICATION

To the memory of
Habib Girgis (1876–1951), a great Coptic reformer,
and Aziz Suryal Atiya (1898–1988),
chief editor of the *Coptic Encyclopedia*

Contents

Editor's Foreword

The Coptic Church is one of the oldest Christian churches and, although it is undergoing somewhat of a renaissance at present, it has long faced—and has had to overcome—considerable adversity. Initially subject to persecution by the Roman Empire, it was able to expand after Emperor Constantine accepted Christianity in 311. However, it repeatedly came under pressure from Byzantium and was on occasionally poor terms with both the Church in Constantinople and that in Rome. But such tension was nothing compared to the consequences of the Arab conquest of 639–641. Once covering all of Egypt and some surrounding areas, the Coptic Church's territory shrank from century to century, affected by actions that ranged from voluntary but strongly encouraged conversions to outright forced ones, with the Copts living until the present day under governments that at best tolerated them and at worst regarded them as enemies. Yet, over recent years, they have flourished in their Egyptian homeland with the creation of more monasteries and a growing interest in Coptic art, literature, and studies. Meanwhile, there has been a continuing diaspora that has resulted in new and sometimes thriving communities in the United States and Europe.

It is this long, complex, sometimes glorious, and sometimes tragic history that is summed up in the *Historical Dictionary of the Coptic Church*. The best starting point is the chronology, which casts a glance over nearly two millennia, marking the high points, the low points, and the turning points. The introduction then takes a broader, more analytical look at the situation of the Church in earlier centuries as well as an emphasis on the present day. Although it is a cursory glance, the introduction provides an excellent context in which to examine many of the details that are then expanded through several hundred dictionary entries. Some of these deal with outstanding figures of today and yesterday—patriarchs and monks, those who determined the mainstream and others who deviated, as well as the councils convened to decide important events of the day. Others look into the basic theology and practices of the Church, its organization and structure, several outstanding monasteries, its literature and liturgy, as well as other salient matters. An extensive bibliography is there for readers who want to follow up on any particular aspects to a greater depth.

This volume was written by one of the most prominent scholars in the field of Coptic studies, Gawdat Gabra. The former director of the Coptic Museum in Cairo, he is the chief editor of the St. Mark Foundation for Coptic History Studies and a member of the board of the Society of Coptic Archaeology. He has taught at various universities in Egypt and the United States and is presently at Claremont Graduate University in California. He has written extensively, and his work includes numerous articles and papers as well as several books, the most recent of which is *The Treasures of Coptic Art in the Coptic Museum and Churches of Old Cairo*. This historical dictionary, of quite a different nature from his other writings, is a further contribution to a lifetime devoted to furthering knowledge of the Coptic Church. In this effort, he was ably assisted on specific aspects by Birger A. Pearson, Mark N. Swanson, and Youhanna Nessim Youssef. Among them, they have covered the important bases and provided a reference book that will be very helpful for Copts wishing to know more about their own church and for outsiders who may finally realize just how important the Coptic Church is in the overall history of Christianity.

Jon Woronoff
Series Editor

Preface

Today, visitors to Egypt are encouraged not only to see its famous and imposing pharaonic monuments but also to enjoy its Christian legacy in many ancient Coptic churches and monasteries throughout Egypt as well as in Cairo's Coptic Museum. Beginning in the early 1960s, the Coptic Church experienced a marvelous renaissance. Its impressive heritage is now known, thanks to numerous publications and, above all, the *Coptic Encyclopedia*.

The Coptic Church's renaissance is most noticeable in the rejuvenation of monasticism, ecumenical activities, and theological discussions with other churches, the establishment of many new dioceses throughout Egypt, and expansion in North America, Australia, Europe, and Africa. The discovery of the Gnostic Coptic library of Nag Hammadi inspired a veritable boom of interest in Coptic studies, including the history of the Coptic Church, at many European and American universities and academic institutions. Exhibitions of Coptic art and artifacts in several European capitals such as Vienna, Paris, Munich, and Budapest resulted in a vastly heightened awareness of the literary and artistic heritage of the Copts worldwide.

The creation of the International Association for Coptic Studies in 1976 emboldened Aziz Suryal Atiya to solicit the assistance of scholars in order to fulfill his dream of a *Coptic Encyclopedia*. The appearance of this eight-volume work in 1991 played a crucial role in facilitating the research of scholars while at the same time providing nonspecialists with information on all aspects of Coptic civilization. Within a few years, however, the *Coptic Encyclopedia* went out of print. Unlike many other encyclopedias, this invaluable tool for Coptic studies is not available on the Internet—nor is there any "handy" one-volume reference work, accessible to the scholar, student, and modern reader interested in the history and heritage of the Coptic Church. Therefore, when Jon Woronoff, senior editor of the Scarecrow series of Historical Dictionaries, contacted me a few years ago to propose that I prepare a *Historical Dictionary of the Coptic Church*, I did not hesitate to accept his suggestion, despite my many other commitments.

The scope of this *Historical Dictionary*, covering nearly two millennia in a single volume, made it mandatory to be selective when choosing subjects to be covered and to exclude others entirely. Although the number of Coptic patriarchs and bishops had to be necessarily limited to those whose impact on the history of the Church was greatest, entries covering major themes such as monasticism and liturgy are comparatively numerous. Many Egyptian scholars who played a role in reforming the Church or in the education of the Copts are mentioned in this work, along with some non-Egyptian figures. The usefulness of the entries on the Coptic Church and its legacy presented in this concise format is enhanced by a bibliography—not only English titles but also many French, Italian, and German titles—in order to enhance the value of the volume and to direct readers to additional sources of information.

I take this opportunity to express my gratitude to three colleagues who contributed to this volume. Professor Birger A. Pearson is responsible for the texts on Gnosticism and the codices of Nag Hammadi. Professor Mark N. Swanson provided all entries relating to the Christian Arabic literature of the Copts. Dr. Youhanna Nessim Youssef assumed the task of preparing all the entries relating to the liturgy and theology of the Coptic Church, as well as the entry on hagiography.

I am also grateful to the Alexander von Humboldt Foundation and the Brigitte and Martin Krause Foundation, Germany, for two generous grants that freed me from other duties and made it possible for me to devote myself to the manuscript's preparation. In writing this volume, I have benefited from the library of the Institute of Egyptology and Coptology in Münster, Germany.

I am indebted to Dr. David Grafton and Howard Middleton-Jones for correcting my English.

Finally, my thanks are extended to the Scarecrow Press and to Jon Woronoff, senior editor, for publishing this volume.

Gawdat Gabra
Saint Mark Foundation for Coptic History Studies
Coptic Orthodox Patriarchate
Cairo

Acronyms and Abbreviations

AACC	All Africa Conference of Churches
A.H.	(anno hegirae) in the year of the hijra of the Islamic calendar.
A.M.	(*anno martyrum*) in the Coptic calendar
BG	Berlin Gnostic Library
BN	La Bibliothèque nationale de France (National Library of France)
CCR	Coptic Church Review
CE	Atiya, Aziz S. (editor in chief). *The Coptic Encyclopedia*, 8 volumes, New York: Macmillan, 1991
IACS	International Association for Coptic Studies
MECC	Middle East Council of Churches
NHC	Nag Hammadi Codices
UNESCO	United Nations Educational, Scientific and Cultural Organization
VP	Vita Plotini

Chronology

30 B.C.   Egypt was conquered by Octavian and became a Roman province, and the main source of grain for Rome in Roman times.

50–60 A.D.   The Gospel preached at Alexandria by St. Mark according to the fourth century *Ecclesiastical History* by Eusebius of Caesarea.

Ca. 120   Papyri first document the presence of Christians in Egypt.

Ca. 180   Foundation of the Catechetical School at Alexandria.

189–231   Patriarch Demetrius appoints three bishops in Egypt.

201   Emperor Septimius Severus issues an edict forbidding conversion to Christianity, resulting in the first persecution of believers in Egypt and endangering the Catechetical School of Alexandria.

250–260   First major persecutions of Christians initiated during the reign of Emperor Decius (249–251), and death sentence for those refusing to make sacrifices and libations to the emperor.

260   Edict temporarily puts an end to persecution.

Ca. 290   Foundation of the Fortress of Babylon by Emperor Diocletian.

303–311   Major administrative and economic reforms of Emperor Diocletian. He attempts to impose religious uniformity on the inhabitants of the entire empire in the form of emperor worship. The worst wave of persecution of Christians in Egypt is unleashed toward the end of Diocletian's reign (284–305). His accession to the throne marks the beginning of the "Era of Martyrs" (the Coptic calendar) because of the martyrdom of countless believers.

311   Emperor Constantine the Great accepts Christianity.

Ca. 313 St. Antony, the father of the monks, withdraws into the desert near the Red Sea.

313 Edict of Milan allows freedom of religion throughout the Roman Empire.

320s–330s Initial moves in Egypt toward the development of monasticism. St. Pachomius (292–346) establishes the first community of monks at Tabennisi in Upper Egypt.

325 First Ecumenical Council of Nicaea condemns the heresy of Arius and formulates the declaration of the faith (Nicene Creed).

328 Athanasius, an outspoken church leader who suffered five periods of exile because of his faith, becomes Patriarch of Alexandria. He wrote *The Life of St. Antony*, which introduced monasticism to the West. Athanasius' relations with several emperors are turbulent.

330 Byzantium, renamed Constantinople, becomes the capital of Eastern Christendom.

361–363 Emperor Julian (known as "the Apostate") tries to revive paganism.

392 Emperor Theodosius makes Christianity the official religion of the Roman Empire. Christians attack the Serapeum at Alexandria in 391.

395 Empire divided into Western and Eastern halves; the Eastern half includes Egypt.

415 Christians fear the influence of pagans and Jews in Alexandria and attack both groups. Synagogues in Alexandria are converted into churches. The philosopher Hypatia is killed.

431 Church Council at Ephesus. Cyril, Patriarch of Alexandria, formulates a doctrine that proposes a union of the manhood and divinity of Christ, emphasizing the role of the Holy Virgin Mary as Theotokos (God-bearer).

451 The Council of Chalcedon is summoned to resolve the continuing problems arising from the definition of the nature of Christ. The Patriarchs of Rome and Constantinople prefer the formulation that two natures, divine and human, coexist in Christ. A schism results when the

Egyptians reject this doctrine in preference to a belief in the single nature of Christ as formulated by Patriarch Cyril. Egypt's Christians split into an anti-Chalcedonian faction, representing the majority of believers, and a pro-Byzantine (Melchite) faction, supported by the emperor and the state.

476 Fall of Rome. Byzantium/Constantinople claims sovereignty over the empire in its entirety.

527 Justinian becomes emperor and reorganizes the administration of the empire. Foundation of the monastery in Sinai, known later as that of St. Catherine. Justinian's wife, Empress Theodora, supports the anti-Chalcedonians.

535–537 Closure of the last pagan temples in Egypt on the Island of Philae.

619–629 Persians occupy Egypt and destroy many monasteries.

629 Egypt reclaimed by Byzantium.

631–639 Persecution of the Copts under the Byzantine patriarch and civil governor. Coptic Patriarch Benjamin flees to Upper Egypt.

639–642 Arab invasion of Egypt, capture of Alexandria, and establishment of the first Islamic capital in Egypt, al-Fustat, north of the Fortress of Babylon. Egypt becomes a province of the Arab Islamic Empire. Beginning of Arab rule by governors appointed by the caliph of Medina. Copts are considered *dhimmis*—that is, "protected people"—in return for a payment of the poll tax in addition to the land tax

626–665 Benjamin, Patriarch of the Coptic Church, is in exile for 13 years (631–644) in Upper Egypt. He returns to Alexandria after the Arab occupation of Egypt and restores monasteries and churches.

661–750 Rule of the Umayyad caliphs from Damascus. Arabization of the administration by Umayyad Caliph Abdel-Malik (685–705). Weakening of the Coptic Church's economic and social status. Monks have to pay the poll tax for the first time in 705.

726–780/815–843 Iconoclasm in the Byzantine Church, apparently without effect on Christians in Egypt.

750–969   Abbasid caliphate, with Baghdad as the capital of the Islamic world. Egypt enjoys a certain degree of independence under the Tulunid and Ikhsid rulers. Copts occupy some important administrative offices.

832   Brutal crushing of the last Coptic revolt of the Bashmurites by Caliph al-Ma'mun and conversion of many Copts to Islam.

969–1171   Fatimid army invades Egypt from Tunisia. Foundation of al-Qahira (Cairo). The Fatimid caliphs are generally tolerant and Copts occupy important positions in the government.

996–1021   Interim persecution of Christians under the fanatic Caliph al-Hakim. Destruction of churches and monasteries.

11th century   Patriarch Christodoulus (1047–1077) moves his residence from Alexandria to Cairo to be closer to Egypt's ruler.

1099–1187   First Crusade, capture of Jerusalem, and the establishment of the Latin Kingdom of Jerusalem.

1131–1145   Patriarch Gabriel (Ibn Turayk) insists that bishops teach their people the doxology, the Lord's Prayer, and the Nicene Creed in Arabic, since many Copts no longer understand Coptic.

1168   Al-Fustat put to the torch to prevent its occupation by the invading Crusaders.

1187   Salah al-Din (Saladin), founder of the Ayyubid dynasty, recaptures Jerusalem.

Ca. 1249   Ayyubid authorities pull down the famous Cathedral of St. Mark in Alexandria on the pretext that the Crusaders might fortify themselves in it should they descend on Alexandria.

1250–1517   Mamluk dynasty rules Egypt. Successive waves of persecution of Copts with destruction of churches. Copts suffer sporadic violence, including plunder of goods and confiscation of properties. Mass conversions of Copts to Islam. Coptic finally dies out as a living language. Copto-Arabic literature flourishes at the beginning of this period.

1321   Muslims destroy, pillage, and burn over 60 of the main churches and monasteries throughout Egypt. Conversion of many Copts to Islam.

1453   End of the Byzantine Empire with the capture of Constantinople by the Ottoman Turks, who rename the city Istanbul.

1517–1798   Egypt becomes a province of the Ottoman Empire. Mamluk beys rule in effect under an Ottoman governor. Abandonment of the majority of Coptic monasteries. Transport of treasures and manuscripts, as well as skilled artisans, to Istanbul. Cairo looses its cultural significance. Some Copts such as Ibrahim al-Gohary (?–1795) enjoy high positions in the administration of the country. Construction, restoration, and renovation of many Coptic churches.

1745–1801   General Ya'qub forms the Coptic legion and defends the Coptic quarter in 1800 against Muslim mobs. He is the first Egyptian in modern times who spoke of an independent Egypt.

1798–1801   The French under Napoleon occupy Egypt. Their short stay in Egypt represents a turning point toward its modernization.

1801–1914   Egypt reverts to the Ottoman Empire. Mohammed Ali (1805–1848) modernizes Egypt. His dynasty rules Egypt until 1952. Copts flourish and restore their churches and monasteries.

1854–1861   Renewal of the Coptic Church under Patriarch Cyril IV, known as the Reformer. Foundation of modern Coptic schools. Regular theological discussions for the clergy. Import of the second printing press from Austria into Egypt. Restoration and renovation of many churches and monasteries. Completion of the reconstruction of the Old Coptic Cathedral of St. Mark at al-Ezbakiyah, Cairo.

1855   Abolition of the poll tax (*jizyiah*) imposed on the Copts by Muslim rulers. Copts attain full citizenship.

1875   Foundation of the Clerical College in Cairo.

1882   British occupation of Egypt, with the Ottomans retaining only nominal control over the country.

1910   Establishment of the Sunday School system and introduction of the study of the Christian religion to Coptic students in government schools by Habib Girgis (1876–1951).

1908   Marcus Simaika founds the Coptic Museum in Old Cairo.

1919 Revolution against the British occupation and national unity of Muslims and Copts under its leader, Sa'd Zaghlul.

1952 Forced abdication of King Farouk.

1953 Declaration of the Republic by Gamal Abd al-Nasser.

1954 Foundation of the Higher Institute of Coptic Studies.

1956 Nationalization of the Suez Canal.

1959–1971 Patriarch Cyril VI. The Coptic Church becomes a member of the World Council of Churches and the Middle East Council of Churches. Beginning of the monastic renaissance. Foundation of a few Coptic churches in America and Australia. Inauguration of the Cathedral of St. Mark by Patriarch Cyril and Ethiopian Emperor Haile Selassie I on the occasion of the transfer of the relics of St. Mark the Evangelist from Venice to Cairo.

1971– Pope Shenouda III. Repopulation of many of the abandoned monasteries and a remarkable renaissance in Coptic monasticism. Reorganization of the Church's institutions and establishment of many new dioceses. Expansion of the Coptic Church in the United States, Canada, Australia, Europe, and Africa. Excellent relations with other churches.

Introduction

Today's Copts, members of the Coptic Orthodox Church, comprise the largest Christian community in the Middle East. Unofficial sources estimate their number at 9 million or more. The term "Copt" and the adjective "Coptic" derive from *qibt*, an abbreviated, Arabic transliteration of the Greek word for the indigenous inhabitants of Egypt (Αἴγυπτος)/"aigyptioi" (Egyptians), itself a phonetic corruption of ancient Egyptian "Hikaptah," a name for Memphis, the ancient capital at the apex of the Nile Delta. After the Arab conquest of Egypt in 641, the term *qibt* came to distinguish the native Christians from the Muslim Arabs. When the majority of Egyptians converted to Islam during the following centuries, they naturally ceased to be Christians (*qibt*). The term "Copt" is relatively elastic as used in historical, ethnic, religious, cultural, and social contexts. Because some other churches that are in communion with Rome are also labeled "orthodox," scholars apply the phrase "Oriental Orthodox Churches" to those congregations from Egypt, Armenia, Ethiopia, Syria, and India that refused to acknowledge the Council of Chalcedon. Moreover, the term "Coptic" is also used to designate Christian minorities in Egypt who are members of the Roman Catholic Church and of various evangelical denominations to signal their ethnic identity as Egyptians.

HISTORY

Some historians consider a "Coptic period" of Egyptian history to date from the second century A.D., simultaneous with the formation of the Coptic language; others prefer the benchmark 451 A.D., the date of the Council of Chalcedon. The Arab conquest of Egypt in 643 A.D. is generally taken to mark the end of the Coptic period. Although Copts never ruled Egypt, they contributed, and still contribute today, to all aspects of Egypt's culture so that their history may be said to continue right down to the present.

The Coptic Church cherishes the memory of the Flight of the Holy Family into Egypt and maintains the tradition of their sojourn in the land of the Nile. It takes pride also in the tradition handed down by the fourth-century ecclesiastical historian Eusebius that St. Mark the Evangelist preached the Gospel in Alexandria in the mid-first century, and that he was the first Egyptian martyr. There is, however, very little concrete information documenting the spread of Christianity in the first century, for early Christianity is not archaeologically traceable in Egypt.

Christianity first gained a foothold in Alexandria where, beginning in the late second century, the first and foremost theological school, the Catechetical School, developed, led by great scholars such as Pantaenus, Clement, and Origen. By the end of that century, Christianity had begun to spread in Egypt, and Patriarch Demetrius consecrated the first three bishops. Because Christians refused to sacrifice to the emperor, they were regarded as a threat to the Roman Empire. Between 249 and 260, under the Roman emperors Decius and Valerian, Christians suffered major persecutions. The second wave of persecutions under Emperor Diocletian made such a lasting impression on Egyptian Christians that the Coptic calendar reckons dates even down to the present in terms of the "year of the martyrs" (A.M.) from Diocletian's accession in 284. The commemoration and veneration of martyrs is one of the main factors that enabled the Coptic Church to survive.

The Edict of Milan, issued in 313 by Emperor Constantine I, put an end to persecution and officially recognized the right of Christians to worship freely. Christianity continued to spread in Alexandria and the majority of its inhabitants became Christians in the second half of the fourth century. Alexander I, Patriarch of Alexandria (312–326), assembled about 100 bishops in a synod. Christianity grew in importance also in the hinterland, where about 80 percent of the population had turned to the new faith by the early fifth century.

Alexandria was one of the most important centers that contributed significantly to the formulation of the Christian doctrine. The patriarchs of that great city played a crucial role in the major theological controversies that shaped Christian dogma during the fourth and the fifth centuries. Patriarch Alexander I and his young deacon Athanasius

(328–373), who later became the most important Coptic patriarch of them all, were instrumental in identifying the heretical ideas of Arius, condemned at the Council of Nicaea in 325. The Nicene Creed, which survives to this day, was a result of that council. It expresses the orthodox belief that Christ and the Father are of one substance. At the Council of Ephesus in 431, Patriarch Cyril the Great opposed the theology of Patriarch Nestorius of Constantinople and championed the role of the Virgin Mary as "God-bearer." During the fifth century, the struggle over this fundamental issue proved decisive for the history of Christianity in Egypt. Following the Council of Chalcedon in 451, the dispute over the nature of Christ led to an irresolvable schism and to bloodshed between the Christians in Egypt and those in Byzantium. The patriarchs of Alexandria refused to accept what has been called the Chalcedonian Definition of Faith. By that time, monasticism was flourishing in the Egyptian deserts, and monasteries began to provide the Coptic Church with its spiritual leaders.

During the doctrinal conflict, the Byzantine emperors wanted to fill the See of Alexandria with men who accepted the Chalcedonian Definition, rewarding their loyalty to Constantinople with military support. The Copts and the wealthy monastic establishments backed the opposing patriarch, who often had to leave Alexandria in order to avoid persecution at the hands of the Byzantine authorities. The Persian occupation of Egypt (619–629) brought more difficulties for the Coptic Church. Sources speak of the destruction of more than 600 monastic establishment by the Persian army. The situation deteriorated further when Byzantium appointed Cyrus in 631 as both civil and ecclesiastical head of the country. Cyrus pursued the Coptic Patriarch Benjamin, who fled for 14 years to Upper Egypt.

This wave of Byzantine oppression did not last long, for the Arab army invaded Egypt in 639 and occupied the entire country within two years. The Arab occupation undoubtedly had immeasurable consequences for the history of the Coptic Church. At first, the conquerors respected the Christian community as "people of the Book" or *dhimmis*, and Patriarch Benjamin was encouraged to return to Alexandria. He restored churches and monasteries, but the building of new churches was prohibited.

During the first few decades of the Arab settlement in Egypt, Copts were appointed to most of the high administrative positions in the country, but in later centuries the higher offices were delegated only to Muslims. The principal concern of the Muslim rulers, like their Roman predecessors, was the efficient collection of taxes, irrespective of any other consideration. Copts were obliged to pay a supplementary tax known as the *jizyiah* or poll tax. Initially, monasteries were exempt from this poll tax, but beginning in 705, the monks, too, were obliged to pay it.

When the tax burden became unendurable at times in the eighth and ninth centuries, Copts revolted. However, their rebellions were successfully put down. It seems that the brutal suppression of the last Bashmurite revolt in 832 by the Abbasid Caliph al-Ma'mun resulted in the conversion of a considerable segment of the Coptic population. The dress code imposed for the first time on Copts during the rule of Caliph al-Mutawakkil (847–861) could not have been implemented were Egypt predominantly a Christian country. Moreover, the Church's economy as well as its institutions, and especially the monasteries, had been weakened long before that time. The social status of the Copts, including patriarchs and bishops, had also been considerably lowered.

Initially, the capital of the Islamic caliphal government was at Medina; in 661, it shifted to Damascus, and from Damascus to Baghdad in 750. The caliphs sent governors to rule Egypt. It was not until 870 that Ahmed Ibn Tulun made himself independent of the Abbasid caliph. In general, the Tulunids (870–905), the Ikhshids (935–969), and the Fatimids (969–1171) were tolerant toward the Christian communities. The Shi'ite Fatimid caliphs in particular appointed Copts to the most important positions and allowed them to receive the highest honors. The only exception was Caliph Al-Hakim (996–1021), who ordered the sacking of monasteries and churches and dismissed Copts from government offices. They suffered humiliation and were compelled to wear wooden crosses weighing at least five pounds and distinctive clothing. The Fatimids resided in Cairo, the new city that they established to the north of al-Fustat. It was Patriarch Christodoulus (1047–1077) who moved the patriarchate from Alexandria to the Church of al-Mu'allqa in Old Cairo in order to be near the seat of government, although he—and his successors as well—continued to be known as the Patriarch of Alexandria.

The arrival of the Crusaders in the Holy Land had long-lasting negative consequences for the Christians in the entire region. Syrian Christians fled to Egypt to take refuge with their coreligionists. But in

Egypt itself, the Crusaders did not distinguish between Muslims and the anti-Chalcedonian Christians; Copts were adjudged heretics. At the same time, Crusader victories led to severe retaliatory actions against the Copts, for Muslim rulers did not distinguish between the indigenous Christians and the invaders. When Egypt's first Ayyubid ruler, Salah al-Din (Saladin, 1171–1193), came to power, he dismissed Copts from governmental offices. He obliged all Copts to wear distinctive dress and forbade them to ride horses. The great Cathedral of St. Mark in Alexandria was destroyed on the pretext that the Crusaders might fortify it should they take the city. However, the Ayyubid sultans (1171–1250) were in general relatively tolerant of the Copts, so that in 1218 the Egyptian Christians joined forces with them to battle the Crusaders who had captured the northeastern Delta town of Damietta.

The Mamluks were slaves brought mainly from the region of the Caspian and Black Seas, sold and trained in Egypt as soldiers. They assumed power in 1250 and ruled Egypt until 1517. The fortunes of the Copts declined steadily throughout this period, and by the time of the Ottoman invasion, their situation was catastrophic. They were often dismissed from government offices. Humiliating rules and regulations were frequently enforced. Persecution and conversions to Islam accelerated the dwindling of the size of the Coptic community. Many Christian houses of worship were pulled down under the Mamluks. On one day in 1321, fanatic Muslims sacked and burned over 60 of the main churches and monasteries throughout Egypt. The art of wall painting with its long tradition in Coptic monasteries and churches deteriorated remarkably and finally ceased during this era.

The influence of the Mamluks continued even after the Ottoman conquest of Egypt in 1517. Their leaders served as provincial beys, ruling in effect under an Ottoman governor until the early 19th century. Some Copts occupied significant positions under Mamluk beys; one of them was Ibrahim al-Gawhari (d. 1795), who served as finance minister and was able to restore many Coptic monasteries and churches, as well as to construct new churches. Although the vast majority of Egypt's inhabitants endured one of the most impoverished periods under Ottoman rule, life as a Copt was less miserable than it had been under the Mamluks. At least Christians were left to lead a relatively peaceful existence trying to preserve what remained of their ancestors' religious legacy. A significant factor that sustained the existence of the Copts under the

Mamluk and Ottoman rules was their success in financial administration, coupled with a comparatively pacific disposition.

The French Campaign of 1798–1801 under Napoleon Bonaparte was a watershed: Egypt turned decisively toward modernization. The new ruler of the country, Mohammed Ali (1805–1849), enlisted foreign expertise, established new industries, and introduced new crops and effective irrigation systems. Mohammed Ali and most of his descendants encouraged all Egyptians, regardless of their religious identity, to build a modern Egypt. Copts began to flourish during the 19th century, and in 1855 the poll tax (*jizyiah*), which centuries of Muslim rule had imposed on them, was lifted. The revival was visible in the cultural movement within the Coptic Church initiated by Patriarch Cyril IV (1854–1861). Known as the Reformer, he established many modern Coptic schools, including one for girls in Cairo, and paid special attention to the teaching of foreign languages as well as Arabic and Coptic, and he imported a printing press from Europe.

The contribution of the Coptic elite, educated in the West and in Egypt, to the remarkable economic and cultural development the country experienced during the first half of the 20th century was considerable. The cultured laity's attempt to establish a more democratic system in Coptic community affairs and in the management of Church properties, however, met with less success. In 1910, Egypt's prime minister, Butros Ghali, a Copt, was assassinated by a Muslim partisan of the Nationalist Party. This crime led to serious clashes between Copts and Muslims. National unity was achieved only by the revolution of 1919, which pitted both against the British occupation. The emblem of this uprising—a crescent enclosing a cross—reflected the bond between Muslims and Copts who were exiled with the revolution's leader, Sa'd Zaghlul, and jailed for their part in the struggle for independence. Undoubtedly, Sa'd Zaghlul succeeded in unifying Muslims and Copts in his Wafd party. In 1923, Copts comprised nearly 44 percent of its executive committee. The three decades following the revolution of 1919 represent a liberal period that was characterized by excellent relations between Muslims and Copts.

By contrast, Copts faced many difficulties in the second half of the 20th century. Under the regime of President Gamal Abd al-Nasser (1952–1970), many wealthy Christian families lost their real estate and other property. His land reform also weighed heavily on the Coptic patriarchate and on landholding Coptic monasteries. Copts were dramatically underrepresented in high governmental positions, in the army, and on the faculties of universities. A few "token" Copts were nominated to sit in Parliament to demonstrate that they were represented in the political structure. But for all practical purposes, Copts no longer played a role in politics. Matters became progressively worse during the regime of President Anwar al-Sadat (1970–1981), who furthered the Islamization of national life and favored extreme Islamists, whose influence had greatly increased, particularly at universities. Moreover, he instigated Parliament's adoption of an amendment to the constitution making the Shari'a (Islamic law) the principal foundation of legislation in Egypt.

This amendment, which had already affected many aspects of the Egyptians' everyday existence, represents a sword directed against the Copts. Muslim militants plundered and set fire to Coptic shops, especially jewelers and pharmacies at al-Minya and Assiut, and attacked churches in villages throughout Upper Egypt. When bloody riots resulted in the torching of three churches at al-Zawya al-Hamra, Cairo, in 1981, Pope Shenouda canceled Easter celebrations as a sign of protest. Sadat issued a presidential decree ordering the patriarch of the Coptic Church to retire in Wadi al-Natrun under what was effectively "monastery" arrest. Pope Shenouda was allowed to return to his seat in Cairo only in January 1985. According to statistics compiled by the Center for Egyptian Human Rights, Muslim fundamentalists have committed 561 acts of violence against Copts since 1994. In the past 25 years, militants attempted to assassinate a number of ministers, slaughtered foreign tourists, and attacked churches in their insurgency against the Egyptian government under President Hosni Mubarak. Most Muslim politicians and intellectuals strongly condemn these criminal activities, which have contributed to the emigration of large numbers of Copts to the United States, Canada, and Australia since the 1960s.

HIERARCHY AND ADMINISTRATION

After the Council of Chalcedon in 451, the Coptic Church became a national institution. The hierarchy established at that time has been maintained independently until the present. Throughout its long history, the authority of the patriarch has been understood to continue in a direct line of apostolic succession. The Coptic patriarchs are the successors of St. Mark, just as the monks are the spiritual descendants of the martyrs. Thus Pope Shenouda III is the 117th Patriarch of Alexandria and the 116th successor to St. Mark. The patriarch bears the title "Pope and Patriarch of the great city of Alexandria and of all Egypt, the Pentapolis, Nubia, the Sudan, Libya, Ethiopia, and all Africa, and all countries of the preaching of St. Mark."

The patriarch presides over the Holy Synod, which is the supreme ecclesiastical authority, responsible for the protection of the faith, the preservation of tradition, and the Church's welfare. It is made up of all the Church's bishops. The hierarchy and administration of the Coptic Church is based on the traditional system of bishop, priest, and deacon. The number of bishops varies from time to time, according to the size of the Christian community and the economic state of the Church. The patriarch, traditionally the bishop of both Alexandria and Cairo, is responsible for vacant dioceses. He ordains bishops, usually after they are chosen by their congregations. The vast majority of bishops come from the monastic milieu. It was Patriarch Athanasius of Alexandria (328–373), who first encouraged monks to be ordained as bishops. The dioceses of Egypt usually enjoyed a considerable measure of autonomy. The Church observed Canon 15 of the Council of Nicaea, which forbade the practice of transferring bishops. Throughout the history of the Coptic Church, bishops have stood united behind their patriarchs, supporting them especially in difficult times, except in a few exceptional cases when a bishop cooperated with Muslim rulers against the patriarch. The Coptic priest has nearly all the same duties as the bishop, with the exception of ordination and a few other functions such as the consecration of icons.

WORLD PERCEPTIONS

On 23 October 2001 the Roman Catholic Pope John Paul II was received by Pope Shenouda III in his papal residence that looks out on the Cathedral of St. Mark. The relics of St. Mark are housed in his shrine, which lies behind the cathedral. They were transferred from Venice to Cairo at the order of the Vatican in 1968 as a conciliatory gesture intended to cement goodwill and new relations between the churches of

Rome and Alexandria. Nonetheless, conditioned by history, the Coptic Church seems rather cautious when dealing with "Western Christians." Many unsuccessful endeavors were made before the second half of the past century to bridge the gap between Rome and the Copts. The first, at the Council of Florence (1439–1443), was followed by other attempts during the pontificate of the Coptic patriarchs Gabriel VII (1559–1565), John XIV (1570–1585), Gabriel VIII (1586–1601), Matthew IV (1660–1675), and John XVI (1676–1718) to persuade the Coptic Church to defer to Rome. The Copts apparently preferred a union based in love and so rejected a strict legal subjugation to Rome. In other words, the popes of Rome demanded obedience from the Copts, who held out for the status of an equal partner. Despite the persecution of the Coptic Church and its very critical financial state, its patriarchs did not show any enthusiasm for a union with Rome.

In Ottoman times, Franciscan friars came to Cairo while the Jesuits settled in Upper Egypt. They succeeded only in the conversion of some individual Copts to Roman Catholicism—in 1683 and 1684 the conversion of four men and more than eight women is documented—but not in their greater goal of a union between the two churches. In 1824 Pope Leo XII of Rome consecrated Abraham Khashur as bishop for the Catholic Copts. The introduction of Catholicism to Egypt profited from the political influence of the French advisors in the government of Egypt's ruler Mohammed Ali (1805–1848), who endeavored to unite the Coptic Church with the Church of Rome. He commanded his Coptic secretary and head of finances, Mu'allim Ghali, and his son to proselytize. In 1895, Rome extended its pretensions to superiority over the Coptic Church by establishing a Catholic patriarchate in Alexandria. Cyril Macarius, the new "Coptic" papal nuncio, issued circular letters inviting the priests and congregations of the Coptic Church to recognize the authority of the Roman pope. Beginning in 1879 the Jesuits and the Franciscans founded many seminaries, colleges, and schools throughout Egypt, which benefited the Coptic Catholic community.

The attempt of the Russian Archimandrite to "realize the union between the Orthodox Church and the Jacobite Copts" in 1845 proved unsuccessful. When the Russian ambassador to Egypt offered Patriarch Peter VII (1809–1852) the protection of the tsar, the patriarch thanked him, saying that no other protection was needed than God's own.

The Presbyterian Church of North America began missionary activities in Egypt in 1854. Less than a decade later, in 1863, the Egyptian Presbytery founded a theological school to prepare Egyptian pastors for evangelical work. Beginning in 1882 the Church Missionary of England supported the efforts of the Presbyterian Church in Egypt. Their initial aim was to preach the Gospel to Muslims. But having soon discovered the dangers involved in this virtually impossible task, they turned to proselytizing Copts, who admired the simplicity and clarity of their preaching and benefited from the excellent educational opportunities and social services that the missionaries provided.

Although the two Catholic and Protestant minor communities contributed to some extent to the modern awakening of the Coptic Orthodox Church from centuries of lethargy under Mamluk and Ottoman rule, their primary purpose of preaching the Gospel to Egyptian Muslims changed to proselytizing Orthodox Copts, whose fathers had kept their faith for centuries, surviving repeated waves of persecution. Therefore, it is no wonder that the Coptic Church felt unfairly challenged by "Western Christians."

The current pope, Shenouda III, was instrumental in overcoming centuries of silence by initiating ecumenical activities. In 1973, he and Roman Catholic Pope Paul VI issued a joint statement of Christology in Rome that has led to further dialogue between the two churches. Pope Shenouda visited the Archbishop of Canterbury in 1979, who returned the favor with a trip to Egypt in 1987. Their joint communiqué confirmed the Nicene Creed as the basis of faith. Pope Shenouda called for a meeting between the Coptic Evangelical Community Council and Coptic Orthodox theologians, which took place in 1988 at his monastic residence in the Monastery of St. Pshoi, Wadi al-Natrun. Such fruitful meetings are repeated frequently. The Coptic Church has been an active member of the Church Council of the Middle East since its establishment in 1974 and of the World Councils of Churches since 1954.

CURRENT GEOGRAPHICAL EXTENT

Reliable statistics concerning the Coptic population are unavailable, and any attempt to estimate the number of Copts living in Egypt must be made with extreme caution, especially since a vast discrepancy exists between the figures provided by the Egyptian government and those originating with Church authorities. Unfortunately, the governmental census does not accurately reflect the number of Christians. In 1975 the figures issued by the Egyptian government placed the number of Copts at 2.3 million, while the Coptic Church counted 6.6 million or nearly three times as many. In 2000 the Coptic Church claimed its community numbered 9,817,000.

The tally of Copts who left Egypt for the West in the second half of the 20th century, primarily because of economic and political discrimination, has been estimated at between 400,000 and 1 million. A sizable proportion of them emigrated to avoid the Islamization of Egypt's national life and the increasing influence of Muslim fundamentalists under Sadat. The majority of Copts abroad live in North America and Australia. There are 125 churches in the United States, 27 in Canada, and 37 in Australia and New Zealand. Many other Coptic churches were established in Europe, South America, Africa, and Asia. These congregations are served by Coptic priests with a number of local bishops. The latter are consecrated by Pope Shenouda III, who is keen to strengthen the ties between the "Mother Church" and the "churches in the lands of emigration."

PRESENT AND FUTURE CHALLENGES

The 21st century has not brought any improvement in the lives of the Copts in Egypt. Primary evidence of discrimination is provided by the many restrictions placed on the construction of churches. Procedures to acquire permission to build are notoriously long, sometimes lasting for decades. It is indeed ridiculous that not a single Egyptian university has a Department of Coptic Studies; the American University in Cairo boasts the only academic "minor" in the field. Copts still suffer discrimination, particularly regarding appointments to governmental positions of influence, such as those of provincial governor, city manager, university president, and director of educational districts. Copts are rarely promoted in the ranks of the police or within the army. The new policy of President Sadat in the early 1970s empowered Islamic extremism and led to the reemergence of the Muslim Brotherhood, which now claims 25 percent of the seats in Parliament. This movement strives to implement the Shari'a and to apply it to every aspect of daily life. Instances of Islamic fundamentalist attacks on Coptic churches and the plundering or burning of their properties after the Friday prayer service occur from time to time in the absence of effective protection by government agencies.

The time has come for Copts to become politically active after decades of their effective exclusion from the political life and institutions following the revolution of 1952. They should seek cooperation with those moderate Muslim politicians and intellectuals who strongly condemn the criminal activities of Muslim fundamentalists. Such cooperation is imperative to improving the educational program of schools and universities and to fostering understanding and peaceful social relations between Muslims and Copts in and by means of the mass media. The modernization of the educational and cultural institutions of the Coptic Church will be indispensable in facing the challenges of the decades to come.

THE DICTIONARY

– A –

ABARKAH. Eucharistic wine. An Arabic corruption of the Greek word *aparche*, which means "beginning of a sacrifice" or "first fruit." Coptic tradition uses this word for the Eucharistic wine in order to highlight the symbolism of Christ as our sacrifice and the first raised among mankind. This wine is either made from dried raisins or grapes. It is noteworthy to mention that wine has played an important role in the life of the Coptic community. The site of the **Monastery of St. Jeremiah** at Saqqara contains a **liturgical** calendar indicating the quality of wine issued for each feast.

'ABD AL-MASIH AL-ISRA'ILI (late 10th c.). Apologist. According to the title of his *Book of Induction* (*Kitab al-istidlal*), 'Abd al-Masih was a Jew of al-Raqqah who was led to Christianity by the famous Christian physician Mansur ibn Sahlan (d. ca. 1004), who flourished under the early Fatimid caliphs. A précis (by Samir Khalil, "'Abd al-Masih") of 'Abd al-Masih's unpublished book suggests that it is a compendium of arguments for the truth of the Christian faith (in particular, the doctrines of the Trinity, the **Incarnation**, and the Crucifixion of Christ), much of it gathered from earlier Arabic Christian literature from outside Egypt. The arguments range from the standard "proofs" for the true religion through prophecies and miracles to sophisticated apologetic exploitation of notions found in the (relatively recent) Arabic translations of Greek philosophical and mathematical works. As 'Abd al-Masih becomes better known, he will undoubtedly gain in stature as a pioneer of Arabic Christian apologetic literature in Egypt.

'ABD AL-MASIH, YASSA (1889–1959). He taught in the **Clerical College** and the **Higher Institute of Coptic Studies** and served as the librarian of the **Coptic Museum**. He was a competent scholar who specialized in **Copto-Arabic literature** and the **Coptic language**. He strove for the preservation of the manuscripts of many monasteries and old churches. He prepared some catalogs of the manuscripts in his own handwriting, such as those of the libraries of the **Monastery of St. Antony** and the **Monastery of St. Paul**. With Marcus Simaka Pasha he published the *Catalogue of the Coptic and Arabic Manuscripts in the Coptic Museum, the Patriarchate, the Principal Churches of Cairo and Alexandria and the Monasteries of Egypt*, in two volumes, 1939–1942.

ABLUTION. The ablution, or washing of the hands, is performed by the **priest** twice during the liturgy. The first occurs just before the offering of the bread. The minister (priest or **bishop**) washes his hands and recites from Psalms 50:7–8 or 25:6–7, according to the majority of the manuscripts, although some manuscripts prescribe that he recites Psalm 50:7–10. The second ablution is during the recitation of the **Creed**. The minister again washes his hands and recites the same psalms.

ABSOLUTION. The Absolution is a prayer recited by a **priest** begging from God the remission of the sins of the people or of an individual repentant in accordance with the authority given in the Gospels (Matt. 16:18, 18:18; John 20:23). In the **Coptic language**, the word for this prayer means "freedom." A special feast for the Absolution took place in Middle Egypt, where we find that Christ promised the saint that he will tear up the deed of their (the faithful's) sins. The Absolution is an integral part of any liturgical church service. It is recited during the offering of **incense** (**Vespers** and **Matins**), the mass, the ceremony of matrimony, the **Unction of the Sick**, the **genuflection**, the Liturgy of the Water of the Basin, the burial services, and baptism. On many occasions, the priest reads the Absolution inaudibly. Some Absolutions are addressed to the Son, while others are addressed to God the Father. The former are likely to date from the sixth and seventh centuries when Egyptian monks started to address prayers to the Son. It is important to mention that the priest recites the Absolution after the confession of the repentant.

ABSTINENCE. *See* FASTING.

ABU AL-MAKARIM. *See HISTORY OF THE CHURCHES AND MONASTERIES OF EGYPT.*

ABU DAQN, YUSUF (ca. 1565–ca. 1630). Linguist and historian. He was sent by **Patriarch** Gabriel VIII (1586–1601) to Rome in 1595, at a time when the Church of Rome attempted to reestablish a union with the Coptic Church under its authority. Abu Daqn did not return to Egypt and instead became a Catholic. In Rome, he learned Greek, Latin, Hebrew, Syriac, and Chaldean, in addition to Arabic, his mother tongue, and Coptic, the language of the liturgy of the Coptic Church. He also learned Italian, Spanish, and French. Around 1600 he was appointed a translator at the court of King Henry IV. In 1603, he began to teach Arabic at Oxford University, where he compiled, in Latin, a history of the Coptic Church that appeared in 1675, long after his death. It was translated into English by Sir Edward Sadleir and published in London in 1733. Abu Daqn copied Coptic liturgical texts, probably to use them in his teaching at Oxford, where he remained for 10 years. He prepared an Arabic-Latin lexicon and other volumes in Arabic in Belgium, and taught Hebrew at Louvain. He sojourned in Munich from 1618 to 1620, where he worked At the Grand Ducal Library.

ABU AL-MAJD IBN YU'ANNIS (?–before 1357). Priest, theologian. Abu al-Majd ibn Yu'annis was a priest of Minyat Bani Khasib (present-day Minya) in Middle Egypt. The dates—and even the century—of his activity are not known, although the oldest dated manuscript of his work (from 1357) provides a *terminus ad quem* (a final limiting point in time). At the request of one **Bishop** Ghubriyal of Qus, he wrote a *Commentary on the Creed* that, in response to Jewish objections to Christian use of a nonbiblical text, provides Old Testament *testimonia* for every clause in the symbol of Nicaea (the **Nicene Creed**). Abu al-Majd also on occasion quotes from the

Qur'an and from the Greek sages, which perhaps indicates that he had wider apologetic and catechetical goals for the work.

As Samir has pointed out ("Abu al-Majd," 21), Abu al-Majd's concentration on the Old Testament neatly complements other Copto-Arabic commentaries on the Creed: that of **Sawirus ibn al-Muqaffa'**, written against the background of **Christological** controversy with the Melchites and **Nestorians**, and that of Abu al-Barakat **ibn Kabar** in the second chapter of his encyclopedia, *The Lamp of the Darkness*, which consists largely of quotations from the New Testament.

ABU MINA. A most significant **pilgrimage** center of the Late Antique period. It is located about 45 kilometers southwest of **Alexandria** near Lake Mareotis, where the tomb of St. **Menas** was venerated from the fourth century onward. According to a tradition, St. Menas was an Egyptian recruit in the Roman army who was martyred because of his Christian faith. When a spring of healing water appeared at the tomb site, pilgrims flocked to his shrine. Byzantine emperors erected splendid buildings there. The huge pilgrimage center flourished from the fourth to the eighth century. Its vestiges include churches, colonnaded avenues, arches, streets, several public buildings, hostels, baths, markets, and presses for both wine and oil. The shrine of St. Menas became the Lourdes of ancient times. People came from all over the world, taking home the famous Menas flasks, which were found not only in Egypt but also in Europe. The flasks are decorated with St. Menas between two camels.

ABU SALIH THE ARMENIAN. *See HISTORY OF THE CHURCHES AND MONASTERIES OF EGYPT.*

ABU SALIH YU'ANNIS (late 10th or early 11th c.). Canonist. Abu Salih Yu'annis (or Yunis) ibn 'Abdallah prepared a collection of canon law (in 48 headings) by gathering materials from (probably) Coptic sources and translating them into Arabic. This work was incorporated into the canonical compendium of the monk **Maqara** (active before 1350), who reports that he found it in a manuscript dated to 1028. If this is correct, then Abu Salih becomes one of the pioneers of Copto-Arabic canonical literature, a figure marking the beginning of a trajectory that finds its culmination in the work of **al-Safi ibn al-'Assal** or of Maqara, two and three centuries later respectively.

ACT OF PETER **(BG, 4)**. A Coptic translation of a narrative featuring Peter's healing activity on a certain Sunday, presumably in Jerusalem. Surprisingly, Peter reverses the healing of his invalid daughter in order to preserve her virginity. This narrative was probably part of the lost beginning portion of the apocryphal *Act of Peter* composed in Greek in the second century.

ACTS OF PETER AND THE TWELVE APOSTLES **(NHC VI, 1).** An account of the adventures of Peter and his companion Apostles on a journey taken by them after Jesus' resurrection. In the text, Peter meets a pearl merchant named Lithargoel, and at his bidding, Peter and his companions go to Lithargoel's city. Lithargoel turns out to be the risen Christ, who commissions them for ministry. The title appears at the end of the tractate. Extant only in Coptic, *Acts of Peter and the Twelve Apostles* was composed in Greek. It resembles other apocryphal Acts produced in the second and third centuries. Its provenance is uncertain.

ADAM. The tune to which hymns are sung on Sundays, Mondays, and Tuesdays. The name is taken from the first word of the verse of the **Theotokia** for Monday: "Adam was yet sorrowful of heart."

AJBIYAH. *See* CANONICAL HOURS.

AL-AS'AD IBN AL-'ASSAL (?–before 1259). Biblical scholar, theologian, scholar of Coptic. Al-As'ad Abu al-Faraj Hibatallah ibn al-'Assal was probably the eldest of the **Awlad al-'Assal**. He was married, a skilled scribe, an avid collector of books, and a frequent traveler to Damascus; he may well have been a civil servant in the Ayyubid administration. The only sure dates that we possess for him concern two of his compositions. An early work, *The Treatise on the Soul*, was written in 1231. Al-As'ad's masterwork was composed two decades later, in 1252–1253: a new Arabic translation of the Gospels, made after collating the various Coptic and Arabic translations in use by the different Christian communities of his day (including Arabic translations made from Greek and from Syriac), and supplied with an apparatus reporting readings or translations different from his own. The resulting text is elegant and much superior to the standard Arabic translation of the Gospels from Coptic (the so-called Egyptian Vulgate), but was never accepted into general use. Despite the fact that al-As'ad's translation of the Gospels continues to attract attention and admiration, no critical edition of it has yet been published.

Al-As'ad's bibliography contains a number of other works, including a Coptic grammar, a work on the epact calculation (for working out the date of Easter), and poetic summaries of inheritance and marriage laws. He also assisted the monk Da'ud (the future **patriarch Cyril III**) ibn Laqlaq and **Bulus al-Bushi** in the composition of their *Book of Confession*.

ALEXANDER I, PATRIARCH. He was the 19th **patriarch** of the See of St. Mark (312–326). He succeeded Achillas in the year 312 A.D., just after the end of the great persecution. Alexander faced three problems during his episcopate. He was first troubled over the timing of the Easter observance by a schismatic faction led by a certain Erescentius. Alexander was obliged to write a special treatise on this paschal controversy, referring to previous patristic declarations by Dionysius the Great. This matter remained a sore point until it was settled by the **bishops** at the **Council of Nicaea** in 325. The second problem that faced the patriarch occurred at Lycopolis in Upper Egypt, where Bishop Melitius, who had been calumniating Achillas (his predecessor), continued to do the same to Alexander. This culminated in Melitius lodging a formal complaint against Alexander before the imperial court under Constantine, but the court paid no great attention to it. More seriously, Melitius seems to have established a kind of alliance with the most dangerous of the patriarch's adversaries, **Arius**. Further, Melitius consecrated his own schismatic bishops, ignoring his ecclesiastical superior. The **Melitian schism** remained in full force until it was temporarily settled at Nicaea in 325 A.D. through the wisdom of the patriarch, who made a compromise in order to win the bishop back to the fold, thus ending Melitius' alliance with Arius. The third problem that faced Alexander was the most dangerous of all heretical movements: that of Arius, who was excommunicated by **Peter I**, only to be readmitted by Achillas and appointed as presbyter of the most ancient of the **Alexandrian** churches, at Bucalis. The church was located in the most populous district of the metropolis, where Arius could exercise a great influence on the Christian population. Arius ran as a rival to Alexander at the time of his elevation to the episcopate. Open hostilities between the two broke out when Alexander declared the unity of the Trinity in one of his sermons. Arius at once branded his declaration as mere **Sabellianism**. Since the Father created the Son of God, he argued, the Son could not be coeternal with his Father. This was the beginning of a long argument, which the future heresiarch enlarged to frightening dimensions as he acquired the support of increasing numbers of followers.

Literature and Works. Alexander I is represented most fully in **Eusebius'** *Historia ecclesiastica*. He is also mentioned in the lives and encomiums of his successor, **Athanasius** the Apostolic. These accounts tend to present Alexander in the shadow of his great successor who, as his secretary, would have led the struggle against Arius and his disciples, both at Alexandria and at the Council of Nicaea, if Alexander had not taken the initiative. Of his works, only one collection of letters related to the Arian controversy was known in antiquity, and of these, only two letters have survived. Also, a homily, *De anima et corpore* (On the Soul and the Body), is ascribed to him in a Syriac version, but the Coptic version attributes this work to Athanasius. **Coptic literature** attributes to Alexander an *Encomium of Peter the Alexandrian*, known in five codices: VC62.10 (Bohairic, ninth century), VC62.8 (Bohairic, two fragments, ninth century), and three fragmentary codices from the **White Monastery**. There is also an elaborated Arabic translation to be found in the chapter concerning Alexander in the *History of the Patriarchs*. It is possible to reconstruct the original redaction of this encomium by comparing the various versions in existence. It must have been composed of three segments, characterized as follows: a literary prologue; the main body, which recounts his birth, life, and martyrdom, with vivid descriptions of the many miracles wrought at his birth, during his life, and after his death; and a literary epilogue. Except for a few minor variations, the Sahidic and Bohairic redactions are similar, save that the Bohairic version has excluded the martyrdom and posthumous miracles.

The text appears to be a typical, late construction, filled with biblical allusions, vague traditions, and the portrayal of Peter's Passion. The complexity of the literary structure, the theological competence, and the style make it one of the best examples of literature of this period, and probably one of the first whose date can be proposed as being at the first half of the seventh century.

ALEXANDRIA. Founded in 331 B.C. by Alexander the Great at the western end of the Nile Delta. An Egyptian town, Rakote, already existed there on the shore and was a fishermen's resort. From its very beginning, Alexandria developed rapidly into one of the world's great cities. The city replaced Memphis as the capital of Egypt under the Ptolemies and became a great center of Hellenism and Semitism. The foundation of the famous library of Alexandria by Ptolemy II (283–244 B.C.) made the city the cultural center of the Mediterranean world for many centuries. According to one tradition, it was Ptolemy II who instigated the work in the Septuagint (the Greek translation of the Torah) for the library at Alexandria, where a Jewish community flourished during the centuries immediately preceding the birth of Christ. The Jewish thinker and exegete Philo (ca. 20 B.C.–50 A.D.) was the most important figure among the Hellenistic Jews in the first century. Alexandria was a cosmopolitan city with a large number of Greek inhabitants.

Alexandria is undoubtedly the cradle of Egyptian Christianity, where the famous **Catechetical School** was established in the second century and became a leading center of the allegorical method of biblical interpretation. The first Egyptian Christians undoubtedly spoke Greek. According to the church historian Eusebius, St. **Mark** the Evangelist arrived at Alexandria in 43 A.D. and preached the Gospel there. Tradition would have it that St. Mark the Evangelist brought Christianity to Alexandria in the middle of the first century and was martyred in that city. During Roman and Byzantine times, the city remained the center of classical learning and the intellectual capital of the cultured world until its occupation by Muslims after the **Arab conquest of Egypt** (639–641). It was the home of one of the most famed libraries of antiquity. Many of the early Church Fathers such as Clement, **Origen**, and **Athanasius** were either Alexandrians by birth or adoption. Alexandrine scholars were also influenced by

Gnosticism, as the great city was the home of the two Gnostic teachers, **Basilides** and **Valentinus**. The **Council of Nicaea** assigned to Alexandria a position second only to Rome and superior to Antioch. The **patriarchs** of Alexandria played a significant role in the religious policy and the universal theological controversies of the fourth and fifth centuries. However, the importance of Alexandria was affected by the rise of Constantinople and the **Council of Chalcedon**.

The Christian monuments and religious institutions in Alexandria and its vicinity must have been exceptional indeed. Like many of its other monuments, the ancient churches and monasteries in and around Alexandria have been almost completely destroyed. The Christian monuments suffered much damage during the Persian occupation between 619 and 629. However, Church historian **Abu al-Makarim/ Abu Salih** (13th century) mentions more than 40 churches; among them is the church of St. Mark on the seashore, known as Bucalis, the spot where St. Mark was martyred and buried. That great church was pulled down during the Crusades by the Ayyubid Sultan al-Kamil around 1218 on the pretext that it might furnish the Crusaders with a fortified position in Alexandria. When the Arabs seized Alexandria, the Melchite patriarch Cyrus left the city with the Byzantine army, and the Coptic patriarch Benjamin ended his exile and returned to Alexandria. The great city continued to be the residence of the Coptic patriarch as late as the 11th century, when Patriarch Christodoulos (1047–1077) transferred the patriarchal seat to the **Mo'allaqa** Church in Old Cairo to be closer to the rulers of the country.

AL-GOHARY, IBRAHIM (?–1795). Minister of finance. He was one of the most important and influential Coptic laymen who contributed to the beginning of the renaissance of the Coptic Church in the 18th century. He was born in the district of Haret al-Saqqayen in Cairo, which was predominantly populated by Copts. He worked for two **patriarchs**, Mark VII (1745–1769) and his successor, John XVIII (1769–1796). He began his career during the tenure of Mu'lim Rizq, the administrator of finance of the Mamluk 'Ali Bey in Ottoman Egypt. Under Ibrahim Bey, al-Gohary became the chief scribe of all Egypt, a position that is equivalent to finance minister. Al-Gohary was one of the most influential personalities in the Egyptian state. He was a humanitarian who gave donations to needy families and was affable to everyone. He served the Coptic Church using his financial and political influence. During his lifetime many **monasteries** and churches all over Egypt were restored, and new churches were constructed. Al-Gohary was able to obtain permission from the Ottoman sultan to build the Coptic Cathedral of St. Mark at al-Azbakiah. His brother Girgis completed its construction. When al-Gohary died, Ibrahim Bey was saddened and went to participate in his funeral, although it was improper for a Muslim to do so. The tomb of al-Gohary is located near the Church of St. George in Old Cairo.

ALLOGENES **(NHC XI, 3).** A **Sethian Gnostic** revelation discourse in which a certain Allogenes transmits to his "son" Messos revelations received from a feminine deity called Youel, and then describes his ascent to heaven. Allogenes ("of another race") is probably another name for Seth. The title is given at the end of the tractate. Heavily influenced by second- and third-century Platonism, *Allogenes* was one of the Gnostic "apocalypses" read in Plotinus' school in Rome in the mid-third century (VP 16). Extant only in Coptic, it was originally composed in Greek, probably in the early third century, possibly in Egypt.

AL-MAKIN JIRJIS IBN AL-'AMID (1205–after 1280). Historian. Al-Makin Jirjis ibn Abi al-Yasir ibn Abi al-Makarim, known as Ibn al-'Amid, was a Copt of Syrian Orthodox ancestry who, like his father before him, served in high office in the Egyptian military bureaucracy. Such a position carried risks, and al-Makin lived in especially risky times (in which the new Mamluk rulers of Egypt had to prove themselves in the face of the Mongol invasions from the East as well as continued Crusading activity from the West); whether a victim of circumstance, poor choices, or intrigue, he ended up spending over a decade (1261–1272 or 1276) in prison. After his release, he composed a world history (from the Creation until the accession of the Mamluk sultan Baybars in 1260) in which he drew heavily on earlier sources, including the world history of **ibn al-Rahib**. If not a strongly original work, al-Makin's history has been very influential in both the East and West: it was used by the 14th–15th century Muslim historians ibn Khaldun, al-Qalqashandi, and al-Maqrizi; an Ethiopic translation of the work was made; and, in 1625, the second part of the history (the *Historica Saracenica*) was published by Thomas Erpenius in Leiden, providing Western scholars with an important source for Islamic and Eastern Christian history.

AL-MU'TAMAN IBN AL-'ASSAL (?–last quarter of 13th c.). **Priest**, theologian, encyclopedist. Al-Mu'taman Abu Ishaq Ibrahim ibn al-'Assal was probably the youngest of the three authors of the **Awlad al-'Assal**, and he is the one whose life is best known to us, thanks now in part to the investigations of Wadi Abullif (see the bibliography). Al-Mu'taman was ordained priest (perhaps by **Cyril III ibn Laqlaq**), was widowed at an early age, and on several occasions served the Coptic community in Damascus, where he lost his library during anti-Christian rioting in 1260 (following the Mongol defeat at 'Ayn Jalut).

Al-Mu'taman had already begun his literary production by the 1230s, and a number of his writings—letters, homilies, an introduction to the Pauline epistles, liturgical primers, and a rhymed Coptic-Arabic vocabulary—have been preserved. *Al-Tabsira al-mukhtasira* (The Concise Instruction), composed in 1260, is an apology for the Christian faith, the Triunity of God, and the **Incarnation**. *Al-Tabsira*, however, was simply a foretaste of al-Mu'taman's masterwork: his theological encyclopedia *Majmu' usul al-din* (The Compilation of the Fundamentals of Religion)—now available in Wadi Abullif's critical edition. Its 70 chapters are divided into five parts: fundamental **theology**; the Triunity of God; Incarnation; miscellaneous theological, moral, and liturgical matters; and **eschatology**. Al-Mu'taman draws on a wide variety of identified sources, thereby not only preserving texts otherwise lost but also allowing the reader to sense the catholicity of his theological vision

AL-MUFADDAL IBN ABI AL-FADA'IL (?–after 1357). Historian. Al-Mufaddal ibn Abi al-Fada'il continued the world history of **al-Makin Jirjis ibn al-'Amid** (who may have been his great-uncle), picking up where al-Makin left off with the accession of the Mamluk sultan Baybars in 1260, and continuing through the death of al-Malik al-Nasir in 1341. It is for the most part a secular history that draws from Muslim sources, but it occasionally refers to events within the Coptic community.

Al-Mufaddal wrote his history for his own personal use, and it has only survived in a single manuscript (where it has the Arabic rhyming title *al-Nahj al-sadid wa l-durr al-farid fima ba'd Tarikh Ibn al-'Amid* (The Correct Procedure and Singular Pearl in What Comes after the History of Ibn al-'Amid); the text's publication in the 20th century has provided scholars with an important source for early Mamluk history.

AL-RASHID ABU AL-KHAYR IBN AL-TAYYIB (?–after 1270). **Priest**, theologian. Al-Rashid Abu al-Khayr ibn al-Tayyib worked as a priest, physician, and possibly also scribe to a Muslim notable. He was the author of a number of theological and apologetic works, most notably *Tiryaq al-'uqul fi 'ilm al-usul* (The Theriac of Intellects in Fundamental **Theology**), an explanation of Christian beliefs and practices with responses to questions raised by Muslims. His wide reading is evident in frequent allusions to figures such as Abu Hamid al-Ghazali, Musa ibn Maymun (Maimonides), and Fakhr al-Din al-Razi. Although **al-Mu'taman ibn al-'Assal** speaks very highly of al-Rashid in his theological encyclopedia and quotes extensively from his treatise on free will, others (as we learn from Abu al-Barakat **ibn Kabar**) passed a negative judgment on his apologetic capacity and even his orthodoxy. Perhaps because of this negative assessment, the genuinely popular *Tiryaq* often circulated under the names of others, including Ibn Kabar, the **Awlad al-'Assal**, or **Sawirus ibn al-Muqaffa'**; furthermore, accurate information about al-Rashid's life—including when he lived—has been difficult to come by. The researches of Wadi Abullif ("Al-Rasid ibn al-Tayyib") have now established al-Rashid as an important writer of the period between 1240 and 1270, and one who deserves a renewed assessment after new editions of his works have been published and studied.

AL-SAFI IBN AL-'ASSAL (?–ca. 1265). Canonist, theologian, apologist. The reputation of al-Safi Abu al-Fada'il Majid ibn al-'Assal has long rested on his magisterial canonical collection, the Nomocanon of 1238 commonly known even today as *al-Majmu' al-Safawi* (al-Safi's Compilation); this has allowed brief characterizations of the **Awlad al-'Assal** to refer to the accomplishments of al-Safi in the canonical field alongside those of his brothers **al-As'ad** in the biblical field and **al-Mu'taman** in the theological. Recently, however, the work of Samir Khalil Samir (see the bibliography) in particular has shown us that al-Safi must be remembered for much more than his work in canon law, however important that work was to the future functioning of the Egyptian and (as the *Fetha Nagast* or *Law of the Kings*) Ethiopian churches.

Surprisingly little is known about al-Safi's life; he was a lay theologian who may have worked in one of the government bureaucracies. He had dealings with Patriarch **Cyril III ibn Laqlaq**, writing discourses in honor of the latter's election in 1235 and upon his death in 1243, and serving as secretary at the Synod of Harat Zuwayla in 1238 that sought to reform the **patriarch's** simoniacal practices. What is best known about al-Safi is the course of his research in the 1230s and 1240s. Al-Safi excelled at making epitomes (*mukhtasarat*) of texts, editing them to a fraction of their original length while sacrificing little of their meaning (and sometimes, particularly in the case of treatises by Yahya ibn 'Adi, making the meaning plainer!). His epitomes include works of monastic spirituality, exegetical homilies of St. John Chrysostom, works by Iraqi Arabophone (Arabic-speaking) theologians (including 'Ammar al-Basri, Iliyya al-Nasibini, and especially Yahya ibn 'Adi), and works by Muslim controversialists. The climax of al-Safi's literary career consists of a set of about a dozen apologetic treatises, including responses to well-known *mutakallimin* such as Fakhr al-Din al-Razi, al-Nashi' al-Akbar, and 'Ali al-Tabari. While these have not yet been adequately studied, indications are that al-Safi should be considered "the greatest Coptic apologist of the Middle Ages" (Samir, "Safi," *CE*, p. 2079).

AL-THIQA IBN AL-DUHAYRI (?–after 1267). Scholar of Coptic. Whether or not al-Thiqa ibn al-Duhayri is the Ibn al-Duhayri who was consecrated Metropolitan of Damietta with the name **Christodoulos** by Patriarch **Cyril III ibn Laqlaq**, he is remembered as a scholar who wrote a highly regarded Bohairic grammar, *Muqaddimat al-Duhayri*. Al-Thiqa sought to improve on the earlier grammars of **Yuhanna, Bishop of Samannud**, **Ibn Katib Qaysar**, and **al-Wajih Yuhanna al-Qalyubi**, refining Ibn Katib Qaysar's threefold division of material into nouns, verbs, and particles, and adding many examples. Al-Thiqa corresponded with scholars such as **al-Mu'taman**

ibn al-'Assal, whose Bohairic-Arabic lexicon he praised; his own grammar was judged to be "good" by Abu al-Barakat **ibn Kabar,** and by many others, to judge from the large number of manuscripts in which it is preserved.

AL-TUKHI, RUFA'IL (1701–1787). Bishop, scholar. He was born in Gerga in Upper Egypt to a Coptic family. He converted to Catholicism in his early 20s and was sent to Rome, where he obtained a doctorate in **theology** in 1735. He was appointed a professor at the collegio and taught **Coptic language** and Church rites for more than 36 years. In Rome, he published a Coptic grammar and a number of Coptic liturgical books provided by an Arabic translation. Pope Clement XIII ordained him bishop in 1761. He was buried at the Vatican.

AL-WADIH IBN RAJA' (?–after 1009). Monk, apologist. The *History of the Patriarchs* devotes several pages to the story of al-Wadih, a Muslim who—through the witness of a martyr and the intervention of St. Mercurius—converted to Christianity and became a monk and **priest**. He became a friend of **Sawirus ibn al-Muqaffa'**, with whom he is said to have spent considerable time in reflection and study. He wrote at least three Arabic-language apologetic/polemical works in which he drew on Islamic sources; unfortunately, these works remain almost entirely unknown. Like Sawirus, al-Wadih is one of the pioneers of **Copto-Arabic literature**, but an evaluation of his place in the history of this literature must await the publication of some of his work.

AL-WAJIH YUHANNA AL-QALYUBI (?–after 1271). Biblical and Coptic scholar. Al-Wajih Yuhanna ibn Mikha'il ibn Sadaqa al-Qalyubi is a rather overlooked figure of the "golden age" of **Copto-Arabic literature**, despite his connection to well-known scholars such as **al-Mu'taman ibn al-'Assal**, and despite his extensive scholarly output, which includes a Coptic grammar, a careful new Arabic translation of the Pauline epistles, a commentary on Romans, and other works. His Bohairic Coptic grammar, entitled *al-Kifaya* (That Which Is Sufficient), breaks new ground in assimilating Arabic grammatical categories (with which the Coptic grammarians began) to the peculiar features of the **Coptic language**.

AMOUN (?–ca. 350). Saint, ascetic. He is the founder of anchoritism in **Nitria**. Amoun was an Egyptian orphan who was brought up and forced to marry by his uncle. However, he and his wife lived celibately for 18 years. Around 330, Amoun retired to the mountain of Nitria. He soon attracted many followers and **monasticism** began to flourish there. One of the **Sayings of the Fathers** attributes the foundation of the monastic center of **Kellia** jointly to St. Amoun and St. **Antony**. Patriarch **Athanasius** mentioned him in the *Life of Antony*. According to one tradition, Antony saw Amoun's soul borne up to heaven by angels.

ANAPHORA OF ST. BASIL. The Anaphora of St. Basil is considered one of three official anaphoras of the Coptic Church. Pope **Gabriel ibn Turayk** (1131–1145) declared in his canons that only the **liturgies** of St. Basil, St. **Gregory**, and St. **Cyril** are to be used, and he forbade the Christian inhabitants of Upper Egypt from using their many anaphoras.

There are four groups of this anaphora representing four geographical regions: Egypt, Syria, Armenia, and Byzantium. The Egyptian Anaphora of Basil, in contrast to the other three textual traditions, represents a substantially shorter version of the Basilian anaphora. The earliest manuscript of the Egyptian group is preserved on four small sheets of parchment written around the seventh century and discovered by Jean Doresse. It is written in the Sahidic dialect. Another fragment of the beginning of the anaphora was written on papyrus and discovered in the Monastery of al-Bali'zah. The Bohairic version survives in a rather large number of manuscripts, but they are mostly of a later date. The Greek version of the Egyptian form survives in a dozen manuscripts dated between the 14th and the 19th centuries.

The first edition was published in Rome in 1636 and edited by Rufa'il (Rafael) **al-Tukhi**, but in all his editions, Tukhi did not respect the text of the original manuscripts. The best edition of the Anaphora of Basil was published by Claudius Labib and edited by Hegumen Abd al-Masih Salib al-Mas'udi in 1908. It provided different readings in the apparatus according to the manuscripts. This edition was reprinted several times by Hegumen Attalah Arser.ius al-Muharaqqi in 1956 by the Commission for Publication in Bani

Sueif in 1986, and by Dayr al-Muharraq in 1997. Another edition was published by the Society of the Sons of the Church in 1945, mainly based on the Abd al-Masih's edition with some additional hymns and the Horologion (a fixed schedule of daily prayers or services). The Mahabah Bookshop published several editions of the Euchologion in both Coptic and Arabic of the liturgies of Basil and Gregory.

ANAPHORA OF ST. CYRIL. The Anaphora of St. **Mark (Cyril)** is notable for several features that are peculiar to it among Eastern **liturgies**, differentiating it from the Syro-Byzantine type. These features suggest that the structure of prayer is of considerable antiquity.

These features are as follows:

- The presence of an offering in the preface.
- The position of the intercessions before the *Sanctus*.
- The absence of the *Benedictus* and of any **Christological** thanksgiving.
- The presence of an *epiclesis* immediately after the *Sanctus* with "fill" as a link word rather than "holy."
- The introduction of the *anamnesis* by "proclaiming" rather than "remembering."
- The inclusion of a second *epiclesis*.

There are early Greek and Coptic versions of the Egyptian Liturgy of St. Cyril. The Ethiopian version of this liturgy was clearly developed at a later date.

The earliest manuscripts of this liturgy are Greek fragments on papyrus. These fragments are preserved in the University of Strasbourg and probably date from the fourth century. The British Museum possesses small Greek fragments written in the sixth or seventh century containing part of the Liturgy of St. Mark. A Polish archaeological mission working in the Naqlun Monastery discovered several fragments of the deacon's responses from the Liturgy of St Mark, which probably date from the 9th or 10th century. A Coptic parchment written around the 10th century contained a part of this liturgy. Unfortunately this important piece of history perished in a fire at Louvain University. The John Rylands Library in Manchester possesses a Greek parchment of the second half of the Anaphora of St. Mark. The British museum has a wooden tablet, crafted around the seventh or eighth century, on which a Sahidic Coptic text is engraved containing a quotation from this liturgy. In addition to these early sources, many Coptic medieval manuscripts survive from the complete text of the Liturgy of St. Mark. See the Anaphora of St. Basil for a review of the various editions.

ANAPHORA OF ST. GREGORY. This anaphora belongs to the same Syrian type as the **Anaphora of St. Basil**. It is unique in that its prayers are directed to the Son and not to the Father through the Son, which indicates a sixth-century date. It seems that the Syrian monks who came to the desert of **Scetis** introduced this anaphora to the Coptic Church.

Some Coptic Sahidic fragments, originally from Ashmunein, contain a few lines of the Liturgy of St. Gregory. The Sahidic Euchologion of the **White Monastery** contains two fragments of the Anaphora of St. Gregory. This manuscript may date from the 10th century. Some Bohairic fragments of the Anaphora of Gregory, originally from the **Monastery of Saint Macarius**, may date from the 12th or 13th century. They are now kept in the University and State Library of Hamburg.

The first edition was published in Rome in 1636 and edited by Raphael **al-Tukhi**, but in all his editions, Tukhi did not respect the text of the original manuscripts. The first and the best edition of the Anaphora of Gregory was published by Claudius Labib. After consulting many manuscripts, Hegumen Abd al-Masih Salib al-Mas'udi edited a Euchologion in 1908 with alternate readings in the apparatus. This edition was reprinted several times by Hegumen Attalah Arsenius al-Muharaqqi after 1956, by the Monastery of al-Moharraq in 1997, and by the Bani Sueif Commission for Publications in 1986. Another edition was published by the Society of the Sons of the Church in 1945, mainly based on Abd al-Masih's edition with some additional hymns and the Horologion. The Mahabah Bookshop published several editions of the Euchologion with the liturgies of Basil and Gregory in both Coptic and Arabic languages.

ANATHEMA. This word occurs in the Greek New Testament in Romans 9:3 and I Corinthians 12:3. It means anything (or anyone) devoted to evil. Hence, it is considered a curse. The great curse of the

Coptic Church is excommunicating a person or denouncing a doctrine or practice as damnable. This anathema is pronounced against
heretics, usually by authority of a Church council. Anathemas are
pronounced against those who insist on contradicting the dogma accepted by the council. Among the famous anathemas in the Church
history were the Twelve Anathemas sent to **Nestorius** by St. **Cyril**
and his synod. The last chapter of the *Book of the Professions of
the Fathers* is a compilation of the anathemas of the Fathers of the
Church, such as Gregory the Armenian, Hippolytus of Rome, Cyril
of **Alexandria**, and **Theodosius.**

ANBA RUWAIS. *See* CATHEDRAL OF ST. MARK IN CAIRO.

ANIANUS (THE COBBLER). Patriarch. Tradition says that the
Apostle **Mark**'s first convert in **Alexandria** was Anianus the cobbler. Mark later consecrated Anianus as the first **bishop** of the new
church. **Eusebius of Caesarea** was the first author to mention the
story of the succession of Mark in his book *Church History.* This
tradition is developed in later sources such as the *History of the
Patriarchs* and the Coptic **Synaxarion** to include many details. Unfortunately the entire Coptic version of the *History of the Patriarchs*
did not survive; hence, we do not know exactly the origin of this
story. Anianus is commemorated in the Coptic calendar on the 20th
Hathor. According to Western tradition, the relics of Anianus were
transferred to Venice in the 12th century.

ANOINTING. *See* CHRISM; MARRIAGE; UNCTION OF THE SICK.

ANTHROPOMORPHISM. The followers of Anthropomorphism
believed that God has a human (*Anthropos*) form or shape (*morphe*).
This affair arose in the late fourth century and the beginning of the
fifth century in Egypt, during the **patriarchate** of **Theophilus** of
Alexandria. The three tall monks of **Nitria** followed the allegorical interpretation of **Origen.** Theophilus first supported them. In his
paschal letter of the year 399 A.D., he was inclined to adopt the
incorporeity of God but later he changed his mind. In front of some
monks who assembled in protest, he cried, "Looking at you, I see
God's face." Theophilus then condemned Origenism and persecuted

the followers of Origen. It should be mentioned that most of our knowledge of the reign of Theophilus of Alexandria came essentially from his opponents and especially **Palladius** (a close friend of John Chrysostom). However, monastic sources show him as a holy man and great champion of the monks.

ANTIPHONARION. *See* DIFNAR.

ANTONY (ca. 251–ca. 356). Saint, monk, ascetic. He is known as "the father of the monks." He was born in an Egyptian village called Koma of the Heracleopolite nome in Middle Egypt. As a youth of about 18 years old, Antony heard in the church the Lord's command: "If you want to be perfect, go, sell what you have and give to the poor, and you will have treasure in heaven; and come to follow Me" (Matt. 19:21). Accordingly Antony sold his possessions, gave the money to the poor, and devoted himself to a life of asceticism. He began his ascetic life as a village ascetic, and around 285 he set out for the mountains and withdrew himself to Pispir, about 60 kilometers south of Cairo, where today stands the Monastery of al-Maimoun. By about 313 he had completely retired in the "inner desert" at the Red Sea, where he is said to have struggled with demonic powers. His commitment to God, seclusion, self-denial, and his readiness to be a spiritual guide for the monks made him a complete model for an anchoritic way of life. Antony went to **Alexandria** to strengthen the Christians who were imprisoned at the time of persecution. He supported Patriarch **Athanasius** in his struggle against the Arians. Toward the end of Antony's life, the number of his disciples grew. They settled in the very region where today stands his famous monastery in Wadi Araba of the Red Sea. Athanasius, who knew Antony personally, wrote the *Life of Antony* shortly after Antony's death. Its authenticity, which has sometimes been questioned, is now generally accepted by scholars. Athanasuis introduced the West to this ideal monk through his biography of the great hermit. It had a considerable impact on Christianity: It is sufficient to mention its influence on St. Augustine. *See also* MONASTERY OF ST. ANTONY; MONASTICISM, EGYPTIAN.

APOCALYPSE OF ADAM **(NHC V, 5).** A **Sethian** Gnostic revelation mediated to Adam by three heavenly visitors and narrated by him to his son Seth. Its title is given both at the beginning and the end of the text. Formally, this apocalypse belongs to the "testament" genre common in early Jewish literature, inasmuch as Adam presents his revelation to Seth just before his death. The revelation consists of a salvation history of the (**Gnostic**) "seed of Seth." With no obvious Christian features in the text, the *Apocalypse of Adam* can be seen as a Jewish Gnostic text. Extant only in Coptic, it was originally composed in Greek, probably in Syria, possibly as early as the late first century.

APOCALYPSE OF JAMES **(FIRST) (NHC V, 3).** A **Gnostic** revelation discourse in which the risen Christ presents esoteric revelation to his brother James. The title, "The Apocalypse of James," is given at the beginning and the end of the text, which is followed in the manuscript by another "Apocalypse of James." Among the revelations given by "the Lord" is a prophecy of James' martyrdom in Jerusalem (which actually occurred in the year 62) and his victory over "the archons." In this text "the twelve disciples" are disparaged, and four women are favored: Salome, Mariam, Martha, and Arsinoe. Extant only in Coptic, *1 Apocalypse of James* was originally composed in Greek, probably in second-century Syria.

APOCALYPSE OF JAMES **(SECOND) (NHC V, 4).** A **Gnostic** revelation discourse purportedly spoken in Jerusalem by James the Just, and written down by a **priest** named Mareim, to which is appended a third-person account of the martyrdom of James (which occurred in 62 A.D.). The title, "The Apocalypse of James," is given at the beginning of the text, which is preceded in the manuscript by another "Apocalypse of James." The account of James' martyrdom resembles that of Hegesippus preserved by **Eusebius**. The text concludes with a prayer uttered by the dying James. Extant only in Coptic, *2 Apocalypse of James* was originally composed in Greek, probably in second-century Syria.

APOCALYPSE OF PAUL **(NHC V, 2).** A **Gnostic** apocalypse recounting the Apostle Paul's journey from the 4th to the 10th heaven (he gets to the third in 2 Cor. 12:2). At the various levels, Paul has visionary experiences along the way. Extant only in Coptic, *Apoca-*

lypse of Paul was originally composed in Greek, probably sometime in the second century, possibly in Egypt.

APOCALYPSE OF PETER (NHC VII, 3). A **Gnostic** writing in which Peter gives an account of visions and revelations he has experienced and interpretations of them by the Savior. The title is given at the end. The text, which contains polemics against other Christians—orthodox ("deaf and blind") believers tied to an ecclesiastical establishment—features a **docetic** interpretation of Jesus' crucifixion that has the "living Jesus" laughing at the folly of those crucifying his physical body. *Apocalypse of Peter*, not to be confused with a second-century apocryphal work of the same title, is extant only in Coptic. It was originally composed in Greek, probably in late second- or early third-century Egypt.

APOCRYPHON OF JAMES (NHC I, 2). A "secret book" purporting to be a letter written by James, the Lord's brother, to a recipient whose name is lost in a lacuna. *Apocryphon of James* lacks a title in the manuscript; its current title has been editorially assigned to it on the basis of its content. It contains reports of teachings given by Jesus 550 days after the Resurrection to James and Peter. *Apocryphon of James* is a **Gnostic** writing of uncertain affiliation, originally composed in Greek as early as the mid-second century. Its provenience is unknown, but it could have been composed in Egypt.

APOCRYPHON OF JOHN (NHC II, 1; III, 1, IV, 1; BG, 2). A "secret book" of **Gnostic** revelations attributed to the risen Savior (Jesus Christ) given to his disciple John, son of Zebedee. *Apocryphon of John* is preserved in four Coptic versions, representing a shorter recension (NHC III, 1; BG, 2) and a longer one (NHC II, 1; IV, 1). The title is preserved at the end of all four versions. The revelations are presented in two parts: a revelation discourse on the unknown God and the heavenly world, and the creation of the cosmos; and a revelation dialogue between the Savior and John, who poses a series of questions answered by the Savior. The creation of the world is attributed to a being called Ialdabaoth, abortive son of the fallen Sophia, a parody of the biblical Creator. The revelation dialogue consists for the most part of Gnostic commentary on Genesis 1–7. The first part is almost identical to teachings of certain "Gnostics" as presented by Irenaeus in his treatise *Against Heresies* 1.29. *Apocryphon of John* is the most important source we have for the basic mythology of "**Sethian**" or "classic" Gnosticism. Its core material, originally composed in Greek, dates to the second century, earlier than ca. 185, when Irenaeus wrote his treatise. There is reason to think that the basic material, without the frame story and the artificially composed questions attributed to John, represents an originally Jewish version of Gnostic mythology only secondarily Christianized by the addition of the frame story and the questions. Jesus Christ takes the place of an originally feminine revealer figure. The Christianized version we now have probably dates to the end of the second century or the beginning of the third. A Syrian provenience is likely, at least for the original core material.

APOLLINARIANISM. Apollinarianism is the dogma instituted by Apollinarius of Laodicea. He was a great friend of **Athanasius** of **Alexandria** and rendered him great service, defending orthodoxy against **Arianism**. But under the influence of Arianism, Apollinarius denied the full human nature of Christ by promulgating that the divine Logos took the place of the nous. Apollinarianism was refuted ably and competently by St. Athanasius the Great at the end of his life, in a huge work composed of three volumes. Apollinarianism was criticized strongly by Basil the Great and **Gregory of Nazianzus**. The heresy was condemned by the Synod of **Alexandria** (362 A.D.) and later by the **Council of Constantinople** (381 A.D.). Since then, his name is mentioned as among the heretics in every ecumenical council.

APOLOGIST. Apologists is the title given to a group of the Church Fathers who strove in the second century to defend Christianity against pagan attacks. They tried to explain the principles of religion, showing that Christianity is compatible with good citizenship, contrary to the belief that refusing to worship the emperor constituted a plot against the state. Some of the apologists wrote to defend Christianity from the attacks of the Jews, and they also wrote inviting the heretics to return to the Church.

In the **Coptic language**, only the work of Melito survived. Melito was a **bishop** of Sardis in Asia Minor in the beginning of the second century. According to **Eusebius of Caesarea**, Melito exerted many efforts to defend Christianity before Emperor Marcus Aurelius. Also according to the same author, Clement of **Alexandria** wrote a book on the Passion of Christ, transmitting to his friends the traditions received from Melito of Sardis. In Coptic, we have his homily on the Passion of Christ.

APOPHTHEGMATA PATRUM. See SAYINGS OF THE FATHERS.

APOSTOLIC FATHERS. Apostolic Fathers is a name given to a group of authors who came just after the Apostles, such as Clement of Rome. According to **Origen** and **Eusebius**, Clement was a disciple of St. Paul and was mentioned in the Epistle to the Philippians 4:3. Ireneaus noted that he was the third **Bishop** of Rome after St. Peter. He is commemorated in the Coptic **Synaxarion** on the 29th Hathor. A part of his Epistle to the Church of Corinth survives in Coptic. Of the Epistle to the Virgins, the Greek origins are lost, but the complete text survived in Syriac. The Coptic version contains chapters 1 to 8 wherein the meaning of virginity and the difference between virginity and celibacy is explained.

Ignatius of Antioch is considered the second bishop of this city. During the reign of Trajan (98–117 A.D.), he was taken from Antioch to Rome in order to be thrown to the beasts in the arena. On his way to Rome, he wrote several letters begging the Christian congregations not to intervene with the emperor for his pardon. Part of the story of his martyrdom has survived in Coptic as well as some fragments of his letters.

Hermas lived in Rome in the beginning of the second century. He was the first to mention **penance** as a remedy for those lapsed in sins. In Coptic, we have parts of his book, the Shepherd. According to Eusebius, Polycarp was the Bishop of Smyrna. In his youth, he met St. John the Apostle who later ordained him bishop. He ended his life as a martyr. In Coptic, we have only a fragment of his letter to Smyrna.

APOSTOLIC SEE. An apostolic see is a see that was founded by an Apostle. The number of sees and their names differed from century to century. In the fourth century, Rome, **Alexandria**, Antioch, and Ephesus were considered the four apostolic sees. However, with the foundation of Constantinople as a capital, the emperors started to assert their capital as an apostolic see, especially in the **Council of Constantinople** in 381 A.D. The relics of St. Andrew were later discovered in order to justify their assertion. From the beginning of the fifth century, the other apostolic sees opposed this innovation. This can be detected in the attitude of the Egyptian popes such as **Theophilus** and **Cyril** toward the **patriarchs** of Constantinople, such as John Chrysostom and **Nestorius** (the heretic).

The **Council of Chalcedon** in 451 A.D. declared the famous Canon 28 (rejected for a long time by Rome), which considered the See of Constantinople as the second see after Rome, for it was the "New Rome." Through the machinations of its **bishop**, Juvenal, Jerusalem also became a patriarchate at the same council. Later, Moscow took the title of "New Rome."

In the Coptic tradition, the four apostolic sees are Rome, Alexandria, Antioch, and Ephesus, as mentioned in a Coptic hymn in honor of Julius of Rome, though the manuscripts erroneously attribute the hymn to his namesake, Julius of Akfahs. In the *History of the Patriarchs* of the Egyptian church, there is a quotation from a work by **Severus of Antioch** mentioning the four parts of the garment of Christ as the four (apostolic) seats that exist in the world.

APOSTOLIC SUCCESSION. This term refers to an unbroken chain of spiritual authority of Church leaders that originated with the Apostles and continues to the present-day **patriarch**. It was used as an argument against **Gnosticism** from the second century onward. Hegesippus, in his memoirs against the Gnostics, mentioned for the first time the word *diadoche*, which could mean either a succession from the Apostles or "continuing to receive from hand to hand" (tradition). Irenaeus of Lyons, one of the most important theologians of the second century, presented an extensive treatment of the *Apostolic Tradition* and succession in his book against heresies.

In the Coptic Church, the patriarch is considered to be the successor of St. Mark (who was not among the 12 disciples); in several hymns welcoming the patriarch, the "Successor of St. Mark" is mentioned.

APOSTOLIC TRADITION. The *Apostolic Tradition* is a book traditionally attributed to Hippolytus of Rome. This book is a mine of information about liturgy and canon law. Scholars believe that this text was composed in the year 215 A.D. The original Greek of this text is lost. However, we have a **Coptic** and a **Copto-Arabic** translation as well as an Ethiopian one. In a later era, an anonymous author used it as the basis for the *Canons of Hippolytus.*

ARAB CONQUEST OF EGYPT (639–641). The Arab conquest of Egypt had immeasurable consequences for the Coptic Church. On the eve of the Arab invasion, Emperor Heraclius appointed Cyrus (known to the Arabs as al-Muqawqas) as both civil and ecclesiastical head. He persecuted the Copts as well as their **patriarch**, Benjamin, who had to flee to Upper Egypt for 13 years. Thus the Copts had little motivation to support the Byzantine army. However, there is no evidence for their cooperation with the Arabs during the actual invasion between the end of 639 and the capture of the Fortress of Babylon in April 641. After an armistice of 11 months to evacuate the Byzantine forces and Greek civilians, the great city of **Alexandria** opened its doors to the Arabs and immediately lost its position as a most important cultural city. Although the Arab army under General 'Amr ibn al-'As was much less in number than the Byzantine garrisons, it achieved a relatively rapid expansion in Egypt. By that time, the Byzantine forces in Egypt were ill equipped and trained to operate in the manner of police than as a militia.

The condition for making peace with the countries being invaded by the Arabs was to choose one of three options: paying the poll tax (*jizyiah*), **conversion to Islam**, or war. At first the invaders respected the Copts who ran the government for them during the first few decades of occupation. Patriarch Benjamin came back to Alexandria and was able to restore monasteries and churches. However, like the Romans, the Arabs were interested in the revenues of the country. Copts were considered *dhimmis*, that is, "protected people," in return for a payment of the poll tax in addition to the land tax. By 705 the monks had to pay the poll tax for the first time. In the following centuries, more financial burdens were imposed on the Copts. By the late ninth century, the Copts did not represent the majority of

Egypt's population because of a combination of factors that led to their conversion to Islam.

ARIANISM. Arianism is the doctrine established by **Arius**. It is important to mention that our primary sources on the Arian crisis are very poor. Most of our knowledge comes from his opponents, that is, **Athanasius** of **Alexandria** and others. The Arians played an important role in Church history until their extinction around 395 A.D. Arianism spread throughout the West and most of the Germanic tribes and barbarians who adopted the Christian faith were Arian. Until the sixth century, many kingdoms in the West were Arian, such as the Goths and the Visigoths. The Arians possessed a church in Constantinople itself. Byzantine emperors turned a blind eye to their existence because they depended on them as soldiers in the army. Ironically enough, in the East where it started, and mainly in Alexandria, the Arians lost their defenders soon after Arius' death.

ARIUS. Arius was born in Libya. He studied **theology** in Antioch at the School of Lucian. He returned to **Alexandria** where he was ordained a deacon and then a **priest**. In 318, he started to preach his theological doctrine, which provoked many discussions. His main doctrine was that because the Son was the first creature of God, he is not from the same substance of the Father; hence, the Son is a son in a moral sense rather than a metaphysical sense. In fact, Arius' teachings were another form of Subordinationism. A council convened in Alexandria under its **patriarch**, Alexander, condemned Arius' heresy and excommunicated him. Arius tried to find allies from among his colleagues at the School of Antioch, such as Eusebius of Nicomedia. Emperor Constantine convoked a council in **Nicaea** to discuss the matter. The council condemned Arius to exile, but Arius did not give up. He continued to pressure the **bishops** until he was reaccepted into the Church by the synods of Tyre and Jerusalem in 335. However, he died suddenly just one day before his official reintegration. The Athanasian party saw this event as divine vengeance. Arius was not a prolific writer. His teachings seemed to have largely been transmitted orally. According to Epiphanius of Salamis, Arius wrote a letter to his friend Eusebius of Nicomedia and a creed, which he presented to the Emperor Constantine. Some fragments were partly preserved in the writings of his opponents.

ART, CONTEMPORARY COPTIC. The school of contemporary **Coptic art** was established in Cairo by **Isaac Fanous** in the 1960s. It reflects the deep roots of ancient Egyptian and Coptic arts combined with the Coptic **theology** and culture. **Icons** represent its major production. Wall paintings, mosaics, and stained-glass windows decorate a considerable number of modern Coptic churches. Other famous iconographers are Youssif Nassif and his wife, Budur Latif, who represent an independent trend and have enriched contemporary Coptic art for more than 35 years. The main themes of this art are Christ, the Holy Virgin Mary, angels, Apostles, martyrs, **saints**, and biblical scenes, especially the **Christological** cycle and the Twenty-four Elders. The latter are usually depicted as part of the iconography of the Pantocrator ("the Almighty"). One of the very popular themes is the **flight into Egypt**, which often features the River Nile and the pyramids. Copts in Egypt and abroad take pride in that great event. Contemporary Coptic art avoids scenes of torture and suffering. One of its significant characteristics is the portrayal of the full face and the three-quarters face; the profile is usually used to represent non-beloved persons like Judas Iscariot or the soldiers at the foot of the cross. As in ancient Egyptian art, contemporary Coptic art shows the protagonist, often Christ or the Virgin, larger than the other figures of the scene. As in ancient Coptic art, the figures are accompanied by their names; the heads and eyes are relatively large, and mouth is small. Many artists use blue, red, green, and brown colors set against a golden background. A number of monks and nuns devote their lives to painting the icons. Coptic emigrants in Europe, the United States, Canada, and Australia decorate their churches with icons executed by Coptic iconographers from Egypt, a considerable number of which are painted by Isaac Fanous, Youssif Nassif, and Budur Latif.

ART, COPTIC. Coptic art is a distinctive art associated with Christianity in Egypt. It is the richest art of the Eastern Christian arts. It appeared in the third or fourth century and began to flourish in the fifth century. Coptic art can only be understood and appreciated in the light of Egypt's economic and social circumstances over the centuries. Lacking royal patronage, it is perhaps best characterized as folk art. Various stages of evolution between pagan art and Coptic art are recognizable, especially in the fourth and fifth centuries. Coptic art has been influenced by Greco-Roman art. Mythological scenes and decorative elements, such as vine scrolls and interlaced patterns, were taken from pagan art. The iconography of the majority of the Christian themes derives from early Christian and Byzantine traditions. The styles and fashions of the Byzantine world were adapted with originality and individuality. Some of the motifs, such as the looped cross and the Holy Virgin suckling the Child Christ, reveal ancient Egyptian influence. The **White Monastery** demonstrates affinities with ancient Egyptian temple architecture. By the 10th century, Coptic ornamentation began to assume an Islamic flavor. Scenes from the New Testament are very popular, especially episodes of the **Christological** cycle.

Coptic **liturgy** influenced church decoration during medieval times. Scenes from the Old Testament, such as Abraham's sacrifice and his meeting with Melchizedec, decorate the sanctuary because of their reference to the Eucharist. **Saints** occur often in mural paintings. Coptic art is primarily decorative art and very rich in its geometric and floral designs. Coptic churches, ancient and modern, are decorated with **icons**, wall paintings, carved wood, and architectural sculptures. A considerable part of the images in the Coptic Church has a function within the church building and the liturgy.

Excavations of the **monasteries of St. Jeremiah** at Saqqara and **St. Apollo at Bawit**, yielded architectural sculptures and wall paintings of the sixth and seventh centuries that belong to the most important monuments of Christian art. The new discoveries of wall paintings in the **monasteries of the Syrians** and the Archangel Gabriel have enriched Coptic art, especially of the 8th through the 11th centuries. The 12th and the 13th centuries witnessed the creation of huge Coptic wall paintings in the monasteries of **Wadi al-Natrun** and the **monasteries of St. Antony** and **St. Paul**, and in some churches of Old Cairo. In the 13th century, Cairo was the center of a workshop of Christian painters of several Christian communities, such as Armenians and Syrians. They were responsible for the painting of icons, wall paintings, and manuscript illumination, which attest to the survival of Coptic art in the narrower sense of a purely Christian art in the service of the Church. The art of wall painting ceased for a few centuries and appeared again in the 18th century in the Monastery of St. Paul. Beginning in the same century, icon paintings and manuscript illumination flourished. **Contemporary Coptic art** began and flourished in the second half of the 20th century. Although the majority of Coptic churches and monasteries were demolished and a considerable number of them suffered many waves of persecution in medieval times—when much of their beautiful original murals, woodwork, icons, and valuable liturgical objects were destroyed or plundered by the mobs under Muslim rulers—what remains of the elaborate wooden altars, ciboria, doors, and screens, as well as beautiful objects of metal such as lamps, chandeliers, Bible caskets, and censers is beyond estimation.

ASCLEPIUS 21–29 **(NHC VI, 8).** A Coptic translation of part of a Hermetic text extant completely only in a Latin translation. In the text, Hermes Trismegistus, acting as mystagogue, is providing esoteric teaching to his pupil Asclepius (Tat and Ammon are two others mentioned in the text). The original Greek version was called "The Perfect Teaching"; two fragments are extant. The Coptic excerpt, for which no title is given, has Hermes expound on human nature and refers to Egypt as "the image of heaven." The original version was composed in second- or early third-century Egypt.

ASKEW CODEX (CODEX ASKEWIANUS). A fifth-century parchment codex of 178 leaves inscribed in **Coptic** containing four Gnostic treatises collectively called *Pistis Sophia*. The codex is named after its first owner, a London doctor named A. Askew, who acquired it from a London bookseller in 1772. It was purchased by the British Museum in 1785 and first published in the mid-19th century. Where in Egypt it was originally found is unknown.

ASSUMPTION. According to Coptic Church tradition, the Virgin Mary died on the 21st Tubah. This date henceforth became a feast in honor of the Virgin every 21st of a Coptic month. The Assumption took place on the 16th of Misra. Since the 15th century, the Coptic Church has commemorated this event by **fasting** for two weeks, called the Fast of the Virgin. This tradition is one that characterizes the Coptic Church.

ATHANASIAN CREED. *See* NICENE CREED.

ATHANASIUS, BISHOP OF QUS (second half of 14th c.). Bishop, scholar of Coptic. Athanasius was an active Upper Egyptian church leader during the later decades of the 14th century. His *Qiladat al-tahrir fi 'ilm al-tafsir* (A Necklace of Composition in the Science of Interpretation) is *not* a work of hermeneutics (as its colorful title might lead one to expect) but rather a grammar of the **Coptic language**. It marks the culmination of a century of attempts to bend and shape Arabic grammatical categories into suitable instruments for describing a language that, by Athanasius' day, was no longer used in the everyday lives of most Copts. Originally composed to describe the Sahidic (*Sa'idi*) dialect of Upper Egypt, *Qiladat al-tahrir* has been preserved in Bohairic recensions as well.

Athanasius represents an end of an era: his is one of the last names that can be mentioned for the 13th- and 14th-century golden age of **Copto-Arabic literature**. He may also serve as an example of the shift of the center of gravity of Egyptian Christianity southward during the Mamluk period. It is notable that the greatest of the Copto-Arabic grammars should have been produced, not in Cairo but in Qus (just north of Luxor), and should examine not the northern Bohairic but rather the southern Sahidic dialect of the language.

ATHANASIUS (1923–2000). Bishop and educator. He was born in the city of al-Mahalla al-Kubra in the Delta. He obtained a bachelor's degree in English literature from Cairo University in 1944, and in 1952 received a diploma of psychology from the American University in Cairo. He also obtained a diploma in divinity from the **Clerical College** in 1944. Between 1944 and 1958 he taught in a few secondary schools in Cairo and Aswan. In 1954, he taught the New Testament in the **Clerical College**. In 1958, he joined the **Monastery of the Syrians** at **Wadi al-Natrun**. Patriarch **Cyril VI** appointed him papal representative in Beni Suef in 1962. On September 1962, he was ordained Bishop of Beni Suef and al-Bahnasa. He was a member of the board of the **Middle East Council of Churches** and represented the

Coptic Church in the World Council of Churches Assembly. Bishop Athanasius was a pioneer in developing the social services of his diocese. In 1965, he established a female religious group of active nuns called the Daughters of Mary, who committed themselves to the service of the community. He is the author of many books and articles related to the New Testament (in Arabic). He printed a number of liturgical books of the Coptic Church.

ATHANASIUS I (295–372 A.D). Saint and **patriarch**. He was the 20th patriarch of **Alexandria** (326–372). He is commemorated on the 7th of Bashons. Born in Alexandria in 295 A.D., he probably studied at the School of Alexandria. He assisted at the **Council of Nicaea** (325 A.D.) as a deacon and secretary to his **bishop**, Alexander. He succeeded his bishop in 328. He suffered exile several times in Upper Egypt and in Europe. He was a prolific writer; his works could be categorized as apologetic and dogmatic writings, including his treatise against the Arians, *On the Incarnation of the Word*; ascetical writings such as the *Life of Antony*; correspondence, including several festal letters; and exegetical works on the Psalms. One of the sources of his life is a homily of **Gregory of Nazianzus** and part of it survives in Coptic, as well as a Coptic homily ascribed to **Cyril** of Alexandria. The corpus of Athansius includes several works, which Lefort believed were written originally in Coptic. Among the most complete texts are the *Life of Antony*; a homily on the Nativity, where we find an autobiographical section; exegetical works on the Psalms, the Gospels of Matthew, Luke, John, and the Epistle to the Romans; and the festal letters. Other works ascribed to him include the canons, homilies on the Archangel Michael, some ascetical works, and an apocalypse on future times.

ATIYA, AZIZ SURYAL (1898–1988). Editor-in-chief of the *Coptic Encyclopedia* (8 vols., New York: Macmillan, 1991). He was born in Egypt in a small village in Gharbiya Province, called al-'Aysha. He graduated from the Higher Training College in Cairo in 1927. Atiya was sent by the Egyptian Office of Education to the University of Liverpool in England, from which he earned his BA in medieval and modern history in 1931. He completed his PhD in Arabic and Islamic studies at the University of London in 1933. The University of Liverpool awarded him a LittD in 1938 because of his work *The Crusade in the Later Middle Ages*, published in the same year. Atiya taught at the University of London (1934), the University of Bonn, Germany (1936–1939), and Cairo University (1939–1942). He held a Foundation Chair in Medieval History (1942–1952), and served as chairman of the History Department (1952–1954) at **Alexandria** University. In 1949–1950, Atiya participated in the joint expedition of the Alexandria University and the American Foundation for the Study of Man to microfilm the invaluable manuscript collection of the Monastery of St. Catherine at Mount Sinai. Credit must be given to Atiya for establishing the **Higher Institute of Coptic Studies** in Cairo in 1954. Atiya also served as a visiting professor of Arabic studies at the University of Michigan (1955–1956), Columbia University, New York (1956), Indiana University (1957), and Princeton University (1957–1958). From 1959 until his death, he lived in Salt Lake City, Utah. He established a complete center for the study of Arabic and Middle East cultures at the University of Utah and founded the library that now bears his name. In 1967, Atiya was designated distinguished professor of history in recognition of his great efforts and scholarly achievements. Atiya is internationally recognized as a leading scholar in the area of the Crusades. Of special interest is his work *History of Eastern Christianity*. The creation of the **International Association for Coptic Studies** in 1976 encouraged Atiya to contact scholars to fulfill his long-cherished vision of a *Coptic Encyclopedia*, which appeared after his death. His achievements have made him unforgettable to the Copts.

AUTHORITATIVE TEACHING (NHC VI, 3). A sophisticated Christian treatise on the nature of the human soul reflecting second-century Middle-Platonic teachings on the soul. Its title, in Greek (*Authentikos logos*), occurs at the end. Extant only in Coptic, *Authoritative Teaching* was originally composed in Greek. It should be seen as a product of late second-century **Alexandrian** Christian Platonism.

AWLAD AL-'ASSAL (13th c.). Family of scholars. The term Awlad al-'Assal ("the children of al-'Assal") is conventionally used to refer to four brothers who played a major role in the revival of Coptic thought in the decades between 1230 and 1260. Their father, Fakhr al-Dawlah ("Pride of the State") Abu al-Mufaddal al-As'ad, was a wealthy and generous Coptic notable who provided his children with an excellent education. He was married twice; **al-As'ad** Abu al-Faraj Hibatallah and **al-Safi** Abu al-Fada'il Majid were full brothers to one another, and half-brothers to **al-Mu'taman** Abu Ishaq Ibrahim and al-Amjad Abu al-Majd Fadlallah.

Al-As'ad, al-Safi, and al-Mu'taman were the scholars who made the name Awlad al-'Assal nearly synonymous with the 13th-century golden age or renaissance of the literature of the Coptic Orthodox Church. However, the role of al-Amjad must not be forgotten; he was a high-ranking civil servant who was capable of financing the scholarly activities of his brothers. He maintained a house in Damascus that often served as a kind of research center, commissioned treatises of various sorts, and engaged the future patriarch **Gabriel III** not only as tutor to his son but also as a skilled scribe who copied manuscripts for ongoing projects. Within the family, patronage and talent met.

The Awlad al-'Assal were loyal children of the Coptic Orthodox Church who were involved in the struggles of the Church for institutional well-being (e.g., in the struggles surrounding Patriarch **Cyril III ibn Laqlaq**) and who were greatly interested in the Church's specifically Coptic heritage, as their canonical and Coptic philological production attest. At the same time, they possessed an extraordinary intellectual openness, including a readiness to benefit from earlier Arabic Christian literature of any **Christological** confession. These ingredients, added to the mix of patronage and talent just mentioned, helped to fertilize a glorious flowering of **Copto-Arabic literature**.

– B –

BASHMURIC REVOLTS. *See* COPTIC REVOLTS.

BASILIDES. A Christian **Gnostic** teacher who was active in **Alexandria** in the 130s and probably before that. He is reported by Irenaeus to have brought his heresy from Antioch to Alexandria. An elaborate cosmogonic myth is attributed to him by Irenaeus, and a rather different one by Hippolytus. Irenaeus also attributes to him a doctrine of salvation that involves a **docetic** interpretation of Jesus' crucifixion. The system reported by Irenaeus comes closest to what is known of his writings as quoted by Clement of Alexandria; the version given by Hippolytus is probably by one of his disciples. A commentary on scripture in 24 books (*Exegetika*) is also attributed to him. Fragments of his writings preserved by Clement deal with traditional Christian themes, interpreted with recourse to then-current Greek philosophies—Platonic, Pythagorean, and Stoic. Basilides is the earliest known Christian commentator on scripture. Among his disciples was his son Isidore. Of Isidore's writings only short fragments remain. Basilides was also probably known to **Valentinus**. The Basilidian school did not spread significantly outside of Egypt, but it persisted in Egypt well into the fourth century.

BENJAMIN I. *See* ARAB CONQUEST OF EGYPT.

BERLIN GNOSTIC CODEX (PAPYRUS BEROLINENSIS 8502). A fifth-century papyrus manuscript discovered in Egypt sometime in the 19th century and purchased for the Berlin Museum in 1896 by Carl Schmidt. It contains three **Gnostic** tractates and one non-Gnostic Christian work. These are, respectively, the *Gospel of Mary*, the *Apocryphon of John*, the *Sophia of Jesus Christ*, and the *Act of Peter*. Two of these also occur in the closely related Nag Hammadi collection: the *Aprocyphon of John* (NHC II, 1; III, 1; IV, 1) and the *Sophia of Jesus Christ* (NHC III, 4). The *Act of Peter* was published by Schmidt in 1903 and the rest of the codex by Walter Till in 1955.

BIBLE, COPTIC. The Coptic Church regarded the Old and New Testaments as a single inseparable unit. The basis of the Coptic version of the Old Testament is not a Hebrew text but the Septuagint. The Coptic Bible is based on Greek manuscripts that are older than most of the extant witnesses. However, the Coptic evidence has not yet been systematically applied to a textual criticism of the Greek Bible. Manuscripts of the Coptic Bible are written in several dialects. The oldest extant Coptic biblical text is preserved in a manuscript of the Proverbs that dates from the late third century. A majority of scholars agree that both the New and Old Testaments must have already been translated from Greek into Coptic by the second half of that century.

We do not possess versions of all the books of the Old Testament. A considerable number of manuscripts from the fourth century provide evidence for the existence of larger or smaller portions of several Old Testament books written in the major Coptic dialects, except for the Lycopolitan. Apparently the entire Old Testament had been translated only in Sahidic, but that translation did not survive in its entirety. The Old Testament was also not completed in Boharic, but the following books have completely survived: the Pentateuch, Psalms, Job, the Minor Prophets, Isaiah, Jeremiah, Ezekiel, and Daniel. Proverbs was partly translated. Joshua, Judges, 1–4 Kingdoms, 1–2 Chronicles, Wisdom of Solomon, and Sirach are attested only in liturgical passages. Ruth, Ezra, Nehemiah, Ecclesiastes, Song of Solomon, Esther, Judith, Tobit, and 1–2 Maccabees are not attested. The Psalms are best documented, for they played an important part in the **liturgy** and were learned by heart. There is not yet a complete critical edition of the Coptic Old Testament and no concordance for any dialect.

The Sahidic and Bohairic versions of the New Testament have been completely published by G. Horner (*The Coptic Version of the New Testament in the Southern Dialect*, 7 vols., Oxford 1911–1924; *The Coptic Version of the New Testament in the Northern Dialect*, 4 vols., Oxford 1898–1905). Horner's edition of the Sahidic New Testament does not represent a homogeneous text, having been edited from many fragments with different dates and provenances. After the appearance of Horner's edition, many manuscripts containing the complete Sahidic version of one of the New Testament books were published. They range in date from the 4th or 5th century to the 10th century. Unlike the Sahidic version, there are a number of manuscripts containing complete books of the New Testament written in Bohairic that are unfortunately relatively late. Some manuscripts of other Coptic dialects have been published, such as the Subakhmimic (Lycopolitan) version of the Gospel of John, and the Gospel of Matthew in the Middle Egyptian dialect (Oxyrhynchus).

BISHOP. The Coptic term *episkopos* is a loan word from the Greek that can be translated *bishop, overseer, superintendent*, or *supervisor*.

The Arabic *usquf* derives also from the Greek *episkopos*. According to the **Didascalia**, the bishop should be chosen by the congregation, and his consecration should take place on a Sunday in the presence of the people and the clergy with at least two or three bishops. The bishop's main duties are the instruction of the people and clergy of his diocese, the ordination of **deacons** and **priests**, and the consecration of churches, **liturgical instruments**, and **icons**. The bishop provides for the poor, the widows, and orphans in his diocese. Canon 15 of the **Council of Nicaea** forbids the transference of a bishop from his diocese. The greater majority of Coptic bishops were chosen from among the monks. It was Patriarch **Athanasius** the Apostolic who first encouraged monks to be ordained bishops. According to Bishop John of Ephesus (ca. 516–585), portraits of new bishops were hung in the churches of their dioceses. Unfortunately, only one of the portraits of Coptic bishops survived, which shows Bishop Abraham and dates from the late sixth century. A number of significant Coptic texts represent biographies or encomia on famous bishops such as Macarius, bishop of Tkow (d. 451 or 452) and Pisentius, bishop of Coptos (569–632). The correspondence of the latter and that of Abraham, bishop of Hermonthis show the activities of the Coptic bishop in the sixth and seventh centuries. Bishops played a crucial role in the history of the Coptic Church. Many of them are commemorated in the **synaxarion**. Some were martyrs, such as Patape, bishop of Coptos and Ammonius, bishop of Esna (4th century). **The Monastery of St. Hatre** was built in honor of St. Hatre, who was the Bishop of Aswan in the late fourth century. A number of bishops are scholars, such as **Sawirus ibn al-Muqaffa'** and **Athanasius, bishop of Qus**. The Bishop of **Alexandria** is the **patriarch** of the Coptic Church. *See also* BISHOP'S CONSECRATION; STRUCTURE OF THE COPTIC CHURCH.

BISHOP'S CONSECRATION. This rite includes the imposition of the Gospel, the imposition of the Hand, the ordination prayers, and the concluding ceremonies. The *Apostolic Constitutions* (written around the end of the fourth century) mention that the ordination precedes the full Eucharistic **liturgy** in order that the new **bishop** might preside over the whole of the rite. This custom continues in the Coptic tradition. The imposition of the Gospel book, which is mentioned in the *Apostolic Constitutions*, is restricted in the Coptic rite to the consecration of the Alexandrian **patriarch**. The imposition of hands of bishops on a candidate for the episcopate, which is also mentioned in the *Apostolic Tradition*, is actually observed in the Coptic rite, but the bishops lay their hands on the ordinand's arms.

The text of the first half of the ordination prayers is quite close to the text given in the *Apostolic Constitutions*. The second half contains all the elements common to the Byzantine rite. It seems that a nucleus of this prayer is old enough to have developed in at least two distinct forms prior to the fifth century, as evidenced by the Coptic/ Byzantine version, on the one hand, and the Georgian/Syrian version on the other. The seating (enthronement) of the bishop is one of the concluding ceremonies observed in the Coptic rite and mentioned in the *Canons of Hippolytus* (composed in the fourth century) and the *Apostolic Constitutions*.

The Coptic manuscripts are late, from the 14th century onward. Catholic editions include that of **R. Tukhi** who published the rite in 1761.

BLESSING. The blessing is a **liturgical** gesture by which the **priest** or the **bishop** makes the sign of the cross over the oblation, the water, or **icon**. The blessing may also mean a special prayer for the blessing of food or a house. The blessing is inspired by the gesture of Christ in Mark 10:16. The blessing is also the final prayer of the priest or the bishop for the dismissal of the congregation. This prayer changes according to the season (there is a special one for the **Holy Week**, another for the ceremony of matrimony, etc.). The Coptic **Euchologion** contains several prayers of blessing. For each meaning, the gesture of the priest giving the blessing changes. It is important to note that only priests and bishops are allowed to give the blessing in the Coptic Church.

***BOOK OF THOMAS THE CONTENDER* (NHC II, 7).** A revelation dialogue between the resurrected Jesus and his twin brother, Judas Thomas, purportedly recorded by Mathaias (Matthew?). Judas Thomas is presented as a "contender" (literally, "athlete") for control of bodily passions, an ideal taught by the Savior. The *Book of Thomas the Contender* represents a type of Christianity at home in

Eastern Syria (Edessa), represented also by the *Gospel of Thomas* (NHC II, 2) and the apocryphal *Acts of Thomas*. The text as we have it may be a composite work made up of two sources. Extant only in Coptic, it was probably originally composed in Greek, but Syriac is also a possibility. A third century date is likely.

BRUCE CODEX (CODEX BRUCIANUS). Seventy-eight unbound papyrus leaves purchased in about 1769 in Upper Egypt by the Scottish traveler James Bruce, eventually acquired by the Bodleian Library in Oxford. Inscribed in Coptic, they date from the fourth or fifth century. The papyrus leaves are probably the remains of two independent codices: 31 leaves containing the major portion of an untitled Gnostic work (*Bruce Untitled Text*) and 47 leaves containing parts of another Gnostic work, the *Books of Jeu*. These texts were published by Carl Schmidt in 1892.

BULUS AL-BUSHI (?–ca. 1250). Bishop, theologian. Bulus al-Bushi was a skilled theologian who contributed much to the dawning of the 13th-century golden age of **Copto-Arabic literature**. Little is known of his life before 1216, when after the death of **Patriarch** John VI the scholarly monk Bulus quickly became one of the two leading candidates for the papacy; the other was his monastic acquaintance and colleague Da'ud ibn Laqlaq al-Fayyumi. Due to political machinations, the election was delayed; Bulus eventually withdrew from the contest. In 1235, however, after a vacancy of nearly 20 years, Da'ud was finally made pope as **Cyril III**. Cyril proved so rapacious in his financial dealings that a synod held in 1240 appointed two monks to supervise his activities; one was Bulus, who was consecrated bishop of Misr (Old Cairo).

A number of works by Bulus al-Bushi have been preserved, and they all point to his deep scriptural and patristic knowledge. For example, *Kitab al-I'tiraf* (The Book of Confession), which Bulus coauthored with Da'ud ibn Laqlaq and with contributions by **al-As'ad ibn al-'Assal**, defends the practice of auricular confession; it was Bulus who assembled and translated the patristic materials quoted in the work. Bulus' collection of eight *Sermons for the Feasts of the Lord* has been popular into modern times; three of the sermons were incorporated into an Arabic collection of patristic homilies for the Church year, where Bulus appears with the likes of St. John Chrysostom and St. **Gregory** Nazianzen. His *Commentary on the Apocalypse* may be the first commentary on the Book of Revelation to be composed in Arabic; it was later used by **Ibn Katib Qaysar**. His *Treatise on the Trinity, the **Incarnation**, and the Truth of Christianity* shows us a theologian deeply rooted in the Bible and in the **Alexandrian** tradition of Saints **Athanasius** and Cyril, but capable of expressing his faith in the Arabic idiom of his own day.

BURIAL RITES. The Coptic Church inherited the ancient Egyptian mentality regarding burial rites and ceremonies for the dead, which played an important role in the life of the Coptic congregation. The time of dying is one of the common themes in **Coptic hagiography**. Epitaph inscriptions reflect the mentality of the Coptic Egyptian toward death. Even the doxologies and the glorifications of some saints, such as those for St. Claudius of Antioch, are inspired by the lamentations of Isis.

Burial rites vary according to the status of the deceased person. The Coptic burial rite is similar to the Greek rite in general, but the latter is more elaborate than the Coptic. The Coptic office has a simple structure; it consists of the Prayer of Thanksgiving and lections from the Holy Scriptures with verses from the Psalms, Pauline Epistle, and Gospels. These are followed by the litanies of "Peace," "the Fathers," and "the Congregations," the recitation of the Creed, and then the prayers appropriate to the purpose of the office, that is, the Litany for the Dead. Several hymns may be added to this simple structure according to the status of the deceased person. There are offices for adult men, male children, adult women, female children, women who died in childbirth, **bishops**/metropolitans/**patriarchs**, hegumens/**priests**, deacons, monks, nuns, men who died during the Holy Pascha (Easter), priests who died during the Pascha, deacons who died during Pascha, male children who died during the Pascha, female children who died during the Pascha, and nuns who died during the Pascha. On the third day there is a special rite called the "Lifting of the Mat." This rite is performed in the home of the deceased person. It has a structure that is similar to that described above.

Although there is no critical study of the rite of burial, several fragments from the **Monastery of St. Macarius** and the **Monastery**

of St. Pshoi at Wadi al-Natrun might date from the 13th or 14th centuries.

The first edition was published by Raphael **Tukhi** in 1763. It is, however, not always in agreement with the manuscript tradition. In 1905, Claudius Labib edited the *Book of Mourning*. This book was printed at the command of His Holiness Pope Cyril V in Coptic and in Arabic. Since then, several editions have been published based on this book but with the Arabic text and with only some readings in Coptic.

BUSTAN AL-RUHBAN. *See* SAYINGS OF THE FATHERS.

BUTRUS AL-SADAMANTI (second half of 13th c.). Monk, exegete, theologian. Butrus al-Sadamanti, sometimes also known as al-Armani because of his Armenian origins, was a monk of the Monastery of St. George in Sadamant, in the Fayyum. He is the author of a large number of works in the areas of dogmatic, apologetic, and moral **theology** (including a *Treatise on Doctrine* dated to 1260), as well as **saints'** lives and a collection of prayers and meditations. Although several of these works were published in Egypt by the 19th century, there is a pressing need for modern editions. Butrus' best known work, *al-Qawl al-sahih fi alam al-Sayyid al-Masih* (Correct Speech about the Sufferings of the Lord Christ), is an exegesis of the Gospels' Passion narratives; it was printed in Cairo in 1872 and again in 1926, and has since been frequently reprinted. One of the introductory essays to the work deals with hermeneutical matters, and shows Butrus to be an exegete with a deep respect for the literal sense of the biblical text as well as a homiletician concerned with bringing useful word to his listeners.

BUTRUS SAWIRUS AL-JAMIL, BISHOP OF MALIJ (beginning of 13th c.). Bishop, apologist, hagiographer. The limited information that we possess about Butrus al-Jamil, who perhaps received the name Sawirus upon his consecration as bishop of Malij, points to a polemically minded scholar: his *Kitab al-Ishraq* (The Book of the Sunrise) is a catalog of the errors of other Christian groups (the Melchites, the Franks, the Armenians, the **Nestorians**, and even the Syrian Orthodox), while his *Kitab al-Burhan* (The Book of the Demonstration) is a vigorous response to questions by a Muslim in Cairo, in which Butrus argues for the superiority of Christian ethics and prayer.

According to Shams al-Ri'asa Abu al-Barakat **ibn Kabar**, the Copto-Arabic **Synaxarion** had been attributed to Butrus al-Jamil. While this attribution has not been verified, it is not impossible that Butrus made a compilation of **saints'** lives ordered by date, and that this compilation was later used by others such as **Mikha'il**, Bishop of Akhmim and Malij, who is usually given major credit for the work.

– C –

CALENDAR. *See* COPTIC CALENDAR.

CANON. The word *canon* in Coptic tradition has more than one meaning. It means a type of hymn that should be recited by two choirs, such as the **Canon of the Twelfth Hour** and **Good Friday**. It means also the "canon-law" or codified law governing a church. Thus, there are the Apostolic canons and the Ecclesiastical canons of the Apostles, or the **Didascalia** and the Testament of the Lord. Moreover, there are the canons on the Ecumenical councils, such as **Nicaea**, or the canons of local councils, such as Gangra, or the canons of a patriarch, such as the Canon of **Athanasius**, Basil, or **Gabriel ibn Turayk**. It means also a punishment as introduced by a spiritual father; this consists of more prayers or fasting. A canon means also a spiritual plan, especially for a monk.

"CANON OF THE TWELFTH HOUR," GOOD FRIDAY. The hymn of the "Canon of the Twelfth Hour" of **Good Friday** begins with "Golgotha in Hebrew and Calvary in Greek; the place where you were crucified, O Lord." This hymn is not mentioned in the encyclopedia of **Ibn Kabar**, *The Lamp of the Darkness*. The second stanza refers to a tradition that the **Trisagion** was first spoken by Joseph and Nicodemus: "The righteous Joseph and Nicodemus came and took away Christ's Body and placed ointment on Him, wrapped Him and placed Him in a tomb, praising Him, and saying: 'Holy God, Holy Mighty, Holy Immortal, Who was crucified for us, have mercy upon us.'"

The first Coptic author to mention this tradition is Ibn al-Saba', who took it from the Syrian Orthodox author Yahya ibn Garir (11th century), who in turn was the first to introduce it in Arabic. This author took it from Thomas Bar Képha, who mentioned that this tradition existed before the ninth century. Later (between the 14th and the 17th centuries), this tradition was introduced into the "Canon of the Twelfth Hour" of the **Holy Week**, replacing two other canons mentioned by Ibn Kabar.

No manuscript known from before the 18th century includes this hymn, which was published for the first time by **Tukhi** in 1736 and subsequently appears in all Coptic Orthodox publications of the rite of the Holy Week after that date.

CANONICAL HOURS (BOOK OF). The first Christians followed the Jewish tradition of praying at fixed times of the day. The prayers for the third, sixth, and ninth hours may have been adopted first in Egypt, where the Jews who converted to Christianity followed the Jewish custom. In the third century, Clement of **Alexandria** (ca. 150–ca. 215) was the first to mention set times for prayers at the third, sixth, and ninth hours, as well as on rising, before retiring, and during the night. In the fourth century, **Athanasius** of Alexandria confirmed the existence of cathedral vigils that were comprised readings, responsorial **psalmody**, and prayers and attended by monks as well as laity. John Cassian, who lived in the monastic centers of Egypt, mentioned that in Egypt there were daily morning and evening prayers (**Vespers** and **Matins**). He gave a detailed description of the two daily offices practiced in **Scetis** by the end of the fourth century. At both offices, 12 psalms were recited followed by two readings, one from the Old Testament and the other from the New Testament. The Gloria Patri was used to conclude the office.

John Cassian wrote,

> There are some, too, to whom it has seemed good that in the day offices of prayer viz., Tierce, Sext, and Nones, the number of Psalms and prayers should be made to correspond exactly to the number of the hours at which the services are offered up to the Lord. Some have thought fit that six Psalms should be assigned to each service of the day. And so I think it best to set forth the most ancient system of the fathers which is still observed by the servants of God throughout

the whole of Egypt, so that your new monastery in its untrained infancy in Christ may be instructed in the most ancient institutions of the earliest fathers.

Palladius wrote in his *Historia Lausiaca*, "there were four prayers in the Monasteries of Upper Egypt."

St. **Shenute** the Archimandrite (fifth century), in his *Monastic Precepts*, speaks of "those who are the first at church in the morning, in the evening at mid-day and at the requisite hour."

It is mentioned that St. John Kame "established for [the brethren] canons and holy laws, and set up for them a meeting place where they should meet together in the middle of the night and should sing psalmody and spiritual songs until the light break. And he bade them moreover one and all that they should pray each one apart."

Yuhanna ibn Abi Zakariyya ibn Sabba', in his book the *Precious Pearl of the Ecclesiastical Science*, mentioned in chapter 35, the time of prayer for the man is seven times per day and night. Ibn Sabba' gave the reason for each prayer, such as the Pentecost for the Third Hour. He did not mention the Prayer of the Veil.

Ibn Kabar, in his encyclopedia *The Lamp of Darkness for the Explanation of the Service*, started by mentioning the prayer of the sunset and the prayer of dawn. For him, the prayer of the matins is established for the following reasons: "On the one hand, it is the time that Adam and Eve dressed by the skin and started to work, on the other hand, this is the time of Resurrection." For the third hour, Ibn Kabar also gave two reasons: "On the one hand it is the time of the creation of our father Adam and his entrance to the Paradise, and on the other hand it is also the time when Pilate condemned our Lord." (He did not mention the Pentecost as Ibn Sabba' had). Ibn Kabar used to make the comparison between Jesus Christ (the new Adam) and Adam the first creation, which is not mentioned in other books.

It is hard to follow the development of each part of the Horologion. Some examples are given here.

The **Troparion/Doxology** of the Prime: Most of the manuscripts used to insert the Doxology **Adam** "O true light" after the Gospel of the Matins. A manuscript from the ninth century, preserved in the Monastery of St Catherine's library, contains this doxology. It was established according to the Palestinian tradition of St. Sabas and introduced to the Coptic Church through the **Monastery of St. Antony** (was in the hands of the Melchite in the ninth century). The monks of this monastery continued their tradition of praying this hymn. By the beginning of the 12th century, an editor of the Agpia (the Prayer Book of the Seven Canonical Hours), wishing to follow the pattern of the other prayers, made from some parts of the Doxology Adam a kind of troparion (a short hymn of one stanza or series of stanzas).

The Troparion of the Sext: According to Anton Baumstark, the fact that the troparia appear in both the Byzantine rite and in the Coptic rite indicate that they should be dated no later than the fifth or sixth century. But a special attention shows that the Coptic text uses *Morphy* instead of the actual Greek word **icon**. It can be assumed that during the iconoclastic controversy, some iconodules intentionally made this change. This troparion is used as the Apolyptikion Hymn on the first Sunday of Lent at the Feast of the Orthodoxy (iconodulic feast), which commemorates the triumph of the right faith over iconoclasm.

It is noteworthy to mention that the troparion of the Sext and the None are a prayer to Jesus. The Prayer to Jesus was a subject of a great debate during the **Council of Nicaea**. But in the fifth century, it became more accepted; **St. Shenute** of Atrib used to say, "That those who refuse to direct his prayers to the Son, let his mouth be shut and he is not allowed to pray to the Father." This prayer confirms the dating proposed by Baumstark, that is, the troparia of the Sext and None are from the fifth and sixth centuries.

The troparion and the **Theotokion** of the Midnight Office of the Third Nocturne is not found in the actual Horologion. It occurs in a manuscript from the **Monastery of St. Pshoi at Wadi al-Natrun** preserved in the State University Library of Hamburg:

> At all times, guiding them unto Thee. Likewise, also, those yearn for Thee, guard them, O Compassionate One, in order that we may continually sing to Thee and glorify Thee. "Now and always etc." All generation call thee blessed, O Virgin God-bearer, for the inseparable Jesus Christ was pleased to be in thee. Blessed are we, for thou art a protectress for us day and night, interceding for us, and the arms of our kings are set up through thy prayers. Wherefore, we sing to thee, crying out saying: Hail, thou who art full of grace, the Lord is with thee.

The Prayer of the Veil is a doubling of Complines. It appears first in Ibn Kabar around 1320. The text is in Arabic (a sure sign of its late origin) and is composed of elements from the other hours. It is used only in monasteries.

Manuscripts show that there is more than one version of the Horologion; the main categories are given here without further detail:

1. The recitation of the complete Psalter (Book of Psalms); mainly the hermits observe this practice.
2. Some of the Coptic manuscripts follow the Byzantine type, which distribute the whole Psalter over the week. This tradition can be found in the Psalter's edition of Claudios Labib (and reprint by Shaker Basilios).
3. The "Cairene use" mentioned in a manuscript (now in Hamburg) from the Monastery of St. Pshoi at Wadi al-Natrun, which goes back to the 13th or 14th century: "according to the custom of the inhabitants of Babylon." We can therefore expect that this type is the one described by Ibn Kabar.
4. The Palestinian Ordo contains a different distribution of the psalms.

The Catholic editions include that of Raphael **Tukhi**, who published for the first time the Horologion in 1750, 388 pages in two-column Coptic and Arabic, and another Coptic-Arabic edition that appeared in Cairo in 1930 and was called the "Book of Hours." The Orthodox editions include a first edition that appeared in Cairo in 1892 and was entitled "The Book of the Seven Prayers." It was again published in 1900, 1906, and 1907. In 1975, the Karuz Bookshop prepared a bilingual edition (Coptic and Arabic) that included for the first time several absolutions and troparia by a retroversion from the Arabic text with the help of Ayoub Farag. The English Orthodox editions are published by the Copts in the Diaspora in America, Australia, and Canada.

CANONIZATION. Canonization is the formal declaration of a deceased person's sanctity, whereby his or her name is added to the roll of the **saints** of the Church and commended for veneration by the faithful. In the Roman Catholic Church, the authority to canonize is the prerogative of the Pope of Rome, who follows a very complicated procedure that dates back to the Middle Ages. No historical literature on the process of canonization in the Coptic Church exists. In most of the hagiographical texts, it says that a church was built and named after a certain martyr. In the Coptic tradition, it is stated that St. **Macarius** the Great, according to **Palladius**, invited the brethren to the "martyrdom of the little strangers" (considering them as martyrs and saints). No text can be found in Coptic canon law organizing this procedure. Many relics were venerated (some recently discovered), among them the martyrs of Fayoum and Beshnufa. In recent times, the authority to canonize in the Coptic Church has rested with the Holy Synod.

CARPOCRATES. A Christian **Gnostic** teacher active in **Alexandria** in the early second century. His teachings are summarized by Irenaeus and other Church Fathers. According to them, he taught a typical Gnostic cosmogony according to which the world was created and is governed by inferior creator angels. The soul of Jesus was able to escape their clutches. Carpocrates is reported to have taught a "libertine" ethic according to which salvation is achieved by engaging in all manner of forbidden licentious acts. The souls of those not having sufficient experience of forbidden acts are condemned to be reincarnated. No writings of Carpocrates are known. Among his disciples was his son Epiphanes, who wrote a book *On Righteousness*, in which he taught that wives should be had in common. Fragments of this writing are quoted by Clement of Alexandria. Irenaeus mentions that a Carpocratian female teacher named Marcellina came to Rome and taught there.

CATECHETICAL SCHOOL OF ALEXANDRIA. The origin of the Catechetical School of **Alexandria** is obscure. The first historic attestation of the School of Alexandria is around the year 180 A.D. under the direction of Pantaenus, according to **Eusebius of Caesarea** in his *Church History*. The reputation of this school grew with Pantanenus' successors Clement and **Origen**. The scholars of this school adopted an allegorical interpretation of the Bible. Many Coptic **patriarchs** studied and directed this school. Among the key figures of the school was Didymus the Blind, who was the director of this institution in the fourth century. Among the famous personalities of those who studied in the School of Alexandria was **Gregory of Na-**

zianzus. It is important to mention that the School of Alexandria was Greek in its literature; thus, no Coptic text has been found from any of the key figures of the school except for some writings by Gregory of Nazianzus, not as a scholar of the school but as a Church Father. Some Coptic authors claim that St. **Mark** was the first founder of this school, but there is no historical evidence to support this.

CATHEDRAL OF ST. MARK IN CAIRO. It is located in the most important Coptic center in Egypt, known as Anba Ruwais. The cathedral is the only church in Egypt that was built by an Egyptian government despite the long history of Christianity in Egypt. On 24 July 1965 President Gamal Abd al-Nasser laid its foundation stone. On 26 July 1968 Patriarch **Cyril VI** (1959–1971) and the Ethiopian Emperor Haile Selassie I inaugurated the cathedral on the occasion of the transfer of the relics of St. **Mark** the Evangelist from Venice to Cairo. The Catholic papacy returned the relics to the Coptic Church as a gesture of goodwill between the two churches. The cathedral is one of the largest churches in Africa. Its imposing structure measures 100 meters long, 36 meters wide, and 55 meters high. The belfry is 85 meters high. There are two shrines on the ground floor under the cathedral. One houses the relics of St. Mark and the other the relics of St. **Athanasius** (326–373); on 6 May 1973 Pope **Shenouda III** received the relics from Pope Paul VI in Rome. The papal residence lies in front of St. Mark's Cathedral. This Coptic compound includes the medieval church of St. Ruwais, the **Clerical College**, the **Higher Institute of Coptic Studies**, the new cultural center with the library, and other Coptic institutions.

CHALCEDON, COUNCIL OF. After the death of the Emperor Theodosius II in 450, his sister Pulcheria married Marcian, who accordingly became emperor. The new imperial officials convoked a council at Chalcedon in order to see to the matters of the Eutychians and the **Nestorians**. As a result of this council, the Coptic patriarch **Dioscorus** was deposed and exiled to Gangra. The council also adopted the famous Canon 28, which considered the Church of Constantinople as the "New Rome" and hence held first place among the apostolic sees. The council adopted the *Tome* (letter) of Leo to Flavian as orthodox. The Coptic Church refused to recognize this council, and this caused a schism between the Orientals and the rest of Christendom. In the 20th century, theologians from the East and the West accepted that both the Chalcedonian and the non-Chalcedonian statements on **Christology** are acceptable as orthodox.

CHRISM. After baptism, candidates are anointed with the oil of thanksgiving. Then they go into the church and receive the laying on of hands and are anointed with the chrism of **confirmation**. A **priest** administers this rite in the Coptic Church. The **patriarch** and the **bishops** consecrate the oil of chrism. After a short prayer over the holy chrism, the priest anoints the baptized with it by making the sign of the cross 36 times on different parts of the body.

CHRIST, NATURE OF. *See* CHRISTOLOGY.

CHRISTODOULOS (?–1077). Patriarch (66th, 1046–1077). The importance of Christodoulos (a monk of the **Monastery of al-Baramous** before his consecration as patriarch) to the history of **Copto-Arabic literature** may be seen from two sides. First, the events of his turbulent patriarchate are recounted by **Mawhub ibn Mansur ibn Mufarrij** in the first of two biographies that he composed in Arabic—rather than translated from Coptic—for inclusion in the *History of the Patriarchs*. Second, shortly after becoming patriarch, Christodoulos issued a set of 31 canons—in Arabic. While canonical materials may have been translated into Arabic by Coptic Orthodox scholars before this (see, e.g., **Abu Salih Yu'annis**), the canons of Christodoulos appear to be the first set of canons to be composed in Arabic in the Coptic Orthodox Church. Thus, both as the subject of a patriarchal biography and as an author of canons regulating the life of the Church, Christodoulos' name is associated with the Arabization of the Coptic community; he stands at the beginning of a period of linguistic transition that would continue through the rest of the 11th century and the whole of the 12th century.

CHRISTOLOGY. Christology is the study of all that pertains to Christ. Several dogmas were discussed throughout the history of the Church by the leaders and theologians of the Church concerning the nature of Christ; whether he is God or merely became a son by adoption

(**Bishop** Paul of Samosata). The divine nature was discussed during the Arian crisis in the fourth century and especially at the **Councils of Nicaea** and **Constantinople**. The nature of and the relation between this divinity and humanity in Christ were discussed at the **Councils of Ephesus** and **Chalcedon**. After the Council of Chalcedon, several theological debates and works defending or opposing the definitions of this council appeared. Notable among these are the works of **Severus of Antioch**.

CHURCH, LAYING OF THE CORNERSTONE. A box is prepared, containing the Bible, a silver cross, a current coin, and a certificate containing the names of the **patriarch**, the governor, the **bishop**, the **priest**, and the leaders of the congregations, that is certified by the officials and dated. The bishop then takes the box, puts it under the place of the door of the main sanctuary, and then blesses it. **Incense** is then offered, followed by the Prayer of Thanksgiving, and a reading of the prophecies from Genesis 28:1–31. The Pauline Epistle (Heb. 9:1–11) comes next, followed by the psalm and the gospel. Then the priest prays the Prayers for Peace, the Patriarch, and the Congregations, and then a special prayer and the absolutions. The structure of this rite is identical to other rites such as the rites of burial and marriage. This rite was published for the first time in 1959 by Bishop **Athanasius** of Beni Sueif.

CHURCH CONSECRATION. Consecration, in general, is an act by which a thing is separated from a common and profane to a sacred use. Church consecration is a rite performed by the **bishop** or the pope in order to implore God's blessing on the new church. This rite occurs also in other Eastern and Latin churches. The rite of the consecration of a church is known only from late manuscripts. The most ancient of these dates from the 12th century in the **Monastery of the Syrians**. Another manuscript dates from 1307 and is preserved in Selly Oak College. This rite consists of five major parts: (1) **Vespers**, which is the Prayer of Thanksgiving, followed by Psalms 121–151 and readings from the **Old Testament** and the Apocalypse; (2) consecration of the church, offering of **incense**, chants, readings from the Pauline Epistle, the Catholic Epistle, the Book of Acts, the Gospels (four Gospels), and three intercessions; (3) introductory prayers;

(4) consecration of the altar and unction of the altar; and (5) prayers of thanksgiving. This is followed by (6) Eucharistic **liturgy**. Although the manuscripts are of late dates, several allusions can be found to this rite in the more ancient literature. The **Antiphonarion** of Hamouli, preserved in the Pierpont Morgan Library (dated 892–893 A.D.), mentions a local tradition for the consecration of the Church of Kalamon, and alludes to several themes that occur in the rite of the consecration of the church. The first two parts evoke the heavenly Jerusalem (Rev. 21:10), the third mentions the testament (Exod. 19:10–11), the fourth is a comparison between the Jewish priesthood and Christ (Heb. 9:2–14), the fifth and sixth quote are from the **Theotokia** of Sunday, the seventh quotes Matt. 16:13–19, and the last part is the Prayer of Solomon (II Chron. 6:12). In the life of Samuel of Kalamun, written in the seventh or eighth century, there is an allusion to the consecration of his church using the same themes as the rite of the consecration. The book of the history of the consecration of the sanctuary of Benjamin, written probably by the seventh century and known only from a manuscript of the 14th century, gives some details about the consecration of the altar with Myron oil, the Alleluia, and the use of Psalm 83. (Note: Myron oil is the holy oil used to consecrate altars, churches, and icons. It is also used for the sacrament of Baptism.) In the questions of Theodore to the **patriarch** (seventh century), the latter made allusion to the consecration of the Temple of Solomon while speaking about the church. There is another rite for reconsecration of churches and their altars to be used when they have been defiled or polluted by infidels or heretics.

Editions include Horner's *The Service for the Consecration of a Church and Altar According to the Coptic Rite* (London, 1902) and Burmester's *The Egyptian or Coptic Church Detailed Description of Her Liturgical Services and Rites* (Cairo, 1967, pp. 236–250).

CHURCH OF ST. MERCURIUS (ABU SAYFAYN). The church is one of Egypt's most significant churches and is the largest church in Old Cairo. It was probably erected in the sixth century, and thus it is the only surviving church in Cairo that could have been founded before the **Arab conquest of Egypt. Patriarch** Abraham (975–978) rebuilt the church since it had been partly demolished. In 1080, 47 **bishops** assembled there to establish the ecclesiastical canons to be adopted by the Copts. The church was pillaged and burned by the fanatic mobs in 1168 and was rebuilt in 1174–1175. A number of patriarchs resided in the Church of Abu Sayfayn in the 12th and 13th centuries. In the 16th and 18th centuries, some patriarchs were consecrated in that church, and many were buried there. The church's central sanctuary is imposing. Its unique medieval wooden screen features elaborately carved cruciform ivory plaques. The church is rich in wall paintings representing **saints** as well as Old and New Testaments scenes; some of them are rare, such as the Transfiguration, which may date to the 12th century. It is also famous for its remarkable collection of icons, especially the medieval icons of the 13th and 14th centuries.

CHURCH OF STS. SERGIUS AND BACCHUS (ABU SARGAH). It is the oldest church within the Fortress of Babylon at Old Cairo, dating to the late seventh century. The church is famous for the cave beneath the sanctuary where the **Holy Family** is believed to have taken refuge during their sojourn in Egypt. A number of **patriarchs** were elected there. It served as the episcopal church of the See of Misr that replaced the former See of Babylon. The Church of Sts. Sergius and Bacchus is a basilica with two rows of six monolithic columns surmounted by Corinthian capitals; some of the columns are painted with **saints**, probably Apostles. The wooden screen of the altar is decorated with fine carvings representing three equestrian saints, the Nativity, and the Last Supper; they date to the 13th century. The oldest wooden altar found in Egypt (5th century) was taken from the church to the **Coptic Museum**.

CHURCH OF THE HOLY VIRGIN MARY (MO'ALLAQA). *See* MO'ALLAQA.

CLERICAL COLLEGE (CAIRO). It was inaugurated as a religious school on 3 January 1875. The aim of its establishment was to prepare a new generation of educated Coptic **priests**. The main subjects taught were **theology**, **liturgy**, Church history, ecclesiastical jurisprudence, and rhetoric, in addition to Arabic, Coptic, geography, and mathematics. When in 1918 **Habib Girgis** was appointed a headmaster of the school, he greatly improved its curriculum. He persuaded **Patriarch** Cyril V (1874–1927) to limit the ordination of priests to its graduates. During the pontificate of Pope **Shenouda III** (1971–), the **Clerical College** has attracted many university students, including women, who have joined the evening classes. A number of seminaries in **Alexandria**, Tanta, **Dayr al-Muharraq**, al-Balyana, and others are affiliated with the Clerical College of Cairo. The most significant publications of the college are the Coptic (Bohairic) biblical texts and a number of liturgical books.

CODEX BRUCE UNTITLED TEXT. A Christian **Gnostic** treatise describing the unfolding of the transcendent world and the material creation. It is usually regarded as the latest extant treatise of **Sethian** Gnosticism. A divine being called Setheus plays a demiurgic role in the text, and references are made in it to two Gnostic prophets, Nicotheus, whose "apocalypse" was read in Plotinus' school in Rome in the mid-third century (VP 16), and Marsanes, whose own apocalypse is partially preserved in Nag Hammadi Codex X. Codex Bruce Untitled is strongly influenced by third-century Platonism. Extant only in Coptic, it was originally written in Greek, probably in late third- or early fourth-century Egypt.

COMMUNION. Communion is the act of partaking of the body and blood of Christ. Communion is given many designations in the New Testament, such as, "a new covenant" (Heb. 8:8–12), "eternal life" (John 6:54), a "dwelling in Christ" (John 5:56; 15:5–7), and a "sharing in the Body of Christ" (1 Cor. 10:16–17). Since the early Church, communion was permitted only to the faithful. In administering the body and blood of Jesus Christ to the communicants, the Coptic Church follows as closely as possible the procedure set by Christ when he instituted this sacrament. The two elements, first the bread and then the wine, are separately given. In the Coptic tradition, the **bishop** starts by partaking himself, followed by the rest of the clergy and the deacons, then the congregation—men first, then women. The Church has laid down certain requirements to be met before receiving communion.

CONCEPT OF OUR GREAT POWER **(NHC VI, 4).** A Christian **Gnostic** treatise dealing with "salvation history," from creation to the end of the world. The title occurs at the end, but another title occurs at the beginning: "The Perception of Understanding: The Concept of the Great Power." In this text, "the Great Power" refers to the transcendent God. The tractate shows signs of editorial redaction. Probably dating to the early fourth century as we now have it, earlier sources are reflected in it. Extant only in Coptic, *Concept of Our Great Power* was originally composed in Greek; its provenience is uncertain.

CONFESSION AND PENITENCE. Confession is actually considered one of the sacraments of the Church, where the **priest** gives the **absolution** to the penitent. The Coptic Church believes that Christ gave this authority of loosening and binding to his disciples (Matt. 16:19). After his Resurrection, Christ also sent out his disciples, giving them the authority to forgive and retain sins (John 20:22–23). The pastoral letters of Paul mention the excommunication of Christian sinners (1 Tim. 5:19–22). There may also be an allusion to group confession in Acts 19:18. In the third century, Tertullian was the first Christian author to use the word *exomologese*, denoting confession in front of the congregation with the **bishop** subsequently pronouncing the absolution.

It is well known that a spiritual guide for the monks has always existed. The Eastern tradition, following Clement's and **Origen**'s lead, emphasized the church's ministers as healers and the importance of spiritual direction. According to K. Holl, it was St. Basil the Great who established this practice; however, many scholars reject this idea, showing that it was only for the monks. Theodore of Mopsuestia, in his catechetical homilies, mentioned some words of the auricular confession. The first clear reference in Coptic history is from the 12th century, when there was a debate between **Mikh'il, Metropolitan of Damietta**, and **Marqus ibn Qunbar** about the necessity for auricular confession. Mark borrowed this practice from the Melchite Church in Egypt along with many other things, but he was excommunicated from the Coptic Church and died in 1208. According to **Abu Salih al Armani**, Marqus ibn Qunbar wrote a book entitled *Book of Confessions* and also *Book of the Master and Disciple*. Patriarch **Cyril ibn Laqlaq** published *Book of the Master and Disciple* in the year 1240 with the help of **Al-As'ad ibn al-'Assal** and **Bulus al-Bushi**. The book was considered for a long time as lost but Ugo Zanetti and M. Swantson have identified two manuscripts of this important book.

After a long period of neglect, the sacrament of Confession has recently been revived, and is today practiced by Copts privately in front of a priest, and concluded by the priest reading inaudibly the absolution of the Son.

CONFESSION OF THE FATHERS (ca. 1078). Patristic florilegium (literally a "selection of flowers," like a bouquet; a chain of quotations from selected authorities). The anonymous text known as *I'tiraf al-Aba'* (Confession of the Fathers) is a patristic florilegium. *Confession* is significant as an assertion and defense of the one-nature (Miaphysite) **Christology** of the Coptic Church compiled in Arabic, though largely from **Coptic-language** sources, around the year 1078. It thus takes its place with *History of the Patriarchs* and various canonical works as an instance of what may be seen as a late 11th-century project of putting key resources of the Coptic Orthodox Church into the Arabic language. To judge from the large number of manuscript copies, *Confession* was widely read and used; furthermore, in the 16th century it was translated into Ethiopic and, in Arabic, refashioned in a Catholic adaptation. A noncritical but useful edition of *Confession* was published in 2002 in an inexpensive volume by the monks of the Muharraq Monastery.

The *Confession of the Fathers* presents material from 53 authors, including the great theologians of the early Church (with **Cyril of Alexandria** figuring especially prominently among them), later teachers of the one-nature **Christology** such as **Severus of Antioch**, and the medieval Syrian Orthodox theologians Habib Abu Ra'ita and Yahya ibn 'Adi. The text also preserves a number of the "synodical letters" exchanged by the **patriarchs** of **Alexandria** and Antioch on the occasion of the election of a new patriarch, and thereby provides a window into a relationship that was important to the life of both the Coptic and the Syrian Orthodox churches, especially when other relationships were cut off or made problematic after the **Arab conquest**.

CONFIRMATION. Confirmation is one of the sacraments of initiation into the Coptic Orthodox Church. It is administered immediately after Baptism and before partaking of the Eucharist. In the Coptic Church, it is performed by unction with the holy oil by a **priest** or a **bishop** (in the Catholic Church, it is the right of the bishop or his vicar). There are several references to this sacrament dating as far back as the **apostolic fathers**, such as in the works of Clement of Rome. This rite is also mentioned by Clement of **Alexandria** (ca. 150–ca. 215) in the *Pedagogue* 1:6 and the *Stromata*. The Arabic canons of the **Council of Nicaea** highlighted the importance of this sacrament in Canons 31 and 69. Basil the Great (330–379) mentioned this rite in his treatise on the **Holy Spirit**. We owe also to the catechetical homilies of Cyril of Jerusalem many allusions to this sacrament. Pseudo Dionysius mentioned this sacrament in his book entitled *The Ecclesiastical Hierarchy*.

The Coptic priest makes the sign of the cross over the child 36 times (at different points of the body) using the oil of the **chrism** (Myron) prepared by the **patriarch** while imploring the Father to send the Holy Spirit on the baptized person. The priest then gives the mysteries (**communion**). The deacons sing "Worthy, Worthy, Worthy."

CONFRATERNITY. The members of the confraternity were called in Greek *philoponoi* (the lovers of work) or the *spoudaioi* (the zealots). They were lay people who undertook a variety of services: caring for the poor, building churches, and assisting in worship services. They are mentioned in the time of St. **Athanasius**. The canons attributed to Athanasius and dating from the fifth century mention them also. The *Life of Severus of Antioch*, written by his friend Zachariah the Scholar in the early sixth century, highlights the role of this confraternity in combating paganism. In a homily ascribed to Severus of Antioch on the Archangel Michael, it says that the archbishop sent to the people who had received the faith several **priests**, deacons, and *philoponoi*. This detail is only mentioned in the Sahidic version of the homily but is omitted in both the Bohairic and Arabic versions. Among the famous *philoponoi* was the sixth-century John Philoponus, who wrote several commentaries on Aristotle and composed some works attacking the **Council of Chalcedon**. In addition to the literary sources, several papyri mention the role of the *philoponoi* in economic and philanthropic activities.

CONSECRATION. *See* BISHOP'S CONSECRATION; CHURCH CONSECRATION; PATRIARCH'S CONSECRATION.

CONSTANTINOPLE, SECOND COUNCIL OF. The Second Council of Constantinople took place in the year 553 A.D. during the reign of Justinian. The council anathematized *The Three Chapters* (the works of Theodoret and Ibas of Edessa) and condemned, post mortem, Theodore of Mopsuestia as the real instigator of **Nestorianism**. Some 165 **bishops** attended this council, including five African bishops. The Pope of Rome, Vigilius, was confined and coerced into accepting the decisions of this council, after which he was permitted to return to Rome. Because of these decisions, the bishops of Italy, Illyria, and Africa broke off with Rome for nearly half a century. These decisions did not change the position of the Coptic Church

CONSTANTINOPLE, THIRD COUNCIL OF. The Third Council of Constantinople took place in 680–681 A.D. Egypt was under Arab control and the Coptic Church had been estranged since the **Council of Chalcedon** in 451 A.D., and hence was not represented at this council. Emperor Constantine IV tried to put an end to the monothelite controversy, which started under Heraclius. Some 174 fathers attended and signed the final statement of the council. In the acts of this council, **Dioscorus** of **Alexandria** and **Severus of Antioch** were considered among the heretics.

CONVERSION TO ISLAM. After the **Arab conquest of Egypt** (640–642), the bulk of the Egyptians remained Christian in the first two centuries of Islamic rule. By the beginning of the third century of Arab occupation, however, the resistance of the Copts was broken and their economic status was dramatically weakened because of the financial burdens imposed on them. Their social status deteriorated and their religious leaders were humiliated. The Church economy and its institutions had been systematically weakened. Monks were tortured to the point of having their hands amputated and even to death. **Bishops** and **patriarchs** were sometimes put in shackles and imprisoned. The Arabization of Egypt played a crucial role in the Islamization of the country. Arab tribes settled in various regions and took up agriculture, mingling with Copts especially in eastern Delta. They considered themselves sons of the country and no longer its masters. The Arabization of the administration by Umayyad Caliph Abdel-Malik (685–705) tempted Copts to learn Arabic. With the brutal crushing of the last of the **Coptic revolts** in 832, the conversion of the Copts to Islam increased dramatically. Not long after that year, the Copts had to obey the orders of Abbasid Caliph al-Mutawakkil (847–861) to wear distinctive dress and not to ride horses. Such a measure would not have been implemented were the Copts still a great majority. Under the Fatimids (969–1171) and the Ayyubids (1171–1250), the Copts were a minority community living in a Muslim society. Their lives and properties were protected by Islamic law that demanded from them segregation and subservience. They and their churches were often vulnerable to the attack and plunder of Muslim mobs, they were dismissed from government offices, and they had to wear distinctive dress.

The arrival of the Crusades in the region brought new problems for the Copts. These wars led to a hostile movement against the Christians in the East, especially the Copts, and left a legacy of hatred between them and the Muslims. In the Mamluk Period (1250–1517), Muslim masses frequently destroyed churches and plundered Copts, who were the scapegoat for the hard time of that period, especially under the Bahari Mamluks (1250–1390). By that time the Copts were reduced to a small minority that today represents around 10 percent of Egypt's population.

COPT. The term "Copt" and the adjective "Coptic" are derived from the Arabic *qibt*, which in turn is a corruption of the Greek term for the indigenous population of Egypt (*Agyptos* and *Aigyptioi*). Initially, after the **Arab conquest of Egypt** (639–641), the new rulers of the country used the word as a designation for the country's non-Arabic-speaking non-Muslim inhabitants, who were Christians. When the great majority of the Egyptians gradually converted to Islam, they naturally ceased to be *qibt*. Later, "Copt" and "Christian" became virtually synonymous. This must not obscure the fact that the term "Copt" and its adjective "Coptic" are elastic in an ethnic, cultural, and religious sense. A certain amount of confusion has surrounded the use of the term "Copt" by scholars of several disciplines and sometimes of the same discipline.

In theological parlance, the term "Copt" is used specifically to identify the adherents of the Egyptian Church (the Coptic Orthodox Church), which broke off relations with Constantinople and became a national church after the **Council of Chalcedon**. The term "Copt" applies also to small minorities of Christian Egyptians who have become Catholic and Protestant and belong respectively to the Catholic Coptic Church and the Evangelical Coptic Church. The **Coptic language** is the last stage of the ancient Egyptian language that was the spoken daily language of all the Egyptians, probably as late as the 11th century when it began to be superseded by Arabic. **Coptic art** is a distinctive art that appeared in the third or fourth century and survived as late as the 13th or 14th century. The Ethiopian Church is often called Coptic because it has shared close ties with the Coptic Orthodox Church and recognized its Coptic **patriarch** from the fourth century to as late as 1948. Scholars use the term "Coptic Period" in connection with the history of the Coptic Church or the Copts from the beginning of the formation of the Coptic language, or from the Council of Chalcedon (451), to the Arab conquest of Egypt. However, the Copts enriched the Egyptian civilization throughout their long history, and they still contribute to every aspect of Egypt's culture.

COPTIC ART. *See* ART, COPTIC.

COPTIC BIBLE. *See* BIBLE, COPTIC.

COPTIC CALENDAR. The Coptic calendar, sometimes referred to as the Alexandrian Calendar, is based on the ancient Egyptian calendar of the solar year. This calendar system continued to be used by the Coptic Church. The Coptic year is divided into 12 months of 30 days each, followed by five more days, called e*pagomenai*, as well as the extra day of an intercalary month, making a year of 366 days. The Coptic leap year follows the same rules as the Julian calendar so that the extra month always has six days in the year before a Julian leap. Since the fourth century, Coptic years are counted according to the Era of Diocletian, whose accession to the throne in 284 marks the beginning of "Era of Martyrs" or Coptic calendar because of the mass execution of Christians and the martyrdom of countless believers. It is conventionally abbreviated A. M. (for *anno martyrum*). Thus the Copts mark the 29 August 284 A.D. as the beginning of their history.

The Coptic year starts on 11/12 September, depending on leap years. The twelve months, pronounced in Arabic, are: Tut (11/12 September to 9/10 October), Babah (11/12 October to 9/10 November), Hatur (10/11 November to 9/10 December), Kiyahk (10/11 December to 8/9 January), Tubah (9/10 January to 7/8 February), Amshir (8/9 February to 9 March), Baramhat (10/11 March to 8 April), Baramudah (9 April to 8 May), Bachans (9 May to June 7), Ba'unah (8 June to 7 July), Abib (8 July to 6 August), and Misra (7 August to 5 September). The *epagomenal* or intercalary days are called in Arabic "al-Nasi."

The three seasons of the Coptic calendar are based on the ancient Egyptian three seasons of the agricultural life in the Nile valley: The Nile-flood season, the sowing season, and the harvest season. Although the agricultural system was completely changed after the erection of the High Dam of Aswan, these seasons are still remembered in the **liturgy** of the Coptic Church; for example "Priest: Graciously, O lord, bless the waters of the river, the vegetation, the plants of the fields, the winds of the sky, and the crops of the land this year. . . ."

COPTIC CHURCH REVIEW (CCR). It is a quarterly journal published since 1980 by the Society of Coptic Church Studies, East Brunswick, New Jersey. Dr. Rodolph Yanney, Editor-in-Chief, founded *CCR* in order to address a significant void in English-language scholastic theological literature on the Coptic Church and the Coptic religious heritage. Born in 1929, Rodolph Yanney, M.D. is an internist who has dedicated his life to patristics and contributed extensively to *CCR* and patristics conferences. He is a member of the American Society of Patristic Studies.

CCR presents the Coptic Orthodox Church and its **liturgy, theology**, monastic literature, art, **iconography**, **music**, history, archeology, architecture, and even social and political roles and struggles. *CCR* publishes scholastic papers by authors from around the world and from a variety of religious backgrounds.

Besides topics specific to the Coptic Church, the patristic literature and its critiques have been a special focus of *CCR*, which features prominently the writings and biographies of the universal church fathers. Occasional special issues explore one subject, such as St.

Athanasius the Great (vol. 4, no. 2, 1983); St. **Pachomius** (vol. 5, no. 1, 1984); Life of St. **Antony** (vol. 15, no.1, 1994); Patriarch **Cyril VI** (vol. 17, no. 1, 1996); and St. **Cyril** of **Alexandria** (vol.19, no. 1, 1998).

COPTIC DIALECTS. There are six main dialects: Sahidic, Bohairic, Fayumic, Oxyrhynchite (Middle Egyptian), Akhmimic, and Lycopolitan (Subakhmimic). The number of Coptic dialects has increased with the discovery of more Coptic manuscripts and the intensive research in Coptic dialects, especially in the second half of the 20th century. However, locating the dialects geographically remains a matter of contention, simply because the provenance of the vast majority of Coptic manuscripts is uncertain. Almost all original **Coptic literature** was written in Sahidic, which is a literary standard dialect because of its dialectal neutrality as it shares many features with the other dialects. The oldest Sahidic manuscript dates from the third century. Most of the dialects are not attested in literary texts beyond the sixth century. Fayumic was in continual use in documents until the 9th or 10th century. Sahidic texts were copied as late as the early 11th century, when it was supplanted by Bohairic. The latter was the dialect of western Delta and the monasteries of **Wadi al-Natrun**. Bohairic is still in use today in the **liturgy** of the Coptic Church.

COPTIC ENCYCLOPEDIA. (Atiya, Aziz Suryal, ed., 8 vols., New York: Macmillan, 1991). It is undoubtedly the most important reference tool for Coptic studies. The encyclopedia comprises approximately 2,800 entries signed by 215 scholars. They cover almost all aspects of Christianity in Egypt and as such represent an essential reference tool for anyone interested in Egypt's Christian history, art and archaeology, **Coptic language** and **literature**, **monasticism**, and the Christian Arabic literature of the Copts. It is also a valuable reference tool for many other disciplines, such as Egyptology, papyrology, religious studies, art history, and Islamic studies.

COPTIC LANGUAGE. It is the final stage of the ancient Egyptian language, which was the language of the Egyptians for more than three millennia. All the essential structural aspects of Coptic, syntax in particular, are Egyptian. The knowledge of Coptic played a crucial role in the decipherment of the ancient Egyptian language by Jean François Champollion (1790–1832). In the Roman period, the first steps were taken to compose an Egyptian text using the Greek alphabet, called Old Coptic by scholars, which was attested from the first to the fourth or fifth century in magical, astrological, and religious texts of pagan origin. The Coptic alphabet comprised the entire Greek alphabet and several letters derived from the demotic signs; there are six letters in the Sahidic dialect, some other **Coptic dialects** feature more, and others less. The proportion of Greek words varies from one Coptic text to another; Greek words represent more than 20 percent of some Coptic texts. The translation of the Bible from Greek into Coptic, which occurred probably as early as the third century, played a significant role in the standardization of the spoken language, molding it in a literary style.

Coptic language and **Coptic literature** are important for biblical and religious studies because the Septuagint and the New Testament were translated into Coptic as early as the third century. Thus, the Coptic version is based on Greek manuscripts that are considerably older than the majority of the extant Greek texts. The **Library of Nag Hammadi**, written in Coptic, provides the main source of **Gnosticism**. A number of noncanonical early Christian books are preserved only in Coptic or survive only imperfectly apart from this language. Most remarkable are the *Gospel of Thomas*, the *Dialogue of the Savior*, and the *Apocryphon of James*. The Arabization, Islamization of Egypt, and the **conversion to Islam** occurred gradually over centuries. Beginning in the 11th century, Arabic began to replace Coptic. The latest nonliterary evidence for the use of Coptic comes from the 11th and the 12th centuries. By the 13th century Coptic scholars compiled Coptic grammars written in Arabic. Thus, the Coptic gave way to Arabic, which became the language of the Egyptians to the present day. In the 19th and 20th centuries, there was a movement to revive Coptic that has proved unsuccessful.

COPTIC LITERATURE. *See* LITERATURE, COPTIC.

COPTIC MUSEUM. The Coptic Museum boasts the largest collection of **Coptic art** in the world. In 1908, **Marcus Simaika** Pasha founded the museum on behalf of the Coptic Church. He chose for it a unique spot in Old Cairo within the Fortress of Babylon and surrounded by a number of Cairo's ancient churches. Simaika brought artifacts from churches, monasteries, houses, and private collections to the museum. In 1931, the Coptic Museum became a national museum under the supervision of the Egyptian Department of Antiquities. The greater part of the magnificent Coptic collection in the Egyptian museum was transferred to the Coptic Museum in 1939. In March 1947, a large new wing was opened; its style is similar of that of the Old Wing, with carved wooden ceilings and picturesque fountains. The museum was completely renovated in 2006 after the earthquake of 1992 that affected its Old Wing. The most significant of the museum's monuments came from Ahnas (Heracleopolis magna), **Kellia**, the **Monastery of St. Jeremiah** at Saqqara, the **Monastery of St. Apollo at Bawit**, and from Cairo's ancient churches. The Coptic **Gnostic** codices (the **Library of Nag Hammadi**) represent one of the most valuable papyri collections.

COPTIC REVOLTS. Sources refer to a number of revolts of the Copts against Arab authorities between 693 or 694 and 832. Arab historians have seen these revolts as a reaction to the heavy taxes placed on the Copts and the deterioration of their social status under Muslim rule. The most significant revolts are those of the Bashmurites, who settled in the marshy land of the Delta and lived by selling papyrus, fowling, and fishing. Thus they were not dependent on the central irrigation system controlled by the government. Moreover, their swampy region with its thickets and reeds was not easily accessible for organized armies. When in 749 the Muslim authorities captured and abused the Coptic **Patriarch** Kha'il in Rashid (Rosetta), the Bashmurites burned that city and killed many of its Muslim inhabitants. Their most serious revolt, which flared up in the Delta in 832, was the last one of the Copts. It required the personal intervention of the Abbasid Caliph al-Ma'mun, who had to come from Baghdad to Egypt and brought with him Dionysius of Tell Mahre, Patriarch of Antioch, to unite with the Coptic Patriarch Yusab in convincing the Bashmurites to surrender. They were offered a general pardon with the condition that they be resettled. When the Bashmurites refused, their rebellion was radically crushed, and churches and homes were burned. The Bashmuric Copts who outlived the massacre were sold as slaves in Damascus. Arab and modern historians as well agreed that the ferocious repression of this last Bashmurite revolt was a turning point for **conversion to Islam** in Egypt. It would be misleading to place too much emphasis on the revolts of the Bashmuric Copts, who did not achieve any improvement of the conditions that caused their revolts. However, they tried without any organized army to protect themselves from foreign oppression.

COPTO-ARABIC LITERATURE. This entry consists of four parts. The first addresses the origins and development of the Arabic literature of the Copts. This is followed by introductions to three Copto-Arabic literary genres—**hagiography**, apocalyptic, and popular catechesis—for which texts are usually of anonymous authorship, and therefore unlikely to be otherwise addressed in a dictionary arranged largely by known historical figures. Literary genres such as **theology**, apologetics, biblical exegesis, history, and canon law are mentioned throughout this volume in articles about named authors.

Origins and Development. After the **Arab conquest of Egypt** in the early 640s, Greek- and Coptic-speaking Egyptian Christians gradually became familiar with the language of their conquerors. Some Egyptian Christians learned Arabic quickly: Christian civil servants (who by and large kept their positions under the new Arab administration) would have been obliged to learn the language, especially after Arabic became the official language of record-keeping throughout the Umayyad empire in 705; Christian merchants no doubt saw business opportunities opening up to those with the appropriate communication skills. Still, the process of Arabization of the Christian population was far slower in Egypt than in neighboring Palestine and Syria, due perhaps in part to the difficulty of learning Arabic for Coptic speakers (as opposed to its relative ease for speakers of related Semitic languages such as Aramaic or Syriac), and in part because of religious sentiment: the **Coptic language** was widely regarded as specifically Christian, a mark of Egyptian Christian identity, while Arabic was the language of the Arab conquerors and their scripture, the Qur'an.

Thus it was that while Palestinian Christians were creating an Arabic-Christian literature by the late eighth century, there is little evidence for the religious use of Arabic by Copts before the 10th century, when the civil-servant-turned-monk **Sawirus ibn al-Muqa-ffa'** produced a library of Arabic-language theological materials in which he defended the faith of the Coptic Orthodox Church. Sawirus' theological activity in Arabic now appears to have been ahead of its time, but by the end of the 11th century a clear linguistic shift was in progress: important collections of Coptic-language materials in canon law (see **Abu Salih Yu'annis, Gabriel II ibn Turayk**), doctrinal theology (*Confession of the Fathers*), and church history (*History of the Patriarchs*) had been rendered into Arabic.

It appears that many Egyptian Christians were not only becoming fluent in Arabic but also *losing* competence in Coptic. Simple catechetical texts that taught the faith of the Church in Arabic began to appear around this time. Pope Gabriel II ibn Turayk (70th, 1131–1145) instructed his **bishops** to teach the faithful the **Doxology**, the **Lord's Prayer**, and the **Nicene Creed** in Arabic so that they could pray with understanding and not merely mouth uncomprehended Coptic words. Toward the end of the 12th century, **Marqus ibn Qunbar** infuriated both Coptic and Melchite **patriarchs** but gathered a huge following as a traveling preacher—in Arabic.

The 13th century witnessed a veritable renaissance of Coptic Orthodox literature: a remarkable confluence of theological talent, generous patronage, and outside stimulus led to extraordinary creativity and production within the Coptic Orthodox community (see, e.g., **Awlad al-'Assal, Ibn al-Rahib**). The literature of this renaissance, however, was primarily in Arabic. Although it included grammars and lexicons of the Coptic language, the nature of these materials underlines the fact that Coptic had become, at least for the urban elite, a language to be preserved and learned at school, rather than a language of everyday life.

The later literature of the Copts (from the 14th-century encyclopedias through a long period of decline to its revival in modern times) continued to be, with the exception of a few specialized liturgical genres, in Arabic. This sometimes results in strange ironies. For example, in a collection of Arabic sermons (falsely) attributed to St. **Shenute** the Archimandrite in a 17th-century manuscript preserved in Paris (B.N. 4761), this greatest of *Coptic* writers and orators is again and again made to speak in rhymed *Arabic* prose and to use religious vocabulary that has its roots in the Qur'an!

The Arabic literature of the Copts is only beginning to receive the scholarly attention it deserves. It is important to specifically Coptic studies: complete Arabic translations of important texts have sometimes served as templates, allowing scholars to assemble Coptic fragments (as the picture on a jigsaw puzzle box might allow the near-assembly of a puzzle for which over half the pieces are missing). In many cases, Arabic translations have provided knowledge of the content of works altogether lost in the Coptic original. Beyond its utility to Coptic studies, however, the Arabic literature of the Copts provides a rich array of witnesses to Christian faith, life, identity, and survival in a largely non-Christian environment; as such, it is of historical, sociological, and theological importance.

Apocalyptic. A literary genre common to a number of religious traditions is that of the apocalyptic, in which saintly members of the community have been granted visions or revelations in which they receive exhortation and, very often, an outline of the course of history to its end. Then God's triumphant control of history shall be made manifest, and those who have clung to the true faith despite trials and persecutions shall receive their vindication. For Christians, apocalyptic literature is familiar from the Bible, for example, in passages such as Daniel 7 (the vision of the four beasts), Ezekiel 38–39 (the Gog and Magog oracle), Mark 13/Matthew 24/Luke 21 (the synoptic apocalypse), and the *Apocalypse or Revelation to John.* This and other traditional material has been reworked and elaborated upon in a variety of ways throughout Christian history, resulting in the creation of new apocalyptic texts, especially in times of trial. For Christians who found themselves under Arab rule in the seventh century, apocalyptic proved to be one way of making sense of and providing frank commentary on painful current events: these could be interpreted as the birth-pangs of the end of time, and Christian believers thus exhorted to steadfastness and hope.

The Copto-Arabic apocalyptic tradition is particularly rich and includes texts originally composed in Coptic and later translated, as well as texts written in Arabic in the first place. Typically they are attributed to great saints of the Coptic Church, such as **Athanasius** of **Alexandria**, Shenute of Atripe, Samuel of Qalamun, or Pisentius of Qift; their actual authors, safe behind their pseudonyms, were then free to express their disapproval of the actions of Muslim rulers and especially of developments within the life of the Coptic community. **Priests** come in for scathing criticism in an eighth-century *Apocalypse of Athanasius*; the adoption of the Arabic language and other forms of assimilation to Arabic-Islamic culture are the special targets of the *Apocalypse of Samuel*. The pseudonymous character of the apocalypses allowed their authors to portray their visionary saints as "prophesying" the actual events of subsequent history, including the Arab conquest, particularly painful or memorable events under Arab rule, and even sequences of rulers—although often in elliptical and symbolic language that invited readers and hearers into an exercise that, like a crossword puzzle, had significant entertainment value. The apocalypses bear witness to Coptic reactions to events such as the building of the Dome of the Rock (in an apocalypse included in the Arabic *Life of Shenute*) or the Muslims' coinage reform and tax demands (in the eighth-century *Apocalypse of Athanasius*). Motifs were used and reused, as when a list of 19 Muslim kings, first compiled near the end of Umayyad rule (mid-eighth century), was then reworked and brought "up to date" in the ninth century and again in the 12th. And while some motifs came into Copto-Arabic texts from the apocalyptic traditions of other Christian communities (e.g., the motif of the last Roman emperor), they were refashioned in order to vindicate specifically Coptic beliefs. A particularly memorable scene found in the *Letter of Pisentius* and a late medieval *Vision of Shenute* displays a contest between the Patriarch of Alexandria and the Patriarch of the Byzantines in the presence of the Byzantine and Abyssinian emperors: As they celebrate the **liturgy** side by side, the **Holy Spirit** is visibly seen to descend upon and hover over the altar of the Alexandrian patriarch. Whatever role the (Chalcedonian!) Roman/Byzantine emperor might play at the end of days, according to the wider apocalyptic tradition, the true faith of the Copts would surely be vindicated.

Catechetical Literature in the 11th–12th Centuries. In every time and place throughout the history of the Christian Church, teachers have attempted to explain the doctrines and practices peculiar to the community in a way that nonspecialists in theological and ecclesiastical matters could comprehend. For the Coptic Orthodox community, an especially fruitful period for the production of such texts fell between the 10th and 13th centuries—that is, during the period marked by a shift in linguistic competence within the community from Coptic to Arabic—and therefore, presumably, a pressing need to explain the faith in simple terms in Arabic. An important sequence of catechetical works begins with *Kitab al-Idah* (the Book of the Elucidation), a hugely popular work (to judge from the number and geographic spread of manuscripts) that has usually been attributed—probably falsely—to **Sawirus ibn al-Muqaffa'**. In plain and unsophisticated Arabic prose, the book sets out to explain key Christian doctrines (Trinity, **Incarnation**, and redemption) and practices (prayer and **fasting**) at a time when, as the author notes in a much-quoted preface, many Christians were more familiar with Islamic doctrinal vocabulary (e.g., God as *fard* and *samad*) than with Christian terms (e.g., Christ as "Son of God"). Of special note is the lively and entertaining manner in which *Kitab al-Idah* describes Christ's redemptive work as his cunning deception of Satan, from whom Christ hid his divine power by regularly performing the deeds of weak human beings. In the end, Satan was undone by his own greed: he was stripped of his captives as fitting punishment for his attempt to kill and seize the soul of the crucified Christ—over whom he had no just claim.

Shorter than *Kitab al-Idah* and dependent upon it, the anonymous but popular *Ten Questions That One of the Disciples Asked of His Master*—or simply *The Book of the Master and the Disciple (10 Questions)*—covers the same topics, but with some fascinating new material. For example, for lay men and women who do not know any prayers (presumably in Coptic), it commends a specifically Egyptian threefold form of the "Jesus Prayer"—*in Arabic*: "My Lord Jesus, have mercy on me. My Lord Jesus, help me. My Lord Jesus, I praise and worship you."

The next book in the sequence is *The Book of the Master and the Disciple (Eight Questions)* of **Marqus ibn al-Qunbar**, which teaches the author's characteristic ideas about frequent **communion** after **confession** and performance of **penance** (and thus, the necessity of having a spiritual master or confessor). The auricular confession championed here was later justified in another work sometimes called *The Book of the Master and the Disciple*, this time in 22 chapters (also known as *The Book of Confession*). The principle author of this book, the monk Da'ud who later became Patriarch **Cyril III ibn Laqlaq**, was assisted in its composition by two luminaries of the

13th-century renaissance in Coptic Orthodox literature: **Bulus al-Bushi** and **al-As'ad ibn al-'Assal**. And thus the "arc" of catechetical texts treated here ends in a period of intense Arabic-language theological creativity.

For all their simplicity, the catechetical texts surveyed here played a role in helping medieval Egyptian Christians to "keep the faith" in an age of many challenges. To a certain degree, they continue to play such a role: *Kitab al-Idah* is widely available in Egypt in an inexpensive edition, and parts of Marqus' and Da'ud's works are available as well.

Hagiography. The Coptic Orthodox Church has always celebrated its saints. When the Arabs conquered Egypt in the 640s, they found a culture mapped out both spatially and temporally by saints and martyrs: their shrines, sometimes connected by **pilgrimage** routes, dotted the countryside; their feast days punctuated the calendar. A regular feature of the liturgical celebration of those **feasts** was the reading of an appropriate homily that described the life and exploits of the saint. Such homilies were embellished or summarized; copied faithfully or translated from and into other languages; transmitted singly or gathered into collections—resulting in a rich and enormously complex hagiographical literature.

As Arabic gradually replaced Coptic as the language of the majority of Egyptian Christians, the Coptic literature of the saints (as well as many texts in Greek and Syriac) were translated into Arabic. Much of this work was done anonymously and cannot be dated with any precision. An exception of a sort is provided by the *History of the Patriarchs*, first compiled and edited between 1088 and about 1094, which not only relates the lives of (mostly) saintly patriarchs but also reports on other saints who lived in their days. For example, the compilation's first life to be composed in Arabic (rather than translated from Coptic), that of Patriarch **Christodoulos** (66th, 1046–1077), includes a recitation of about a dozen miracles by the holy monk Bessus of the **Monastery of St. Macarius**.

The mention of postconquest patriarchs and saints makes it plain that the Copts by no means restricted themselves to writing about saints and martyrs of the early Christian centuries. New "Lives" and collections of "Miracles" were regularly composed to celebrate newly (and rather informally) acclaimed saints of the Coptic Orthodox Church. Some Arabic "Lives" (often with "Miracles") that have attracted recent attention are those of the patriarchs Afrahâm ibn Zur'ah (62nd, 975–978, patriarch at the time of the miracle of the moving of the Muqattam hill) and **Matthew I** (87th, 1378–1408); the medieval holy men Barsum the Naked (d. 1317) and Marqus of the **Monastery of St. Antony** (d. 1386), both of whom played a mediatorial role on behalf of the Coptic community in dangerous Mamluk times; or the neomartyrs Jirjis al-Muzahim (executed for apostasy in 978) and Salib (executed for anti-Islamic statements in 1512).

The Coptic Orthodox faithful have, for centuries, celebrated the memory of their saints by visiting their shrines, venerating their relics, and listening to their stories as presented in the liturgical reading of the **Synaxarion**. They continue to do so in our own day, in which Coptic Orthodox bookstores carry a wide range of books and pamphlets—and even movies!—about individual saints. Copto-Arabic hagiography continues to be a lively enterprise.

COPTOLOGIA. An international journal that encourages research in the Coptic heritage, concentrating on Alexandrine **theology** and Coptic **monasticism**. It was founded by Fayek Ishak in 1981. Some of its publications are the Coptic Orthodox Mass and the **Liturgy** of St. Basil, the *Horologion (al-Agbeya): The Book of the Seven Nocturnal and Daylight Canonical Prayers,* and *Selected Hymns (Taranîm) and Lauds (Madayih) of the Coptic Orthodox Church.*

COPTOLOGY AND COPTOLOGICAL STUDIES. Martin Krause, the father of modern Coptology, has defined Coptology as "a scientific discipline in Oriental studies that investigates the language and culture of Egypt and **Nubia** in the widest sense: literature, religion, history, archaeology, and art. Its range extends from late antiquity to the Middle Ages, or even down to the present. It touches on and intersects with a number of neighboring disciplines." Of the latter should be mentioned Egyptology, classical philology, Byzantine studies, religious studies, **theology**, Church history, Islamic studies, Arabic studies, art history, Ethiopic studies, linguistics, history of law, and history of medicine.

Coptic studies go back to the earliest centuries of Christianity in Egypt, when an Egyptian text was composed using the Greek alphabet, with additional letters from the demotic. The early stage of that script was called Old Coptic. Its inventor or inventors are not known. The creation of that new practical writing system was a very significant cultural moment, for it enabled the native Egyptians to read the Old and New Testaments and Greek writings, which were translated from Greek into the **Coptic language**. After a few centuries of the **Arab conquest of Egypt**, Arabic began to supersede Coptic. In order to preserve the knowledge of their language, which is also the language of their Church, a number of scholars compiled Arabic glossaries of Coptic words (*scalae*). Many biblical and liturgical texts, as well other literary works had been translated from Coptic into Arabic. By the 13th century, Coptic scholars were using Arabic and employing Arabic grammatical terminology to prepare and edit Coptic grammars. These glossaries and grammatical summaries proved to be instrumental in beginning Coptic studies in Europe. The manuscript collection of the Vatican, which was founded by Pope Nicholas V in the middle of the 15th century, had already included some Coptic-Arabic bilinguals. **Yusuf Abu Daqn** copied the Coptic text of the liturgy, probably to use it in his teaching at Oxford. He also wrote a history of the Coptic Church in Latin. During the 16th and 17th centuries, European travelers brought Coptic manuscripts from Egypt to Europe that were used by European scholars to study the Coptic language.

It was **Athanasius Kircher** who produced the first Coptic grammar and lexicon in a Western language. In the 18th century, Coptic was studied by many scholars in Europe, playing a crucial role in the decipherment of the ancient Egyptian language by Jean François Champollion (1790–1832). In the same century, **Rufa'il al-Tukhi** published a Coptic grammar and a number of Coptic liturgical books provided by an Arabic translation. In 1845, Moritz Gotthilf Schwartze was named professor extraordinaire of Coptic language and literature at Berlin University. The late 19th and the first half of the 20th century witnessed a remarkable progress in Coptological studies in many universities in Europe, especially in Germany, France, and England, as well as in the United States. During that period many "excavations" were carried out in Coptic sites such as Akhmim and Antinoë, and publications on many ancient monasteries appeared. Of special significance are the **Monastery of St. Jeremiah**, the **Monastery of**

St. Apollo, the **Monastery of St. Hatre**, the **White Monastery**, the **Red Monastery**, and the monasteries of **Wadi al-Natrun**. Moreover, a large number of Coptic texts found their way into museums, libraries, and private collections in Egypt, Europe, and America, including the Manichaean Codices, the Gnostic **Nag Hammadi Library**, biblical manuscripts, and nonliterary texts.

Many Copts strived for the recognition and preservation of the legacy of their Church, notably **Ya'qub Nakhlah Rufaylah, Iqladiyus Labib, Marcus Simaika, Habib Girgis, Yassa 'Abd al-Masih, Georgy Sobhy, Mirit Ghali, Aziz Atiya**, Sami Gabra, and **Murad Kamil**. A number of Coptic institutions had been established, such as the **Clerical College**, the **Coptic Museum**, and the **Society of Coptic Archaeology**. Two exhibitions of **Coptic art** stimulated the interest of both scholars and laymen; one was in Brooklyn in 1941 and the other in Cairo in 1944. In the second half of the 20th century and the first years of this century, Coptological studies have considerably improved. Under UNESCO auspices, scholars from several countries cooperated to work in the Coptic codices of the Nag Hammadi Library in the Coptic Museum, and many scholars studied Coptic in order to investigate **Gnosticism**. In 1954, the **Higher Institute of Coptic Studies** was founded in the Coptic **patriarchate**. The exhibition of Coptic art in Villa Hügel, Essen, Germany, in 1963, began a series of exhibitions in many European cities such as Munich, Zurich, Vienna, Geneva, and Paris, with the latest at the Museum of Fine Arts in Budapest in 2005. These exhibitions engendered a vast awareness of the Coptic heritage worldwide. Scientific catalogues and symposia enhanced the benefits of such cultural events. In 1965, Coptology became an academic major in the University of Münster in Germany; and the universities of Geneva, Rome, and Halle had professorships of Coptic language and literature. Coptologists also teach in other universities, such as Yale, Paris, Munich, and Göttingen. Since its foundation in 1976, the **International Association for Coptic Studies** has organized an international congress every four years to further Coptic studies. The appearance of the *Coptic Encyclopedia* in 1991 considerably facilitated research in the various aspects of the Coptic civilization.

Excavations that were executed in the late 1950s and in the 1960s in **Nubia** led to the discovery of many Coptic and Christian Nubian monuments. Carefully recorded excavations were carried out in many Coptic sites. Of special importance are **Abu Mina, Kellia**, Athribis, **Saqqara, Naqlun**, Antinoe, Abu Fana, Bawit, Thebes, and Esna. Great conservation projects yielded rich monastic wall paintings in Wadi al-Natrun, the **Monastery of St. Antony**, the **Monastery of St. Paul**, and the Red Monastery. A number of publications on the collection of the Coptic Museum appeared. The past few decades have witnessed more involvement of the Copts with their glorious history and legacy. Their cooperation led to the establishment of a professorship of Coptic studies at the American University in Cairo in 2002, where Coptology became an academic minor. In 2005, Macquarie University in Sydney started a unique master of arts program in Coptic studies, while courses are also offered online. *Coptologia* and *Coptic Church Review* were both founded in North America. The **St. Shenouda the Archimandrite Coptic Society** and the **St. Mark Foundation for Coptic History Studies** play a significant role in preserving Coptic heritage and furthering Coptic studies in Egypt and in the United States.

COUNCIL OF CHALCEDON. *See* CHALCEDON, COUNCIL OF.

COUNCIL OF CONSTANTINOPLE. *See* CONSTANTINOPLE, COUNCIL OF.

COUNCIL OF EPHESUS. *See* EPHESUS, COUNCIL OF.

COUNCIL OF FLORENCE. *See* FLORENCE, COPTS AT THE COUNCIL OF (1439–1443).

COUNCIL OF NICAEA. *See* NICAEA, COUNCIL OF.

CREED. *See* NICENE CREED.

CYPRUS. According to the traveler Iohann van Kootwyck, who visited Cyprus in 1598–1599, Copts as well as other Oriental Christians arrived there as fugitives after the capture of Jerusalem by Saladin in 1187. In 1342, the Spanish Dominican Alphonse Bonhome referred to an Arabic *Life of St. Antony* that he found at a Coptic monastery at Famagusta. Documents of Mikha'il, a Coptic metropolitan of Cyprus in 1508, attest to the Audeth family, probably of Syrian origin, which provided donations to **priests** and churches of Oriental communities, in particular four Coptic churches in the 15th century. In 1573, the historian Etienne de Lusignan described a Coptic monastery named after St. **Macarius** as situated outside Nicosia near the village of Platani belonging to the Armenians. An Arabic manuscript on the Pentateuch was copied in 1646 at the **Monastery of St. Antony** at Nicosia. In 1671, the traveler Johann Wansleben (Vansleb) purchased 16 Coptic and Arabic manuscripts for the Royal Library of Paris. However, the census of 1777, carried out by the Turks, does not mention Copts among the population of Cyprus. The priest Zacharia al-Anba Bula founded a Coptic Church at Nicosia in August 2001 that was dedicated to St. Mark

CYRIL I. Saint and **patriarch**. Cyril was the 24th patriarch of **Alexandria** (412–444). He was the nephew of his predecessor, Patriarch **Theophilus**. Part of his "Life" survives in Coptic and the entire "Life" was translated into Arabic in the *History of the Patriarchs*. He studied in Alexandria and he may have spent a few years in **Scetis**. He was elected to the patriarchate soon after the death of his uncle. Cyril was a prolific writer, writing commentaries on the Gospels of John, Luke, and Matthew, the Epistles to the Romans, Corinthians, and Hebrews, as well as commentaries on the minor prophets, the Pentateuch, and the Book of Isaiah. Unfortunately, only a few works of his corpus have been translated into English and published. Cyril also wrote dogmatic works against **Arianism**, such as the *Thesaurus* and *Dialogue on the Trinity*. But his main contribution was against **Nestorianism**, where he played a pivotal role in the movement to affirm the title of **Theotokos** (God-Bearer). Cyril was also a good **bishop** and pastor.

In Coptic we possess part of the Twelve Anathemas from a manuscript of the **White Monastery**, a homily on penitence, a homily on the time of death, a homily on the Apocalypse, a homily on the three young men in the furnace, a homily on St. **Athanasius**, a fragment of the *Thesaurus*, his first festal letter, a homily on the Virgin Mary, a homily on the Nativity, a dialogue with Deacon Anthemus and Stephen, and some letters, attributed to St. Cyril. The Egyptian **liturgy** of St. **Mark** is also attributed to St. Cyril. It seems that Cyril played an important role in revising this liturgy.

CYRIL II (?–1092). Patriarch (67th, 1078–1092). Like his predecessor **Christodoulos**, Cyril II (before his consecration, the monk Jirja of the **Monastery of St. Macarius**) occupies a place in the history of **Copto-Arabic literature** both as a subject of an Arabic-language biography by **Mawhub ibn Mansur ibn Mufarrij** in the *History of the Patriarchs*, and as an author (in 1086) of a set of Arabic-language canons. Cyril's canons, 34 in number, deal primarily with the pastoral responsibilities of **bishops**. They were incorporated into the 14th-century canonical collection of the monk **Maqara**.

CYRIL III IBN LAQLAQ (?–1243). Patriarch (75th, 1235–1243), theologian. Da'ud ibn Laqlaq was a monk of the Fayyum who ran afoul of local clergy, his **bishop**, and Patriarch John VI (74th, 1189–1216) by championing the ancient practice of auricular confession to a father confessor, thus aligning himself with the disgraced **Marqus ibn al-Qunbar** against Church leaders such as Metropolitan **Mikha'il** of Damietta and Patriarch John VI himself. Upon John's death, Da'ud became a candidate for the patriarchate, and, after a long struggle in which he outlasted, outmaneuvered, and outspent his opposition, was enthroned as Pope Cyril III in 1235. Once patriarch, however, Cyril had to find the means to fulfill the pledge of 3,000 dinars by which he had guaranteed the support of the Ayyubid court. As patriarch of a church in which no episcopal consecrations had taken place for 19 years, there was ample opportunity for him to receive money in return for appointment to ecclesial office, ranging from a high of 200 dinars for consecrating a bishop to three dinars for ordaining a deacon. These simoniacal practices alarmed other Copts, who in synods held in 1238 and 1240 sought reform; Cyril shortly afterward retired to the Monastery of al-Sham' in Giza, where he died in 1243. Whatever may have been Cyril's administrative, pastoral, and diplomatic accomplishments during his relatively brief patriarchate, they have been overshadowed by the scandal of simony. Be that as it may, Cyril's role in the history of **Copto-Arabic literature** should not be overlooked. As patriarch he put talent to work, employing, for example, the canonical skills of **al-Safi ibn al-'Assal**, whom he also asked for a response to al-Ja'fari's *Takhjil muharrifi l-Injil* (Shaming the Corrupters of the Gospel). Before becoming patriarch, the monk Da'ud (as he was then known) collaborated with **Bulus al-Bushi** and **al-As'ad ibn al-'Assal** in composing *Kitab al-I'tiraf* (the Book of Confession), also known as *The Book of the Master and the Disciple* (22 chapters). This book justified the practice of confession to a spiritual "master" or **priest**; judging from its presence in at least 50 manuscripts (and a partial edition published in Cairo in 1985), it has been widely read and accepted.

CYRIL IV (1816–1861). Patriarch, reformer. He was the 110th patriarch of the Coptic Church (1854–1861). He was born Dawud in 1816 at Nag' Abu Zaqali, near Akhmim in Upper Egypt. In 1838, he entered the **Monastery of St. Antony** at the age of 22 and became its abbot only two years later. He then opened a school for the monks, as well as for local children at Bush, where the monastery possessed land. In 1851, Pope Peter entrusted him with a delicate task in Ethiopia that lasted 16 months. After the death of Patriarch Peter in 1852, Dawud was raised to the post of a general metropolitan **bishop**. In 1854, he was consecrated Patriarch Cyril IV. His short pontificate of about seven years marked a Coptic renaissance that was visible in the cultural movement within the Coptic Church and its awakening from five centuries of sluggishness under Mamluk and Ottoman rule.

Cyril's reform is indeed a turning point in the history of the Coptic Church, as it paved the way for the renewal and expansion that continue to the present generations. Cyril IV devoted his efforts toward education. He founded modern schools at the patriarchate, at Haret al-Saqqayin, and at Darb al-Wasi' in Cairo. One of those schools was for girls, which was a very progressive step at that time. He paid great attention to the education of the clergy and conducted regular theological discussions for them. The patriarch imported the second printing press from Austria, and he sent four Coptic apprentices to be trained at the government press. He erected new churches and renovated the cathedral in Cairo. The management of the Church's property and finance were reorganized. In 1855, the Copts were freed from the poll tax that had been imposed on them since the **Arab conquest of Egypt**. Khedive Said, the ruler of Egypt, sent the patriarch to Ethiopia to undertake a dangerous mission related to the borders between the two countries. He spent 18 months there and accomplished his mission successfully. In 1861, Cyril was invited by the khedive and died very shortly after that meeting. It is said that Cyril was poisoned.

CYRIL VI (1902–1971). Patriarch and **saint**. He was the 116th patriarch of the Coptic Church (1959–1971). He was born 'Azir Yousseef 'Ata in 1902 at the village of Tukh al Nasara in Lower Egypt. He played a large role in the renaissance of the Coptic Church. He joined the **Monastery of al-Baramous** in **Wadi al-Natrun** at the age of 25. In 1931, he was ordained a **priest** and was known as Father Mina, the solitary from al-Baramous monastery. Between 1936 and 1942 he lived as a hermit in a deserted windmill in Old Cairo. People sought his blessings and miraculous powers. It is said that many miracles happened during that period. He attracted graduate students who wished to be monks and advised them to join the **Monastery of the Syrians** in Wadi al-Natrun. Among the students, who were influenced by him were **Matta al-Miskin**, Bishop **Samuel**, and Pope **Shenouda III**, the present patriarch of the Coptic Church.

Cyril was elected patriarch on 19 April 1959. In 1960, Cyril VI issued a decree that all the priests must be graduates of the **Clerical College**. He was able to secure permission from President Gamal Abdel-Nasser to build 25 churches each year, and thus he avoided the long complicated process of obtaining such permissions. On 26 July 1968, he and Ethiopian Emperor Haile Selassie I inaugurated a new cathedral on the occasion of the transfer of the relics of St. **Mark** the Evangelist from Venice to Cairo and the 1900th anniversary of his martyrdom. Moreover, Cyril VI solved the problem of the administration of the *Waqfs* (property or land endowed to the Church) by establishing an independent board to control the *Waqfs*. During his pontificate the Coptic Church became a member of the World Council of Churches and the **Middle East Council of Churches**. One of his innovations was the consecration of three extradiocesan **bishops** for social affairs, higher education, and religious education. Although Coptic canon law only allows the **canonization** of a saint at least 50 years after her or his death, Cyril VI was considered a saint not long after his death. He is buried in a huge modern church in the new

Monastery of St. **Menas** at Mareotis, to which many people flock, seeking his intercession.

– D –

DAYR AL-MUHARRAQ. The Monastery of the Holy Virgin (Dayr al-Muharraq) is situated near the towns of al-Qusiyah and Gabal Qusqam in the present governorate of Assiut. According to medieval sources, this area is believed to be the Holy Family's southernmost stop, where they dwelt for six months at the end of their **flight into Egypt**. The main source for this tradition is *The Vision of Theophilus*, which is attributed, very probably in a later date, to Patriarch **Theophilus** (385–412). The text describes Dayr al-Muharraq as the "holy mountain" and compared it to Mount Sinai and the Mount of Olives in Jerusalem. The *History of the Churches and Monasteries of Egypt* provides a tradition that Christ, accompanied by his mother and the Apostles, consecrated the church in which the Holy Family dwelt for six months. Each year on 15 November the monks of Dayr al-Muharraq commemorate Christ's post-Resurrection visit to Qusqam as a fulfillment of the prophecy of Isaiah 19:19, "On that day there will be an altar in the center of the land of Egypt." However, the date of the foundation of Dayr al-Muharraq and its early history are not known. The *History of the Churches and Monasteries of Egypt* (early 13th century) refers to the restoration of the monastery's keep. **Patriarchs** Gabriel IV (1370–1378), **Matthew I** (1378–1409), Matthew II (1452–1465), and John XIII (1484–1524) had been chosen from among the monks of al-Muharraq. In medieval times, Ethiopian monks stopped at al-Muharraq on their way to Jerusalem. The monastery is one of the most popular **pilgrimage** centers in Egypt, which is visited yearly in June by hundreds of thousands of the faithful. There is a theological seminary at Dayr al-Muharraq that is affiliated with the **Clerical College** of Cairo.

DEACON, ARCHDEACON, ORDINATION OF. The ordination of the deacon in the Coptic Church is performed after the Prayer of Reconciliation and before the Kiss of Peace, that is, immediately before the beginning of the anaphora, and is based on the ordination prayer from the *Apostolic Constitutions*. It provides an explicit description of the ministry as being related to the altar, as well as some further elements from the Syrian rite. The earliest manuscript is Ms 253 Liturgica of the Coptic Museum, dated 1364 A.D. The first edition was edited by R. **Tukhi** (Catholic) in 1761 with an Arabic translation. However, the accuracy of this edition is suspect. Its content is sometimes artificial, and it is not a reliable source for the liturgist. The first Orthodox edition was edited by Athanasius, Metropolitan of Beni Suef in 1959, and reprinted with minor changes by his successor bearing the same name in 1992.

The deacon is the first rank of the Coptic priesthood. Originally deacons were in charge of administrative and charitable affairs (Acts 6:1–6). However, in early history, they also played an important role in the field of evangelism. In the Book of Acts, the mission of Philip in Samaria (Acts 8:4–8) is referred to. In the Epistle of St. Paul to Timothy (1 Tim. 3:8–13), the first mention of the deacons as a clerical rank is found. The ecumenical councils issued several decrees concerning deacons. Thus, the First **Council of Nicaea** forbade their transfer from city to city (Canon 15, which confirmed Apostolic Canons 14–15). They are not allowed to practice usury (Apostolic Canon 44) and they should not administer the Eucharist to presbyters or be seated above them (Canon 18). In the Middle Ages, Ibn al-'Assal, in his nomocanon, collected all the relevant synodical decrees and collated them in a compendium for deacons. From the extant papyrological documents, it can be seen that deacons played an important role in the activity of the Coptic Church, especially before the Arab conquest.

DESERT FATHERS. *See* SAYINGS OF THE FATHERS.

DIALOGUE OF THE SAVIOR **(NHC III, 5).** A **Gnostic** revelation dialogue featuring "the Savior" (Jesus Christ, though he is not named) presenting esoteric teaching to his disciples Judas, Mary, and Matthew. Traditional sayings of Jesus, some paralleled in the canonical New Testament and the *Gospel of Thomas*, are expanded into larger discourses. The title is given at both the beginning and the end of the text. Mary (Magdalene) is given a special place in the text, though the disciples are counseled to "destroy the works of womanhood," that is, eschew physical generation. *Dialogue of the Savior* is in a poor state of preservation. Extant only in Coptic, it was originally composed in Greek sometime in the second century, perhaps in Egypt.

DIASPORA, COPTS IN THE. The largest communities of Coptic emigrants are in the United Stated, Canada, and Australia. Statistics concerning their population are unavailable. However, according to unofficial sources, they number between 400,000 and 1,000,000. A considerable number of the Copts left Egypt for the West because of discrimination; others left because of the nationalization policies of President Gamal Abd al-Nasser (1952–1971) and the subsequent economic deterioration that was combined with overpopulation. The majority of the Coptic emigrants took advantage of President Anwar al-Sadat's "open door" and wanted to avoid the Islamization of Egypt's national life and the increasing influence of the Muslim fundamentalists under Sadat (1971–1981) and President Hosny Mubarak (1981–). According to the statistics of the Center for Egyptian Human Rights, such groups committed 561 violent incidents against Copts between 1994 and 2004. A large number of the Coptic emigrants are university graduates and thus are engaged in professional jobs such as medicine, commerce, and engineering.

When the Copts settle abroad, they prepare a place to pray, as without a Coptic priest **Eucharist** cannot be received and children cannot be baptized. As in Egypt, the Coptic churches in the Diaspora are decorated with the **contemporary Coptic art**, especially the **icons**. Today, there are 125 churches in the United States, 27 churches in Canada, and 37 churches in Australia, in addition to many churches in Europe, South America, Africa, and Asia. These churches are served by Coptic **priests** with a number of local **bishops**. The latter are ordained by Pope **Shenouda III**, whose many pastoral visits reinforce the ties between the "churches in the lands of emigration" and the "Mother Church" in Egypt. Within less than three decades, a considerable part of the texts of the liturgical books of the Coptic Church have been translated into English, French, and German, especially those texts that are frequently used in the **liturgy**. Some theological seminaries, monasteries, and Coptic schools have been established. The liturgy is often performed in Arabic, **Coptic**, and one of three European languages. However, it is very probable that **Coptic**, unlike Arabic, will continue in the churches of the emigrants as English already became the mother tongue of the third generation; **Coptic** is considered by the Copts as the language of the Church and the ancestors.

The emigrants are aware of their Coptic heritage. The *Coptic Encyclopedia* was initiated by a Coptic scholar in the United States. The **St. Shenouda the Archimandrite Coptic Society** and the St. Mark Foundation for Coptic History Studies support and promote Coptic studies worldwide. A number of periodicals and magazines are published by Copts in North America such as *Coptologia* and the *Coptic Church Review*. The weekly newspaper *Watani* includes some pages in English written and edited by Copts in Egypt and in the Diaspora. Cooperation between the Coptic Church in Australia and Macquarie University led to the establishment of the first online master of arts degree program in Coptic studies. The Coptic community of the region of Los Angeles is strongly supporting Coptic studies in Southern California, especially at Claremont Graduate University and the University of California at Los Angeles.

DIDACHE. *Didache* is a Greek word meaning the "teaching of the Apostles." It was written in the second century. The Metropolitan of Nicomedia, Philotheus Bruennios, discovered it in 1883. The author of this text is likely to have been of Hebraic origins. Many Fathers of the Church such as Clement of **Alexandria**, **Eusebius**, and **Athanasius** used quotations from this book. Serapion, **Bishop** of Thmuis, quoted it in his **liturgy**. In Egypt, the Oxhyrhynchus papyri contain the first two chapters of this book, and a Coptic translation of the text is preserved in the British Library. The unique complete manuscript was copied in the 11th century. The *Didache* starts with a discussion of how one should live one's life, then describes liturgical practices, prayers, and the Eucharist, and concludes with pastoral instructions.

DIDASCALIA. The book contains the duties of the **bishops**, the widows, and the **deacons**. It also gives some details concerning **fasting** and **Holy Week**. The *Didascalia* was written in Greek and later translated into Syriac, Latin, and Arabic. It is believed to reflect the situation of the Church of the third century. It belongs to the group of the Church instructions such as the *Didache* and the *Apostolic Tradition* of Hippolytus.

DIFNAR (ANTIPHONARION). A liturgical book that contains a collection of hymns for the whole year. The hymns of the Difnar are sung in the service of the **Psalmodia**, which follows the office of Complines after the *lobsh* of the **Theotokia**. The hymns are arranged according to the Coptic calendar. There are two hymns for each day, one in the Batos tune and another in the **Adam** tune. The title of this book means that the hymns are sung antiphonically. It seems that the Difnar was composed before the **Synaxarion**. The compilers of the Difnar have repeated different hymns in order to cover the whole year. Hence, the hymns for Pesynthius are used for Lazarus, and those of **Theodosius** are used for **Cyril** of **Alexandria**. If a **saint** has more than one **feast** in the year, the same hymns are used for both occasions. This is the case for the Virgin Mary, John the Baptist, **Severus of Antioch**, and others. The earliest manuscript is from the collection of the Monastery of the Archangel Michael in Hamuli and now preserved in the Piermont Morgan Library (M575) and dated 893. This manuscript is in the Sahidic dialect. The **Monastery of St. Antony** possesses a complete Bohairic version of the Difnar dated 1385. In 1922, the monk Domadius al-Baramusi published the first six months of the year. His edition contains the first two stanzas in Coptic and a complete translation in Arabic. The edition of De Lacy O'Leary (1926–1928) contains the Coptic texts and Arabic titles with an index in the last volume. In 1984, Fr. Gabriel Anba Bishoy published the second part of the year. In 1985, **Bishop** Matthaus published the whole text according to a manuscript preserved in the **Church of Sts. Sergius and Bacchus** (Abu Sargah) dated 1746, and two manuscripts from the **Monastery of the Syrians** and the **Monastery of St. Pshoi at Wadi al-Natrun**.

DIOSCORUS I. Saint and **patriarch**. He was the 25th patriarch of **Alexandria** (446–454). Our best reference about his life is the Coptic version of the *History of the Patriarchs*. He was a disciple of **Cyril** of Alexandria and a vigorous opponent of **Nestorian** doctrines. Eutyches also argued against the Nestorian parties but he was condemned by a synod of **bishops** headed by Flavian, Bishop of Constantinople, on 8 November 448. Eutyches asked for support from Dioscorus. A synod was assembled in **Ephesus** in 449. Here, a **Christological** formula based on the Twelve **Anathemas** of Cyril was edited. But this synod caused confusion. The teaching of Dioscorus is Orthodox, but at **Chalcedon** he used the same distinction as Eutyches: "I accept the phrase 'from two natures' but not 'the two natures.'" Dioscorus was also a writer. We have an encomium on Macarius Bishop of Tkow, which survives in two **Coptic dialects**, Sahidic and Bohairic. To him also is attributed a letter to Sapianus, another to St. **Shenute**, and some fragments. The Syriac tradition attributes to him several works that reflect his theological dogma.

DISCOURSE ON THE EIGHTH AND NINTH (NHC VI, 6). An initiatory Hermetic tractate featuring a dialogue between Hermes Trismegistus as mystagogue and his "son" (Tat) as initiate. The tractate lacks a title; the one now in use has been editorially assigned on the basis of content. The "eighth" and the "ninth" refer to the spheres above the planetary cosmos wherein the initiate might approach the transcendent divine realm, presumably located at the 10th level. Extant only in Coptic, *Discourse on the Eighth and Ninth* was originally composed in Greek, and is closely related to other texts in which the god "thrice-greatest Hermes" reveals gnosis to his initiates, such as might have been used in a Hermetic conventicle. It was certainly composed in Egypt, possibly as early as the second century.

DOCETISM. Docetism is derived from a Greek word that means "it seems." In this context, it refers to the belief that Christ did not have the same flesh as we do, but only seemed to. Docetism, like **Gnosticism**, is of non-Christian origin, but it invaded Christianity. Tertullian, in his work entitled *On the Flesh of Christ*, tried to defend the Orthodox views. These ideas were adopted later by **Apollinarianism**.

DORMITION OF THE VIRGIN MARY. The Coptic calendar has two **feasts** for the Holy Virgin, the 21st of Tuba, the Dormition of the Virgin, and the 16th of Misra, the **Assumption** of the Virgin. The earliest manuscript, which contains a homily on the Assumption of the Virgin, is a papyrus preserved in the Pierpont Morgan Library. It probably dates from the seventh century. We have a collection of homilies on the subject attributed to Cyril of Jerusalem; Evode, Pope of Rome; **Theodosius** of Alexandria; **Theophilus** of Alexandria; **Cyril** of Alexandria; Cyriacus of Bahnasa; and Theophilus of Landra, as well as a number of anonymous fragments. This relatively huge literature is from the collections of the libraries of Hamuli (Fayoum), the **White Monastery**, the **Monastery of St. Macarius**, and Edfu. Such liturgical books as the **Synaxarion**, the **Antiphonarion (Difnar)**, the *Psalis*, and the **doxologies** commemorate these two feasts. Several apocryphal books in the Coptic Church mention the Dormition and the Assumption of the Virgin Mary. It is noteworthy that this tradition is also accepted in the other Oriental churches as well as the Roman Catholic Church.

DOXOLOGY. The word *doxology* is composed from two Greek words: *"doxa"* meaning "good report, glory," and *"logos,"* meaning "word, expression." Hence, the combined meaning is "the expression of glory." The doxology is a hymn used in the Coptic Church to commemorate an event or a church personality. It is usually a short hymn of 5–10 stanzas. There are two types of doxologies. The first is the doxology to the Batos tune, sung during Vespers, Matins, and **Psalmodia**. The second is the doxology to the Adam tune sung especially during the Rite of Glorification. The doxologies provide a valuable background to Coptic literature, giving a brief summary of the martyrdom, miracles, and so forth of many **saints**. Some doxologies, such as the Doxology of St. Pshoi, are a historical reference. This doxology narrates the translation of the relics of St. Bshoi from Upper Egypt to his monastery during the patriarchate of the **Patriarch** Joseph (831–849 A.D.). The doxology to the Adam tune used for the morning service, which occurs also in the Byzantine rite, was introduced to the Coptic Church by the **Monastery of St Antony**. It seems to be a late translation from Greek to Coptic. It is hard to date the doxologies. The Doxologies of St. Pshoi and the Morning Doxology were written in the ninth century. For editions, see also Psalmodia and **Theotokia**.

DOXOLOGY TO THE HOLY TRINITY. "Glory be to the Father and the Son and the **Holy Spirit**." According to the historian Philostorgius, around 350 the Nicene opponents of Leontius of Antioch composed the **doxology** "Glory be to the Father and to the Son and to the Holy Spirit," emphasizing that both the Son and the Holy Spirit were consubstantial with the Father. This was in contrast to the traditional Antiochene version, "Glory be to the Father through the Son and in the Holy Spirit," which seemed to imply a subordination of the latter two to the Father.

– E –

EMIGRANTS, COPTIC. *See* DIASPORA, COPTS IN THE.

EPHESUS, FIRST COUNCIL OF (431). After the **Arian** crisis of the fourth century, theologians started to discuss the nature of the humanity of Christ. Among them was Apollinarius of Laodicia, one of the participants of the **Council of Nicaea**, who suggested that if Jesus is the true God then he could not be a perfect man. At the School of Antioch, Theodore of Mopsuestia taught the coexistence of two different natures in Christ, which would make it acceptable that the human nature of Christ was born from the Virgin and had been crucified. When the seat of Constantinople became vacant after the death of Sisinius in 427, Emperor Theodosius II decided to nominate a popular preacher from Antioch named **Nestorius**. Although he appears to have been a good monk, Nestorius was not a good theologian. He was also narrow-minded and he started to persecute the Arians, who had been tolerated by his predecessors. He also defended the theological point of view of the School of Antioch but in his homily he mentioned that the Virgin should not be called the Mother of God (Theotokos) but the Mother of Christ (Christotokos). This assertion upset many people, including Proclus of Cizicus. He also entered into a contention with the Empress Pulcheria when he reproached her behavior. In the same year (428), **Cyril of Alexandria** sent his famous letter to the monks, where he explained the mystery of Christ and how it is suitable to call the Virgin the Mother of God, although Cyril avoided mentioning Nestorius. But Nestorius unwisely received the complaints of some monks coming from Egypt. Worse, he did not send the synodical letter to his Alexandrian counterpart.

The Roman Pope Celestinus (422–432) then became involved in the matter; both Cyril and Nestorius submitted to him the relevant documents. The documents of Cyril were translated into Latin while Nestorius' documents were in Greek, and required some time and effort to be translated in Rome. Celestinus sided with the Alexandrian point of view. Cyril wrote a letter to Nestorius, asking him to sign it within 10 days. This letter included his Twelve **Anathemas**. Pulcheria supported the Roman-Alexandrian popes while the emperor and his wife supported Nestorius. The situation became more confused, so the emperor ordered the convocation of a council in Ephesus on 7 June 431. The choice of this city was not favorable to Nestorius. Memnon, the **bishop** of the city, was not happy that the See of Constantinople had risen in stature above his own see since the Council of Constantinople in 381. Cyril presided over the council with the support of Memnon, and John of Antioch was late in coming to the city. Nestorius was condemned by the council, but upon the arrival of John of Antioch and his Syrian colleagues, they declared that this condemnation was void and proceeded to excommunicate Cyril and Memnon. The emperor decided to send both parties into exile, banishing Cyril, Memnon, and Nestorius. Cyril fled to Alexandria and Nestorius was exiled to Antioch first and after that to the Great Oasis (Kharga) in Upper Egypt, where he spent the rest of his life. After a long discussion between Cyril of Alexandria and John of Antioch, the relations between the two seats were restored. From the correspondence between these two **patriarchs** emerged a definition of faith that was accepted by everybody. *See also* EPHESUS, SECOND COUNCIL OF.

EPHESUS, SECOND COUNCIL OF (449). Eutyches was an archimandrite from Constantinople who started to voice complaints against Nestorius in 428. He was the spiritual father of the grand chamberlain, the eunuch Chrysaphius. In 448, a law was promulgated that forbade any **Christological** scheme not in accord with **Nicaea** or the **First Council of Ephesus**. He opposed **Bishop** Flavian of Constantinople. Flavian censured Eutyches for having an unbalanced **theology**. Eutyches was condemned, appealed to Emperor Theodosius, and a council was summoned. The Second Council of Ephesus took place in 449 under the presidency of **Dioscorus** of **Alexandria**.

He restated the Cyrillian doctrine, mainly from the Twelve **Anathemas**, which disagreed with the Antiochene doctrine of **Nestorius**. Eutyches was restored and all his opponents were deposed. But Flavian died shortly after and the Pope of Rome rejected this council, calling it the robber council. After the sudden death of Theodosius in July 450, imperial officials convoked another, greater council in 451 at Chalcedon, which simply reversed the decisions of the council held in Ephesus in 449.

It is important to note that our knowledge of the Second Council of Ephesus comes mainly from the opponents of the council. The acts of this council are included in the acts of the Council of Chalcedon. Hence, it is very hard to attain a true idea of what happened. Also worthy of note is the fact that most of the attendees of this council later attended the **Council of Chalcedon** and changed their allegiance, claiming that Dioscorus had previously applied pressure on them.

EPHESUS, THIRD COUNCIL OF (476). After the death of Emperor Leo I (457–474), his two successors, Basilicus the Usurper (474–475) and Zeno (474–475, 476–491), intervened in the conflict between the supporters and the opponents of the **Council of Chalcedon**. In 468, an anti-Chalcedonian delegation of Egyptian monks and clergy sought to recall **Timothy Aelurus**, **Bishop** of **Alexandria**, who had been banished to Cherson. The attempt was successful and Timothy regained his seat after 16 years of exile. A large number of bishops assembled in 476 in order to reverse the decisions of the Council of Chalcedon. The Coptic Church considers it a meeting rather than an ecumenical council. Several recommendations were addressed to the Emperor Basilicus but the restoration of Zeno in 476 prevented the application. Timothy returned to Alexandria, where he died in 477.

EPIPHANY, LITURGY OF THE. The Epiphany, in the Coptic Church as in the Eastern churches, commemorates the Baptism of Christ. It seems that it was introduced into the Church calendar by the fourth century. The canons of **Athanasius** and the festal letters mention it for the first time. By the end of the fourth century it had become widely celebrated. **John Cassian** gave a detailed description of the festivities. Some scholars see in this **feast** a continuity of ancient Egyptian festivals, while others think that it was introduced to replace the Jewish feast of the Tabernacles. In the Middle Ages, the Feast of Epiphany became one of the great national festivals in Egypt. Maqrizi, a Muslim historian, described this ceremony and blamed the Christians for their misbehavior. The rite of these ceremonies was performed on the banks of the Nile. Later, due to the persecutions, the rite came to be performed in the church. In the 17th century, the Dominican Father Vansleb attended this ceremony in the **Church of St. Mercurius** in Old Cairo. He described it thus:

> Then comes the benediction of the water, various prayers and lessons recited over it: moreover the pontiff censes it and stirs it crosswise with his pastoral staff, as do also other **bishops** present in due order. This benediction lasts about two hours, but when it was over, the **patriarch** blesses also all the clergy and the congregation, sprinkling them with the holy water. Originally the custom was for the people to rush tumultuously into the water, each striving to be one of the three whom the patriarch dipped thrice, and who were thus supposed to receive a special **blessing**. Those who failed of that distinction dipped themselves: and when the men had finished, they retired to the choir, while the women came and disported themselves quite unclothed. After the immersion follows the ordinary office of **matins** and a festival of the *qorban* [**Eucharist bread**].

The actual rite in the Coptic Church consists of a **liturgy** over the basin (*lakane*). According to **Sawirus ibn al-Muqaffa'** in his book *The Order of Priesthood*, in the Church, this basin represents the Jordan River. The liturgy has the same structure of the Eucharistic prayers. It begins with the prayers of thanksgiving, then readings: the prophecies, the Pauline Epistle, **Trisagion**, the psalm, and the gospel. The **priest** prays the prayers for the peace of the church, the **patriarch**, and the congregation, and the Creed, followed by a special prayer for the Epiphany. Among the special hymns of this feast is a hymn praising John the Baptist, and this hymn makes allusion to a homily of the Patriarch **Theodosius** (sixth century), which survives in a manuscript in the collection of the Pierpont Morgan Library. **Rufa'il al-Tukhi** included the rites of the Epiphany in his edition of the pontificals of 1761. The first Coptic Orthodox publication was edited by Hegemon Bakhum al-Baramusi and 'Arian Farag in 1921.

ESCHATOLOGY. Eschatology is the study of last things, hence the destiny of the world. In Greco-Roman culture, this theme was a favorite subject, and in apostolic times, Paul had to act several times to correct the erroneous eschatological views of the Corinthians. The conversion to Christianity of many pagans and Jews brought with it an intrusion of eschatological apocrypha into Christianity. These books were always ascribed to one of the Apostles, such as the *Ascension of Paul*, the *Apocalypse of Peter*, the *Apocalypse of Thomas*, the *Apocalypse of Stephen*, and the *Apocalypse of Bartholomew*.

ETHIOPIAN LITURGY. The Ethiopian **liturgies** are translated from the Arabic, which in turn are translations of Coptic originals. There are in fact 14 liturgies used by the Ethiopian Church: the Anaphora of the Apostles; the Anaphora of the Lord; the Anaphora of John, Son of Thunder; the Anaphora of St. Mary; the Anaphora of the Three Hundred; the Anaphora of St. **Athanasius**; the Anaphora of St. Basil; the **Anaphora of St. Gregory**; the Anaphora of St. Epiphanius; the Anaphora of St. John Chrysostom; the **Anaphora of St. Cyril**; the Anaphora of St. Jacob of Sarug; the Anaphora of St. **Dioscorus**; and the Anaphora of St. Gregory II.

EUCHARIST. This is considered as one of seven sacraments in the Coptic Church. The Coptic Church believes that in the Eucharist, the bread and wine are no longer mere bread and wine but become the true Body and Blood of the Redeemer, Jesus Christ as being the sacrifice of Christ for all humanity. The Eucharist is known as the sacrament of thanksgiving, the Lord's Supper, the Lord's table, Christ's table, the sacred table, Holy Communion, the holy sacrifice, the divine mystery, the Lord's bread, the heavenly bread, Christ's Body, the Precious Blood, and the redemptive chalice.

According to the Gospel, Christ himself has instituted this sacrament. It is the firm belief of the Orthodox Church that after the consecration of the oblations and the descent of the Holy Spirit upon them, they become the Body and the Blood of Christ. Many church fathers from the second century and onward mentioned the Eucharist in their writing, such as Ignatius of Antioch, Cyril of Jerusalem, Dionysius of Alexandria, **Cyril** of Alexandria, and many others. The Eucharist must be denied to unbelievers, the not baptized, and believers who are impenitent or unprepared to receive the Sacrament. The Eucharist is celebrated daily in most Coptic churches and monasteries; a few churches, however, celebrate it only on Sunday, Wednesday, and Friday.

EUCHARIST BREAD. The Eucharistic bread (called *qorban*) is baked from white flour and yeast in a round shape. It has in the middle a large cross (symbolizing Christ) surrounded by 12 small crosses symbolizing the 12 Apostles. The Greek inscription "Holy God, Holy Almighty, Holy Eternal" surrounds the circle containing the 12 crosses. The Eucharist bread is baked on the same day as the Eucharistic celebration. It should be perfect, without blemish. The psalms are recited during the baking of the Eucharistic bread. The **priest** chooses the most perfect loaf out of a number of loaves of Eucharistic bread (no fewer than three should be baked) for the consecration, and the rest are distributed to the congregation at the end of the liturgy as a **blessing** (*Eulogia*).

EUCHARIST FAST. According to canon law as expressed in the *Apostolic Constitutions*, "It is forbidden to partake of the **communion** unless the person is **fasting**, and whoever dares to eat breakfast and then partake of the Holy Communion will be excommunicated eternally from the Church of God." The canons of Hippolytus state, "It is important that every believer be sure that he did not taste anything before communion."

EUCHARISTIC VEILS, VESSELS, AND IMPLEMENTS. There are four types of Eucharistic veils used in the Coptic Church: altar veils, chalice veils, mats, and the paten veil. The Eucharistic vessels and implements are the chalice, paten, asterisk, spoon, and ark used at the altar in the celebration of the Divine **Liturgy**. The Eucharistic vessels must be consecrated before being used in the church. These vessels, though usually made of silver, may alternatively be made of more precious metals, glass, or terracotta.

The ark is a wooden box that always stands in the middle of the altar. The top has a round hole for the chalice. The four sides carry religious paintings. It must be stressed here that, in accordance with the practice of the Coptic Church, the ark is to house the chalice only during the prayers of the liturgy, and not to hold the Precious Body and Blood following their consecration.

The paten is a flat, shallow, circular dish, with a turned-up edge. It is used to hold the **Eucharist bread**, which is consecrated during the celebration of the liturgy and is transformed into the Body of Christ.

The asterisk (in the Greek church, "star") consists of two half-circles in the form of a dome, intersecting at right angles, and riveted together with a small cross at the top. It folds so as to be conveniently stored. During the liturgy, it is set over the consecrated oblations in the paten to prevent the veil from touching them. It bears a mystical significance to the Star of Bethlehem that led the wise men to the infant Savior while he was lying in the manger.

The chalice is the wine cup used in the celebration of the **Eucharist**. At the celebration of the Eucharist, the **priest** pours the wine into the chalice from the cruet, fills the empty cruet partially with water, and adds the water in turn to the wine in the chalice, which sits inside the ark on the altar. The wine and water refer to blood and water (John 19:34, 1 John 5:6).

The spoon is used for administering the Precious Blood to the communicants.

EUCHARISTIC WINE. *See* ABARKAH.

EUCHOLOGION. The Euchologion is a book containing the pre-anaphoral and anaphoral parts of the Divine **Liturgy** as well as several diaconal hymns and prayers used on different occasions.

EUGNOSTOS THE BLESSED **(NHC III, 3; NHC V, 1).** A revelatory **Gnostic** treatise composed in the form of a letter by "Eugnostos, the Blessed, to those who are his." The text deals with the heavenly world and its various emanations. It is a non-Christian work, probably of Jewish Gnostic origin. The text of *Eugnostos* was subsequently "Christianized" with additional material in which the risen Christ reveals gnosis to his disciples in another **Nag Hammadi** tractate, the *Sophia of Jesus Christ* (NHC III, 4; BG, 3). Extant only in Coptic, *Eugnostos* was originally composed in Greek as early as the late first century, probably in **Alexandria**. It was probably known to the

Gnostic teachers **Basilides** and **Valentinus**, active in Alexandria in the early second century.

EUSEBIUS OF CAESAREA (ca. 265–ca. 340). Bishop, theologian, historian. He is famous for his *Ecclesiastical History*. The Coptic Church takes pride in the tradition recorded by him, that St. **Mark** the Evangelist preached the Gospel in **Alexandria**. He was a pupil of Pamphilus, who had attended the **Catechetical School of Alexandria** under **Origen**. Eusebius had been influenced by Origen and by the theological traditions and style of Alexandrian **theology** through Pamphilus. In ca. 314, he was ordained Bishop of Caesarea, where he wrote three of his largest works—a refutation of paganism, an examination of the fulfillment of Old Testament prophecy in Christ, and his chronicle of world history until 303. He also wrote a "Chronicle" and a "Life of Constantine." Eusebius attended the **Council of Nicaea** in 325, and he did not accept the *homoousios* formula of the Nicene Creed but signed this only under pressure from Constantine, and never completely sympathized with it. Thus he joined the camp opposing Patriarch **Athanasius** of Alexandria. Of great value are his apologetic and dogmatic works, especially the *Preparation for the Gospel* and the *Proof of the Gospel*. Another important work of Eusebius is the *Martyrs of Palestine*.

EVAGRIUS PONTICUS (345–399). Monk, ascetic. He was born at Ibora in the province of Pontus. He studied under the Cappadocian Fathers Basil of Caesarea and **Gregory of Nazianzus**. The latter ordained him deacon. After visiting Jerusalem, Evagrius became a monk in the Egyptian desert in 383. He lived two years in **Nitria** and then moved to **Kellia**, where he remained until his death. He claimed to be a disciple of **Macarius** the Great. Evagrius, a highly educated classical scholar, was one of the most prominent figures among the monks of the Egyptian deserts. He was well known as a keen thinker and a sophisticated, gifted writer. He did not suffer the exile that was imposed on the **Origenist** monks for he died before the intervention of Patriarch **Theophilus**. However, he was posthumously condemned for Origenism by the fifth ecumenical council at Constantinople in 553, a century and half after his death.

A number of the sayings of the *Apophthegmata patrum* are attributed to him. Some of his works survived in Greek, especially those that deal with asceticism. Nearly all his books were translated into Syriac and Latin, some into Armenian and Arabic. Although Evagrius played a significant role in making the ascetic teaching of Egyptian monks known throughout the Christian world, it seems that only a few of his works were translated into Coptic. His treatise "On the Eight Spirits of Malice" was known to Coptic-speaking monks. Evagrius' teachings on asceticism and prayer had a crucial impact upon both Christian East and West.

EXCOUCONTIANS. The Excoucontians were an **Arian** sect of the fourth century, and were combated by St. **Athanasius**. This sect died out after the return of Athanasius to **Alexandria** in 363.

EXEGESIS ON THE SOUL **(NHC II, 6).** A **Gnostic** tale relating the fall of the soul from heaven and her life in a brothel until she repents and is mercifully restored to heaven by the Father. The text contains a number of extensive quotations from the Bible, both Old and New Testaments, and from Homer's *Odyssey*. The title occurs at the end of the tractate. Extant only in Coptic, *Exegesis on the Soul* was composed in Greek, probably in third-century Egypt.

– F –

FANOUS, ISAAC (1919–2007). Educator and founder of **contemporary Coptic art**. He was born on 19 December 1919 in Cairo. He obtained a bachelor of arts degree from the Higher School of Applied Art of Cairo in 1941 and a diploma in art education from the Institute of Education of Cairo in 1946. He worked in both the **Coptic Museum** and the Egyptian Museum. He joined the **Higher Institute of Coptic Studies** in 1954 and obtained his doctorate in 1958. In the 1960s, he studied and trained in Paris under the famous Russian iconographer Leonid Uspensky. After 1967, he taught at the Higher Institute of Coptic Studies. He founded the School of Contemporary Coptic Art, which attempts to provide a conscious fusion of ancient Egyptian and Coptic conventions with contemporaneous twist. The icons of Isaac Fanous and his pupils have spread to many of the Coptic churches in Egypt, and can be found in most of the churches that the Coptic emigrants established in the United States, Canada, Australia, and Europe.

FARAJALLAH AL-AKHMIMI (first half of 14th c.). Canonist. Farajallah is the compiler of a nomocanon preserved in a single manuscript (Paris, Bibliothèque Nationale, arabe 250), dated to 1357. It consists of a first part (on strictly ecclesial matters) in 26 chapters and a second part (of a more secular nature) in 50 chapters. For the most part, the work closely follows *The Book of Spiritual Medicine* attributed to **Mikha'il, Bishop** of Atrib and Malij, with some materials taken from other sources, notably the nomocanon of **al-Safi ibn al-'Assal.**

FASTING. The first references concerning fasting in the Coptic Church are the paschal letters of St. **Athanasius** from the beginning of the fourth century, wherein Athanasius introduced the date of the Holy Lent. This tradition was continued by his successors such as **Theophilus** and **Cyril.** In all these documents, mention is made of Lent and the weekly fast on Wednesdays and Fridays only. A homily ascribed to Theophilus of **Alexandria** and kept in the Freer Collection at the University of Michigan, says, "My beloved, let everyone of you guard his bed pure during the Sabbath and the Sundays as well as the feast days and the meeting days according to the Canons of our holy fathers, the Apostles. And after these the forty holy days and the two fasts and the other dominical **feasts**." It seems that this was a practice that did not survive the commentary of the edition of this text: "i.e. The Pascal fast, at that time separate and beginning on the Friday before the Palm Sunday, and the fast of Jonas, or Nineveh, occurring one week before Lent" is not accurate, as the fast was introduced in the 10th or 11th century. In the year 513, Homily 48 of **Severus of Antioch** mentioned that the homily was delivered during the fast of the Apostles before the feast of the Pentecost. In the 10th century, the first Coptic **bishop** writing in Arabic, Severus of Ashmunain, in his book *The Lamp of the Intellect*, provided a list of the fasting days. However, it seems that there is a later interpretation of this list.

In the Middle Ages, the **patriarchs** issued a series of canons. Among them were those of **Christodoulos**, who is precise in his instructions:

- Canon 15: "Likewise the Fast of the Holy Nativity shall be from the Feast of St. Mena [Mîna] i.e. The fifteenth day of Hatur to the twenty-ninth day of Kîhak."
- Canon 6: "The believer shall conduct himself during the Fast of the Pure Forty [days] as our Lord and our God and our Saviour Jesus Christ fasted—to Him be glory—and this is asceticism and humility. And during it [the Lent]."
- Canon 7: "and in **Holy Week** there shall not be any **baptism** or burial service."
- Canon 13: "And the Fast of the Apostles which is after Pentecost is obligatory for the faithful, in thanksgiving to God that He has granted us the gift of the **Holy Spirit**, fasting continuously until the fifth of Abib; and they shall celebrate the Feast on it as is the custom."
- Canon 14: "And if that day falls on a Wednesday, they shall celebrate the Feast, but they shall not break the fast until the accustomed time for breaking the fast on fasting days. And if the feast is a Friday they shall not break it before the time of the fast, which is customary on it."
- Canon 19: "And it is not allowed for any of the faithful to fast on Saturday, except one Saturday in the whole year, and this is the Holy Saturday which is the end of the Lent."
- Canon 20: "Fasting is obligatory on Wednesday and Friday always throughout the year, except the Fifty Days only."

The *History of the Patriarchs* of the Coptic Church also mentions the fasts of Advent, Wednesdays and Fridays, and of the Apostles. The fasts of the Virgin and of Jonah are not included. **Cyril II** issued a series of canons that exhorted the Christian congregation to fast the 40 days in a decent way, the fasts of the Apostles and the Nativity (Advent), as well as the Wednesdays and the Fridays, except during the Khamasin time (the 50 days after the Resurrection). The last medieval author to provide a list of fasting days is **Ibn Kabar** in his encyclopedia *The Lamp in the Darkness for the Explanation of the*

Service. This list includes for the first time also the Fast of Jonah, and there is a mention of a Fast for the Virgins, which became later the Fast of the Virgin.

According to the **Lectionary** of the Lent, the Fast of Jonah was introduced by Patriarch Afraham the Syrian, Ibn Zur'ah. The detailed history of this fast is included in an Arabic manuscript preserved in the Vatican Library and published by Joseph Simeonis Assemani. According to the manuscript, this fast was promulgated by the Maphrian of Syria in the year 847 of the Calendar of Alexander (536 A.D.) for there was a plague. According to Bar-Hebraeus, there was a dispute between some people and Abu al-'Abbas al-Fadl ibn Sulayman concerning the Fast of Jonah (Ninevah) in the year 290 AH (902 A.D.). They later wrote to the Catholicus asking him the reason for this fast as well as the Fast of the Virgins.

According to Gregory Bar-Hebraeus in his *Ethicon* (1282 A.D.),

On the Number and the Days of the Fasts.

Besides the Wednesday and the Friday the Syrian people have five renowned periods of fasting: First: the fast of the Forty [days]. Second: the fast of the Apostles. Third: the fast of the Departure [of Mary]. Fourth: the fast of the Nativity. Fifth: the fast of Nineveh. As the fast of the Forty [days] is followed by the week of the Redeeming Passion, its days are completed in 48 days. The people in the West [of Syria] observe the fast of the Apostles from the Monday after the feast of Pentecost till the 29th of Hzîrân which is the feast of Peter and Paul, the people in the East till the completion of fifty [days?]. About this [fast] the Holy Jacob [of Edessa] said that it is not compulsory; otherwise, anyone not keeping this fast would be blameworthy. But perhaps because our Lord said to his Apostles: the sons of the Bride chamber . . . shall fast (Mt. 9:15), therefore, when our Lord ascended and the Spirit came, the Apostles fasted and this was accepted as a custom, but not prescribed.

We observe the fast of the Departure [of Mary] from the first day of Ab till its full moon.

Some people observe the fast of Nativity forty days from the full moon of Teshrîn the second, others twenty-five days from the beginning of Kânûn the first and still others two weeks from the 10th of Kânûn the first. The people in the East observe the fast of Nineveh from Monday in the third week before the great fast till the morning of Thursday, the people in the West till the morning of Saturday.

In addition to literary works, inscriptions from the Monastery of Epiphanius mention fasting twice: "Apa Shenute: If your word be true, that it is a sin to fast in the Pentecost, for that it is a [festival]; know then rather it is a far greater iniquity [wherein?] ye transgress, early [the] forty holydays . . ." and "[the] holy [forty] days fast . . . The eight weeks . . . [the day] of Me[chir . . . according to the] Egyptians. We will begin . . . [the] holy [. . .] of the fasts, to wit . . . in number pleasing unto."

FEASTS. The number of the dominical feasts changes according to the tradition. In the Byzantine tradition, there are 12 feasts, whereas in the Coptic tradition there is the existence of seven dominical major feasts and seven dominical minor feasts, and this has been attested since the 12th century. **Abu al-Makarim** mentioned that in the Church of Haret Al-Rum there is an **icon** depicting the seven dominical major feasts. In his encyclopedia, **Ibn Kabar** gave a detailed description of the **liturgical** practices of the major and minor feasts. However, this number varied throughout the ages. In 518 A.D. **Severus of Antioch** states, in Homily 125, that Palm Sunday and the Feast of the Presentation of the Lord in the temple are of a recent date. It is known that the Feast of the Nativity was introduced in the Coptic Orthodox Church by the late fourth century. The feasts that are observed by the Coptic Church fall into four main divisions:

1. The Lord's major feasts: the Annunciation (29 Baramhat), the Nativity (29 Kiyahk), the Epiphany (11 Tubah), Palm Sunday, Easter Sunday, Ascension Day, and Pentecost.
2. The Lord's minor feasts: Circumcision (6 Tubah), the Marriage Feast at Cana (13 Tubah), **Maundy Thursday**, Thomas' Sunday, the **Flight into Egypt** (24 Bashans), Candlemas (8 Amshir), and the Transfiguration (13 Misra). One may find iconographic representations of these feasts in the form of wall paintings in the **Monastery of the Syrians** and the **Monastery of al-Baramous** as well as in the Church of Haret Zuwelah (Old Cairo) and the **Church of St. Mercurius**.
3. The Marian feasts.
4. The feast days of the **saints** and martyrs.

FESTAL DAYS, MONTHLY. Traditionally, the Coptic Orthodox Church would celebrate two **feast** days for prominent martyrs, the timing of which would generally fall during the summer and winter. One feast day would commemorate the **saint's** martyrdom, and the second would be the consecration of the saint's church. This practice was later extended to incorporate a monthly festal celebration. The most significant monthly festal celebrations include the commemoration of the Archangel Michael on the 12th of each month, the commemoration of the Virgin Mary on the 21st of each month, and the commemoration of the Annunciation, Nativity, and Resurrection, all of which are remembered on the 29th of each month. Some liturgical manuscripts contain "the Monthly **Lectionary**," which was adopted by the Ethiopian Church and became a popular tradition.

FILIOQUE. Latin, meaning "and [from] the son." In the sixth century, **Arian** barbarians (Goth and Visigoth) invaded the western empire and introduced many heretical dogmas and expressions. In 589 A.D., the Council of Toledo included details in the **Nicene Creed** concerning the procession of the **Holy Spirit** from the Father and the Son in order to emphasize the divinity of Christ. This addition of "and the Son" (*filioque*) was accepted by the West before this council. In the seventh century, the *filioque* became a matter of debate between the East and the West, when **Patriarch** Photius of Constantinople raised the issue within the empire, and it was only in the ninth century that the Western world responded. In the 11th century, the Franks imposed *filioque* on the papacy and the West, while the East rejected it, hence resulting in a schism between the East and the West. The Coptic Church, then under Islamic dominance and having been separated from imperial Christianity since the **Council of Chalcedon** in 451 A.D., did not take part in the *filioque* debate, which caused a schism between the two Chalcedonian strongholds in Rome and Constantinople.

FLIGHT INTO EGYPT. Many Coptic churches commemorate the flight into Egypt by celebrating the mass on the 24th of the Coptic month Bachons, corresponding to the first day of June. This great event is glorified in the liturgical book the **Difnar** and the **Synaxarion**

of the Coptic Church. The scripture (Matt. 2:13) provides no information about the duration of the Holy Family's stay in Egypt and the sites that were blessed by them. This was left to tradition that developed throughout the centuries. In the early third century, Hippolytus of Rome states in his *Commentary on Matthew* that Christ remained in Egypt three years and a questionable number of months in his flight to Egypt. Around 400, an anonymous author of the *History of the Monks in Egypt* speaks of the Upper Egyptian city of "Hermopolis, to which the Savior along with Mary and Joseph came fulfilling the prophecy of Isaiah" (19:1). People sought an "itinerary" of the Holy Family's sojourn in Egypt. Many medieval sources, mainly in Arabic, mention fascinating details of the journey with its miraculous incidents. The most important **pilgrimage** centers with association with the Holy Family are the **Church of Sts. Sergius and Bacchus** in Old Cairo, the Church of the Holy Virgin Mary at Musturud near Cairo, the Church of the Virgin at Gebel al-Tayr, **Dayr al-Muharraq**, and the Church of the Virgin at Durunkah near Assiut. They attract hundreds of thousands of pilgrims annually.

FLORENCE, COPTS AT THE COUNCIL OF (1439–1443). This council was an unsuccessful attempt to bridge the gap between Rome on one side and the Copts and the Ethiopians on the other. In September 1440, Pope Eugenius IV sent the Franciscan friar Albertus to Cairo to meet Coptic **Patriarch** John XI. The latter gave Albertus a letter to Pope Eugenius in which he appointed Andrew, abbot of the **Monastery of St. Antony**, to represent the Copts in the Council of Florence. On 4 February 1442 at the Church of Santa Maria Novella, the Latin text of the bull (papal correspondence) of the union with the Copts was read out, followed by an Arabic translation. The bull was signed by Pope Eugenius IV, 20 cardinals, and 51 prelates. Andrew signed the Arabic text in the name of the Jacobites and his patriarch. The **Council of Chalcedon** was accepted, together with several other later councils. The bull commanded the Copts to obey all ways and adhere faithfully to the **Apostolic See**. The Copts understood this as a reunion of equal partners. However, the act of the union remained in abeyance, for the rejection of the Council of Chalcedon had been an essential part of the Coptic dogma for a millennium.

FRACTION. A liturgical prayer recited after the anaphora and prior to **communion**. The Fraction prayers are first attested in Serapion's fourth century **Euchologion** and they are recited in many Eastern liturgies such as the Liturgy of **Mark**, Gregory, Basil, John Chrysostom, and James. In the printed edition of the Euchologion, there are 20 Fraction prayers, with each **liturgy** containing one prayer and with 17 in an appendix. The most recent is translated from Syriac to Arabic and finally to Coptic. In editing the Euchologion, Hegumen Abd al-Masih Salih al-Mas'udi mentioned the existence of many prayers. He made a critical study to choose the most well known that corresponded to the dogma and traditions of the Coptic Church.

– G –

GABRIEL II IBN TURAYK (1084–1145). Patriarch (70th, 1131–1145). Abu al-'Ala' Sa'id ibn Turayk was a learned, generous, and pious layman who served as an administrator in various government bureaus before being chosen, in 1131, to be the 70th patriarch of the Coptic Orthodox Church under the name Gabriel. During his patriarchate he issued a number of sets of canons (in Arabic) that displayed his administrative skill, his zeal for reform of the Church and community, and his concern for the religious life of the laity. For example, in the set of 32 canons issued shortly after he became patriarch, Gabriel forbids simony and concubinage and takes steps to ensure that prayers are offered and attended with reverence and in good order. Concern for the laity may be seen in Gabriel's insistence (Canon 3 of the 32) that **bishops** teach their people the **Doxology**, the **Lord's Prayer**, and the **Nicene Creed** in Arabic (since many of them no longer understood Coptic), and in his reform of the **Holy Week** **liturgy** (*The Book of the Pascha*), which takes into account the work schedules of Coptic civil servants unable to dedicate the entire week to prayer.

Gabriel's nomocanon, once considered lost but now available in a critical edition, is important for understanding the history of Copto-Arabic canonical literature. Gabriel identifies his sources, which allows us to see him gathering materials from canonical collections that had already been translated into Arabic by the early 12th century, including the Arabic *Didascalia* (*al-Disquliyya*), the *Canons of the Apostles*, the *Canons of the Kings*, the canons of the **Council of Nicaea** and regional synods, as well as the collections attributed to Hippolytus, Epiphanius, Basil, and John Chrysostom.

GABRIEL III (?–1271). Scribe, **patriarch** (77th, 1268–1271). Before his election as patriarch, Gabriel was a monk (at the **Monastery of St. Antony**), **priest** (who served for a time at the Church of the Resurrection in Jerusalem), and scribe (who was a client of the **Awlad al-'Assal**, who championed his elevation to the patriarchate). His contributions to **Copto-Arabic literature** are largely in the scribal realm, as he copied books for the Awlad al-'Assal and their friends; scattered manuscript notices dated from 1249 to 1271 apprise us of his activities. However, Ethiopic sources claim that after the disputed election of 1262 that elevated Gabriel's rival John VII to the patriarchal throne, Gabriel withdrew to the Monastery of St. Antony and—according to one witness—then to the **Monastery of St. Paul**, where he translated the *Pandektes* of the 11th-century Byzantine monk Nikon from Greek into Arabic. This story, even if apocryphal, is indicative of the ecumenical horizons of the Coptic scholars of the 13th century: they rejoiced in the discovery of theological books, even those of non-Coptic provenance, and made creative use of them.

GABRIEL V (?–1427). Patriarch (88th, 1409–1427), liturgical reformer. Gabriel V was patriarch during a period of political instability, economic difficulties, and repeated outbreaks of plague, during which the Coptic community, like other *dhimmi* communities in Egypt, was regularly scapegoated and shaken down for funds. The Muslim historian al-Maqrizi reports that Gabriel was obliged to travel barefoot from village to village in order to beg for aid. Still, Gabriel found the time and energy to reform the **liturgy** of the Coptic Orthodox Church by producing a *Kitab Tartib* or *Ordo*, setting forth the major offices of the Church and specifying prayers and gestures with great precision. This *Ordo* represents a gathering as well as a unifying and standardizing of earlier traditions. It was approved at a synod at the Church of Abu Sayfayn in Old Cairo on May 3, 1411. *See also* CHURCH OF ST. MERCURIUS.

GAIANUS, JULIAN. Bishop. The controversy within the anti-Chalcedonian parties between Julian of Halicarnasus and **Severus of Antioch** led to the choice of two episcopal candidates after the death of the Patriarch **Timothy** of **Alexandria** (517–535): **Theodosius** (for the Severian party) and Gaianus (for the Julianist party). Although Theodosius received the most number of votes, his consecration was not accomplished due to a revolt, and hence Gaianus was instated. However, even his appointment was short-lived, for an imperial decree banished him to Carthage. Nevertheless, Gaianus received strong support in Alexandria until the year 580 A.D.

The doctrine of Julian of Halicarnasus intimates that Christ has one divine nature, and hence an incorruptible nature. Accordingly, his doctrine assumes that Christ did not have a human nature. The information that has been passed down regarding the doctrines of Julian of Halicarnasus comes predominantly from his opponents, such as Anastasius Sinait and John of Damascus. The *History of the Patriarchs*, which was written long after these events, provides a simplistic overview.

GANGRA, COUNCIL OF (ca. 340). The Council of Gangra was a local synod and, accordingly, the Coptic Church did not take part in its discussion. This council condemned extreme ascetical practices such as the condemnation of marriage, deprivation of eating meat, and so on. Although medieval sources attest that the decisions resulting from this council were received by the Coptic Church and were entered into Coptic canon law at quite an early date, there are no surviving Coptic manuscripts reflecting this. It is the medieval canonical collections such as the books of Ibn al-Assal and **Ibn Kabar** that mention them.

GENUFLECTION. The Prayer of Genuflection is performed in the Coptic Church on the eve of Whitsunday (the **Feast** of Pentecost) to indicate the end of Eastertide, during which prostration does not occur. This prayer signals another period in the liturgical calendar, during which prostration is permitted.

Ireneaus **Bishop** of Lyon wrote, "Do not kneel on the Lord's Day as symbol of the resurrection, through which by Christ's grace we have been freed from our sins." In the third century, Tertullian wrote, "As for ourselves, according to our tradition, only on the day of the Lord's resurrection should we refrain from this custom [of kneeling]. . . . The same holds for the season of Pentecost, that is marked by the same joyous celebration." **Eusebius of Caesarea**, expounding the Gospel of Luke, wrote, "Wherefore we are not allowed to toil during this festival. . . . Consequently, we neither bend the knee at prayers nor afflict ourselves with **fasting**." The Armenian **Lectionary** of the fifth century states that on the eve of the Feast of the Pentecost, there are three genuflections and a reading from the Gospel of John (16:5–15). **Severus of Antioch** at the beginning of the sixth century composed a hymn for this occasion by saying that we do not bend our knees during Eastertide. Hence, the tradition of kneeling or prostration on the eve of the Feast of the Pentecost is well attested by the Church Fathers.

The Coptic prayer book of genuflection mentions an incident that occurred during the patriarchate of a certain Macarius of Antioch. While the **patriarch** was reciting his prayers on the eve of Pentecost, a storm arose three times and the believers understood this as God's will for prostration to take place three times. Although the practice of genuflection is well attested as early as the second century, this legend is simply considered another demonstration for the practice.

Manuscript 42 Vatican is dated 1032 A.M. (1316 A.D.) and was originally from the Church of the Virgin Mary in Haret Al-Rum, Old Cairo. A manuscript from the Church of the Virgin Mary in Haret Zuweila, Cairo, is dated 1177 A.M. (1461 A.D.) and, in addition to an incomplete manuscript also from Haret Zuweila, is now located in the Italian city of Pisa. This rite of genuflection is mentioned by Abu al Barakat **ibn Kabar** in his encyclopedia entitled *The Lamp of Darkness for the Explanation of the Service* (chapter 19).

There exists in the Greek Church a rite for the necessity of performing seven prayers. According to Coptic rites, there are three liturgical segments (sections), each of which contains readings from Deuteronomy, a Pauline epistle, a psalm, and a gospel reading. Each segment then concludes with the prayers found in the rites of the Greek Church. Each prayer of the Coptic genuflection follows the same structure. Within the prayers, several themes are apparent, such as fire, speaking in tongues, feast of the weeks, kneeling, and the ministry of the Apostles, all of which are relevant Pentecostal themes. Important to note is that the first prayer of genuflection consists of some prayers taken from the Vesper **Psalmody**:

First Genuflection	Second Genuflection	Third Genuflection

Prophecy
  Deut. 5:23–33, 6:1–3
These commandments
  the Lord spoke in a
  great voice to your
  whole assembly on
  the mountain out
  of the fire.
	Prophecy
	  Deut. 6:17–25.
	You must
	  diligently keep the
	  commandments of
	  the Lord your God
	  . . . and you may
	  enter and occupy the
	  rich land, which the
	  Lord promised by
	  oath to your
	  forefathers.
		Prophecy
		  Deut. 16:1–18.
		Observe the month of
		  Abib and keep the
		  Passover to the Lord
		  Your God . . . Seven
		  weeks shall be
		  counted from
		  the time.

I Cor. 12:28—13:1–12.
God has appointed, in
  first place apostles,
  in the second place
  prophets. . . . I may
  speak in tongues of
  men or of angels, but
  if I am without love.
	I Cor. 13:13, 14:1–17.
	And now abides faith,
	  hope, love, these
	  three; but the greatest
	  of these is love. I
	  would that you all
	  spake with tongues
	  but rather that you
	  prophesied.
		I Cor. 14:18–40.
		I thank my God, for I
		  speak with tongues
		  more than you all.
		  . . . Wherefore,
		  brethren, covet to
		  prophesy, and forbid
		  not to speak with
		  tongues. Let all
		  things be done
		  decently and in
		  order.

Psalms 96:8, 1.
Worship (kneel) Him
  all you angels. Zion
  heard and was glad.
  The Lord reigns.
	Psalms 115:9–10–13.
	The Lord remembered
	  us and He blessed
	  the house of Aaron.
	  He blessed them that
	  fear the Lord, both
	  small and great.
		Psalms 65:4, 72:11.
		All the earth shall
		  worship (kneel) Thee
		  and shall sing unto
		  Thy name. You, all
		  kings will kneel
		  down in front of Him
		  and all nations will
		  worship Him.
		
		(continues)

First Genuflection	Second Genuflection	Third Genuflection
John 17:1–26. As you sent Me to the world even so have I *sent* them to the world. . . . I in them and Thou in Me that they may be made perfect in one; and that the world may know that Thou hast *sent Me*, and hast loved them, as Thou hast loved Me.	Luke 24:36–53. And as they thus spake, Jesus Himself stood in the midst of them and saith unto them, 'Peace be unto you.' . . . And He led them out as far as Bethany, and He lifted up His hands and blessed them. And it came to pass while He blessed them; He was parted from them and carried up into heaven. And they *worshipped* (kneeled) Him and returned to Jerusalem with great joy.	John 4: 1–24 When therefore the Lord knew how the Pharisees had heard that Jesus made and baptised more disciples than John . . . But the hour comes, and now is, when the true *worshippers* shall *worship* the Father in Spirit and in truth: for the Father seeks such to worship Him. God is Spirit and they that worship Him must *worship* Him in spirit and truth.
First and Second prayer	Third and Fourth prayer	Fifth, sixth and seventh prayers

This rite was first published by R. **Tukhi** in his pontificale, vol. II, pp. 326–415.

GERONTICA. *See* SAYINGS OF THE FATHERS.

GHALI, MIRRIT BOUTROS (1908–1992). Founder of the **Society of Coptic Archaeology**. He was one of the important Coptic personalities of the 20th century. He studied law and political science in Paris and joined the Egyptian Ministry of Foreign Affairs. In 1938, he published a significant book entitled *The Policy of Tomorrow* (in Arabic), in which he criticized successive Egyptian governments for ignoring the economic and social needs of the people. He was a member of Parliament (1950–1952) and a minister for social affairs. He was instrumental in the negotiations between the Coptic and Ethiopian Churches in the 1940s. Mirrit Ghali is one of the editors of the *Coptic Encyclopedia*.

GIRGIS, HABIB (1876–1951). Reformer, educator, preacher. He was born in Cairo and joined the Coptic school of Harit al-Saqqayin, which Patriarch **Cyril IV** had established. He was educated in the **Clerical College** of the Coptic Orthodox Church and became a professor of **theology** from 1898 in the same college, and then its principal from 1918 until his death. He published *al-Karma* (1906–1923), a weekly magazine that radiates his teachings. At the turn of the 20th century, he founded the Sunday School system to teach Coptic children the Christian faith. Habib Girgis played a key role in the introduction of the study of the Christian religion to Coptic students in government schools and provided the Ministry of Education with a two-volume manual as a teacher's guidebook. He strove for the reform of the Coptic Church and succeeded in persuading **Patriarch** Cyril V (1874–1927) to take steps to limit the ordination of **priests** to graduates of the Clerical College.

Girgis is the author of numerous articles and books in Arabic related to the theology and **liturgy** of the Coptic Orthodox Church. His most significant work, entitled *Practical Means for Coptic Reformation: Aspirations and Dreams Which Could Be Realized in Ten Years* (in Arabic), appeared in Cairo in 1942 and was reprinted by the Sunday Schools Press in 1993. Many of the disciples of Habib Girgis continued his work, in particular as Sunday School leaders, including the present **patriarch** of the Coptic Church, Pope **Shenouda III**, who highly appreciates him.

GLORIFICATIONS, RITE OF. This rite is performed before an **icon** of a **saint**, either after Vesper prayers or after the Eucharistic **liturgy**. Sometimes the rite is performed during a visit of the tomb or the **pilgrimage** center of a saint. In commemoration of the saint, the faithful chant the **Doxology Adam** — a glorification of the saint's life, virtues, miracles, and homilies. The **priest** then reads a homily or a collection of miracles performed by the saint, after which the faithful sing hymns of praise for the saint commemorated.

GNOSTICISM IN EGYPT. The term "Gnosticism" was first coined in the 17th century to refer to an early Christian heresy described by the Church Father Irenaeus of Lyon in his five volumes *Against Heresies* (ca. 185). Historians of religions use the term to refer to a religion that probably developed around the turn of the era from Jewish roots and took on various forms—Jewish, Christian, and others. In this religion, gnosis ("knowledge") is the prerequisite to salvation, and consists of revelations concerning the true nature of God and the human self. The traditional God is split between a transcendent deity and a lower creator deity responsible for the creation of the material world. The true human being (soul or spirit) is regarded as a divine spark that originated in the divine world and is now imprisoned in a material body. Salvation consists of an escape from the cosmic prison and a return to the soul's divine origin. All of this is given expression in an elaborate mythology.

In Christian forms of Gnosticism, Jesus Christ is the heaven-sent revealer of gnosis. Early adherents of this religion referred to themselves as *gnostikoi*, "Gnostics," that is, those in possession of saving gnosis. The sources for our knowledge of ancient Gnosticism consist of reports and refutations by Christian fathers, especially Justin Martyr, Irenaeus, Hippolytus, Tertullian, Clement of **Alexandria**, **Origen**, and Epiphanius. Thanks to manuscript discoveries, we now have primary sources available in Coptic versions found in the **Nag Hammadi Codices**, the **Berlin Gnostic Codex**, the **Bruce Codex**, and the **Askew Codex**. The religion of the Mandaeans (Gnostics) of Iraq and Iran is the only surviving remnant of the ancient Gnostic religion. Gnosticism was especially prominent in Egypt, first in Alexandria and then spreading into the *chora* (Hinterland, not Alexandria). Indeed, the first Christian teachers in Egypt known to us by name were Gnostic "heretics" active in Alexandria in the early second century: **Basilides** and his son Isidore, **Carpocrates** and his son Epiphanes, and **Valentinus**, who moved to Rome ca. 140. While several forms of Christian Gnosticism existed in Egypt, two were especially prominent, as reflected in our primary sources: "Sethian" or "classic" Gnosticism, in which the heavenly Seth plays an important role as revealer of gnosis and spiritual progenitor of the Gnostic "race"; and Valentinian Gnosticism, which originated as a more specifically Christian adaptation of classic Gnosticism and is reflected in the writings of Valentinus and several prominent pupils of his, such as Ptolemy, **Heracleon**, **Theodotus**, and several others. Heracleon and Theodotus were probably active in Alexandria in the mid-second century. Valentinian Christianity spread to all parts of the Roman Empire and beyond, and persisted in some areas into the seventh century.

The first Christian teacher in Alexandria to label Christian Gnostic teachings as a deviant "heresy" was Clement of Alexandria, who taught in the last quarter of the second century. His writings reflect the influence of Irenaeus' treatise *Against Heresies*. Ecclesiastical opposition to Gnostic teachings seems to have been sponsored by **Bishop** Demetrius of Alexandria (189–232). The official position of the Alexandrian **Patriarchate** on Gnostic and other "heresies" was adumbrated by St. **Athanasius** in his paschal letter of 367, in which he proscribed heretical and "apocryphal" writings and established the contours of the biblical canon of scripture. Even so, Gnostics could be found in Egypt for some time after that. Around 600, John of Paralos wrote a polemical treatise against Gnosticism and other heresies.

A special form of the Gnostic religion, Manichaeism, founded by the prophet Mani (216–277), was brought by disciples of Mani to Egypt from Mesopotamia around 270. Several Manichaean writings exist in Coptic versions preserved in fourth- and fifth-century manuscripts found in the 20th century. The first Egyptian Christian refutation of Manichaeism was penned by Bishop Theonas of Alexandria (282–300), but Manichaeism persisted in Egypt for several centuries.

GOOD FRIDAY. The Friday before Easter and the anniversary of the crucifixion of Jesus Christ. Ibn Kabar's description of the rites of Good Friday is as follows:

> the prayer of the first hour is performed according to the rite of the Passover with readings from the four gospels and the prophecies, followed by sermons that are relevant for this hour. In the third hour, black veils are hung on the iconostaces and on the doors of the sanctuary. Seven censers are also hung upon the door of the iconostaces. The icon of the glorified crucifixion is placed outside of the sanctuary, signifying that Christ had been crucified outside of the city. The icon is surrounded by aromatic herbs and flowers. The readings of the hour (and each hour) include prophecies, gospels, sermons and the hourly commentary, followed by concluding prayers. During the sixth hour and after the reading of the prophecies, the congregation chant, "To You is the power and glory." Censers are prepared by the priests who offer incense before the icon of the crucifixion, in accordance with

their ranks. The gospel is then read in a sorrowful tune. The Pauline text of this hour is from the Epistle to the Galatians which begins with, "I should not boast of anything except the Cross of our Lord Jesus Christ . . ." (Galatians 6:14). Some chant this Pauline in a combination of sorrowful and normal melodies; however, this is incorrect. Following the Pauline, the congregation chant the "Agios" of crucifixion three times in a long tune. This is consistent with what is performed in the Greek Church. The stanza of the Sext [sixth hour] as in the Horologion [*Agbiah*] is also chanted. Following this, a psalm and gospel is chanted, after which a sermon appropriate to the hour is given with the hourly commentary, and the hour concludes with supplication prayers and the "Agios" of crucifixion chanted in the short tune.

The congregation are seated during which the confession of the thief on the cross, "Remember me O Lord," is sung in Greek and Arabic. After each stanza, the cantors respond to the reader in two choirs, one in Coptic and the other in Greek. When the confession is completed, the congregation chant the hymn of the repentant thief: "Blessed are you Demas the thief more than anybody." The Paralex is also sung, which begins, "It happened when they crucified our Saviour. . . ." The candles and lamps are put out during this hour until the ninth hour, to represent the darkness in all the land that is recorded in the gospels.

If time permits, a homily of **Bishop** James of Sarûg on the confession of the thief and his entrance to Paradise with the Lord, as well as other homilies and sermons focusing on the gospel accounts of the Crucifixion, may be read for the edification of the believers.

Following this is the None [ninth hour]. Prior to chanting the psalms, some stanzas from the Book of Hourly Prayers [*Agbia*] are chanted in the usual tune.

According to tradition, the prophecies and gospels of the 11th hour are to be read by the eldest deacons; the Gospel of John (19:31–37) read by the archdeacon. Following the 11th hour are the prayers of the 12th hour. All the readings of this hour are done by the priest, and the Gospel of John (19:38–42) is read by the **patriarch** if he is present, or the bishop of the diocese, and the archdeacon reads the Arabic version.

The custom in the Hanging Church [Al-Muallaqah] in Old Cairo, is that the patriarch should read the *Cathedra* [*ambon*] and that the *tubh* [supplications] is read. The cross is then raised as the congregation chanted "Kyrie Eleison" [Lord have mercy] 400 times: 100 times whilst facing east, 100 times whilst facing west, 100 times whilst facing north, and 100 hundred times whilst facing south. The chant is said in the tune of Passover. Following this, the clergy and the congregation face east and continue with a further 12 Kyrie Eleison chanted in a long tune of great melody. The canon of the cross, "By Your Cross . . . ," and "They Nailed You to the Cross . . ." is then chanted. Following the recitation of this hymn, the patriarch or the highest ranking priest reads the first three psalms, after which the congregation depart the church in peace. The patriarch places the cross in a piece of cloth to symbolise the burial of the body of our Lord. The cross is placed amidst much aromatic herbs and rose petals to symbolize the anointments that are placed on the body during burial.

The whole Book of Psalms is read by the priests who begin and the deacons who follow. At Psalm 148, the highest ranking priest reads the last three psalms, and the patriarch or the bishop read Psalm 151 [in Coptic], followed by the archdeacon who reads the Arabic version. Following this, the Book of Psalms is placed in a silk veil. The deacon holds it to his head, and together with the other deacons, proceeds around the church with candles whilst chanting "Lord have mercy" in the tune of Passover. It is better to sing, "Let us praise" until the procession deacons return back to the place where the highest ranking priest is. The cantiques are then read one after the other.

In Upper Egypt, all the cantiques are read by the archdeacon. In the churches of Old Cairo, the archdeacon reads them in Arabic. Ibn Kabar then provides a detailed description of the rite of the Passover in the **Monastery of St. Macarius**.

According to the linguistic study of Anton Baumstark, the hymn of Demas the thief, "Remember me, O Lord, when You come in Your kingdom" dates back to the seventh and eighth centuries.

GOSPEL OF JUDAS. Its text is extant in only one manuscript, known as *Codex Tchacos*, an early fourth-century Coptic papyrus manuscript that surfaced in the 1970s. It is reported that the codex was discovered during an illegal search for treasures in a burial cave near the village of Qarrara north of al-Minya in Middle Egypt. The manuscript was badly mistreated and partly damaged before its restoration. The text has been released to the public in 2006 after its purchase from the antiquities market and conservation. It is one of the most important contributions to early Christianity since the discovery of the **Nag Hammadi Codices** in 1945. Around 180, Irenaeus, bishop of Lyons, criticized some Christians, who produced a fabricated work that they entitled the Gospel of Judas. The Coptic text, a **Gnostic** gospel, is a translation of an earlier Greek version that is probably from the second century. Unlike the canonical gospels, the gospel of Judas portrays Judas Iscariot as a divinely appointed instrument of a predetermined purpose. The text is identified on the first page as "The secret account of the revelation that Jesus spoke in conversation with Judas Iscariot during a week three days before he celebrated Passover."

***GOSPEL OF MARY* (BG, 1).** A **Gnostic** revelation discourse between the risen Jesus and his disciples, followed by a report by Mary Magdalene of a special revelation given to her by the Savior. The title occurs at the end: *"Gospel According to Mary."* The *Gospel of Mary* is poorly preserved (10 of the original 18 pages are missing), but enough is left to show that Mary, whose chief antagonist is Peter, is preeminent among Jesus' Apostles in the tractate. A third-century papyrus fragment of the original Greek version is known. The *Gospel of Mary* was probably written in second-century Egypt and translated into Coptic in the early fourth century.

***GOSPEL OF PHILIP* (NHC II, 3).** A Valentinian **Gnostic** anthology of statements on aspects of **Valentinian theology** and ritual life, including 17 sayings attributed to Jesus. The subscript title, "The Gospel According to Philip," probably derives from the fact that Philip is the only Apostle named in the text. Extant only in Coptic, the *Gospel of Philip* was originally composed in Greek sometime during the third century, probably in Syria.

***GOSPEL OF THE EGYPTIANS* (NHC III, 2; IV, 2).** A **Sethian** Gnostic tractate containing a mythological account of the heavenly world and its various emanations, a cosmogony, and an account of the saving activity of Seth on behalf of his "race" (**Gnostics**). The text also contains allusions to Gnostic ritual activity. The title, "Gospel of the Egyptians," obviously secondary, occurs at the beginning of a colophon at the end of the text, but there is also a subscript title at the very end, "The Holy Book of the Great Invisible Spirit," which reflects phraseology found in the opening passage. This tractate is to be distinguished from an apocryphal Gospel of the Egyptians, of which only fragments remain. Extant only in Coptic, it was originally composed in Greek, probably in third-century Egypt.

GOSPEL OF THOMAS (NHC II, 2). A collection of 114 "secret sayings" attributed to Jesus, said to have been written down by Didymos Judas Thomas. The *Gospel of Thomas* is completely preserved only in Coptic, but three copies of a Greek version are represented by Greek papyrus fragments found at Oxyrhynchus. Some of the sayings have parallels in the canonical gospels, but most do not. It is possible that some of the sayings represent an Aramaic sayings tradition that is very early, though the *Gospel of Thomas* as we now have it represents a later mystical type of Christianity at home in eastern Syria, for which Judas Thomas, Jesus "twin," is the chief apostolic authority. The original **eschatological** teaching of Jesus is thoroughly de-eschatologized in the *Gospel of Thomas*. Some scholars hold that the *Gospel of Thomas* was composed in Syriac, but no Syriac version is extant. As the Oxyrhynchus fragments attest, the *Gospel of Thomas* was brought to Egypt sometime during the second century. Some of the sayings also have parallels in apocryphal gospels composed in **Alexandria**, the Gospel of the Hebrews and the Gospel of the Egyptians (not the same as the **Nag Hammadi** tractate of the same title). A likely date of composition for the *Gospel of Thomas* (whether composed in Greek or Syriac) is around 140.

GOSPEL OF TRUTH (NHC I, 3; XII, 2). A homiletic meditation whose title is given in its opening words: "The Gospel of truth is joy for those who have received from the Father of truth the grace of knowing him." Preserved only in Coptic, the *Gospel of Truth* was composed in Greek early in the second century, probably in **Alexandria**. Similarities in the text to the extant fragments of the writings of the Christian **Gnostic** teacher **Valentinus** have led some scholars to attribute the text to him.

GREGORIUS (1919–2001). Bishop and educator. Born Wahib Atalla Girgis, he obtained a bachelor's degree in **theology** from the **Clerical College** in 1938, and a bachelor's degree in philosophy from Cairo University in 1951. The University of Manchester awarded him a

PhD in Coptic studies in 1954. He taught at the Clerical College and he became the head of the Section of Theology at the **Higher Institute of Coptic Studies** in 1963. Pope **Cyril VI** ordained him Bishop for Christian Education and Coptic Culture in 1967. He represented the Coptic Church in many international conferences and in the World Council of Churches Assembly. Bishop Gregorius is the author of numerous books and articles related to the Coptic Orthodox dogma, the history of the Coptic Church, and the Coptic culture (in Arabic). His valuable contribution to Coptic studies is "Greek Loan Words in Coptic," *Bulletin de la Société d'archéologie copte* 17, (1963–1964): 63–73; 21(1971–1973):33–53.

GREGORY OF NAZIANZUS (329–389). Saint, theologian, and **bishop**. Gregory was born near Nazianzus in Cappadocia. He was educated at Caesarea and **Alexandria**, where he became familiar with the works of **Origen**. After studying in Athens, he returned home, where he was baptized in 358. He was ordained a **priest** against his will in 362. His friend Basil, the great Archbishop of Cappadocia, ordained him as the bishop of a small city named Sasima. He withdrew to Seleucia in order to live as a contemplative there. In 379, he became the spiritual father of the Nicene congregation in Constantinople. In 381, the Second Ecumenical **Council of Constantinople** confirmed him as Bishop of Constantinople. However, because the transferal of a bishop from one diocese to another is not canonical, Gregory resigned from his responsibilities in order to avoid possible conflict and disturbance. He died near Nazianzus. In Coptic there exist various homilies that have been attributed to Gregory of Nazianzus, such as a homily on St **Athanasius**, a homily on charity to the poor, a homily on St. Basil of Cappadocia, a homily on the Passion Week, and a homily on the Archangel Michael. There also exist fragments of homilies, theological treatises, and letters. The **Anaphora of St. Gregory**, certain prayers of exorcism, and some commentaries on the gospels have also been ascribed to him.

GREGORY OF NYSSA (ca. 335–ca. 394). Saint, theologian, and **bishop**. Gregory is commemorated in the Coptic calendar on the 17th of Babeh. He was the younger brother of Basil the Great. He was first an orator. However, under the influence of his friend

Gregory of Nazianzus, he withdrew from the world. His brother consecrated him a Bishop of Nyssa in 371. Gregory was accused of mismanaging his diocese and was deposed, but the Synod of Antioch entrusted him to visit the diocese of Pontus. The Coptic version of his works is relatively poor compared with his corpus in other languages, mainly Greek. His homily on Gregory the Thaumaturgus survived in two versions—Bohairic and Sahidic. There exist also fragments on his homilies on the Book of the Song of the Songs and a homily on the **Holy Spirit**.

– H –

HABACHI, LABIB (1906–1984). A renowned Egyptologist, he was born in Mansura where he was educated at the Coptic School. He studied Egyptology at Fouad I (later Cairo) University. In 1927, he visited the monasteries of **Wadi al-Natrun**, the **Monastery of St. Antony**, and the **Monastery of St. Paul**, and published, with Zaki Tawadrus, a book on these monasteries (in Arabic) in 1929. In 1930, he was appointed as an inspector in the Egyptian Antiquities Service, where he pursued his career and was promoted to subdirector of fieldwork and excavations in 1958. In 1960, he resigned from the Antiquities Service and was appointed archaeological consultant of the Nubian expedition of the Chicago Oriental Institute. Habachi published more than 170 articles and books related to the ancient Egyptian monuments and civilization. He was chosen a member of a number of significant archaeological institutions, such as the German Archaeological Institute. He was awarded a number of prizes from Egypt, European countries, and the United States. He was a member of the board of the **Society of Coptic Archaeology** and was elected permanent honorary president of the **International Association for Coptic Studies** in 1978. He was one of the consultants of the *Coptic Encyclopedia*.

HADES. Hades is the place where the souls rest before the Last Judgment. For Egyptians, life after life is an important aspect and has been since pharaonic times. For this reason, the ancient Egyptians created many myths concerning the afterlife, and great importance was placed on texts such as the Coffin texts or the Book of the Dead, for the words were believed to facilitate the journey of the deceased through the netherworld and hence to immortality. With Christianity, such ideals survived through many apocryphal texts. In Coptic **hagiography**, the Archangel Michael plays an important role in protecting martyrs and later in taking their souls to Paradise. The accounts of the lives of the **Desert Fathers** contain many stories of and allusions to Hades, examples being the conversation Abba **Macarius the Great** had with the skull of a pagan **priest** concerning the netherworld and the conversation Abba Pieties had with an ancient Egyptian mummy. In Late Antique Egypt, Coptic tombstones included funerary formulas of Christ destroying the gates of Hades. In funeral services conducted in the Coptic Church, the priest beseeches Christ to open the gates of Paradise to welcome the deceased's soul into the bosom of Abraham, Isaac, and Jacob.

HAGIOGRAPHY, COPTIC. Egypt was influenced by the Greek culture, hence many of the hagiographical texts were written first in this language and translated later into Coptic. It is important to use the classical hagiographical tools such as *Bibliotheca Hagiographica Orientalis* and the *Bibliotheca Sanctorum* (16 vols., Rome 1965–1976), in addition to the bibliography in each issue of the *Analecta Bollandiana*. There are several methods to approach the study of the Coptic hagiography, but the preferred one is to choose the liturgical aspect or how the Coptic Church presents its saints through the Coptic liturgical books.

The saints are commemorated through several rites, such as the **Rite of Glorifications**. This book contains various hymns in honor of saints. A short account of their life is included in the **Synaxarion**. It contains the lives of saints according to the Coptic calendar. There are two versions, one of the Lower Egypt and another one from Upper Egypt. The **Antiphonarion** (in Arabic, **Difnar**) is a collection of hymns for the whole year. The hymns of the Antiphonarion are sung in the service of the Psalmodia, which follows the office of Compline. For the liturgical celebration, the Coptic Church possesses the synaxis (assembly) of the saints, where the Virgin Mary asks for their intercessions and their prayers; another synaxis is also recited before the mass during the midnight prayer. *See* GLORIFICATIONS, RATE OF.

The commemorated saints in the Coptic Church can be put in several categories:

1. The Virgin Mary. There exists the **feast** of her birthday, the feast of her entrance in the temple, the feast of her resting, the feast of the **Assumption** of her body, and the consecration of the church named after her in the city of Philippi. In addition to that, the month of Kiahk, preceding the feast of the Nativity, is consecrated to praising the Virgin Mary and comparing the image of the Virgin symbols in the Old Testament.

2. The angels and the heavenly creatures: the Archangels Michael, Gabriel, Raphael, and others.

   - The Archangel Michael (12 Hathor, 12 Baunah) is the most popular heavenly creature among the Copts. He inherited several characters from the ancient Egyptian religion, such as a special cake that was presented in ancient times to Osiris. According to Coptic tradition, Michael is the angel who announced the Resurrection to the women. Michael is also the angel of the Last Judgment, holding a balance with his hand like the god Anubis. Several churches and monasteries are named after him.
   - The Archangel Gabriel (22 Kiahk) is the angel of the Annunciation, hence his commemoration is included in the Fast of the Advent, during the month of Kiahk, and also for the feast of the Annunciation. In art, he is always represented with the Virgin for the Annunciation, or with a sword in front of the **icon** of Michael.
   - The Archangel Raphael (3 Nasi), in the Coptic mentality, is assimilated to the story of Tobit, so he is always presented as a guardian angel.
   - The Archangel Suriel, according to the Coptic tradition, is the trumpeter of the Apocalypse.
   - The Four Bodiless Creatures (8 Hathor)—only a few churches are dedicated to them, such as the ancient church of the **Monastery of St. Antony**.
   - The Twenty-four Elders of the Apocalypse (24 Hathor) represent the **priests** on Earth; their **doxology** is used to welcome the new priest and **bishops**.

3. John the Baptist (2 Thot, 2 Baunah, 30 Baunah, 30 Meshir, 26 Thot): the precursor of Christ has a very special place among the Coptic synaxis. The Coptic Church asks his intercession, as it does the Virgin, the angels, and the heavenly creatures, while for the other saints it is only a prayer.

4. The infants of Bethlehem (3 Tobeh): assimilated to the 144,000 of the Apocalypse.

5. The prophets of the Old Testament: Abraham, Isaac, Jacob (28 Mesori), Moses (8 Thot), Jeshua, son of Nun (4 Thot), Isaiah (6 Thot), Jonah (25 Thot), Joel, Nahum, Haggi, David, Obiedias, Hosoe, Daniel, Ezechiel, Joachim, Jeremiah, Samuel, Joseph the carpenter, Eziachias, and Micha. Most of their biographies in the Synaxarion are inspired from the Bible and sometimes from apocryphal texts.

6. The Apostles: Peter, Paul, Philip, Andrew, Barnabas, James son of Alpheus, Ansemus, Matthias, James son of Zabadee, James the brother of the Lord, Thomas, Titus.

7. The 70 disciples: Stephen, Philipp, and others.

8. The Evangelists: Matthew, Mark, Luke, and John the evangelist.

9. The martyrs: Hippolyte Delehaye traces the history of the persecution by comparing the Coptic texts with the Greek and Latin Passions. He analyzed the texts and concluded that they were written in **Alexandria** by a Greek Egyptian. De Lacy O'Leary listed all the saints in the Copto-Arabic Synaxarion and gave some details about the manuscripts of each saint. Baumeister compared the Coptic texts with the ancient Egyptian mentality and concluded that there is what can be called the "Coptic consensus."

A. Martyrs before the Diocletian era: Few martyrs before the Diocletian era are included in the Coptic calendar; most of them are foreigners, such as Ignatius of Antioch under Trajan, and St. Mercurius and the Seven Sleepers of Ephesus under Decius. There is the legend of the martyr Eudoemon, who was from Erment in Upper Egypt. An angel informed him of the presence of the Lord Jesus, Joseph, and the Virgin Mary in Ashmunaun, fleeing Herod. He went to their place and worshipped Christ. After his return to his village, he refused to worship the pagan gods and suffered martyrdom. The tradition of this martyrdom occurs only in the Synaxarion of Upper Egypt.

B. Martyrs during the great persecution:
  i. The martyrs of Egypt.
    a. The clergy: This category is very important. Historically, we have the martyrdom of Phileas, Bishop of Thmui. The Coptic calendar includes also several bishops such as Serapamon, Bishop of Nikiou; Pisoura, Bishop of Masil; Macrobius of Nikiou; Psate, Bishop of Psoi; Gallinicus, and Ammonius.
    b. Nobles such as John of Sanhout (8 Bachans) and Isaac of Tiphre (6 Bashans).
    c. Soldiers such as Apa Dios (25 Tubah), Ischyrion of Qallin (7 Baunah), Abakradjon (25 Abib), and St. **Menas**.
  ii. The martyrs of Antioch (the **Basilides** family): These martyrs are considered members of the legendary royal or noble family of Basilides. There are several genealogies included in their martyrdoms but without any consistency. This cycle includes the martyrdoms of Claudius, Basilides, Apater and Iraaie, Macarius, Eusebius, sometimes Theodore, Victor, Besamon, Apoli, and Justus.

C. The group of Julius of Aqfahs: This group is attributed to a person called Julius of Akfahs. In fact, the study of this corpus shows that these martyrdoms were written between the 6th or 7th century and the 11th century. The study of the events, administrative titles, geography, and persons demonstrates that this corpus can be subdivided in homogenous groups. The first group is the martyrs from Middle Egypt, such as Epima, Shenoufe, Heraclides, Didymus, Pansnew, and Chamoul. It shows that the compiler knew very well the geography of this district; they have a common beginning and end, but there is an evolution toward the presentation of Julius of Akfahs. The second group is composed of the texts of Ari and Anoub. It was written in Lower Egypt. Julius is presented in a few lines and the author did not give any useful data for the geography of administrative titles. The third group is Paese and Thecla. It has a different style—the story of a brother and a sister—and it seems that the text we have is a compilation of at least two narrations. Macarius of Antioch and Nahrawa are the fourth group. It is characterized by the exaggeration—hence, the judge is the emperor himself—and the events are in Antioch (the capital). The martyrdom of John and Simon is from the 11th century and ascribed to Julius of Akfahs. There are also several texts in Arabic attributed to Julius of Akfahs, but it is hard to determine their authorship. Mention can be made of Mirhch, Apa Ischyrion, and Kastor.

D. The foreign martyrs
E. The post-Diocletian martyrs, Alladius (3 Baunah)
   i. The non-Roman martyrs: St. George, James Intercicus, and Helias
  ii. The martyrs against the heresies (against **Arianism**, Chalcedonianism)
 iii. The new martyrs (or martyrs during the post–Arab conquest) such as John of Phanidjoit, Salib (3 Kiahk), and George al-Mozahim (19 Baunah). The text of their martyrdom is more or less realistic; there are no outstanding miracles, atrocious tortures, or heroic answers. The general schema of these martyrdoms is that the saint was falsely accused; to keep his life, he has to renounce his faith and become Muslim (some of them adopted for a while the Islamic religion either as from Islamic origin, such as George al-Mozahim, or by proselytism). An outbreak of the mob or fanatical caprice of some rulers or searching for a scapegoat cause the martyrdom of these saints. Geographical and historical data are, generally speaking, accurate.
 iv. The Confessors, such as Agapetus (24 Amshir)

10. The monks: Egypt is the cradle of the **monasticism**, and the Coptic sanctoral includes many monks. Foremost is St. **Antony** the Great, but there are also other important monks such as St. **Macarius**, St. **Paul** the Hermit, St. John Kama, and St. Simeon the Stylite. The monks could be grouped either using the geographical criterion; hence, we can say the monk of

Lower Egypt, **Scetis**, **Nitria**, and **Kellia**; the monks of Middle Egypt; the disciples of St. Antony and those of the Fayyumic regions; and the monks of Upper Egypt such as **Pachomius** and Shenute. The last category includes all the rest, including the foreigners. They could also be grouped according to their order or the rule that they follow; hence, one finds the hermits, the semihermits (cross-bearers), the monks in the community, and the stylites. Finally, the monks can be categorized using historical criterion; hence, starting with the monks of the fourth century, the fifth century, and so forth.

11. Fathers of the Church. This category regroups the several Fathers of the Church. As opposed to the martyrs, the Fathers of the Church are historically authentic. We may notice that some of them are local **patriarchs**, while other are broadly known (Basil the Great) and the group of the Fathers who played an important role in the Monophysite movement.

    A. The patriarchs of the Coptic Church, such as **Peter I, the Seal of the Martyrs**, Agathon, Cosman, Demetrius, Khayil, Macarius, **Alexander**, and Damian.
    B. The bishops who suffered for their faith: John Chrysostom, Basil the Great, **Athanasius**, Gregory the Amenianm Liberius, and Felix.
    C. The bishops who established the faith: This category is mainly formed from the Eastern Fathers in addition to the Alexandrian patriarchs, such as **Cyril** of Alexandria, **Severus of Antioch**, Dionysios of Alexandria, **Dioscorus** of Alexandria

12. Contemporary saints and martyrs: During the 19th and 20th centuries, various riots of the Muslim mob produced several martyrs. Under rule of the President Anwar al-Sadat (1970–1981), the Islamic fundamentalist movements were on the rise. These groups started a systematic persecution, especially in Upper Egypt. These persecutions produced many martyrs; some of them are known by name while others remain anonymous. The following can be mentioned among them:

    • Sidhum Bishai (1804–1844). He served as clerk at the port of Damietta when a Muslim-instigated revolt erupted. He was accused of insulting Islam. His incorruptible body reposes in the Church of the Holy Virgin in Damietta.

- In March 1978, in the province of Minya, a priest, Father Marcus Aziz, was killed in the city of Samalut.
- On 3 August 1978 in Qalubyia Province, in Mansha Delo, two Copts were killed.
- On 4 September 1978 in al-Minya Province, in the city of Samalut, Father Gabriel Abd al-Mutagaly, a woman, and a child were killed.
- On 24 November 1978, in Assiut Province, in the city of Abu Tig, Father Ruweiss Fakher, parish priest of the Church of Dweina in Abu Tig, was massacred when he refused the pressure of Islamic groups to close his church except on Sunday.
- In March 1981 in Cairo, in the Zawyia Hamra suburb, six months before the assassination of President Sadat, an everyday conflict started between a Coptic family and a Muslim that turned quickly to a religious war; about 25 Christians perished and three churches were burned.
- In April 1990, about seven Copts died in an attack against a Coptic Church in Alexandria.
- In September 1991 in Embaba, Cairo, several Copts were murdered and their homes destroyed.
- In May 1992 in Dayrout-Assiut, 12 Coptic students along with their teacher were murdered inside the classroom.
- In January 1993 in Dayrout-Assiut, a Coptic man was murdered.
- In January 1993 in Dayrout-Assiut, a Coptic shopowner was murdered and three others were wounded by members of a Jihadist Islamic group.
- In June 1993 in Sohag, a clash between one Moslem and a Christian family resulted in the killing of two Copts.
- In July 1993 in Assiut, a Copt was murdered by Islamic radical militants.
- In August 1993 in Dayrout-Assiut, a Copt was murdered by Islamic radical militants.
- In August 1993 in Dayrout-Assiut, a Coptic school viceprincipal was murdered.

- In August 1993 in Dayrout-Assiut, the Coptic manager of a detention center hospital was murdered by the al-Gama'a al-Islamia.
- In August 1993 in Assiut, a Coptic jewelry store owner was murdered.
- In October 1993 in Assiut, a Coptic liquor store owner and his son were murdered.
- In October 1993 in Assiut, a Coptic secret service policeman was murdered.
- In October 1993 in Dayrout-Assiut, a Coptic pharmacist was murdered and two others were wounded in an attack by Islamic radical militants.
- In October 1993 in Assiut, a Coptic policeman was murdered.
- In March 1994 in **Dayr al-Muharraq**, Dayrout-Assiut, an armed assault on the visitors and the fathers of the monastery resulted in the death of five Copts. Islamic radical militants carried out the assault.
- In February 1996 in al-Badary-Assiut, five Copts were murdered.
- In February 1997 in al-Fekrya Abu Qurqas, in al-Minya Province, an armed assault on a Coptic Church during Sunday School service resulted in the murder of 10 parishioners inside the church.
- On 13 March 1997 in Nag Hammadi-Quena, eight Copts were murdered.
- On 23 April 1997 in al-Minya, two Copts were murdered.
- In January 2000 in al-Kosheh, Sohag Province, 21 Copts were murdered and tens of stores and shops were destroyed as a result of a random and armed raid on Copts.

There is no procedure for **canonization** in the Coptic Church. Several Fathers are venerated by the Coptic people as saints, among them:

A. 'Abd al-Masih al-Makari (1892–1963). He was a monk in the **Monastery of St. Macarius** but dwelt in several monasteries. He served as a parish priest in the village of al-Manahra. He used to do some strange acts to hide his holiness. He is venerated as a wonder worker. He is buried in the Church of al-Manahra.

B. Abraham Bishop of Fayyum (1829–1914). He was the abbot of the Monastery of al-Muharraq in Upper Egypt. Accused of mismanagement, he was chased to the **Monastery of al-Baramous**. He was ordained Bishop of Fayyum by Patriarch Cyril V. He is known for his charity to the poor and as a wonder worker. He is buried in Dair al-'Azab, Fayyum.

C. **Cyril VI** (1959–1971). He was a monk in the Monastery of al-Baramous and became a hermit in the hills near Cairo. During World War II, he was forced to leave his cell in the windmill and live in Cairo. He built a church named after St. Menas. After his enthronement, he built the Monastery of St. Menas, the Cairo Cathedral, and during his patriarchate, a part of the relics of St. **Mark** was returned to Egypt. In 1968, the Virgin Mary appeared in the Church of Zeitun-Cairo. He is venerated as a wonder worker. His shrine in the Monastery of St. Menas as well as his cells in the Monastery of al-Baramous and in the windmill attract many pilgrims.

D. Mikha'il al-Buhayri (1847–1923). He was a monk in the Monastery of al-Muharraq and a disciple of Anba Abraham, Bishop of Fayyum. He observed silence all his life.

13. The newly discovered saints and martyrs: the criteria of identification are not clear, sometimes resulting from the vision of a monk, or a dream, or a pure coincidence in a historical book.

A. While restoring the **Church of Sts. Sergius and Bacchus** in Old Cairo, some bones were discovered on 25 April 1991. They were identified as the relics of St. Bashnufa mentioned in the ***History of the Patriarchs*** who suffered martyrdom in 1164. The **Naqlun** martyrs: On the Polish archaeological mission working in the site of the Monastery of St. Gabriel, Naqlun Fayyum discovered 13 complete bodies of men, women, and children that bore traces of tortures. There were considered as martyrs but the circumstances of their martyrdom are not known.

B. Simeon the Tanner: His relics were discovered in the Church of the Virgin Babylon al-Darag in August 1991.

Coptic hagiography is not a closed book. As can be seen, every day there are new saints added to the list of saints, martyrs, and miracles workers.

HEGUMEN. Today *hegumenos* means "abbot," or the head of a monastery. The *hegumenos* is usually chosen by the monks from their own community and approved by the patriarch, metropolitan, or bishop within whose jurisdiction the monastery lies. The *hegumenate* is the highest rank of the priesthood to which priests, married or celibate, serving in cathedrals or large parishes, may be raised. The Arabic equivalent term for *hegumenos* is *qummus* (protopriest). The term derives from the Greek *hegoumenos*, whose primary meaning was "ruler," well known in pagan Greek and also used by Christian authors to denote a bishop. In late Greek texts from Egypt and in Coptic texts, this title referred to clerics and monks and was given to whoever played the leading role in the group. Hence, *hegumenos* actually corresponded to *archipresbyteros*, a term rarely used in Egypt, or to the even rarer *protopresbyteros*. The Hegumen is in charge of several priests. In the **Historia Monachorum in Aegypto** some monks are described as "fathers of many monasteries," although here "monastery" has a different meaning from the one given to it later on. However, Palladius, who was in Egypt at the same time as the author of the *Historia monachorum* at the end of the fourth century, used *hegumenos* with the technical meaning that was to become usual later on.

HEGUMENOS ORDINATION. The hegumenos (hegomen or proto-**priest**) is ordained in the Coptic Church to serve the altar, and to instruct and admonish the congregation. The ordination begins after the Prayer of Reconciliation and before the Kiss of Peace, that is, prior to the anaphora. The candidate bends his knee and prostrates himself before the **bishop**, who stands in front of the altar. The bishop begins by praying the **Prayer of Thanksgiving** and offers

incense together with a special prayer invoking God to help the candidate be worthy of this ministry and to serve the priesthood as a hegumenos. The earliest known manuscript is Ms 253 Liturgica of the **Coptic Museum**, dated 1364. The first edition was edited by R. **Tukhi** (Catholic) in 1761 with an Arabic translation. This edition can hardly be accepted as valid witness, for its content is at times artificial, and hence is not a reliable source for the liturgist. The first Orthodox edition was edited by **Athanasius**, Metropolitan of Beni Suef in 1959, and reprinted with minor changes by his successor bearing the same name in 1992.

HENOTICON. When Emperor Zeno returned to Constantinople in 482, he issued his famous Henoticon to the Christians of the world in **Alexandria**, Egypt, Libya and Pentapolis. In it, he confirmed the faith of the Fathers of the **Councils of Nicaea** and **Constantinople**; nothing, however, is mentioned concerning the **Councils of Ephesus** and **Chalcedon**. Zeno condemned both Eutyches and **Nestorius** and confirmed the faith of St. **Cyril** as expressed in the 12 chapters. The Henoticon confirmed also the title of Theotokos for the Virgin Mary, and refuted the formula of the one hypostasis (person) in two natures, which was rejected by the Alexandrians. The text was balanced in a way for it to be accepted by Chalcedonians and non-Chalcedonians. It avoided difficult theological issues and aimed to restore a position prior to that of Chalcedon. Peter Mongos accepted the Henoticon in Alexandria. Although Zeno did not succeed in his attempt, he is well thought of and remembered in the Coptic Church. According to tradition, his daughter Hilaria went to **Scetis** and disguised herself as a monk. She interceded for the construction of the monastery fortresses. She is commemorated in the Coptic Church on the 21st of Tubah.

HERACLEON. A pupil of **Valentinus** the **Gnostic** who was active during the mid-second century. He was referred to by Clement of **Alexandria** as "the most esteemed member of the school of Valentinus." He wrote an important commentary on the Gospel of John that was excerpted by **Origen** in his own commentary on John. Although he is reported by Hippolytus to have been a member of the "Western" or "Italic" branch of the Valentinian School, he was probably an Alexandrian, and his commentary was probably composed in Alexandria between 160 and 180.

HEXAPLA AND TETRAPLA. Origen is the first author in the Church to arrange a critical edition of the Old Testament. He organized in six columns the Hebrew text of the Old Testament, in Hebrew and Greek, and incorporated the translation of Aquila (a Jew of the time of Hadrian), and the translation of Symmachus and the Septuagint. According to **Eusebius**, he later published another edition containing only four columns that is called the Tetrapla. This scientific work was used by many Church Fathers, among them Didymus the Blind in his commentaries on the Psalms, as well as **Eusebius of Caesarea** and **Jerome** for his commentaries on the Psalms. It is regretful that only a fragment of this work has survived. A Syriac translation of the text of Paul, the **Bishop** of Tella, survives.

HIERARCHY, CHURCH. The hierarchy is the collective body of the ecclesiastical ranks including **bishops** (**patriarchs**, metropolitans, and bishops), **priests** (presbyter and **hegumen**), and deacons (archdeacons and deacons). The rite of ordination of each rank prescribes the role of each member. The ecumenical councils issued several decrees in order to organize their work. In the fifth century, a writing ascribed to Dionysus the Aeropagite was entitled *The Ecclesiastical Hierarchy*; chapter 5 of his work presents and interprets the ceremony of the consecration of those in the hierarchy. The author compares the Church clergy with the celestial hierarchy. In the 12th and 13th centuries, Ibn al-Assal in his nomocanon codified all the previous texts taken from the councils, canons, and tradition.

HIERARCHY AND ADMINISTRATION. *See* STRUCTURE OF THE COPTIC CHURCH.

HIGHER INSTITUTE OF COPTIC STUDIES. This institute was founded by **Aziz Suryal Atiya**, assisted by **Murad Kamil** and Sami Gabra, on 21 January 1954 in a building at **Anba Ruwais** belonging to the Coptic **patriarchate**. The aim was to launch a study program in **Coptology**, a field long neglected in Egypt. The institute's sections are **Theology, Coptic Language** and Literature, Coptic History,

Coptic Archaeology and Architecture, Sociology, African Studies, Coptic Law, Coptic **Music**, and **Coptic Art**. The institute holds a specialized library that offers research opportunities in Coptic studies. The most flourishing sections are that of the Coptic Music, which documented the music of the Coptic Church under **Ragheb Moftah**, and of Coptic art under **Isaac Fanous**, whose **icons** have spread to most of the Coptic churches in Egypt, the United States, Canada, Australia, and Europe. The institute has awarded doctoral degrees to many researchers under the auspices of Pope **Shenouda III**.

HISTORIA LAUSIACA. *See* PALLADIUS.

HISTORIA MONACHORUM IN AEGYPTO (HISTORY OF THE MONKS IN EGYPT). This work describes a number of journeys made to different monastic settlements in the Thebaid and in Lower Egypt during the winter of 394–395 by a party of seven persons; the writer is one of them. Apparently, they went directly by the Nile to Assiut (Lycopolis), which seems to be the southernmost site that they reached. They stopped at several monastic sites and visited many monks, especially in the district of Oxyrhynchus. They reported on such famous monks as John of Lycopolis and Apollo. They visited **Kellia** and probably **Nitria**. The majority of scholars agree that Rufinus translated the Latin text of the *Historia monachorum in Aegypto* from a Greek origin. Like the *Historia Lausiaca*, this work served as a **pilgrimage** itinerary. It had a profound impact on the spread of the fame of Egyptian monks throughout Europe. A number of versions in Syriac and Armenian had been preserved; in Coptic, only five leaves from a Sahidic codex have survived.

HISTORY OF THE CHURCHES AND MONASTERIES OF EGYPT (late 12th–early 13th c.). An important source for the history of the Coptic Church. The *History of the Churches and Monasteries of Egypt* is a remarkable collection of geographically arranged entries concerning churches and monasteries (primarily in Egypt, but with entries as far-flung as Abyssinia, Palestine, and Rome), and sometimes the people and events connected with them. Den Heijer has shown that Melchite and Muslim sources as well as Coptic ones (the *History of the Patriarchs* in particular) were used by the compilers—whoever they were. Indeed, many details about the composition of the work are obscure: Three layers of text range in date from about 1160 to 1220, and the full text may have been reedited over a century later. The names of **Abu al-Makarim** Sa'dallah ibn Jirjis and **Abu Salih the Armenian** have been attached to the work, but their precise contributions are unknown. All this is complicated by the fact that the text has been preserved in a single manuscript that was divided in two and from which pages amounting to about 15 percent of the total have been lost. One part of the manuscript (now in Paris) was edited and published by Basil Thomas Alfred Evetts in 1894, but it was another 90 years before the contents of the other part of the manuscript (now in Munich) were made available in Egypt through a modest volume published by the monk Samu'il al-Suryani (later Bishop **Samuel** of Shabin al-Qanatir). Despite the puzzles posed by the text, it is a vast store of information in which readers have found treasures. The *History of the Churches and Monasteries of Egypt* is, for example, one of our most important sources for the career of **Marqus ibn al-Qunbar**. In an age in which many Egyptian Christians are assiduously studying the history of their holy places, including the itinerary of the Holy Family in Egypt, the *History* has become a major resource. And when handled with sensitivity, the text bears quiet witness to the fragility of a community that had suffered during the 12th century (from Crusaders and the transition from Fatimid to Ayyubid rule) and that continued to delineate, claim, and celebrate its sacred geography. *See also* MONASTICISM, EGYPTIAN.

HISTORY OF THE PATRIARCHS. Major source for Coptic Church history. The *History of the Patriarchs* is the principal source for the history of the Coptic Orthodox Church during the first six centuries of Islamic rule. The work came into existence toward the end of the 11th century through the labor of a team led by **Mawhub ibn Mansur ibn Mufarrij**; the biographies of the first 65 **patriarchs** of the Coptic Church (beginning with St. Mark the Evangelist) were compiled from Coptic-language sources and translated into Arabic, while Mawhub added original Arabic-language biographies of Patriarchs **Christodoulos** (66th, 1046–1077) and **Cyril II** (67th, 1077–1094), contemporaries with whom he was well acquainted. After Mawhub, the *History* continued to grow as continuators added biographies, although most of the entries after **Cyril III ibn Laqlaq** (75th, 1231–1245; a lengthy "Life" is devoted to him in one manuscript) are simply brief notices. (The biography of **Matthew I** [87th, 1378–1408] is an exception to this rule.)

The *History of the Patriarchs* is a well-known work. Western scholars have been using it since the 18th century, two editions were published early in the 20th century, and inexpensive copies circulate in Egypt today. Recent research (especially by David W. Johnson and Johannes den Heijer; see the bibliography) has elucidated the nature of the work as a compilation of materials and has denied its attribution to the 10th-century theologian **Sawirus ibn al-Muqaffa'**. This research has served to emphasize just how precious the *History of the Patriarchs* truly is: it preserves material by a number of different authors who were intimately acquainted with at least some of the people and events they describe. For example, the biographies of the patriarchs who served during the first 60 years of Arab rule in Egypt were written by one George the Archdeacon, who was the spiritual son of Patriarch John III (40th, 677–686) and scribe of Patriarch Simon I (42nd, 689–701). There thus is eyewitness testimony for a critically important period in the history of the Coptic Church. If this testimony is not wholly "objective," it is tremendously revealing of how Christians imagined themselves and their Church within the "new world order" of the *Dar al-Islam*.

HOLY CROSS DAY. The Coptic Church celebrates the **Feast** of the Cross on the 17th of Tut (27 September) and on the 10th of Baramhat (19 March). The first date commemorates the discovery of the Cross by Queen Helena, the mother of Constantine the Great, in the fourth century. The second date commemorates the recovery of the Holy Cross from the Persians by the Roman Emperor Heraclius in the seventh century. Although these two feasts are Byzantine par excellence, the Coptic Church has a special rite for these days. The tune of Palm Sunday is used for these feasts as well as for the procession. There is a hymn praising King Constantine, who ordered the closing down of the idol temples and the reopening of the churches of the

Christians. It seems that the cult of Constantine was imported from the Byzantine church.

HOLY FAMILY. *See* FLIGHT INTO EGYPT.

HOLY SPIRIT, COPTIC DOCTRINE OF THE. The Holy Spirit is one of the Holy Trinity. He is consubstantial, coeternal, coequal, and coadorable with the Father and the Son. **Origen** may be considered as a good starting point on this subject. He treated the nature of the Holy Spirit, who is the "Paraclete" (or Comforter) in his book *The Principles*, as well as in his homilies on the Gospel of Luke. In the West, Tertullian also wrote on the same subject. After the Peace of the Church in 313 and the involvement of the Church in combating such heresies as **Apollinarianism**, **Arianism**, and Macedonianism, the Fathers of the Church consecrated a great part of their literary activities to writing about the Holy Spirit, which they treated under three main topics: the Trinity, **Christology**, and pneumatology. In Egypt, **Athanasius**, Didymus the Blind, and **Cyril** of **Alexandria** were among the writers. Outside of Egypt, Basil the Great and **Severus of Antioch** were the spokesmen and great theologians.

The Church of Alexandria played an active role in the Second Ecumenical **Council in Constantinople** (381 A.D.), and adopted its official creed of faith concerning the Holy Spirit: "Truly we believe in the Holy Spirit and in the Lord, Giver of life, Who forthly proceedeth from the Father; we worship and glorify Him with the Father and the Son; who was spoken of by the Prophets." This creed is recognized and affirmed by all members of the World Council of Churches as an ecumenical declaration of the apostolic faith. In addition to the dogmatic treatise, the Holy Spirit is invoked in all liturgical rites and sacraments of the Coptic Church. The troparion of the prayer of the third hour, "O heavenly King," is the unique prayer addressed to the Holy Spirit. This troparion contains quite a few Basilian expressions. It is also said in the Byzantine rite.

HOLY WEEK. Holy Week falls between Palm Sunday and Easter Sunday. The first description of the rite of the Holy Week is given by Egeria, a European woman from France who visited the Holy Lands between 381and 384. She provided a detailed description of the places she visited and the ceremonies that she attended. It is noteworthy to mention that Coptic rites are similar in structure to the Jerusalem rites of the fourth century.

Among the canons of **Athanasius** written around the year 370, which are preserved in Coptic fragments and in Arabic translation, one finds that in Articles 57–60 some arrangements concerning the Holy Week; for example, they show that there were long prayers based essentially on psalms and readings from both the Old and New Testaments. The churches were so crowded that it was very difficult for the deacons to keep order. **Pachomius**, the founder of cenobitic **monasticism**, established a monastery at Tabennisi in the Thebaid ca. 320. He wrote the first monastic rule in Coptic. His life and writings describe Holy Week during Late Antique times in Upper Egypt. It is one of the rare Coptic sources on this topic. St. Theodore, the disciple of St. Pachomius, would assemble with brethren during the days of the Passover.

The actual rite consists of five hours in the morning and five hours in the evening. Each hour starts with the prophecies and the chanting of "To You is the power and glory," 12 times. A deacon reads the psalm preceded by the words, "In order to make us worthy to hear the holy gospel, we beseech our Lord and our God. Listen to the holy gospel, in wisdom." One of the most ancient sources on the history of hymns during **Good Friday** is a Syriac manuscript preserved in the British Library that dates to 411. (This manuscript is a translation of a lost Greek original that goes back to the year 362 and belongs to the Church of Nicomedia, where Egypt and **Alexandria** are mentioned 19 times in four folios.) It mentions that "Good Friday after the Passover, the remembrance of the martyrs is performed." This remark can explain the resemblance between the tune of the hymn of the Glorification of the **Saints** and the introduction to the Coptic gospel during the Holy Week. It is probable that these hymns were originally one.

Under the following **patriarchs** of Alexandria—**Christodoulos** (1047–1077 A.D.), **Cyril II** (1078–1092 A.D.), **Gabriel II** (1131–1146 A.D.), and **Cyril III** (1235–1243 A.D.)—many new important canons were added to Coptic canonical law. The first of this series of new canons was promulgated by Christodoulos, the 66th patriarch, in Alexandria on Sunday the 8th of Misri, A.M. 764 (1 August 1048 A.D.). Two of these canons deal with the rite of the Holy Week:

[Canon 8:] And after the completion of the **Liturgy** [Quddas] on the Sunday of Olives [Palm Sunday] there shall be read the gospel and the Diptych for the dead after the Apostle [the lesson from the Pauline Epistles] of Paul appointed for the dead, and after this there shall be read over the assembly of the people the Absolution, because in Holy Week neither **Absolution** nor the diptych nor the burial service is allowed until the **Feast** of Easter is completed.

[Canon 9:] On **Maundy Thursday** the Liturgy [Quddas] shall be [celebrated] in fear and trembling and quietness without either Kiss [of Peace] or the hand touching. [At the Kiss of Peace, the members of the Congregation touch one another's hands] and the Prosphorin shall not be said, but instead there shall be said "meta-phobou" without the Absolution either at the beginning or at the end.

Shams al Riasah Abû al-Barakat **ibn Kabar** wrote his book *The Lamp of Darkness for the Explanation of the Service*. Only a few chapters have been published scientifically, where can be found the detailed description given below and taken from the oldest manuscripts of this book (from Paris dated to 1363 and another in Upsalla dated 1546 but copied from an earlier manuscript dated 1357).

The Rites of Monday, Tuesday, and Wednesday:

The rites of the day and evenings of Monday, Tuesday, and Wednesday are identical, as follows: For each prayer, we read the readings of the Prophets and the Arabic translation and then "Kyrie Eleyson," "Glory Be to God," "Our Father," and "To You Is the Power and Glory" (12 times). The psalm and the gospel is sung in sorrowful tune.

After the reading of the psalm and before the gospel, they sing: "In order to be worthy to hear the holy gospel; Our Lord, our God, have mercy upon us and make us worthy to hear the holy gospel, a chapter from the gospel of . . . The Evangelist." And when it is finished, the commentary of the hour is read. If there is a sermon, it will be said after the gospel reading.

The reader says before the reading of the *Tubuhat* [*see* **Tubh**]: "Bow your knees" (four times) and the people prostrate four times for each hour except for the first and the third prayer of the night because they follow the break of **fasting**.

The **priest** or an archdeacon reads the *Tubh*, which are 18 in total:

Pray that God have mercy upon us; for the prayer for establishment of this place; the prayer for this holy place; for the sick members of our congregation; for our fathers and our brethren who travelled abroad; for the fruits; for the granting of God's mercy; for our fathers and our brethren who had fallen asleep; for those who are in positions of authority; for the holy, apostolic father and patriarch; for the holy apostolic Church; for those who are assembled here; for those who suffer from imprisonment; for everybody present; for everybody who has asked us to pray for them; for the raising of the water of the river; and for this holy Pascha. Some priests pray only 12 of the litanies.

Then they pray "God have mercy upon us," and Kyrie Eleison 48 times stanza by stanza. This is followed by 12 "God have mercy upon us," then the "Our Father," and finally the priest says in Coptic, "Make charity, bow your heads to receive the Lord's **blessing**. May the Lord bless you," before giving the benediction and dismissing the congregation. (It is important to mention that the number and the arrangement of the *Tubuhat* differs from the actual edition which includes more *Tubuhat*).

The prophecies in the Church of Egypt (Old Cairo) are arranged for the **Matins** (morning prayer) and the None (ninth hour) of the days only and some hours for the night. For the Passover at Sandamant, the prophecies are arranged for every hour of day and night. The sermons are generally read during the Matins and the None of the days.

If the patriarch is present, he reads the first prophecy of the first hour of Monday and the gospel of ditto and the gospel of the None of the day of Tuesday, which is the section of Sandaliyah, and the first prophecy of the first hour of Wednesday. On Tuesday night, the Gospel of Matthew is read and during Wednesday night the Gospel of Mark is read. On Thursday night the Gospel of Luke is read.

We owe another description to another Coptic writer called **Yuhanna ibn Abi Zakariyya ibn Sabba'**. He is the author of a book called *Precious Pearl in the Ecclesiastic Science*. He provided a brief and useful description, while **Ibn Kabar** gave a detailed description of the rite as performed in the Monastery of Shahran, the **Mo'allaqa** Church, the rite in Upper Egypt, and in the **Monastery of St. Macarius**. Maqrizi is a Moslem historian from the 15th century. He compiled his "Chronicles" from Coptic and other sources in addition to his own observations. Concerning the Passover he wrote, "This is the great feast for them and they pretend that the Christ-peace be on him—when the agitated Jews wanted to kill him, they crucified him on the cross."

Textual Structure of the Rite of the Holy Week. The textual structure of the rite of the Holy Week is like a fabric with threads running

Rite	Sext	None	Remarks
1st lesson	Num. 21:1–9 Bronze Serpent		Notice the first and the last lesson of Sext
2nd Lesson	Isa. 53:7→ He was led like a *sheep led* to the *slaughter* . . .	Jer 11:18, 12:13 I had been like a *sheep* led	Deals with the exceptional events of this hour.
3rd lesson	Isa. 12:2,13:1–10→ And so you shall draw *water* with joy from the *springs* of deliverance . . .	obedient to the *slaughter* Zech. 14:5–11. On that day *living water* shall issue from Jerusalem . . .	Lessons 2 and 3 are complementary readings.
4th Lesson	Amos 8:9–12. I will make the sun go down at noon . . .		
1st Hymn	This *golden and pure censer* bearing the aroma is in the hands of Aaron the priest, who offers up incense on the altar↓	The *golden Censer is the Virgin;* her *aroma is our Saviour.* She gave birth to Him, He saved us and forgave our sins.	One may notice that the hymn of the Sext could be completed either by reading the corresponding hymn in the None or the following hymn in the same hour.
2nd Hymn	This Who offered Himself upon the Cross as an acceptable sacrifice for the salvation of our race.	This Who offered Himself upon the Cross as an acceptable sacrifice for the salvation of our race.	

(continued)

Rite	Sext	None	Remarks
	His Good Father *smelled* His aroma on Golgotha in the evening . . .		
Pauline Epistle	Gal. 6:14–16. I should not *glory except in the Cross of our Lord Jesus Christ* . . .	Philippians 2:5–11. He humbled Himself and became obedient to the point of death even the death of the Cross. *Therefore God also has highly exalted Him.*	
Troparia	O Thou Who on the 6th day, at the 6th hour, was nailed to the Cross, because of the sin which Adam dared (to commit) in the Paradise, tear up the handwriting of our sins, O Christ our God, and deliver us.	O Thou Who didst taste death in the flesh about the 9th hour on account of us, slay our corporal thoughts, O Christ our God and deliver us.	
Troparion	O Only Begotten Son and the Word of God . . . *Save us*		Especially for the Sext
Trisagion	As usual	As usual	
Psalm/Gospel			
Litany/ conclusion	As usual	As usual	
Confession of the Thief			Especially for the Sext

horizontally and vertically. We will give examples by comparing the rite of the Sext and None of the Good Friday according to the earliest manuscript of the **Lectionary** in order to demonstrate the possibility of reading each section either horizontally or vertically.

HOLY WEEK SATURDAY. The first allusion of the rite of the Holy Saturday is the description of Egeria: "Those who are able to keep the vigil do so until the dawn. . . . The clergy keep watch there, and hymns and antiphons are sung there through all the night until the morning." It is mentioned in the canons of **Christodoulus** (11th century): "And the Liturgy [Quddas] of Holy Saturday the diptych and the absolution are included, but the kiss of peace is omitted." **Ibn Kabar** (14th century), in his encyclopedia *The Lamp of Darkness for the Explanation of the Service*, gives a similar description of the rite of the Holy Saturday (or the Saturday of Joy):

the altar is covered with white veils and prayers commence with the offering up of **incense**. Psalm 50 and the **Doxology** of **Matins** is prayed, followed by the Prayer for the Departed, the *Psalis*, the **Theotokia** and Saturday *lobsh*, the hymn of the angels and the doxologies. The creed is recited followed by three "Lord have mercy" chanted in the long, great tune, while the procession of deacons proceeds around the church. A reading from a Pauline epistle (said in sorrowful and annual tunes) takes place, followed by the chanting of the **trisagion**, a psalm and the gospel reading. Prayers conclude with the absolutions and the final canon. Prayer of the Third and Sixth hours then commence.

In the monasteries, the monks begin by praying psalms from the Horologion [*agbia*, or the Book of Hours], while the people of Upper Egypt read the prophecies and the gospels of previous hours of the **Holy Week**. As people assemble in the church, seven lamps are lit and seven censers are prepared, after which the Apocalypse is read. Incense is offered, and relevant hymns are sung. After the conclusion of the Ninth Hour prayer, the **priest** celebrates the **liturgy** without reciting the Prayer of Reconciliation.

Yuhanna ibn Abi Zakariyya ibn Sabba' provides a similar description with the addition of praying Psalm 50 and chanting the Hymn of the Three Youths in the Fiery Furnace.

Maqrizi described the Saturday of Joy as follows: "This feast is the day before the Passover, and they [the Christians] pretend that the light is coming out of the tomb of Christ in the Church of Resurrection in Jerusalem [al-Qods] during which they would light the lanterns of the Church. But after investigation by some trusted people, it was concluded that this is a Christian invention."

It is important to mention that most of the edited books and even the manuscripts mention a commentary for the Saturday of Joy that is not relevant to the event (even at the time of **Ibn Kabar**). It was J. Muyser who discovered the original commentary.

HOMOEANS. In the controversy between **Athanasius** and the **Arians**, a group tried to find a middle solution. Instead of *homoousios* (from the same substance), which occurred more than 25 times in the Apology against Apollinarius, this group under Acacius of Caesarea preferred the term *homeousios*, or "like God." They played an important role in the political life of the Church. Acacius wrote many books as well as the acts of the Synod of Constantinople of 360 A.D., but sadly all his works are lost. The term of *homoios* first occurred in 345 A.D.

HOSANNA. Hebrew word, meaning "save us." In the Coptic **liturgy**, it relates to Palm Sunday. In the 12th century, **Abu al-Makarim** wrote his book, the *History of the Churches and Monasteries in Egypt*. The feast of Palm Sunday was a special ceremony in his church (Church of the Holy Virgin in Haret Zuwylah in Old Cairo):

> The **priest** and the laity of that church are accustomed to assemble in the church on the feast of the Olive every year, where they pray in the early morning. Then they come out of the church to the street in which that church stands carrying the olive branches, the Bible, the crosses, the censers and the tapers, where they pray and read the Bible. They pray on behalf of the Caliph and his vizier. Then they return to the Church to spend there the rest of the day. They repeat the same rite on the second and the third days of the feast of the Cross, which is celebrated on the 17th of Thot every year.

All these **feasts** were abolished during the dynasty of al-Ghuzz and al-Kurds in the year 565 A.H. (1169 A.D.).

The same author mentioned that the Procession of the Olive during Palm Sunday in **Alexandria** would start at night in the city:

They used to cross the city from the **Church of St. Sergius** [Abu Sargah] to the Church of Soter [the Savior] with supplication and reading. But the Muslims who attacked this tradition caused many troubles, and they prevented it for 25 years. Then the Procession of the Olive [Palm Sunday] reappeared during the reign of Mizwa in the year 444 A.H. [1053 A.D.] during the patriarchate of **Christodoulos**, the 66th **patriarch** of Alexandria, and again appeared during the reign of al-Amir. The rite continued for many years, before being abolished during the dynasty of al-Ghuzz and the Kurds in the year 565 [1169 A.D.].

Ibn Kabar in his encyclopedia *The Lamp of Darkness for the Explanation of the Service* states,

We pray the Asheya [**Vespers**] in the night of Lazarus Saturday. We sing the tunes of the feast of the Cross. We sing a hymn of the above mentioned feast which is, "Go on the highest mountain . . ." We pray the rite of **Psalmodia** and we go in procession with the olive branches around the Church. We gather the olive branches and the palm. We stop in front of the altar, the **icons** and at every station we stop in a place we sing the Psalm and the Gospel in Coptic in addition to some hymns and the commentary of the Feast with the tune of [feast] the Cross.

Some do this after the Psalmodia and before the **Matins**, others do this after the Matins and before the Prayer of the Gospel (which is actually observed). The readings of the gospel while processing the palm are different from one church to another. The custom in the Church of **Mo'allaqa** in Old-Cairo, is to read the story of Zaccheus from the Gospel of St. Luke whilst standing before an icon of Palm Sunday; the gospel passage speaking about the end of the world is read before the icon of John the Baptist together with the passage commemorating his memory. Before the door on the right of the iconstacles [women's section], the story of the centurion is read from the Gospel of St. Luke. The story of the Annunciation is read whilst standing before the icon of the Theotokos [Mother of God]. The ceremony continues in front of every icon and other stations. In the Monastery of Shahran, they would read a suitable part before each icon and altars in the monastery. Near the kitchen is read the story of the five loaves and the two fish. Besides the tombs are read passages relating to burials. In the **Monastery of Saint Macarius**, the custom is to go in procession holding palms in and around the monastery (when processing to the cells outside).

The tradition of people of Upper Egypt has the hermenia and dog-mata, composed from the Psalms of David, which are mentioned in a book called El-Kafus. They choose parts from the psalms and they sing according to the place where they pass, river, sand, hill, green grass, tree and other things.

Here is the tradition of the Egyptians [those of Old Cairo]: After the procession, they return back with the olive to the main altar. They pray the litany for the gospel and they sing the psalm and hence they finish the matins and celebrate the liturgy. The best is the **Anaphora of St. Gregory**, which is more suitable for the **feasts** of our Lord. When they finished the liturgy and during **communion**, they do not say Psalm 150 but instead pray the funerary rite, that is, the Epistle of Paul, the Psalms, the gospels of the funerary rite, up until the time the Eucharist is offered. The reason of this rite is that during **Holy Week** the church does not officiate funerary services, but in the case of a death, the church will only do a reading from the law (Pentateuch). For this reason, the fathers instituted these prayers during Palm Sun-day. We read the whole or a part of the service, according to the time. Beginning with vespers, tunes of the Holy Week are used.

Ibn Sabba' (**Yuhanna ibn Abi Zakariyya ibn Sabba'**) gave a shorter description of the rite of Palm Sunday in his book *Precious Pearl in the Ecclesiastic Science*. He mentioned that the reading from the four Gospels before the liturgy should be done in the four corners of the church and added that no procession should take place on this day, but only during the feasts of the Cross. It is hard to examine this local tradition. The traditions mentioned by **Abu al-Makarim** and other authors show clearly that there was a procession on this day. Maqrizi is a Muslim historian from the 15th century. He compiled his chronicles from various sources; some of them are Coptic in addition to his own observations. Concerning the Coptic Passover he wrote regarding Palm Sunday:

> the feast of Olive known also to them as the feast of Hosanna [Shaanin] means the proclaiming. It is the seventh Sunday of their lent and ac-cording to their tradition in the Feast of Shaanin they go out of the church with palm branches. They say that this is the day in which Christ entered into Jerusalem [al-Qods] and Zion riding on a donkey followed by the multitudes singing Hosanna. . . . In this feast, the Christians in Misr [Old Cairo] used to decorate their Churches. It hap-

pens when it was the last day of Rajjab 378 A.H. [989 A.D.], the feast of Shaanin [Hosanna], Hakim Bi-Amar alla Abû Ali Mansûr ibn al Aziz Bi-allah forbade Christians from decorating their Churches and to go in procession with the palm branches according to their custom.

We may notice that the processions with palms branches used to be around the city. A comparison between manuscripts shows clearly that each church and monastery has its own stations in the procession of Palm Sunday. The first publication of the Book of the Procession was edited by Philotheus al-Maqari, Barnabah al-Baramusi and Claudius Girgis in 1921. No Catholic edition has been published to date.

HYPOSTASIS. This word was known in classical Greek. It is composed of two parts: *hypo* meaning "under" and *stasis* meaning "setting." In **theology**, it developed to mean reality, substance, nature, or essence. This word occurs 20 times in the Septuagint but only one of them can be regarded as theologically significant. At the beginning of the fourth century the word *hypostasis* and the word *ousia* had pretty much the same meaning. St. **Cyril** denoted the hypostatic union, that is, the union of two distinct levels of reality, being divine and human in Christ, while **Nestorius** understood the word as a "physical connotation." As for the Antiochene, in the time of St. Cyril this term had only a concrete meaning, hence "physis." The diversion between the two conceptions led to the schism and the misunderstanding in the **Council of Chalcedon**.

HYPOSTASIS OF THE ARCHONS (NHC II, 4). **Sethian** Gnostic tractate presenting an esoteric interpretation of Genesis 1–6. Its subscript title reflects a phrase in the opening sentence, "the reality [*hypostasis*] of the rulers," a reference to the creator Archons of **Gnostic** mythology. A prominent figure in the text is Norea, sister-consort of Seth, who receives a heavenly revelation from an angel called Eleleth. *Hypostasis of the Archons* as we now have it is probably a Christianized version of an originally Jewish Gnostic work. Extant only in Coptic, it was originally composed in Greek, probably in third-century Egypt.

HYPSIPHRONE (NHC XI, 4). A **Gnostic** revelation partially preserved in six fragments of the heavily damaged codex. Its title (partially preserved) occurs at the beginning. The opening passage indicates that the text contains a first-person report of a feminine revealer called Hypsiphrone ("high-minded"). Known only in this poorly preserved Coptic version, *Hypsiphrone* was originally composed in Greek, perhaps in second- or third-century Egypt.

– I –

IBN AL-RAHIB, AL-NUSHU' ABU SHAKIR (ca. 1210–ca. 1290). Encyclopedist, historian, theologian, scholar of Coptic. The Coptic polymath Nushu' al-Khilafa Abu Shakir, known as Ibn al-Rahib ("Son of the Monk"), was the son of al-Shaykh al-Sana' Abu al-Majd, a high-ranking civil servant who became a monk and who provided leadership to the Coptic Orthodox Church during the two-decade interregnum between the **patriarchates** of John VI (74th, 1189–1216) and **Cyril III ibn Laqlaq** (75th, 1235–1243). Ibn al-Rahib was a civil servant like his father, but remained a layman (although a deacon at the **Mo'allaqa** Church in Old Cairo). The on-going research of Adel Sidarus (see the bibliography) is revealing the breadth, creativity, and impact of Ibn al-Rahib's scholarship, which may especially be seen in four major works composed between 1257 and 1271, perhaps after being dismissed from government service (under the Mamluks).

His *Kitab al-Tawarikh* (Chronology) deals at length with astronomical and chronological matters before turning to world and ecclesiastical history; it was used by later Christian (Coptic and Ethiopian) and Muslim scholars. In the area of linguistics, Ibn al-Rahib compiled a (now lost) Coptic-Arabic lexicon that apparently surpassed previous attempts both in the range of vocabulary included and in its systematic presentation; it was prefaced by a highly original (and extant) introduction to Coptic grammar. His *Kitab al-Shifa-fi kashf ma-statara min lahut al-Masih wa-khtafa* (The Book of Healing: Of What Is Veiled and Hidden of Christ's Divinity, Revealing) is an exegetical florilegium that preserves patristic and medieval Arabic commentary on biblical passages of **Christological** importance, while the encyclopedic *Kitab al-Burhan* (The Book of the Demonstration) deals with a wide range of theological, moral, and **liturgical** issues in its 50 "questions" or chapters. Ibn al-Rahib's intellectual openness is everywhere evident: *Kitab al-Shifa* quotes freely from the great 11th-century scholar of the (**Nestorian**) Church of the East, Abu al-Faraj 'Abdallah ibn al-Tayyib, while the treatment of theodicy in *Kitab al-Burhan* is conversant with the well-known Muslim *mutakallim* Fakhr al-Din al-Razi.

IBN KABAR, SHAMS AL-RI'ASA ABU AL-BARAKAT (?–1324).
Priest, encyclopedist, scholar of Coptic. The writer known to contemporaries as al-Shams ibn Kabar provides one of the last great examples of the flowering of Arabic-language Coptic Orthodox literature in the 13th and early 14th centuries. Ibn Kabar served for a time as scribe to the Mamluk Emir Baybars al-Mansuri (d. 1325) and is reported to have helped him to write his multivolume narrative of Islamic history, *Zubdat al-fikra fi tarikh al-hijra* (The Quintessence of Thought in Islamic History). Although the precise dates of this secular service are unknown, in 1300 Ibn Kabar was ordained priest with the name of Barsum (probably after the great **saint** of the day, Barsum the Naked) and served at the **Mo'allaqa** Church in Old Cairo. Many of his sermons (in rhymed Arabic prose) have been preserved. He escaped pursuers unharmed during the anti-*dhimmi* disturbances of 1321, but he died a few years later in 1324.

Ibn Kabar is especially remembered for two works. His Bohairic-Arabic vocabulary *al-Sullam al-kabir* (The Great Ladder or Scala Magna) is a high point of Coptic lexicography, much used and preserved in many manuscripts. It has played a huge role in European Coptic studies, thanks to its publication (in Rome, 1648) with a Latin translation by the Jesuit scholar **Athanasius Kircher**. Ibn Kabar's other great work is the ecclesiastical encyclopedia *Misbah al-zulma wa-idah al-khidma* (The Lamp of the Darkness and the Illumination of Service). Wadi Abullif points out (Wadi, "Abu al-Barakat," 242) that this title reflects the work's content: It moves from dogmatic and canonical considerations (chapters 1–6, a "lamp" in "the darkness") to practical and **liturgical** matters of importance to deacons and other servants of the Church (chapters 8–24, an "illumination of service"). The break between these two major sections comes at chapter 7, "Eminent Christians and Their Writings," which is a catalogue of Christian books known to Ibn Kabar from the Church Fathers to the

Arabophone theologians of his own day—and a precious resource for all students of Arabic-Christian literature down to the present time

IBN KATIB QAYSAR (?–after 1260). Biblical and Coptic scholar. 'Alam al-Ri'asa Abu Ishaq Ibrahim, known as Ibn Katib Qaysar (because his grandfather was secretary to the Emir 'Alam al-Din Qaysar), was a contemporary and colleague of scholars such as **al-Mu'taman ibn al-'Assal.** He is remembered in the first place for a Bohairic Coptic grammar entitled *al-Tabsira al-mukhtasira* (The Concise Instruction). This is perhaps the first true Coptic grammar; Ibn Katib Qaysar moved beyond the paradigms of **Yuhanna, Bishop of Samannud,** by making use of Arabic grammatical categories (as had recently been described by the great grammarian Ibn al-Hajib, d. 1249) in order to describe the **Coptic language.** The other major work for which Ibn Katib Qaysar is known is a *Commentary on the Apocalypse,* which is systematic in its treatment of words and categories, attentive to historical context, and ecumenical in its use of sources. It was published in Egypt in 1898 and again in 1939. Ibn Katib Qaysar may also have composed a commentary on the Pauline and Catholic epistles and the Acts of the Apostles. The theological encyclopedia of **al-Mu'taman ibn al-'Assal** quotes from or alludes to yet other works, including epitomes of treatises by Yahya ibn 'Adi and a contribution to the debate—ongoing in the Coptic Church since the time of **Marqus ibn al-Qunbar** and **Mikha'il of Damietta**—about auricular confession to a **priest.**

ICON. The word *icon* derives from the Greek *eikon,* meaning "image," "portrait," or "likeness." Generally, Coptic icons are made of panels of wood painted mostly in tempera. Encaustic (hot wax) was also used, and the panels may be covered with a layer of gesso. The greater majority of Coptic icons represent portraits such as images of Christ, the Holy Virgin Mary, and the Apostles. Narrative icons that depict events of their lives are less frequent. All Coptic monasteries and churches, ancient and modern, are decorated with icons. The vast majority of the Coptic icons date from the 18th and 19th centuries. A considerable number of important medieval icons dating from the 13th and 14th centuries were conserved and published beginning in the late 1980s and through the 1990s. It is generally accepted that the oldest Coptic icons derive from pagan mummy portraits that incorrectly were known as the "Fayoum Portraits." These portraits, usually encaustic, sometimes tempera, show the deceased's head and shoulders on a thin wooden board that is placed on the mummy with bandages. They date between the first and the fourth centuries. According to the Arab historian al-Maqrizi (1364–1442), Patriarch **Cyril I** (412–444) hung icons in the churches of **Alexandria** and in the land of Egypt. Bishop John of Ephesus (ca. 516–585) stated that portraits of new **bishops** were hung in the churches of their dioceses. Unfortunately, only one of the portraits of Coptic bishops survived, which is preserved in the Museum of Byzantine Art of the National Museums in Berlin. It shows Bishop Abraham and dates from the late sixth century. The monastery of St. Catherine at Mount Sinai preserves some of the oldest and most valuable icons of the Byzantine Period, dating from the sixth and seventh centuries, which were not affected by the iconoclastic controversy of the eighth and ninth centuries as Sinai came under Islamic rule about 640.

Icons are objects of veneration rather than displayed for their aesthetic values. They are an indispensable part of the **liturgy** of the Coptic Church. Shrines are built to house icons, where candles and **incense** are burned. There is usually an icon of Christ to the right of the door of the principal sanctuary of the church, the Royal Door, and an icon of the Virgin Mary with the Christ Child to the left of the door. Icons of the 12 Apostles flank the scene of the Last Supper atop the wooden sanctuary screen above the Royal Door. Icons from the **Christological** cycle as well as icons of **saints** decorate the walls of the church. The consecration of the icon is usually performed by a bishop, who anoints it with the **chrism** "holy oil," saying three times: 'Receive the Spirit.' During the evening and morning offering of incense, the **priest** censes the icons of the Holy Virgin Mary and of John the Baptist.

Icons play an important role in the celebrations during festival days and **pilgrimages**. They are carried in the procession of the **feasts** of the Holy Cross, Palm Sunday, Easter, Ascension, and Pentecost. On **Good Friday** the priest envelops the icon of the Crucifixion in a white veil of linen and places it on the altar. In the service on Holy Saturday, the icon of the Resurrection is carried in a procession around the altar and the church seven times while priests and deacons carry crosses, gospels, censers, and candles. During pilgrimages, especially to sites believed to be blessed by the Holy Family, thousands of Copts venerate an icon of the Virgin by singing a song of praise. Upon entering a church, a devote Copt goes directly to the principal sanctuary and touches its curtain while prostrating himself to pray. Then he touches one of the icons and kisses his fingers afterward. A number of Coptic icons became famous in medieval times for their miracles.

There is no evidence that the Coptic Church suffered iconoclasm (destruction of icons), a movement that was initiated by Emperor Leo III (717–741), who issued the first edict against the use of images in 726. The controversy over the nature and function of the icons agitated the Church within the Byzantine Empire from 731 to 843, during which time religious art greatly suffered. However, Coptic icons must have suffered the many waves of persecutions in medieval times when Muslim mobs attacked the churches and plundered them. Coptic monasteries and churches are also decorated with wall paintings. The Coptic liturgy influenced the mural decorations in medieval times; for example, the sacrifice of Abraham was chosen to decorate the sanctuary because of its reference to the Eucharist.

ICONOCLASTIC CONTROVERSY. *See* ICON.

INCARNATION. The doctrine of incarnation—that God the Son took flesh and became man—is the central point of Christian **theology**. It is attested in the New Testament (John 1:14; 1 Tim. 3:16). During the fourth century there was a great debate about the incarnation of Christ, especially after the **Arian** heresy. The **Nicene Creed** (325 A.D.) was composed in order to combat this heresy and states precisely, "We believe in one Lord Jesus Christ, . . . who for us men and for our salvation came down from heaven; he was incarnate of the **Holy Spirit** and of the Virgin Mary; and he became man." The **apostolic fathers** of the Church, such as Ignatius of Antioch in his epistle to the Ephesians, studied this dogma. One of the masterpieces of the Christian theological books is the work of **Athanasius** of **Alexandria**: *On the Incarnation of the Word*. This theme was also treated by **Cyril** of **Alexandria** and by **Severus of Antioch**, the great

Church theologian. This dogma could be summarized in the beautiful hymn attributed to him:

O only begotten Son and Word of God, immortal and everlasting, accepting everything for our salvation; the incarnated from the Mother of God, the ever **Virgin Mary**; without change, Christ God, becoming man and crucified; through death, trode on death, One of the Holy Trinity, glorified with the Father and the Holy Spirit, save us.

INCENSE. Incense is a substance producing a pleasant aroma when burned. **Yuhanna ibn Abi Zakariyya ibn Sabba'** (14th century), the author of a book called *Precious Pearl in the Ecclesiastic Science*, mentioned that four sorts of incense are permitted in the Coptic Church: sandarac, benzoin, aloe, and olibanum. The first had never been offered to idols. Olibanum was offered to Apollo but is offered to God as the creator of heaven and earth. The aloe and the benzoin are the most fragrant aromats. This incense is offered in the same way as the magi offered a gift of frankincense to Christ, having seen his star in the east. **Mikha'il, Metropolitan of Damietta** (12th century), mentioned among the exclusively Coptic observances that he offered the incense of *sandarah* only, and argues against using olibanum or *mi'ah* (styrax) because they were used in the offering of incense to idols. Regarding aloe wood and mastic, he says that the Fathers did not allow these to be offered as incense to God, but that they were later permitted because they were believed to repel devils and destroy the works of the magicians.

INTERNATIONAL ASSOCIATION FOR COPTIC STUDIES (IACS). IACS was founded in Cairo during the First International Congress of **Coptology** (11–17 December 1976) under the auspices of the Egyptian Antiquities Organization. It is a nonprofit organization designed to promote Coptic studies. The IACS publishes a newsletter that provides information about Coptologists and their work. It sponsors congresses at four-year intervals. There have been eight International Congresses of Coptic Studies: Cairo, 11–17 December 1976; Rome, 22–26 September 1980; Warsaw, 20–25 August 1984; Louvain-la-Neuve, 5–9 September 1988; Washington, D.C., 12–15 August 1992; Münster, 21–26 July 1996, Leiden, 27 August–2 September 2000; and

Paris, 28 June–3 July 2004. The Ninth International Congress of Coptic Studies will be held in Cairo in September 2008 under the auspices of His Holiness Pope **Shenouda III.**

INTERPRETATION OF KNOWLEDGE **(NHC XI, 1).** A **Valentinian Gnostic** homily addressed to a Christian community apparently riven by factions. The author utilizes the writings of the Gospels and the Pauline epistles to rectify the situation. The title occurs at the end of the tractate. Extant only in Coptic, *Interpretation of Knowledge* was originally composed in Greek, probably sometime in the second century. Its provenience is unknown.

– J –

JAR, RITE. This rite is performed by a **priest** in the case of one who committed grave sins and seeks repentance and reconciliation. After relevant readings and special prayers, the priest pours some oil in a jar full of water, saying "In the name of the Father and the Son and the **Holy Spirit,** blessed is the Almighty Father, blessed is holy Son Jesus Christ our Lord, blessed is the Holy Spirit the Comforter," after which he sprinkles the water over the penitent. This rite is a sort of "second" baptism; it is not published in the actual printed **liturgical** books but it is mentioned only in few manuscripts. However, it is no longer in use.

JEROME (ca. 349–ca. 419). Monk, biblical scholar. He was born at Strido, near Aquileia at the head of the Adriatic. He studied in Rome, where he was baptized. He devoted himself to asceticism. He moved to the Syrian Desert near Chalcis, where he began learning Hebrew and Greek with intense study of the scriptures. In Egypt he attended the **Catechetical School of Alexandria** under **Origen** and visited Coptic monasteries. From 382 to 385, he was back in Rome, where he became a secretary to Pope Damasus I. Jerome's greatest achievement was the translation of most of the Bible into Latin from Greek and Hebrew. The vulgate Bible became the version that the Roman Church used almost exclusively throughout its history until modern times. Jerome wrote many biblical commentaries and translated several works of Origen and **Eusibius of Caesarae** into Latin, and continued the *Historia ecclesiastica* of the latter. He combated fiercely **Arianism, Pelagianism,** and Origenism. In 404, he translated the cenobitic, or communal, rules of St. **Pachomius** into Latin from a Greek translation, which had been made for him from the Coptic text.

JEU, BOOKS OF. Two **Gnostic** texts partially preserved in Coptic in the **Bruce Codex**. At the end of the first book is a title, "The Book of the Great Mystery-Message." The current title, the Books of Jeu, was applied to the texts by Carl Schmidt, reflecting his view that they are "the two books of Jeu" mentioned in the closely related Gnostic work *Pistis Sophia*. A divine being called "Jeu" is prominent in the texts. *1 Jeu* is a revelation dialogue between the risen Jesus and his disciples in which he refers to various divine emanations called "Jeu" and gives them instructions on how to reach the 60 "treasuries" of the heavenly world. In *2 Jeu*, Jesus initiates his disciples into the mysteries of water baptism, fire baptism, and spirit baptism. The Coptic text of both books is accompanied by cryptic diagrams called "seals." Extant only in Coptic, *1–2 Jeu* were originally composed in Greek, probably in late third-century Egypt.

JIRJIS IBN AL-'AMID AL-MAKIN (late 14th c.). Priest, theologian, encyclopedist. Sometimes referred to as "al-Makin the Younger" in order to distinguish him from the 13th-century historian of the same name, Jirjis was a physician from a well-connected Coptic family who later became a monk. He is best known as the author of a theological compendium entitled *Mukhtasar al-bayan fi tahqiq al-iman* (The Brief Exposition in Faith's Verification), or for short—and perhaps more accurately—as *al-Hawi* (The Compiler). The work begins by addressing **Christological** matters, but then goes on to treat a great variety of topics. Its recent publication in Egypt (by the Muharraq Monastery, in four substantial volumes totaling over 1,600 pages) will undoubtedly encourage the study of this witness to Coptic theological culture in late medieval Egypt.

JOHN THE LITTLE (339–409). Saint and monk. He is a renowned figure among the **Desert Fathers**. He is known from the *Apophthegmata* *partum*, which preserves nine sayings under his name, and a Coptic "Life" attributed to Zacharias, the eighth-century **Bishop** of Sakha. He is also commemorated in the Arabic **Synaxarion** of the Copts. John was born in the village of Tesi in the region of Oxyrhynchus. In 357, when he was 18 years old, he came to **Scetis** and became a disciple of Abbot Ammoes. About 380–385, St. John established his own community. In the early fifth century, he became "Father of Scetis." The virtues that were most highly valued by him are obedience, humility, and compassion. Three fears were with him all the time: the fear of the time of the separation from the body, the fear of meeting God, and the fear of Judgment Day. Following the invasion of the nomads in 407, St. John had to leave Scetis for the Clysma area near Suez, where he seems to have died. His monastic settlement was one of four settlements that developed into the oldest four monasteries of **Wadi al-Natrun**. The Monastery of John the Little was empty of its monks in 1493. Some of its buildings, including a church, were discovered in 1995. Excavations resumed a few years ago after nearly 10 years of interruption.

JOHN XI (?–1452). Patriarch (89th, 1427–1452), ecumenist. John XI presided over the Coptic Orthodox Church during a difficult period marked by coerced conversions away from the Church, confiscation of the property of Copts and other *dhimmi*s, and the destruction and pillaging of churches. Especially tragic for the Coptic community was the destruction in 1436 of the famous Marian **pilgrimage** center of Dayr al-Maghtis, near Lake Burullus in the north of the Delta.

In the midst of such difficulties, John's contacts with Christian leaders outside Egypt took on special importance. He received the Syrian Orthodox patriarch in 1430 and was in regular contact with the great Ethiopian Emperor Zar'a Ya'qob (1434–1468), although this sometimes aroused the suspicion and ire of the Mamluk authorities. In 1440, a delegation from Roman Catholic Pope Eugene IV invited John to join the union that had just been concluded between the Latin and Greek churches at the **Council of Florence**. John responded with a letter in Arabic to Pope Eugene, which he sent to Florence with a delegation of Coptic and Ethiopian monks led by Andrea, superior of the **Monastery of St. Antony**. John's letter, which has recently been edited with a commentary (by Philippe Luisier; see the bibliography), was the first of many written by Coptic patriarchs to Latin popes and high officials over the next three centuries. Although fulsome in its (often rhymed) expressions of respect for and gratitude to the Roman pope, John's letter clearly reflects the medieval Copto-Arabic theological tradition and makes no concessions to the Latins, either on matters of papal primacy or on matters of **Christology**. All the same, in 1442 a bull of union between the Latin and Coptic churches, *Cantate Domino*, was signed by their representatives in Florence.

– K –

KAMIL, MURAD (1907–1975). A Semitist, who taught at Cairo University, the Coptic **Clerical College**, the **Higher Institute of Coptic Studies** in Egypt, and the University of Freiburg in Germany. Professor Kamil played an important role in the negotiations between the Coptic Church and the Ethiopian Church. He wrote a book on the Coptic civilization (Cairo, 1967). He bequeathed his valuable library to the Coptic **patriarchate**.

KELLIA. The archaeological remains that were discovered in Kellia represent the largest complex of Christian monasteries and hermitages known to date. The monastic site, which is situated about 18 kilometers south of modern al-Barnuji, the ancient **Nitria** in the western Nile Delta, was partly excavated, examined, and documented between 1965 and 1990. Unfortunately, the encroachment of the cultivation destroyed nearly the entire site. According to one of the **Sayings of the Desert Fathers**, Sts. **Amoun** and **Antony** founded Kellia. **Palladius** stated that hundreds of monks were living at Kellia by the late fourth century. Kellia flourished from the fourth to the seventh century and began to decline in the eighth century. The monks' cells extended over a territory of more than 100 square kilometers and the population of monks numbered thousands there. Archaeologists discovered more than 1,500 hermitages and a number of churches. In addition to a bedroom, **oratory**, kitchen, storeroom, and a latrine, each hermitage included a well and a garden. Thus the monks were living independently and met only on Saturday and Sunday to celebrate Mass. **Evagrius Ponticus** was the most illustrious figure who lived in Kellia. The documentation of this huge **monastic** site, including buildings, wall paintings, inscriptions, and ceramics, provided invaluable material for the study of monastic life in Egypt during its golden age. The **Coptic Museum** possesses a number of wall paintings and some fine examples of pottery from Kellia.

KHURUS. An Arabic word derived from the Greek *choros.* It is a transverse room reserved for the clergy between the altar room in the sanctuary area and the nave with the side isles or the *naos.* It developed in the Coptic Church in the seventh century. It had been used primarily to separate the clergy from the congregation.

KIRCHER, ATHANASIUS (1602–1680). Jesuit scholar, professor. He was born in Geisa in Germany, and took his vows as a member of the Society of Jesus at Paderborn in 1620. In 1630 Kircher became a professor of philosophy, mathematics, and Oriental languages at Würzburg. He produced the first Coptic grammar and lexicon in a Western language, which are considered major works in the field of Coptic studies. Kircher tried and failed to decipher Egyptian hieroglyphics. However, he aroused interest in ancient Egypt. His Coptic studies were of immense importance in the 1630s and 1640s. His *Prodromus Coptus sive Aegyptiacus* (Coptic or Egyptian Forerunner, 1636) and *Lingua Aegyptiaca Restituta* (The Restored Egyptian Language, 1643) were successful and became primary sources for Coptic studies at least for two centuries.

KRAUSE, MARTIN (1930–). Coptologist and educator. He is the father of modern **Coptology**. He was born in Planitz near Zwickau, Germany. He studied **theology**, Egyptology, and the history of religion in Berlin and Leipzig and obtained a PhD (Berlin) in 1956 and a ThD (Leipzig) in 1958. In 1958, he joined the German Archaeological Institute in Cairo, where he stayed until 1963. He began the work of preserving and listing the **Nag Hammadi Codices** in the **Coptic Museum**. He was instrumental in the documentation and publication of these remarkable **Gnostic** papyri. In 1965, he established a Department of Coptology at the Westfälischen Wilhelms-Universität Münster in West Germany, which boasts the largest library in Coptic studies. In order to ensure this unique academic major in Coptology,

Brigitte and Martin Krause arranged to bequeath their entire estate to that university. He is one of the founders of the **International Association for Coptic Studies** and was elected its first president. He is one of the major editors of the *Coptic Encyclopedia*. Krause wrote numerous books and hundreds of articles on the various aspects of Coptic civilization that related to both the literary and material culture of Christian Egypt and **Nubia**.

– L –

LABIB, IQLADIYUS (1873–1918). He was born in the village of Mir, which is located near the famous Monastery of the Holy Virgin Mary (**Dayr al-Muharraq**). His visits to that monastery may have motivated him to be interested in the **Coptic language**. Pope Cyril V made the **patriarchal** library of manuscripts in Cairo available to him. Labib insisted on speaking Coptic with his family. He encouraged the laity to use Coptic as a spoken language. He published a Coptic grammar, a number of Coptic biblical texts, and some **liturgical** books of the Coptic Church. His most valuable contribution to Coptic studies is a Copto-Arabic dictionary.

LABIB, PAHOR (1905–1994). Director of the **Coptic Museum**, educator. He was born in Cairo. His father was **Iqladiyus Labib**, who used to speak only Coptic with his family. He studied Egyptology at Cairo University and obtained his PhD from the University of Friedrich Wilhelms, Berlin, in 1934. He was appointed lecturer in the Institute of Archeology at Cairo University in 1935. In 1945 he held the post of keeper in the Egyptian Museum, Cairo. From 1951 to 1965, he directed the Coptic Museum. One of his important achievements is the excavation in the **pilgrimage** center of **Abu Mina**, which he started in 1951 and which was continued by the German Archaeological Institute of Cairo. The greatest achievement of Pahor Labib is the protection of the **Gnostic Nag Hammadi Library** in the Coptic Museum, and his cooperation with the International Committee of scholars under UNESCO to document and publish these invaluable Coptic texts. He taught Coptic at the Faculty of Archaeology of Cairo University for many years, and was a member of several high committees in the Egyptian Ministry of Culture and the Egyptian Antiquities Organization.

LECTIONARY. In the Coptic Church, a lectionary is a book containing lessons to be read at the service of evening and morning offering of **incense** (namely a Psalm-Verside and a gospel, readings), and the Divine **Liturgy** for which there are readings from the Pauline Epistles, the Catholic Epistles, the Acts of the Apostles, a Psalm-Verside, and a gospel reading.

The yearly lectionary is comprised of two parts: 40 services for Sundays and 366 daily services. The days are distributed according to the Coptic calendar. The daily services follow the calendar and commemorate the day's **feast** or **saint**. The Lenten lectionary normally includes the four days of Jonah's Fast and Lent, which lasts for seven weeks. There is no evening offering of incense, but Old Testament selections are read at the morning offering of incense on fast days. The **Lectionary of the Holy Week** has a special particularity that all the Gospels of the liturgy are taken from the Gospel of John. The readings for the days and the Sundays are given together. A "monthly lectionary" was published by R. **Tukhi**, but Tukhi's edition does not follow the Coptic manuscript and thus cannot be used as a reference.

The earliest manuscript of the **Holy Week** lectionary is Ms 253 Liturgica of the **Coptic Museum**, dated 1364 A.D. The first edition was edited by R. Tukhi (Catholic) in 1761 with Arabic translation. This edition can hardly be accepted as a valid witness. Its content is sometimes artificial and it is not reliable for the liturgist. The first Orthodox publication was edited by Claudius Labib in 1912 and reprinted with minor changes several times.

LECTIONARY OF THE HOLY WEEK. The **Holy Week** lectionary service covers services from **Palm Sunday** to Easter. Each day of the Holy Week has five "five night hour" and "five day hours," each of them with special readings, and a "burial service" conducted after Palm Sunday Eucharist. This last service is for those who pass away during this week. The British Library holds the most ancient complete Bohairic **lectionary** of the Holy Week, Manuscript N Add.

5997, dated A.M. 990 (1273 A.D.). Some fragments of the Sahidic Holy Week lectionary has also survived.

According to a tradition mentioned in the Holy Week lectionary, this book was compiled by the Patriarch **Gabriel II** (1131–1146) with the help of the monks of the **Monastery of St. Macarius**. Further lessons and also a number of short homilies or exhortations were afterward added to the lectionary by a certain Peter, **Bishop** of Behnasa. The attribution to Gabriel II contradicts an event known in the biography of this **patriarch** mentioned in the *History of the Patriarchs of the Egyptian Church*. When Gabriel went to the Monastery of St. Macarius, he added one extra word to the Confession that is said over the oblation. A discussion took place between the patriarch and the monks. If adding one word to the holy liturgy had caused such a reaction, then we would expect greater reactions if the patriarch had "dared" to produce a new book. Moreover, the *History of the Patriarchs* would have also mentioned this event. In addition to this, some of the Sahidic fragments of the Holy Week are earlier than this date. In the 14th century, **Ibn Kabar** mentioned a different system of reading the Bible during Holy Week in the Monastery of St. Macarius. It would have been quite unusual that the monks of the monastery who prepared the lectionary did not use it. To conclude, we have the most ancient lectionary from the 13th century, and in the 14th century Peter of Behnasa added new lessons. But it is hard to believe that Gabriel II had created or compiled this book. It is probable that his role involved approving a local tradition, rather than creating a new liturgical book.

LETTER OF PETER TO PHILIP (**NHC VIII, 2**). A **Gnostic** revelation dialogue between the risen Christ and his disciples, preceded by a short letter addressed by Peter to his "fellow Apostle" Philip. The title occurs at the beginning: "The Letter of Peter which He Sent to Philip." Jesus' revelation consists of various topics of Gnostic mythology, concluding with a commission to the Apostles to go out and preach. Extant only in Coptic, the *Letter of Peter to Philip* (*Ep. Pet. Phil.*) was originally composed in Greek, probably in the early third century, possibly in Egypt.

LIBRARY OF NAG HAMMADI. *See* NAG HAMMADI CODICES.

LITERATURE, COPTIC. Comparatively little Coptic literature, which is almost entirely religious, has survived. Coptic literature flourished from the fourth to the ninth century. The 10th and the 11th centuries did not witness new literary works; literary activity was limited to editing and compiling older works. Most of the Coptic literature is written in codices, the pages of which are made of papyrus or parchment, and a small part is written on scrolls or *ostraca* (chips of limestone or pieces of broken pottery with inscriptions). A small part this literature is written on paper. Many lists of manuscripts reflect the richness of the libraries of ancient monasteries in significant literary works that have been lost. The provenance of the vast majority of the Coptic manuscripts is unknown; most of the relatively few manuscripts of known origin came from the monasteries of **Wadi al-Natrun**, the **White Monastery**, and the Monastery of the Archangel Michael at Phantoou in the region of Fayoum. Many Coptic manuscripts are still unpublished.

Coptic literature is written in the **Coptic language**. However, a significant proportion of this literature is preserved only in Arabic translation. A considerable part of the Coptic literature consists of translations from the Greek of the Holy Bible, the apocrypha, **Gnostic** works, and Manichaean scriptures, as well as some paragraphs from the writings of Clement of **Alexandria** and Hippolytus, and of another 35 Church Fathers; of the latter, a few texts had been translated from the Syriac. The surviving few works of **Pachomius** are the oldest Coptic texts of the original Coptic literature. Numerous literary works have been attributed to dozens of **patriarchs**, **bishops**, famous monks, and great personalities of the Coptic Church, the last of them being Patriarch Mark III (799–819). St. **Shenute** is the most significant Coptic writer, whose numerous sermons and letters greatly enriched the Coptic literature. Among the important original works that survived in this literature are the lives of **saints**, canons, homilies, liturgical texts, monastic rules, and Church history. Poetry and medical, arithmetical, alchemical, and magical texts are also represented in Coptic literature.

LITURGICAL INSTRUMENTS. The **patriarch** or a **bishop** must consecrate the liturgical instruments of the Coptic Church, as well as everything worn or used during the services, as part of the general process of consecration. The liturgical instruments consist of the following:

- Basin and ewer: used to wash the **priest's** hands before the Divine **Liturgy**.
- Candelabrum: a large ornamental candlestick.
- Censer: a metal bowl in which **incense** is added to the glowing coals. Three chains are attached to it, which end with a small domelike lid and a hook. (Sometimes the censer is not considered a liturgical instrument).
- Cross: a small cross held in the hand of the priest or the deacon.
- Cruet: a small vessel with a secure lid, where wine and water are placed.
- Eucharistic bread basket: a large wicker basket, with a cross-embroidered lining, used to hold the loaves baked for the Eucharist.
- Fan: made of ostrich or peacock feathers, or linen cloth woven at times with fine threads of metal. Used in the church during the Divine Liturgy to drive away flies and other insects from near the chalice. It usually carries a drawing of the six-winged cherubim.
- Gospel: a case of shiny metal that is placed on the altar during church services. Within it is contained a copy of the New Testament, or just the four Gospels, in either the Coptic or Arabic language.
- Incense box: used to place incense and is usually made of silver or carved wood. It is placed on the altar on the right side of the officiating priest. A small spoon for scooping the incense onto the coal is usually placed in the incense box.

However, Severus of Ashmunein in his book *The Order of the Priesthood* did not include the censer, the cruet, the incense box, or the throne of the chalice among the consecrated instruments of the altar.

LITURGY IN THE COPTIC CHURCH. The etymological origin of the word *liturgy* is from *leitos*, "public, relating to the people," and *ergon*, "work." It is used in the New Testament as a religious (priestly) service in Luke 1:23: "When the days of his *ministry* were accomplished, Zechariah returned to his house." In Acts 13:2 we read that at Antioch, the prophets and teachers held a worship service (doing service to the Lord) and appointed Paul and Barnabas as missionaries. Hebrews 8:2, having described the resurrected Christ as the heavenly high **priest**, calls him *"Leitourgos"* of the sanctuary of the true tabernacle. Hence we can conclude that this word means a religious public service.

The beginning of the Coptic liturgy is obscure and it is difficult to find the origin of the liturgy before the final Peace of the Church (312 A.D.). We will give a list of the most important direct sources of the liturgy followed by the indirect sources.

A. Direct Sources
    1. The New Testament. The New Testament remains our foremost liturgical source giving information about the life of the first Christians and their faith. Here and there, parts from hymns are to be found. The use of the Psalms derives from the Jewish background. It is important to mention that the Eastern liturgies are primarily related to the liturgy of Jerusalem, which had widespread influence. Since the time of Constantine, Jerusalem and Palestine generally had been the pilgrimage places par excellence. Even the beginning of the Church of **Alexandria** is always related to Jerusalem, as evidenced by the Book of Acts (2:10).
    2. The *Apostolic Tradition*. The *Apostolic Tradition*, attributed to Hippolytus of Rome and usually dated to ca. 215, can be regarded as providing reliable information about the liturgical activity of the Church of Rome. Unfortunately the original Greek text has not survived, but a few isolated fragments from Coptic, Arabic, and Ethiopian texts have survived, which shows that at one stage it was used in the Alexandrian Church.
    3. The Canons of Hippolytus. The Canons of Hippolytus, which are derived from the *Apostolic Tradition*, were composed in Egypt between 336 and 340. Only an Arabic version survives, which provides important liturgical data.
    4. The *Apostolic Constitutions* (**Didascalia**). This is a reworking of the *Apostolic Tradition* written in the fourth

century, probably in Syria, and shows the development of the liturgy.

5. The **Euchologion** of Sarapion of Tmuis. This collection of prayers traditionally is regarded as the work of Sarapion, **Bishop** of Tmuis in Lower Egypt and a friend of **Athanasius** of Alexandria.

6. The travel journal of Egeria. In the journal of her travels, Egeria gives a detailed account of the services during the weekdays and on Sunday. She describes also in details the rite of the Passion Week in Jerusalem. According to Egeria, the monks took part in communal worship together with the clergy and the congregation.

B. Indirect Sources

1. The paschal letters. Since the middle of the third century, the **patriarchs** of Alexandria were accustomed to writing letters announcing the date of Easter and giving some moral lessons to the congregation. These writings, especially those of Athanasius and **Cyril** of Alexandria, contain much liturgical material.

2. Monastic literature. There are liturgical materials in monastic literature and especially in the rules of **Pachomius** for the monks.

3. Hagiographical texts. The lives of saints and especially of monks and bishops contain several quotations from liturgical texts. A detailed study of the Coptic liturgy scattered through **Coptic hagiography** would be highly profitable.

The Church in Egypt was divided by the **Christological** controversy, which came to a head in the **Council of Chalcedon**. The Coptic Church maintained its liturgical particularity, but the Syrian Church, sharing the same faith, influenced it to a certain extent; hence, it is important to mention some of the sources of the Syrian tradition.

1. Cyril of Jerusalem delivered 24 catechetical lectures that explained Christian initiation and contained some liturgical details.

2. John Chrysostom's works, especially his initiation catecheses, are rich in liturgical information as well as his festal homilies.

3. Ephrem the Syrian was an inexhaustible hymn writer.
4. **Severus of Antioch**, well known for his dogmatic controversies, was a great liturgist. He wrote several hymns and liturgical texts, and his cathedral homilies contained a great deal of liturgical information such as his explanation of the *Trisagion*.

The Coptic liturgy comes to our knowledge through four groups:

1. Greek texts, including anaphoras such as the Anaphora of St. Basil, and hymns for several occasions.
2. Sahidic texts, including the anaphora and the liturgy before the mass **(Psalmodia)** in addition to several excerpts. We have several papyri from the seventh and eighth centuries, although most of the texts in this group date from the ninth and tenth centuries. Some hymns survive from the rite of concoction of the Myron from the year 1374.
3. Bohairic texts, including nearly all the liturgical texts. The Egyptian popes moved their residence to Cairo in the Middle Ages, and the Bohairic dialect became the official dialect of the Coptic Church. The manuscripts of this group are of a late date. The most ancient manuscripts date from the 12th century.
4. Arabic texts, consisting of some late hymns for the month of Kiahk and other occasions.

It is impossible to mention, in this limited space, the full list of the Coptic liturgical manuscripts. The reader should start with W. Kammerer's *A Coptic Bibliography* (1951). For manuscripts the reader should refer to De Lacy O'Leary's *Primary Guide to Coptic Literary Material* (1938). In addition, we have the following:

A. Khater and O. H. E. Burmester, *Catalogue of the Coptic and Christian Arabic Mss preserved in the Cloister of St. Menas at Cairo* (1967).

A. Khater and O. H. E. Burmester, *Catalogue of the Coptic and Christian Arabic Mss preserved in the library of the Church of the All-Holy Virgin Mary known as Qasriat Ar-Rihan at Old Cairo* (1973). The church was destroyed but some manuscripts were rescued and are preserved in the **Coptic Museum** and Coptic patriarchate.

A. Khater and O. H. E. Burmester, *Catalogue of the Coptic and Christian Arabic Mss preserved in the library of the Church of Saints Sergius and Bacchus known as Abu Sargah at Old Cairo* (1977).

B. Layton, *Catalogue of Coptic Literary Manuscripts in the British Library Acquired since the year 1905* (1987).

L. Depydt, *Catalogue of Coptic Manuscripts in the Pierpont Morgan Library* (*Corpus of Illuminated Manuscripts*) (1993).

A. Elanskaya, *The Literary Coptic Manuscripts in the A. S. Pushkin State Fine Arts Museum in Moscow* (1994).

Koptische Handschriften, 1–2 by O. H. E. Burmester (1975), L. Stork (1995, 2002).

The reader is also referred to the reports on the liturgical studies published every four years in the Acts of the International Congress of Coptic Studies. The last published report was H. Brakmann's "Nueue Funde und forschungen zur Liturgie der Kopten," *Agypten und Nubien in spatantiker und christlicher Zeit, Akten des 6. Internationalen Koptologenkongress* (1999, pp. 451–468). *See also* ETHIOPIAN LITURGY; LITURGICAL INSTRUMENTS.

LOBSH. Meaning "crown" or "consummation." It is the title given to the final stanzas of certain hymns used in particular for odes and the Theotokias.

LORD'S PRAYER. The Lord's Prayer is the model that Jesus Christ gave to his disciples. It is mentioned in the Gospel of Matthew 6:9–13 and in the Gospel of Luke 11:2–4, but in different context. This prayer has been used in the liturgy since the early days of Christianity. The book of the **Didache** includes this prayer with the final **doxology**, "Through our Lord Jesus Christ, for . . ." In the third century, **Origen**, in his book on *Prayer*, gave a detailed interpretation of this prayer. St. Cyprian and Tertullian wrote detailed interpretations on this prayer. In the Coptic **liturgy**, there is not a single rite where this prayer is not recited at the commencement and conclusion of service.

– M –

MACARIUS THE GREAT OR THE EGYPTIAN (ca. 300–ca. 390). Saint, ascetic.

He is one of the great figures of Egyptian **monasticism**. Macarius was a villager from the southwestern part of the Delta. Around 330 he withdrew into **Wadi al-Nartun (Scetis)**, about 80 kilometers south of **Alexandria**. He lived for a time in a cave in the area of Wadi al-Natrun near where the **Monastery of al-Baramous** stands today. Finally he prepared for himself a cave in the very region where there is an extant monastery bearing his name. Disciples joined Macarius soon, and monasticism began to flourish there. Macarius' monasticism was a form of semianchoritism, between the anchoritic life of **Antony** and the cenobitic or communal monasticism of **Pachomius**. Monks lived alone in independent cells but gathered on Saturdays and Sundays to celebrate mass and to take part in a common meal. Many of Macarius' sayings and anecdotes about him are found in the **Sayings of the Fathers**. Macarius was highly appreciated by **Evagrius of Ponticus**. When Macarius died in 390 there were four monasteries in Scetis: Macarius, Pshoi, **John the Little**, and the Monastery of al-Baramous. Today, the **Monastery of St. Macarius** is one of the most prosperous monasteries in Egypt. Beginning in 1969 it flourished greatly under **Matta al-Miskin**. Its modern printing press produces many important publications in Arabic, in addition to the monthly magazine *Saint Mark*.

MAQARA (active before 1350). Monk, canonist. Maqara was a monk of the Monastery of St. **John the Little** in the **Wadi al-Natrun** who dedicated great energy to gathering the canons of the Coptic Orthodox Church—as well as materials from other ecclesial communities—into one great Arabic-language compendium. This compendium includes the canonical collections attributed to the Apostles and Fathers of the Church; the canons of the early ecumenical councils and synods; the canons of the Coptic patriarchs **Christodoulos, Cyril II, Gabriel II ibn Turayk**, and **Cyril III ibn Laqlaq**; and collections by the Copts **Abu Salih Yu'annis** and **Mikha'il, Metropolitan of Damietta**. We do not know Maqara's dates for certain, but he may have been younger than Shams al-Ri'asa Abu al-Barakat **ibn Kabar** (d. 1324), who does not mention him in his *Lamp of the Darkness*.

At the same time, the oldest manuscript of Maqara's canonical collection dates to 1350, indicating that he was active in the first half of the 14th century.

MARK. Apostle, evangelist, and **saint.** According to the Coptic tradition, St. Mark is the founder of the Coptic Church in Egypt. This tradition is supported by the testimony of **Eusebius of Caesarea** in his *Church History.* A Coptic manuscript preserved in Paris contains a detailed story of St. Mark. This manuscript was copied in the 11th century but reflects an ancient tradition. This manuscript contains a description of St. Mark: "Tall in his appearance, his nose was long, his speech was obvious, and his beard was long and thick. He became grey haired." In the sixth or early seventh centuries, John, **Bishop** of Ashmunein, delivered a homily on the life of St. Mark, where he accumulated the different traditions concerning St. Mark at that time. According to these traditions, St. Mark, originally from Pentapolis, returned to Palestine, where he met Christ and became one of his 70 disciples. He came to Egypt where he preached the good news. He traveled also to **Cyprus** and then to Rome, where he met Peter and Paul. He suffered martyrdom in **Alexandria** in an insurrection of the pagans.

St. Mark's relics remained in Alexandria until the Venetians took them in the ninth century. According to Coptic tradition, his head remained in Alexandria. It played an important role for the consecration of the **patriarchs** of Alexandria. The name of St. Mark is mentioned in all the Coptic **liturgical** books. In the absolution of the ministers, his name appears after the 12 Apostles. In the commemoration of the saints in the anaphora, his name follows those of the Virgin Mary, John the Baptist, and St. Stephen the protomartyr.

In the 20th century **Cyril VI**, the 116th patriarch of Alexandria, requested from Paul VI, Pope of Rome, the return to the Coptic Church of the relics of St. Mark, which reposed in the Cathedral of St. Mark in Venice. The request was accepted and part of the relics of St. Mark was received by a Coptic delegation. The relics are preserved under the altar of the **Cathedral of St. Mark** in Cairo, where a **wall painting** in neo-Coptic style, executed by **Isaac Fanous**, narrates the story of the martyrdom of the saint as well as the return of the relics to Egypt in 1968. One of the most beautiful icons in the

Coptic Museum is the icon of St. Mark with a severed head, dating to the 15th century.

MARK, LITURGY OF SAINT. *See* ANAPHORA OF SAINT CYRIL.

MARQUS IBN AL-QUNBAR (?–1208). Priest, reformer. Marqus ibn al-Qunbar ("son of the lark"), sometimes referred to as "Marqus the Blind," flourished in the final third of the 12th century as a traveling priest and spiritual teacher who gathered a following known as the "Qanabira." Falling afoul of Coptic **Patriarch** Mark III ibn Zur'ah (73rd, 1166–1189), he and his followers went over to the Melchite Church. Later, perhaps after another round of switching allegiances, he attempted to return to the Coptic Church but was refused; having antagonized the hierarchies of two churches, he spent the last years of his life quietly at the Melchite Monastery of al-Qusayr, south of Cairo, where he died in 1208.

Marqus is an interesting witness to the language shift that was taking place among the Copts in the 12th century: He gathered great crowds to himself by teaching and interpreting the Bible in Arabic at a time when Coptic Christian **theology** and culture were still largely bound to the **Coptic language**. His importance to Coptic Church history lies especially in a cluster of ideas that he insistently promoted (as can be seen from his allegorical *Commentary on the Pentateuch* and from the catechetical *Book of the Master and the Disciple* in eight chapters): that every Christian should partake of the Eucharistic elements frequently, though only after confession to a spiritual master and performance of **penance**, necessitating that every Christian have a spiritual master or father-confessor. Although Marqus' ideas (including a number of Melchite teachings that he adopted) were firmly rejected by **Mikha'il, Metropolitan of Damietta**, his insistence on recovering the ancient practice of auricular confession to a priest—which had fallen out of practice in the 12th-century Coptic Church—began a debate that continued into the next century, when auricular confession received support in *The Book of Confession*, written by Da'ud al-Fayyumi (before he became Patriarch **Cyril III ibn Laqlaq**), **Bulus al-Bushi**, and **al-As'ad ibn al-'Assal**.

MARRIAGE. Marriage is actually considered as one of the sacraments, a spiritual bond between a man and a woman, sanctified by the grace of the **Holy Spirit**, joining them into an indissoluble unit for the purpose of establishing a caring and harmonious Christian family. Despite that, we possess a large number of documents relating to marriage contracts in Coptic; however, detailed description of marriage is lacking in Coptic tradition. This might be because most of the literary documentation is relating to monks and monasticism or to martyrs. A section in the martyrdom of Apater and Iraie his sister reflects the custom of marriage in Egypt in the time of writing this text:

> Some days later, after Apater left his house, a mighty young man, tribunus, whom the king loves greatly, called Constantine, came to the king Diocletian asking him the sister of Apater for marriage. But her mother refused saying that 'Apater my son is not here and his sister is exiled also. . .' Having heard these words, Constantine was very sad and so the king. The latter called Romanus, the father of saint Victor. . . . Romanus went to the house of mother of Calonia, took the hand of Calonia, the sister of Apater, and gave it to Constantine as bride.

The text mentions precisely the profession of the young man, and how he should ask the person in charge of the family, and in case of refusal another person interferes. It shows also that in case of mourning or absence of one the family, the wedding is delayed.

The rite of marriage is performed in front of the sanctuary or in a private house. The Coptic wedding ceremony is called "the coronation ceremony." A papyrus in the collection the National library of Strasbourg contains an inventory of a church that mentions three crowns of copper. The eve of the wedding day is called "Night of the Henna," where a trained woman prepares the bride for marriage. Only women are invited. A parade of the most important gifts of the bride is organized that includes furniture . . . etc. During the ceremony the bridegroom wears a long cape embroidered in white, waits in the chancel for his bride, who approaches on the arm of her father or a relative. She is preceded by the choir and clergy dressed in festive habits and singing to the accompaniment of cymbals and triangles. She takes her place at the right in one of the chairs on the platform. In front of the couple is a table holding the New Testament, a golden cross, the wedding rings, and incense. The marriage service begins. The structure of the rite is typical of the morning incense. The ceremony starts with the Thanksgiving prayers, the Pauline epistle, the **trisagion** and the Gospel, and then some litanies asking for the blessing of the marriage, taking many quotations from Old Testament, while the deacons sing appropriate hymns. At the end, after everyone has recited the **Lord's Prayer**, and the **absolution**; the **priest**, preceded by the choir of deacons singing, leads the newlyweds to the exit. There is a special reading for the Eucharistic liturgy if the bride and the bridegroom will partake the **communion** after this ceremony; which is from John 2:1–11: the wedding of Cana. Sometimes a lavish dinner is served, usually in the home of the bridegroom or under a tent especially erected for the occasion or in a large hotel. On the following morning, friends and relatives call at the bridegroom's house to present their gifts to the newlyweds. Gifts used to consist mainly of cash, which was carefully recorded for reciprocation on later occasions. After forty days, the new family is visited by the priest who reads an absolution of the bride asking for a blessing in order that she will have children and good health.

MARSANES (NHC X, 1). A **Sethian** Gnostic revelatory work written by, or in the name of, the **Gnostic** prophet Marsanes. Very poorly preserved, it is the only tractate in the codex, which is extremely fragmentary. The title is partially preserved on a fragment from the last page. Marsanes recounts an ascent to heaven and visions seen along the way. Heavily influenced by second- and third-century Platonism, *Marsanes* may have been one of the Gnostic "apocalypses" read in Plotinus' school in Rome in the mid-third century (VP 16). Extant only in Coptic, it was originally composed in Greek, probably in the third century, either in Syria or in Egypt.

MARY THE EGYPTIAN (5th century). Saint and ascetic. She left home at the age of 12 and went to **Alexandria**. After a career of infamy there, as an actress and courtesan for 17 years, she was converted on the threshold of the Holy Cross in Jerusalem. She spent the rest of her long life as a penitent in extreme asceticism in the desert of Jordan. After 47 years, a devote monk called Zosimus met her there by chance. She asked him to come to see her in the following year to give her the **communion**. But when he came, he found her dead body. He buried her, helped by a lion. Mary is commemorated in the Arabic **Synaxarion** of the Copts in the sixth of Baramudah. She is venerated by the Church as a great image of repentance.

MASS OF THE CATECHUMENS. In the early Church, the **Liturgy** of the Catechumens is the part of the liturgy that is attended by those initiated in Christianity. After the reading of the gospel and the homily, they would take their leave.

MASS OF THE FAITHFUL. This is the entire **liturgy** that concludes with the Holy Eucharist. No catechumen was allowed to attend it.

MATINS, LITURGY OF THE. The **Vespers** and the Matins are called the "Offering of **Incense**" in the Coptic Church. They are very similar. They appeared under one section in the edited **Euchologion**. They begin with the Prayer of Thanksgiving, followed by a hymn called "The Verses of the Cymbals" (Arba' al-Naqus). The **priest** then prays the Vesper prayers (Prayer for Intercessions). The congregation chants the **doxologies**, followed by the recital of the **Nicene Creed**. The priest prays "O God have mercy upon us," followed by the Litany for the Gospel, and then the gospel reading. The Vesper prayers conclude with the Litanies for the Church, for the **patriarch**, and for the congregation, and finally the **Lord's Prayer** and the absolutions.

MATTA AL-MISKIN (1909–2006). Abbot, spiritual writer. He was born Youssef Iskander in the Banha, Qalyubia, governorate in the Delta. He graduated in pharmacy from Cairo University in 1944 and later owned a pharmacy in Damanhour. In 1948, he sold his pharmacy with all that he had, gave the money to the poor, and devoted himself to asceticism. He was the first university graduate of his generation who had chosen the monastic life. For three years, he remained in the Monastery of St. Samuel of Qalamun in the southwest of the Fayyum. In 1951, he joined the **Monastery of the Syrians** and was consecrated Monk Matta al-Miskin. **Patriarch** Yusab II (1946–1956) appointed him as a patriarchal representative in **Alexandria**, where he established an office for social services and a clerical school. In

1956, he withdrew again to the Monastery of Samuel of Qalamun and built 30 cells there. From 1960 to 1969, a dozen hermits, led by Matta al-Miskin, lived at **Wadi al-Rayan**, which connected to the depression of the Fayyum. Their ambition was to emulate the hermits of the Egyptian deserts of the fourth and fifth centuries.

In 1969 Mikhail, **Bishop** of Assiut and abbot of the **Monastery of St. Macarius**, suggested that they should develop that monastery, which was dilapidated and occupied by only six elderly monks. After the approval of Patriarch **Cyril VI**, they made a great effort in restoring the monastery's old buildings and in establishing more than 150 modern monastic cells, beautiful guesthouses, a new sizable library, and a printing press. In the 1990s, there were more than 150 monks in the monastery. Matta al-Miskin has written about 50 books and pamphlets on history, **theology**, and spirituality. Two important works by him have been translated from Arabic into English: *The Communion of Love* (New York, 1984) and *Orthodox Prayer Life: The Interior Way* (Crestwood, New York, 2003). He was one of three nominees to be patriarch of the Coptic Church in 1971. He believed that any attachment to politics is against the spirit of Christianity and that the 20th-century Coptic revival was too socially and politically oriented. For him the main duty of Coptic clergy is to support the believers through prayer and to persuade them to repent and confess.

MATTHEW I (1336–1408). Saint and **patriarch** (87th, 1378–1408). Matthew is perhaps the greatest of the late medieval Coptic popes, a saintly monk who, as patriarch, organized major charitable operations, cultivated good relations with the Mamluk Sultan al-Zahir Barquq (1381–1399), and strove to serve and stabilize a Coptic community that had been declining in numbers and influence. His patriarchate was also marked by a wave of voluntary martyrdoms that began in 1380 and that claimed, in all, 49 lives. As a figure in the history of **Copto-Arabic literature**, Matthew is remembered for a number of sermons that have been preserved in manuscript form, and more so for the panegyric sermon and "Life" that were composed shortly after his death. The "Life" was incorporated into the *History of the Patriarchs*, where it provides that compilation's only extensive biography for a patriarch of the Mamluk period. Furthermore, as patriarch, Matthew was surrounded by several remarkable saints: the monks Marqus al-Antuni and Ibrahim al-Fani of the **Monastery of St. Antony** and the urban ascetic Anba Ruways. Their "Lives" have also been preserved and, together with that of Matthew, provide a vivid picture of the Coptic community in often difficult times.

MATTHEW THE POOR. *See* MATTA AL-MISKIN.

MAUNDY THURSDAY. The hymn of Judas is sung in Greek in the **Matins** of the Maundy Thursday; according to Baumstark, this hymn may be dated to the sixth or seventh century. A manuscript from the John Rylands Library in Manchester contains a Prayer for the Basin "without sprinkling the lentils" (the interpretation of this phrase is difficult). According to the text, this prayer is taken from "The Book of Joseph," presumably either the owner of the book from which it was copied or the author of some **liturgical** work.

This prayer seems to be an ancient prayer addressed to God the Father through the Son, because the prayers addressed directly to the Son appeared only in the sixth century and hence this prayer is older than those addressed directly to the Son. The words of this prayer are not in pure Sahidic dialect but most likely belong to a local tradition. The words "without sprinkling the lentils" assumes that there was a local tradition at a precise time to sprinkle the lentils.

Ibn Kabar in the 14th century gives this description in his encyclopedia, *The Lamp of Darkness for the Explanation of the Service*:

> For the Matins a chapter from the Law of Moses is read and after that To You Is the Glory is sung. The sanctuary that is clothed by a black veil is opened. The **priest** says the Thanksgiving prayer and raises up **incense.** Psalm 50 is read and the priest offers incenses towards the congregation without the liturgical kiss of peace and he prays the litanies for the Offerings and for the Sacrifice, after which a chapter from the Acts of the Apostles is read with a special tune, and the prophecy of Isaiah is read in the tune called the Great **Trisagion** after the Praxis. The Psalm is chanted in Idribi, which is the tune of burial and the gospel is read in sorrowful tunes. Prayers conclude usually with a sermon and the commentary followed by the Litanies and Kyrie Eleison.
>
> [His description does not differ from the actual practice.]
>
> The prayers of Terce, Sext, and None are performed, then the basin is filled with water. When the priests are assembled around it, they begin praying the **Prayer of Thanksgiving** followed by Psalm 50,

after which readings from Genesis 18:1–23, Exodus 14:15, Joshua 1:3, Isaiah 4:1–4, Ezekial 36:25–28, Ezekial 47:1–9 are read. [Note that the actual rite contains additional readings from Proverbs 9:1–11, Isaiah 55:1–13, and Exodus 36:25–28, in addition to a sermon. [Actually the readings are double those of the 14th century.]

The Pauline Epistle of I Timothy 4:9–16 and 5:1–10 is read. Then Agios is sung followed by the Prayer for the Gospel. The gospel psalm begins with, "Take hyssop and sprinkle me, that I may be clean . . ." The gospel reading is from John 13:1–17. The gospel is sung with the annual tune and when the reader arrives at the words, "He tied the towel around Him. Then he poured water into basin," the priest ties a towel around himself and pours water in the basin in the shape of the cross thrice. And after the interpretation (the reading of the text in Arabic); the priest raises the cross and the congregation chants Kyrie Eleison ten times with the great tune.

The seven litanies and the sixteen supplications concerning the basin are then prayed:

1. Who girded Himself with a towel.
2. Who by His love for mankind.
3. Who prepared for us the way of life.
4. Christ our God.
5. Who bears light like a garment.
6. Misere nobis; Domine, secundum magnam misericordiam tuam.
7. Lord our God the almighty.
8. Who gathered water.
9. Who put the waters in His hand and the sky in His palm.
10. For the sources to become rivers.
11. And also who truly gives.
12. Irrigate the harvest and make their fruits plentiful.
13. Give joy to the face of the Earth.
14. Let the Land of Egypt rejoice.
15. Rescue Your people.
16. Give security to the king.

After each supplication the congregation recite "Lord have mercy." The priest then concludes the supplication and the congregation chants Kyrie Eleison one hundred times.

The three long prayers are then said: the Prayer for Peace, for the Fathers, and for the congregations, followed by the Creed. The priest says: "The Lord be with you" and makes the sign the cross on the water. The priest begins with saying "Right and worthy" three times,

followed by a prayer which begins with "Lord God our Saviour."
The deacon responds: "You seated stand up" and the priest continues
in prayer. When the deacon says: "Look towards the East," And the
congregation chants: "*Agios agios.*" And the priest prays a prayer this
is followed by, "Our Father" and the priest say the Absolution of the
Son. The deacon says: "*meta foboy*" (which means "With the fear
. . ."), and the priest blesses the water with the cross, saying, "One is
the Holy Father . . ." followed by Psalm 150 according to the tradition.
The priest washes the feet and the hands of the people individually
and greets them, saying, "Let God make you live." The congregation
sing the six stanza hymn which begins with "Our Saviour put down
his clothes" in the annual Batos tune. They are sung with the tune of
the *lobsh* of the **Theotokia** of Thursday, which is, "The One from the
Trinity," and they are chanted with a melody of sadness because this
day is the commemoration of the New Passover and the future joy, that
resulted in the washing of our sins and the humiliation of the Lord of
glory for the salvation of mankind.

The priest then prays the **Prayer of Thanksgiving** on the basin, that
begins with, "Lord God the Almighty," and when the deacon says,
"Let us pray," the priest concludes the prayer. The clergy enters to the
sanctuary for the *Prothesis* of the *qorban.*

The washing of the feet ritual takes place before the offertory is
done, to symbolise that our Lord first washed the feet of His disciples,
and then He broke the bread, blessed it, and gave it to His disciples
before consecrating the same with the chalice. This ritual is done in
accordance with the holy words of the Gospels. In fact, the Gospels
of Matthew, Mark, and Luke did not mention the foot washing but
only the breaking of the bread and the giving out of the chalice. John
mentioned the foot washing without mentioning either the bread nor
the chalice but noted that the Lord, having washed their feet, returned
back to [the] table. And hence, . . .

For the *proemium* [prelude] of the liturgy, they read the Pauline
epistle with both the annual and sadness tunes. There are some people
who read all the texts according to the annual tune and others according to the melody of sadness. Neither the Catholicon nor the Praxis are
read. It is mentioned that they were read formerly, however, a manuscript of the Passover, which contains a lesson of the Catholicon from
the Epistle of Peter 3 (This assumes that in the 14th century this lesson
was not observed) begins with, "What credit is there in fortitude when
you have done wrong and are beaten for it," and ends with, "But now
you have turned towards the Shepherd and Guardian of your souls." I

Peter 2:20–25. The Praxis is read during the matins, with the addition of, "He was counted with the twelve." The majority of the churches read only the Pauline epistle.

The Trisagion is sung, followed by the psalm and gospel according to the annual tune. The gospel is from section 32 of Matthew. [According to the editor of the text of Ibn Kabar, this is an error and it should be corrected as the Gospel of John. The gospel chapters differ from what is actually in use.] They do not kiss the Gospel on this day because of the kiss of Judas. They do not say the Prayer of Peace which is the Aspasmos, and there is no mutual kiss between the people, and they do not say the Diptych of the Dead.

When the priest says, "Remember O Lord those who offered these oblations . . ." the congregation responds, "As it was." The priest continues and says, "For this . . ." after which he concludes the liturgy with the Holy Eucharist. They do not read Psalm 150, and there is no dismissal, but rather, a lesson from the prophecy of Isaiah the prophet, followed by a psalm and a reading from the Gospel of John chanted in the melody of sadness.

During the first hour of the night, four lessons of the Paraclet from the Gospel of John are read. These readings are reserved for the priests according to their ranks. For the other hours of the night, they read four lessons from the holy gospel; one from each.

Maqrizi, a Muslim historian from the 15th century, compiled his "Chronicles" from various sources; some of them are Coptic and others are his own observations. The following is what he wrote concerning the Coptic Passover on Maundy Thursday:

Three days before the Passover [the Christians would celebrate] is Maundy Thursday and according to their customs, they would fill a basin and pray on it before washing the feet of all Christians. They pretend that the Christ did so with his disciples on this day in order to teach the humility and he got their oath to be humble towards each other. The common people in Misr [Old Cairo] call this day the Thursday of Lentil, because Christians cook lentil and sometimes the Christians gave to each other and to the Muslims a variety of fish with lentil soup, but this custom has been abolished.

MAWHUB IBN MANSUR IBN MUFARRIJ (ca. 1025–ca. 1100). Historian. Mawhub ibn Mansur ibn Mufarrij was a wealthy and well-connected Coptic notable of **Alexandria** who played a significant role in the life of the Church in his days. His father had once played a heroic role in saving a precious relic, the head of St. Mark, from confiscation; the governor of Alexandria entrusted Mawhub and his uncle with the key to the Church of St. George at a time when all the other churches of Alexandria had been closed; and he made a major contribution to the expenses of the impoverished **patriarchate** after Pope **Christodoulos** had been kidnapped, tortured, and held for ransom by the Lawati Berbers.

For Copto-Arabic studies, Mawhub (and not **Sawirus ibn al-Muqaffa'**, thanks to the research of Johannes den Heijer; see the bibliography) is now recognized as the "general editor" of the Arabic-language *History of the Patriarchs*, and therefore the first major Arabophone historian of the Coptic Church. Mawhub and his collaborators, primarily the deacon Abu Habib Mikha'il ibn Badir al-Damanhuri, gathered Coptic-language sources for the history of the Egyptian Church, and then translated and edited these materials together as the "Lives" of the first 65 patriarchs. This work, begun in 1088, was completed a few years later. Mawhub then added original Arabic-language biographies for the two patriarchs of whom he was a contemporary, Christodoulos (66th, 1047–1077) and **Cyril II** (67th, 1077–1092); these are precious historical sources that reflect a profound awareness of (and involvement in) internal Church politics and the complexities of the Church's engagement with contested and changing Islamic authority. Mawhub's project of creating an Arabic-language history of the Coptic Orthodox Church was roughly contemporary with the creation of other Arabic-language ecclesiastical resources, such as collections of canon law or the **Christological** compilation known as *The Confession of the Fathers*. Together, the development of these resources may be seen as a pivotal point in the history of the Coptic Orthodox Church; henceforth, the most important contributions to the literature of the Coptic Church would be in Arabic.

MELCHIZEDEK (NHC IX, 1). A Sethian **Gnostic** apocalypse written in the name of Melchizedek, "**Priest** of God Most High" (see Gen. 14:18). Its title occurs at the beginning. Codex IX is quite fragmentary; much of the text is lost in lacunae. The text reflects influence from early Jewish lore concerning Melchizedek, but also features

Jesus Christ, with whom Melchizedek is ultimately identified. It also includes cultic invocations of various divine beings of **Sethian** Gnostic mythology. Extant only in Coptic, Melchizedek was originally composed in Greek, probably in third-century Egypt.

MELITIAN SCHISM. Melitius was the **Bishop** of Lycopolis (Assiut) during the **patriarchate** of **Peter, the Seal of Martyrs** (300–311). He opposed the patriarch of **Alexandria** on two issues. The first was the admission of the *Lapsi* (those who under torture deny Christ), and the second issue was the authority of the bishops to consecrate other bishops. Melitius consecrated many bishops during the persecution era. Regarding the first issue, Melitius adopted the rigorist point of view of the Donatists in North Africa and the Novatianists in Rome. Melitius was exiled during the persecution and upon his return organized a schismatic church. In 325, **Alexander**, the Bishop of Alexandria (313–328), submitted this affair to the **Council of Nicaea**. The council decided on the sixth canon, referring to ancient custom, that the Bishop of Alexandria has authority over all the bishops of Egypt, Libya, and Pentapolis. The council approved the bishops ordained by Melitius. Papyri attest the activity of the Melitians in the fourth century among the monks. According to Ugo Zanetti, the Saracote monks mentioned in the life of John of **Scetis** in the seventh century could be Melitians. This sect disappeared in the eighth century.

MELITIUS. *See* MELITIAN SCHISM.

MENAS, ST. *See* ABU MINA.

MIDDLE EAST COUNCIL OF CHURCHES (MECC). It was established in 1974 and the first General Assembly took place in Nicosia, Cypress, in May 1974. At the beginning it consisted of the Eastern Orthodox churches, the Oriental Orthodox churches, and the Protestant churches. In 1990, the seven Catholic churches of the region joined the council. The churches are represented by 94 members, who meet every four years. The council has offices in Amman, Beirut, Cairo, and Limassol. An elected executive committee with a general secretary is responsible for the administration of the council during each interim period. In 2003, Guirgis Saleh, a Coptic theologian and professor, was elected general secretary.

MIKHA'IL, BISHOP OF ATRIB AND MALIJ (13th c.). Bishop, theologian. We know little about the life and career of Mikha'il apart from the fact that, in the mid-1240s and before his consecration as bishop, he wrote a series of 12 treatises explaining Christian beliefs and practices to Muslim questioners. He is best known, however, for the connection of his name with two important works: the Copto-Arabic **Synaxarion** (*al-Sinaksar*) and a handbook of penitential discipline—"a fine product of a pastoral mind," according to Cöln ("Nomocanonical Literature," 128)—that has circulated under the title *Kitab al-Tibb al-ruhani* (The Book of Spiritual Medicine). Mikha'il's name is found in a number of Arabic manuscripts of the Synaxarion, and its Ethiopic translation goes so far as to specify that Mikha'll compiled it in 1246–1247. As for *The Book of Spiritual Medicine*, it is again an Ethiopic translation (*Mashafa faws manfasawi*, made before 1620) that provides the strongest attribution of the work to Mikha'il. Although much more research is necessary to illuminate the processes by which these compilations came into existence and Mikha'il's role in them, both the Synaxarion and *The Book of Spiritual Medicine* serve to illustrate the importance of Copto-Arabic works in the transmission of the Christian tradition to Ethiopia. Greek to Coptic to Arabic to Ethiopic was the course taken by many hagiographical, ascetic, and canonical texts as they made their way up the Nile.

MIKHA'IL, METROPOLITAN OF DAMIETTA (?–after 1208). Bishop, theologian. Mikha'il, an active defender of the Coptic Orthodox faith in the late 12th and early 13th centuries, was the first Coptic bishop to receive the title "metropolitan" (Arabic: *mutran*). His best known works include a collection of canon law that, while of great merit, was soon overshadowed by that of **al-Safi ibn al-'Assal**, and works of controversy (such as his *Usages That Distinguish the Orthodox Copts*) occasioned especially by the activities of a convert to the Melchite church, the popular preacher **Marqus ibn al-Qunbar**. Against Marqus' insistence on the necessity of auricular confession of sins to a spiritual master, Mikha'il defended the practice—fairly recent in the Coptic Church of his day—of confession to God alone. Other Coptic particularities that Mikha'il defended included circumcision, the **marriage** of first cousins, and making the sign of the cross with one finger (representing Christ's one nature) from left to right (indicating the believer's hope of joining the sheep at Christ's right hand rather than the goats at his left; Matt. 25:31–33). The distinction between this and the Melchites' two-fingered right-to-left crossing could not have been clearer.

MINA, TOGO (1906–1949). Egyptian Coptologist. He was born in Assiut in Upper Egypt. He obtained a diploma of Egyptology from Cairo University in 1929. Between 1930 and 1934 he studied at the École Pratique, École du Louvre, and Institut Catholique in France. His dissertation "Le martyr d'Apa Epima" was published in Cairo in 1937. He was appointed assistant to **Marcus Simaika** in the **Coptic Museum** in 1934. After the death of the latter in 1944, he became the museum's director. Mina excavated in **Abu Mina** and in west Thebes. In 1942, he published his important contribution "Inscriptions coptes et grecques de Nubie" in Cairo. He started the process of acquiring the **Nag Hammadi Codices** for the Coptic Museum before his death.

MO'ALLAQA. The Church of the Holy Virgin is known as al-Mo'allaqa, "the Suspended One," because it was built upon the south gate of the Babylon fortress in Old Cairo. It is the most famous ancient church in Cairo. The church was erected after the **Arab conquest of Egypt** (640–642). We know from the biography of **Patriarch** Joseph (Yusab I, 830–849) that the governor of Egypt ordered the demolition of its upper section down to the columns. From the 11th to the beginning of the 14th century, the Coptic patriarchs resided in Old Cairo at al-Mo'allaqa or at the Church of Abu Sayfayn. During that period, many patriarchs were elected, consecrated, or enthroned at al-Mo'allaqa, and the holy **chrism** (sacred oil) was consecrated several time there. A number of synods were held there as well. Abu al-Barakat **ibn Kabar**, a celebrated Coptic scholar, was a **priest** at that church.

The church has been restored several times over the centuries. Al-Mo'allaqa is also significant for its artistic heritage, such as magnificent medieval wooden altar screens that are decorated with fine geometric designs and inlaid with small pieces of ebony and ivory, a beautiful 13th- or 14th-century **wall painting** of the Nativity, a

14th-century **icon** of St. **Mark**, and many other 18th- and 19th-century icons. A number of Coptic artifacts were transferred from al-Moʻallaqa to the British Museum and the **Coptic Museum**.

MOFTAH, RAGHEB (1898–2001). Musicologist, educator. He was born to a wealthy Coptic family on 21 December 1898 at Al-Faggala in Cairo. In 1991, he was sent to Germany to study agriculture at the University of Bonn, but his great passion was **music**. After his earning a bachelor's degree in agronomics, he obtained degrees in music at Bonn and in Catholic Southern Germany at the University of Munich. Muftah's most important achievement is the recording of the entire corpus of Coptic **liturgical** music, including the hymns and chants for the celebration of the Great Lent, the Pascha or **Holy Week** through the chants of Bright Saturday to the magnificent Resurrection chants. Moftah found a willing companion in the traditionalist Coptic music teacher Muʻalim Mikhail Girgis al-Batanouny, who worked with him from 1907 to 1957. From 1927 to 1936 Moftah collaborated with Oxford-trained musicologist Ernest Newland Smith, who used a Nile houseboat while investigating the structure and notation of Coptic music. They produced 16 volumes of musical notation that could be read by any trained musician. They lectured on Coptic liturgical music at Oxford, Cambridge, and London universities in 1931. In 1940, Moftah founded the first Coptic choir, and five years later he established two centers in Old Cairo and Bab al-Hadid (now Ramses Square) to teach Coptic liturgical chants and hymns. He was one of the founders of the **Higher Institute of Coptic Studies**, and established the Music Division in 1954. In 1970, Muftah entrusted the Hungarian ethnomusicologist Margit Toth to transcribe the notation of the Coptic Orthodox Liturgy of St. Basil that he recorded. This colossal project took 30 years and the work was published by the American University in Cairo Press in 1998. The Library of the Congress, the American University, and the Higher Institute of Coptic Studies possess archives preserving Moftah's collections of recordings, documents, writings, and letters.

MONARCHIANISM. In the dogmatic controversies during the early centuries of Christianity, some heretics denied the distinction of the Father, the Son, and the **Holy Spirit** in the Trinity. Modalists denied any differences and they took their model from the monarchy in the Roman Empire, being singular. The other group of Monarchians, "the Adoptionists," claimed that Jesus was a mere man born of a virgin according to the counsel of the Father. After he had lived a life common to all men and had become preeminently religious, he received at His baptism "the Christ" in the form of a dove. This gift enabled Him to manifest miraculous powers, which He had not shown before, and after His death He was "adopted" into the Godhead. Jesus was therefore entirely human, though controlled by the Spirit. He was to be revered as the greatest of all the prophets, but whether He was to be worshiped "as God" was questionable. The Fathers of the Church such as Hippolytus of Rome, Tertullian, and Epiphanius of Salamis combated both heresies.

MONASTERY OF AL-BARAMOUS. It is the northernmost of the monasteries in **Wadi al-Natrun**. It occupies the place where the oldest **monastic** community in Wadi al-Natrun stood. The Arabic name Baramous is a transliteration of the Coptic *Pa-Romeos*, "that of the Romans," referring probably to the two Roman **saints** and children of the Roman Emperor Valentinian I (364–357), Maximus and Domitius, whom St. **Macarius** received and consecrated their cell by building a chapel after their death. The monastery is significant for its oldest church in Wadi al-Natrun that originates from the late sixth century or the beginning of the seventh century. It is dedicated to the Virgin Mary. Its nave features scenes of the Great **Feasts**: the Annunciation, the Visitation, the Nativity, the Baptism of Christ, and the Entry into Jerusalem, as well as the Pentecost. The sanctuary is decorated with the scenes of the sacrifice of Isaac and the meeting of Abraham and **Melchizedek**. They date to about 1200. The sanctuary's apse is occupied by Christ enthroned in the upper register, and below is the Holy Virgin flanked by two angels. There is a feretory against the north wall of the *khurus* that contains the relics of Sts. Maximus and Domitius. The monastery's keep is the oldest extant keep in Wadi al-Natrun and probably dates from the ninth century. *See also* MONASTICISM, EGYPTIAN.

MONASTERY OF ST. ANTONY. It is located at the foot of the Wadi Araba near the Red Sea. The monastery is named after the famous figure of **monasticism**, St. **Antony**. Probably in the second half of the fourth century a monastic community gathered around the site where the **saint** lived. Historian Sulpicius Severus (ca. 360–420) reported the existence of the monastery. In 407, St. **John the Little** fled from **Wadi al-Natrun** to the Monastery of St. Antony because of the attack of nomads. At the beginning of the 13th century, Church historian **Abu al-Makarim/Abu Salih** stated that the monastery was fortified and that the cells of the monks looked onto a garden. Many European travelers visited the monastery, he reported, noting that Syrians, Ethiopians, Franciscans, and Armenians lived there in medieval times. It was abandoned and pillaged in the time of **Patriarch** John XIII (1484–1524) and repopulated under Patriarch Gabriel VII (1525–1568). Most of the patriarchs of the 17th, 18th, and 19th centuries were chosen from among its monks. The monastery's library is comprised of some 1,863 manuscripts that are of great value for the study of the **Copto-Arabic literature**.

An old church is the most significant building in the monastery. One of its wall paintings represents Christ flanked by the busts of the Apostles and dates from the seventh century. The church boasts the most complete program of wall paintings that has been preserved in Egypt. It dates to 1232 or 1233 and is the last important artistic achievements of the Copts before the waves of persecution under Mamluk rule. The murals represent scenes from the Old and the New Testaments, such as the sacrifice of Abraham; the meeting of Abraham and **Melchizedek**; the three Patriarchs Abraham, Isaac, and Jacob; the sacrifice of Jephtah; Pantocrator surrounded by angels and cherubim; the Four Living Creatures; the Twenty-four Elders of the Apocalypse; the Virgin and Child; and women at the tomb. Many equestrian saints, such as Sts. Theodore the Stratelate and Mercurius, and some of the great figures of monasticism—including Antony, **Paul, Pachomius, Shenute, and Macarius**—are also depicted. The portraits of St. **Mark** the Evangelist and St. **Athanasius**, Patriarch of **Alexandria**, dominate the two lateral sanctuaries.

MONASTERY OF ST. APOLLO AT BAWIT. The archaeological site of Bawit is located about 300 kilometers south of Cairo on the west bank of the Nile. In the late 19th century and early 20th century, the site was known to dealers in antiquities as a source of monuments and beautiful artifacts. Between 1901 and 1904 and again in 1913, archaeologists explored only a small part of the site, identifying two constructions that were called the North and South Churches. In addition, several small buildings were found scattered over the site. The monastery flourished from the sixth to the 10th century. The Monastery of Bawit consisted of many small monasteries with cells and a little church along with several other building complexes that were encircled by an enclosure wall. The majority of scholars agree that the large monastic community in Bawit was led by St. Apollo, who was mentioned in the *Historia monachorum in Aegypto* as a man who was more than 80 years old around 395 A.D. The architectural sculptures of some of the Bawit structures, such as engaged columns and the capitals, friezes, door jambs, and lintels, were brought from older buildings. However, the reuse of beautifully carved pieces cannot be shown to account for all the Bawit sculptures. A considerable number of the Bawit sculptures date from the sixth and the seventh centuries. The excavations yielded a large number of murals that represent one of the largest collections of Coptic paintings. The most common scenes show Christ and the Virgin Mary. They feature the Annunciation, Visitation, Nativity, the Massacre of the Innocents, Christ's Baptism, and the Last Supper, as well as Christ in the Majesty and Virgin and Child flanked by Apostles. Angels, Apostles, and **saints** occur in the murals. Old Testament scenes such as the three Hebrews in the fiery furnace and David's exploits are also represented there. Secular themes such as hunting lions or gazelles do not lack at Bawit. Dating of the wall paintings is based only on a stylistic analysis; they are assigned by scholars to the period between the sixth and the eighth centuries. The monuments of the Monastery of St. Apollo are now preserved in the **Coptic Museum**, the Louvre in Paris, and in the Museum of Late Antique and Byzantine Art of Berlin. They represent a major source for the study of **Coptic art**. Beginning in 2003, a joint mission of the Louvre and the French Archaeological Institute in Cairo started new excavations at Bawit. *See also* MONASTICISM, EGYPTIAN.

MONASTERY OF ST. HATRE AT ASWAN. It is situated on the west bank of the Nile facing the Island of Elephantine. The monastery is named after its patron, St. Hatre, who was the **Bishop** of

Aswan in the late fourth century. Later it was given the name of St. Simeon by archaeologists and travelers. It is not known when the monastery was established. However, the earliest wall paintings in the grotto representing **saints** are from the sixth or seventh century. The remaining church was built in the first half of the 11th century. Its construction provides the most significant example of the domed oblong church in Egypt. The church's paintings were executed probably in the 11th or the 12th century. The eastern semidome of the sanctuary is decorated with a scene of Christ in the *mandorla* (an oval enclosing a scene or painting) that is held by two angels. There are the remains of a scene of the 24 **priests** (elders) on the sanctuary's north wall. The monastery's upper terrace serves as a keep or a tower that consists of three stories and comprises the monks' cells, the refectory, the kitchen, and other facilities. It is the largest keeplike lodging complex in Egypt. There is a room containing a reservoir that is a part of a water supply system including bathrooms, latrines, and laundering facilities. About 200 tombstones were discovered in the monastery's cemetery, which provide important material for the study of Christian tombstones in Egypt and **Nubia**. The monastery ceased to be occupied by monks around the end of the 13th century. *See also* MONASTICISM, EGYPTIAN.

MONASTERY OF ST. JEREMIAH. It is situated at Saqqara, the necropolis of ancient Memphis. It was founded probably in the early sixth century, flourished in the seventh and eighth centuries, and was abandoned around the middle of the ninth century. Excavated in 1906, 1910, and the 1970s, it represents one of the few communal monasteries that has been archaeologically investigated. The monastery included churches, one or more refectories, facilities for baking bread, a kitchen, workshops, a wine press, storerooms, and other buildings, the functions of which remains obscure. The main church was built in the second half of the seventh century. The monks lived in cells with oratories that feature niches in their eastern walls. Some of the niches were decorated with paintings of Christ enthroned and the Virgin Mary with the Christ Child on her lap, flanked by archangels or holy men. A few biblical themes such as the sacrifice of Abraham have been preserved on the north wall of the refectory. The sixth- or seventh-century pulpit that was discovered in the monastery is the only freestanding example in stone to have survived virtually intact. The excavations also yielded many fascinating architectural sculptures, such as lintels, friezes, niches, and column capitals, of which a considerable number had been taken from late Roman sepulchral buildings. The majority of the sculptures and paintings that have been preserved are exhibited in the **Coptic Museum**. *See also* MONASTICISM, EGYPTIAN.

MONASTERY OF ST. MACARIUS. It is the southernmost monastery in **Wadi al-Natrun**. The monastery bears the name of its patron St. **Macarius**, who died in about 390. This monastery became an official occasional residence for the Coptic **patriarchs** toward the middle of the sixth century when the Byzantine authorities did not allow them to reside in **Alexandria**. Thirty patriarchs were chosen from among the monks of the Monastery of St. Macarius, and many patriarchs consecrated the **chrism** there. Epiphanius of Jerusalem (ca. 800) speaks of "a thousand cells" dominated by a fortress at the site of the monastery. The old church of St. Macarius was dedicated in later times to St. John the Baptist and Patriarch Benjamin I (626–665). Its 12th-century paintings feature interesting scenes from the Old and New Testaments: Moses and Aaron, the sacrifice of Abraham, the meeting of Abraham and **Melchizedek**, the purification of Isaiah, Jacob's dream, Job, the three Hebrews, John the Baptist holding a medallion containing "the lamb," the Annunciation to Zachariah, the Annunciation, the Nativity, Christ and Nathanael, Christ flanked by the Apostles and evangelists, the Resurrection, the Ascension, the Twenty-four Elders of the Apocalypse, and many **saints** as well. The monastery's keep or tower is one of the best preserved of its kind in Egypt. It dates from the 13th century and contains a number of chapels and a church. Some of the chapels are decorated with the figures of famous Coptic saints such as Sts. **Antony**, **Paul of Thebes**, and **Pachomius**. By the middle of the 14th century, the monastery began to decline because of the Black Death, the Mamluk persecution, and the impoverishment of the Coptic Church. The monastery's library possessed valuable manuscripts for the **Coptic literature** and **liturgy**, of which the vast majority were removed to Europe. Beginning in 1969 the monastery witnessed a "renaissance" when Father **Matta**

al-Miskin and his disciples started to revive monastic life there. *See also* MONASTICISM, EGYPTIAN.

MONASTERY OF ST. PAUL. It is located about 39 kilometers southwest of the Red Sea lighthouse station of Za'farana. St. Paul, who is known as the "first hermit," is presumably **Paul of Thebes**, whose biography was composed by St. **Jerome**, probably in 375 or 376. The cave church is the oldest and most venerated element of the monastery where St. Paul lived, and was first mentioned in 401 by Sulpicius Severus. An anonymous pilgrim from Placentia visited the "cave of the blessed Paul" in 570. **Abu al-Makarim/Abu Salih** (13th century) reported that monks came from the **Monastery of St. Antony** to celebrate the **liturgy** in the Monastery of St. Paul by turns. Beginning in the 14th century, a number of European travelers reported on the monastery, such as Ogier de St. Chéron and Signeur d'Anglure, who found 60 monks there in 1395. The monastery was abandoned and sacked by the Bedouins during the patriarchate of John XIII (1484–1524). **Patriarch** Gabriel VII (1525–1563) repopulated the monastery, but the Bedouins sacked it again during his lifetime. The monastery remained in ruins and uninhabited probably for more than a century. Beginning in the patriarchate of Patriarch John XVI (1676–1718) the monastery prospered. It was he who restored and repopulated it. For most of the monastery's history, abbots of the Monastery of St. Antony administrated it. In 1974, Pope **Shenouda III** consecrated **Bishop** Agathon to supervise the monastery.

The architecture and decoration of the cave church are unusual. Its most ancient part is mainly underground and carved into the rock. It consists of the sanctuary of St. Paul and his cenotaph, the sanctuary of St. **Antony**, a corridor, and a central room. The 13th-century paintings depict the enthroned Christ with the Four Living Creatures, the Annunciation, the Massacre of the Innocents, angels, evangelists, **saints**, and monks. Patriarch John XVI (1676–1718) restored the existing cave church and extended it with three domed rooms on its north side. Recent research has shown that Abdel-Sayed al-Mallawani, a monk at the monastery who became Patriarch John XVII (1726–1745), was responsible for the paintings scheme and the inscriptions of the 18th-century new extension. His painting program and the inscriptions in the dome of the martyrs, the central nave, and in the sanctuary of the Twenty-four Elders are based on the **liturgical** book of the **Psalmody**. The 18th-century paintings and inscriptions of this monastery provide evidence for the very beginning of the renaissance of the Coptic Church in many respects. *See also* MONASTICISM, EGYPTIAN.

MONASTERY OF ST. PSHOI (ANBA BISHAY) AT SOHAG. Situated about three kilometers to the north of the **Monastery of St. Shenute** at Sohag. It is known as the Red Monastery owing to the color of its outer walls, which were built of red bricks. Al-Maqrizi (1364–1442) used the two names of the monastery: "Red Monastery also called monastery of Abu Bishai." St. Pshoi was an older companion of St. **Shenute**. It is not known whether St. Pshoi was actually the founder of the monastery or if it was only dedicated to him. The monastery lived in the shadow of the celebrated monastery of St. Shenute. Therefore, information about its history is scarce. A Coptic manuscript dated to A.M. 807 (1091 A.D.) shows that the monastery was inhabited in the 11th century. In 1301, the painter Mercurius inscribed his name in the sanctuary of the church. In 1672, Johann Wansleben visited the monastery and found the church's nave ruined. The Mamluks set fire to the monastery in 1798.

The church of the monastery dates from the late fifth century; the columns in the nave and the surrounding walls are probably a little younger, belonging to the sixth century. It is of a Basilican type with a triconch sanctuary and a long narrow hall along the south wall (The term *triconch* in architecture refers to a square, circular, or oblong room expanded on three sides by semicircular rooms.). Beautifully sculptured friezes decorate the northern and southern entrances. The architectural sculptures of the sanctuary are the most significant as they belong to the church's original structure. The walls are decorated with columns in two rows and between the columns are niches. The walls are painted and the colors enhance the effect of the architectural sculptures, adding an imitation of stone patterns or decorative designs. A project to clean and preserve the monastery's murals was initiated in 2002. The eastern semidome depicts the enthroned Christ with the Four Living Creatures, flanked by archangels. The northern semidome shows a monumental enthroned nursing Virgin Mary flanked by angels and the four prophets Ezekiel, Jeremiah, Isaiah, and Daniel with their open scrolls. Their texts make reference to the miracle of the Virgin birth. This unique scene can be dated to the late seventh or early eighth century. The southern semidome features the enthroned Christ flanked by John the Baptist and his father Zacharias, angels, evangelists, and **patriarchs**. After the completion of the conservation of the church's murals, this monastery will be one of the most beautiful ancient monasteries of the world. *See also* MONASTICISM, EGYPTIAN.

MONASTERY OF ST. PSHOI AT WADI AL-NATRUN. It is one of the four original monasteries of **Wadi al-Natrun**. St. Pshoi was one of the early settlers in **Scetis**; he lived mainly in the fourth century and died in the first decades of the fifth century. When in 407 the tribes of the Libyan Desert attacked Scetis, St. Pshoi fled to Antinopolis in Upper Egypt where he died. We are told that his body was transferred to his monastery at Wadi al-Natrun. Pope **Shenouda III** spends two or three days a week in this monastery. Therefore, it attracts thousands of Copts who visit Wadi al-Natrun. The tower, which dates to the 13th century, is the most significant building in the monastery. On its second floor there is a church dedicated to St. Michael. Some parts of the monastery's main church, which is dedicated to St. Pshoi, might have been erected before the ninth century. **Patriarch** Benjamin II (1327–1339) restored the monastery. Remains of wall paintings can be traced in the "Chapel of Benjamin." They date from the 12th century and depict three of the Twenty-four Elders of the Apocalypse, the three Hebrews in the fiery furnace, and some **saints**. A church of St. Iskhyrun was added, probably in the 11th century. The monastery possesses three refectories and a bakery. Its millhouse represents the most complete example of its kind in Wadi al-Natrun. *See also* MONASTICISM, EGYPTIAN.

MONASTERY OF ST. SHENUTE AT SOHAG. It is known as the "White Monastery" and is located about eight kilometers to the west of Sohag. The monastery was founded by St. Shenute's uncle, Pjol. After his uncle's death in 385, **Shenute** became the monastery's abbot. The monastery grew considerably under Shenute and became a significant religious center with many acts of philanthropy. It continued to be in use probably as late as the 14th century.

By the 15th century, the monastery was ruined and nothing remained except the church, which is the most significant Christian building to have survived in Upper Egypt. The nave is separated from its two side aisles by two rows of columns. The remaining steps of the oldest stone *ambon* (pulpit) in Egypt stand at the north aisle. The church's exterior resembles a pharaonic temple built of limestone blocks of a considerable size. The façade of the blocklike structure features a slight batter, topped with a cavetto cornice and provided with waterspouts. But the architectural sculpture of the interior derives from Hellenistic and Roman sources. It is comprised of approximately 40 beautifully decorated niches with semicolumns (or pilasters), capitals, and gables. The structure of the sanctuary is a *triconch*, flanked at the north by a staircase and at the south by an octagonal chamber with a baptismal basin. It features profusely ornamented entablatures. A considerable part of the church's splendid architectural sculptures were executed in the middle of the fifth century. The semidomes of the *triconch* sanctuary are ornamented with murals that date from the 11th or the 12th century. They show the enthroned Christ with a shell motif over his head and cross-flanked by the Virgin Mary and John the Baptist (*Deesis*). *See also* MONASTICISM, EGYPTIAN.

MONASTERY OF THE ARCHANGEL GABRIEL AT NAQLUN. It is situated about 15 kilometers southwest of the city of al-Fayyum. Church historian **Abu al-Makarim/Abu Salih** (early 13th century) referred to two churches of the Archangels Michael and Gabriel there. In 1672, Johann Wansleben found the monastery completely ruined except for the Church of the Archangel Michael, which he admired because of its paintings. The church was probably built in the ninth century and designed as a basilica with three aisles. Its eastern part features a *khurus*, main apse, and two lateral sanctuaries. The limestone Corinthian capitals of its columns were taken from older monuments.

In the 1990s, its wall paintings were conserved, and superimposed layers of wall paintings were discovered. The Coptic foundation text indicates that the church was renovated and decorated with murals during the reign of **Patriarch** Zacharias (1004–1032). Some of the wall paintings are unique, such as St. Peter standing in the apse among the Apostles and wearing the **bishop's** garb and a monk's cap. The text identifies him as Archbishop Petros, which shows that he represents both the Apostle and the martyr patriarch of **Alexandria**. In the narthex, the Virgin is depicted between the Archangels Gabriel and Michael, while unusually two doves appear behind her throne. Eighty-nine hermitages scattered in the valleys of Gabal al-Naqlun are cut in the rocky hills. Some of them were inhabited by hermits as early as the fifth century and continued to be in use until the 12th century. The texts, pottery, textiles, and murals discovered in Naqlun provide invaluable material for the study of **monasticism** over almost 1,000 years.

MONASTERY OF THE SYRIANS. Built in the sixth century in **Wadi al-Natrun** as a result of a schism caused by Theodosian monks, who left the neighboring **Monastery of St. Pshoi**. By the second half of the ninth century, the monastery was simultaneously inhabited both by Syrian monks and Coptic monks. One of its most important abbots was Moses of Nisibis (ca. 907–943), who originated from North Syria. He brought 250 Syriac manuscripts from Mesopotamia and North Syria to the monastery in 932. He constructed the wooden doors of the sanctuary of the Church of the Holy Virgin Mary and very probably the entire sanctuary, which is decorated with stucco ornaments that are reminiscent of the earlier decoration of Samara. The *khurus* of this church is the oldest of its kind in Egypt.

Beginning in 1991 several segments of wall paintings layered on top of each other were uncovered there, together with Coptic and Syriac inscriptions. These murals range in date from the 7th or 8th century to the 13th century. The majority represents scenes from the Old and the New Testaments, Apostles, **saints**, **patriarchs**, and **bishops**. Some of them provide very interesting iconographies that do not occur frequently in Egypt, such as the scene of the Annunciation with the Prophets Isaiah, Ezekiel, Moses, and Daniel flanking the Virgin and the Angel Gabriel; the scene of Abraham, Isaac, and Jacob in Paradise; the scene of Abgar of Edessa holding the *mandylion* (a holy relic of a piece of cloth. It is believed that an image of the face of Jesus was imprinted upon it, perhaps similar to the Shroud of Turin); and the conversion of the eunuch of Candace. A Dormition scene is indeed unique. It shows the Virgin lying in bed surrounded by the 12 Apostles and six women, three on each side, swinging censers. The Coptic text describes these women as "virgins." It is well known, however, that handling of censers is confined to men in the Orthodox churches.

In 1088, there were 60 monks in the monastery. In 1515–1516, 43 monks inhabited the monastery, 18 of whom were Syrians. The new ongoing projects to discover and conserve more significant murals and Syriac manuscripts makes this monastery one of the most important Christian monuments. *See also* MONASTICISM, EGYPTIAN.

MONASTIC AND LITURGICAL VESTMENTS. Many sources show the evolution of the monastic and liturgical vestments, which are attested in Egypt as early as the fourth century. The description of **Evagrius**, **Palladius**, and the **Saying of the fathers** gave the names of some monastic vestments in Lower Egypt. The Middle Egyptian tradition of the period is attested by the life of **Antony** and the **historia monachorum in aegypto**. In the fifth century, the life of **Pachomius** and the life of **Shenoute** provide some illusions to the monastic garment in Upper Egypt. The evolution of the monastic vestment may be witnessed in the homily of Basil of Pemdje on abbot Loginus; the vestment became more simplified, while the panegyric on Apollo shows that there is no change in the tradition of the Middle Egyptian monasticism. From this period survived the first two icons showing monks and bishops, one is the icon of abbot Menas in the Louvre museum and the other is that of Abraham in Berlin Museum. The monastic sites of Bawit and Saqqarah provide us with a large number of wall paintings, wherein monks and bishops are depicted.

From the 10th century survives the body of a monk (Bisada) in the monastery of Qalamun, the monks wear a special turban and robe. From the 12th century to the 14th century, the rite of consecration the monk and that of the patriarch provide the reader with a complete list of the different items. In the 17th century, two Western travellers, Richard Pocock and Johann Wansleben (Vansleb) made description of all the monastic vestments. Pocock also made a drawing of a Coptic priest, which shows clearly that there are minor changes. In the 18th century, the two masters, the icon-writer Ibrahim the scribe and Hanna the Armenian painted many icons depicted monks such as Shenoute, Pachomius, Macarius, Apollo, and Abib. However, the

Century	Lower Egypt	Middle Egypt	Upper Egypt	Remarks
Fourth–fifth	Evagrius (+ 399) and Cassian (+420) *Cuculion* a kind of mantlet with hood. *Lebiton* a linen tunic that is also called *Colobion*. It does not have sleeves *Analobos*: put on the shoulder as cross *The belt.* *Melotes*: a mantle with a goat or sheep skin used while traveling	*Life of Antony* (after 356AD): §46 a linen garment §47 (from hair) §91–92 *Melotes* *History of the monks in Egypt*: (written 394–395): *Lebiton* *Cuculion* over the head. *Melotes* over the shoulder and sometimes used as a bag		Semi-hermitic system
	Lausiac history Of Palladius (420) *melotes, sack* *Apophthegmata Patrum* *Skema:* *Lebiton*: tunic without sleeves *Colobion* *Melotes* (not frequent) belt (rare)			

(continues)

Century	Lower Egypt	Middle Egypt	Upper Egypt	Remarks
fifth			Life of Pachom Two tunics one in linen without sleeves. Melotes Belt Two cuculia A staff and sandals	Cenobetic
Seventh–ninth century	Basil of Pemdje, the Virtues of Saint Longin Mantle or anabolos, dead skin or melotes, hood Life of Hilaria Tunic The skin tunic Belt	Panegyric on Apollo Archmandrite of the monastery of Isaac by Stephen of Heracleopolis Magna Lebiton A skin Cuculion Belt Staff Life of Samuel of Kalamun by Isaac the Presbyter Schema, The skin tunic Cuculion		Semi-hermitic system

Seventh–ninth century Icon and wall painting	Icon of the Abbot Menas in the Louvre (seventh century). Wall painting from Saqqarah and Bawit, the Coptic Museum (three monks).		
Seventh–ninth century		The body of saint Besada (monastery of Saint Samuel Kalamun)	
12th–14th century	Rite of ordination a monk Lebiton *Cuculion* *Belt* And later *the Schema* *and the mantle* Rite of ordination a patriarch *Tunic* *Cuculion* *The schema which* *is bound over* *the shoulder*		

Century	Lower Egypt	Middle Egypt	Upper Egypt	Remarks
	The leather belt over the kidney *The mantle*			
12th–16th centuries	Beam icon in the **Church of Saint Mercurius** (XIII century) Wall painting saint Macarius (XVI century)	Wall paintings **Monastery of Saint Antony** (XIII century)	Wall paintings of the monastery of al-Fakhury	
14th and 15th centuries	Abu al-Barakat Ibn Kabar, the lamp of Darkness			Only commentary
17th and 18th centuries	The Western travelers Wansleb Pockok			
18th century	Icons of Ibrahim al-Nasikh and Yuhanna al-Armani		Icons from Akhmin	

monastic vestments reflect more Greek influence rather than Coptic tradition. The Coptic Clergy wears a black turban (an evolution of the *cuculion*), a black tunic and a mantle with large sleeves.

MONASTICISM, EGYPTIAN. Christian monasticism is a distinctive form of spiritual discipline that seems to have been originated in Egypt. St. **Antony**, the "father of the monks," is usually regarded as its founder. As a youth of about 18 years old, he responded to a gospel reading (Matt. 19; 21), began his hermitic life as a village ascetic, and around 285 he set out for the mountains. By about 313 he had moved to his "inner" mountain at the Red Sea. His seclusion set the standard for an anchoritic way of life that attracted many followers who came to live near his cave. The influential *Life of Antony*, written by Patriarch **Athanasius** shortly after the **saint's** death, was responsible for introducing the monastic ideal and Egyptian monasticism to the West. Another form of monasticism began in about 320 when St. **Pachomius** established the first communal system at Tabennisi in Upper Egypt. This cenobitic, or communal, monastic system is based on precise rules governing almost every aspect of monks' lives. The monks had everything in common, living together in houses, each with a steward assigned special duties. There were set times for prayer, meals, work, mass, and sleep; literacy was obligatory. **Patriarch** Athanasius supported the growing monastic movement and acknowledged its leaders. In 404, St. **Jerome** rendered the Pachomian Rule into Latin. Thus, the rules of Pachomius influenced monasticism in Europe.

Some great figures of early Christianity lived among the monks in the Egyptian deserts; these include St. Basil the Great (ca. 330–379), St. John Cassian (ca. 360–435), St. Caesarius of Arles (ca. 470–542), and St. Benedict of Nursia (ca. 480–ca. 550). After John Cassian visited Egypt, he founded the monasteries of St. Victor for men and St. Salvador for women in Marseilles. The Western monastic tradition—in particular, the order of St. Benedict of Nursia, the "patriarch of Western monasticism"—owes much to Coptic monastic traditions. Monasticism is indeed Egypt's most considerable contribution to Christianity.

During the fourth and the fifth centuries, a form of semianchorism evolved and then spread in Lower Egypt. The desert area along the western edge of the Delta became renowned for the **Desert Fathers** who practiced their ascetic life in **Nitria, Kellia,** and **Wadi al-Natrun (Scetis)**. Many monastic colonies were established in these sites around famous ascetics such as **Amoun, Macarius,** and **John the Little**. Monks lived alone in independent cells, enjoyed an undisturbed meditation during the week, and met on Saturdays and Sundays to participate in the Eucharistic **liturgy** and to take part in a common meal (*agape*). During that time many ascetics had the talent of expressing spiritual truths in anecdotes or memorable sayings, which are known as the "**Sayings of the Fathers,**" or the *Apophthegmata partum*. The Sayings of the Fathers provide significant material for understanding the cultural and social milieu of the monks in Nitria, Kellia, and Wadi al-Natrun. They influenced monastic life both in the East and the West.

Many monasteries and monastic colonies were established along the desert fringes in Upper Egypt. One of the great figures of Egyptian monasticism is St. **Shenute** (d. 464 or 465) whose monastery, known as the **Monastery of St. Shenute** or White Monastery, received thousands of refugees when the Blemmye/Beja tribes attacked inhabitants of Upper Egypt. St. Shenute is regarded as the most significant Coptic writer. The imposing church of his monastery bears witness to a great monastic community that prospered during his time. By the end of the fourth century, the monks rapidly became numerous. **Palladius** speaks of 5,000 monks in Nitria and 600 in Kellia. The *Historia Monachorum* reports 10,000 monks at Oxyrhynchus. St. Jerome reported that 50,000 Pachomian monks attended the annual meeting. Although these numbers may be exaggerated, it is nevertheless certain that the monastic population during the golden age of Egyptian monasticism before the **Arab conquest of Egypt** was quite numerous. Many of the monasteries began to decline and gradually deteriorated, or were even abandoned after the poll tax was imposed in 705 for the first time on the monks.

Monastic buildings represent a considerable part the Christian architectural heritage in Egypt. When anchorites lived in groups of cells without an enclosure wall, such a congregation is called *laura*. Several types of hermitages have been discovered in Kellia, **Naqlun, Abu Mina,** Esna, and elsewhere. Literary sources tell us that Pachomian monks lived together in larger buildings where each monk had his own room. Meals were served in a refectory. Monks practiced their careers before joining the monastery in workshops. The guest-house was located outside the enclosure wall. A further type of mo-nastic dwelling is exemplified by the remains of the eighth-century Monastery of al-Balaiza. A large number of monks inhabited several levels with large sleeping halls. In the **Monastery of St. Jeremiah** at Saqqara, the monks lived in cells supplied with an **oratory**. An en-closure wall protected the monks' cells, churches, one or more refec-tories, a kitchen, a bakery, workshops, a wine press, storerooms, and other buildings. The imposing tower of the **Monastery of St. Hatre at Aswan**, which dates from the 10th and 11th centuries, represents the climax of the development of the towerlike lodging complex in Egypt. It includes cells, a refectory, a kitchen, and other facilities. With the deterioration of security in the ninth century in the region of Wadi al-Natrun, the monasteries there had to be protected by ap-propriate enclosure walls.

Female ascetics were known in Egypt. Some of the Sayings of the Fathers are attributed to the female ascetics Theodora and Sara. Pachomius founded nine monasteries for men and two for **women**. Mary, Pachomius' sister, became the "mother" of a monastery. Sources tell us that there were 2,200 monks and 1,800 nuns under Shenute. The Monastery of St. Jeremiah at Saqqara had regular con-tact with a nunnery.

Monasteries are the major source of **Coptic art**. They provide valuable material for the study of Coptic architectural sculpture. The vast majority of Coptic wall paintings are monastic. Beginning in the 1980s, wonderful monastic paintings have been discovered, es-pecially in the **Monastery of the Syrians** and the **Red Monastery**. The monasteries possessed libraries, and some of them had scriptoria where copyists transcribed manuscripts. Some libraries were exten-sive, such as those of the **Monastery of St. Macarius** and the Mon-astery of the Archangel Michael at Naqlun, or the Monastery of St. Shenute. Monastic libraries preserved Greek, Syriac, Coptic, Ethio-pian, Armenian, Old Nubian, and Arabic manuscripts. They provide evidence for the multiethnic character of Coptic monasteries.

Monasticism is one of the important factors that led to the continu-ity of Christianity in Egypt. Monks played a crucial role in the his-tory of the Coptic Church. The majority of its patriarchs and **bishops** came from the monastic milieu. Many Coptic monks participated in ecumenical councils and were often involved in theological controversies. Coptic monasteries have experienced a strong cultural renewal in the past few decades, and the number of monastic institution is still growing. This is not surprising, for the **structure of the Coptic Church** is based mainly on monks, and thus its future lies to a great extent in the future of the monastic movement.

MONOPHYSITISM. This word is derivate from the Cyrillian statement, "One nature of the incarnated Word of God." It is used to designate those who, in opposition to the two-natures doctrine of Chalcedon, confess the formula of St. **Cyril**, which has been adopted by the Coptic Church: "One Nature for the Word God incarnated." Hence, Christ has one nature, and out of it there is divinity and humanity without mingling, confusion, or alternation—while for the Chalcedonians, Christ is in two natures, divine and human. Some scholars assumed that the schism was mainly for nationalistic reason. However, some others rejected this idea.

The Coptic Church never accepted this title; it prefers the title "Miaphysite." Monophysite means "one nature" and if Christ has one nature, it should only be divine; in the Coptic thinking, Christ has one nature from two natures. The title "Miaphysite" came from the definition of St. Cyril "Mia Physis": "One nature for the incarnated Word of God." The Fathers such as Cyril of **Alexandria, Severus of Antioch, Timothy Aelurus**, and **Theodosius** explained this definition. It is now admitted by Chalcedonian and non-Chalcedonian denominations that the formulation of this dogma is orthodox, according to a pioneer study conducted by **Bishop** Lebon. *See also* CHALCEDON, COUNCIL OF.

MU'AQQUB, AL. Al-Mu'aqqub are hymns sung on Saturday evenings during the month of Kiahk. The last verse of each stanza is repeated as a precursor to the next stanza. The edited **Psalmodia** of Kiahk includes several hymns of Mu'aqqub, one being of Old Cairo, some of which are in Arabic attributed to Abu al-Sa'ad from Abu Tig, Gabriel from Qay, **Patriarch** Mark, and others.

MUHARRAQ. *See* DAYR AL-MUHARRAQ.

MULID. *See* PILGRIMAGE.

MUQAWQAS. *See* ARAB CONQUEST OF EGYPT.

MUSIC. The Coptic Church uses more than one tune. The yearly tune, is used for all days except some feasts, **fasting**, and other occasions. The tune of Joy (*Faraihi*) is used from the first day of Tut, the beginning of the year, until the feast of the Cross, then in the dominical feasts and in the 29th day of every Coptic month, except for the month of Tubah and Amshir. The tune of *Sha'anini* is used for the feast of the cross and the **Palm Sunday**.

The tune of the Month of Kihak or the advent tune is used from the first day of Kihak until the 28 of Kihak. The tune of the Lent (*Siyami*) is used for the fast of Jonah and the lent.

The tune of Sorrow (*Hazaini*) is used during the **Holy week** and for the burial service.

For each category, there are two main subcategories: the melody Batos and Adam tunes. The first is used from Wednesday to Saturday every week and the last is used for the rest of the week. There are three primary traditions, from which Coptic music very likely absorbed elements in varying proportions: the Jewish, the Greek, and the ancient Egyptian. Hans Hickmann maintained that a system of *chironomy* that dates from the Fourth Dynasty (2723–2563 B.C.) is still employed. However, not all scholars have shared this opinion.

As Coptic music is transmitted orally, we are totally depending on the literary texts treating this topic. Clement of Alexandria in the third century had banished the Music that breaks the souls and provokes carnal sentiments. St. Athanasius was for a psalmody closer to speaking rather than singing. In his letter to Marcelinus on the interpretation of Psalm 27, he says: "Some of the simple ones among us . . . think that the psalms are sung melodiously for the sake of good sound and the pleasure of the ears. This is not so."

The attitude of the **Desert fathers** was similar; **Pambo** rebukes his disciple who appreciates the hymns of Alexandria, i. e., canons and *troparia*. Paul of Cappadocia complains that he is not able to sing hymns as is habit.

Apparently, there were two traditions in Egypt, the first is the Cathedral tradition of beautiful melodies, and the monastic tradition that consists of the recitation of Biblical texts, such as the **psalmodia**. In a later stage, these two traditions fused together to form one tradition. It is very hard to determine when this happened because all the manuscripts record only texts and rubrics. No known notation exists designed specifically for Coptic music, though manuscripts bearing ancient Greek notation have been found in Egypt. The music has passed from one person to another, and from one generation to the next by oral teaching and rote learning. Thus, Coptic music has always depended on a continuous oral tradition. According to Hickmann, this music was held as a sacred trust by those who learned it, and indeed, was purposely not transcribed lest it fall into the wrong hands. For the most part, the instruction must have been very strict and rigid, as it is today.

The Coptic Church uses for her rites Coptic, Greek, and recently Arabic and other languages as well. Texts are sung interchangeably in different tongues, the melodies remain essentially intact. Because members of the clergy were not equally talented as singers, it became and has remained the tradition to entrust performance of the music to a professional cantor (Arabic: *'arif,* "one who knows," or *mu'allim,* "teacher"), who is employed and trained by the church to be responsible for the correct delivery of the hymns and responses in all the services. He is usually blind, due to the popular belief dating from ancient times that the sensitivity of eyesight was transferred from the eyes of a blind person to his ears, and that such transference enhanced musical skills. Little is known about the cantors prior to 1850. However, at that time, it became apparent that the music and texts had often been rendered incorrectly by untrained and/or careless cantors. Patriarch **Cyril IV** (1853–1861), concerned about this situation, made the training of cantors a matter of prime importance to the church. In 1859, he published the first edition of the book *The Services of the Deacons* with the help of Deacon Iryan Jirjis Muftah, teacher of Coptic in the Patriarchal College. In 1893, at Mahmashah, Cairo, Patriarch Cyril V (1874–1927) opened the theological Seminary, of which one branch was the Saint Didymus Institute for the Blind. Blind cantors joined the institute for their training, which is now located in Shubra, Cairo.

The Copts have preserved their music over the centuries essentially by means of oral tradition. Only in the 19th century did scholars begin to transcribe Coptic melodies using the notation system established for Western music. Guillaume Andre Villoteau, a French scholar who was part of Napoleon's expedition to Egypt, was the first to attempt such a transcription when he devoted some five pages of his *Description de l'Egypte* (1809) to an Alleluia from the Divine Liturgy. Later, toward the 19th century, other transcriptions were made by Jules Blin and Louis Badet . In 1916, Kamil Ibrahim Ghubriyal published a small volume of transcriptions of hymns and *responsoria*, *Al- Tawqi'at al-Musiqiyyah li-Maraddat al-Kanisah al-Murqusiyyah*. Unlike previous transcribers, Ghubriyal, a lieutenant in the Egyptian army, was a Copt, and deeply steeped in the musical tradition of his church. He designed his transcriptions for Coptic youth, and in an effort to make them more attractive to his audience. He adapted them for piano, adding a rhythmic accompaniment. Ghubriyal is to be recognized for his pioneering efforts as a Copt seeking to notate the music of his people. Nearly one generation later, one of the most ambitious efforts in this regard was undertaken by the English musicologist Ernest Newlandsmith, who came to Egypt at the invitation and sponsorship of **Ragheb Moftah** for the express purpose of transcribing the music of the Coptic services. From 1926 to 1936, he compiled through listening to the best Coptic cantors sixteen folio volumes of music, which include the entire Liturgy of Saint Basil and other important hymns and *responsoria* reserved for special **feasts**. Among other scholars are Hans Hickmann and René Ménard, who, working both separately and together, transcribed a few short pieces.

In 1967, Ilona Borsai went to Egypt to collect materials for study and analysis. During her short span of ethnomusicological studies, she was able to publish some 17 articles containing transcriptions and observations on facets of Coptic music never before touched upon. In 1969, Margit Tóth came to Cairo to study Coptic music. Working with Ragheb Moftah, she, like Newlandsmith, notated the entire Liturgy of Saint Basil. In 1976, Nabila Kamal Butros, violin teacher in the Faculty of Music Education at Helwan University and a member of the Arabic Classical Music Ensemble, completed a master's thesis, "Coptic Music and Its Relation to Pharaonic Music," in which she made a comparative transcription and analysis of one hymn as sung by several different choirs.

Although Western notation was not designed for transcribing Coptic music, it may be the form in which this ancient music from the Near East will at last be written. By comparing the various transcriptions of dedicated scholars, one can at least glimpse the complexity and variety of the Coptic musical tradition.

– N –

NAG HAMMADI CODICES. A group of 12 papyrus codices plus eight leaves dating from the fourth century and inscribed in Coptic. The manuscripts were discovered in a buried storage jar by fellahin (farmers) in 1945 some 10 kilometers from Nag Hammadi, and are now housed in the **Coptic Museum** in Old Cairo. Publication of the manuscripts, some of which are very fragmentary, was completed in 1977, but work on the texts is ongoing. Three international projects—based in Claremont, California; Berlin, Germany; and Québec, Canada—have been preparing critical editions of the texts. Many scholars believe that the manuscripts belonged to monks of a **Pachomian** monastery near the site of the discovery and were buried as a result of the proscription of heretical books by Bishop **Athanasius** of **Alexandria** in 367. Athanasius' letter was circulated in Egyptian monasteries and was presumably enforced by local leadership. The Nag Hammadi collection consists of 46 different tractates (some in more than one copy), most of them unknown before the discovery of the codices. All of the tractates are Coptic translations of Greek originals dating to as early as the second century or even earlier. Most of the writings represent varieties of **Gnosticism**: "**Sethian**" (a), **Valentinian** (b), and other types (c). There are two texts from the Thomas tradition originally at home in Syria (d), three from the Hermetic tradition of Egyptian origin (e), and miscellaneous other writings, non-Gnostic (f). Closely related to the Nag Hammadi Codices in terms of religious content is the **Berlin Gnostic Codex**, which contains two tractates also found in the Nag Hammadi collection.

A complete inventory of the Nag Hammadi and Berlin tractates is as follows (with religious affiliation in parentheses according to the preceding categories): *The **Prayer of the Apostle Paul*** (NHC I,

1) (b); *The Apocryphon of James* (I, 2) (c); *The Gospel of Truth* (I, 3; XII, 2) (b); *The Treatise on the Resurrection* (I, 4) (b); *The Tripartite Tractate* (I, 5) (b); *The Apocryphon of John* (II, 1; III, 1; IV, 1; BG, 2) (a); *The Gospel of Thomas* (II, 2) (d); *The Gospel of Philip* (II, 3) (b); *The Hypostasis of the Archons* (II, 4) (a); *On the Origin of the World* (II, 5; XIII, 2) (c); *The Exegesis on the Soul* (II, 6) (c); *The Book of Thomas the Contender* (II, 7) (d); *The Gospel of the Egyptians* (III, 2; IV, 2) (a); *Eugnostos the Blessed* (III, 3; V, 1) (c); *The Sophia of Jesus Christ* (III, 4; BG, 3) (c); *The Dialogue of the Savior* (III, 5) (c); *The Apocalypse of Paul* (V, 2) (c); *The (First) Apocalypse of James* (V, 3) (c); *The (Second) Apocalypse of James* (V, 4) (c); *The Apocalypse of Adam* (V, 5) (a); *The Acts of Peter and the Twelve Apostles* (VI, 1) (f); *The Thunder, Perfect Mind* (VI, 2) (c); *Authoritative Teaching* (VI, 3) (f); *The Concept of Our Great Power* (VI, 4) (c); *Plato, Republic 588A-589B* (VI, 5) (f); *The Discourse on the Eighth and Ninth* (VI, 6) (e); *The Prayer of Thanksgiving* (VI, 7) (e); *Asclepius 21–29* (VI, 8) (e); *The Paraphrase of Shem* (VII, 1) (c); *Second Treatise of the Great Seth* (VII, 2) (c); *Apocalypse of Peter* (VII, 3) (c); *The Teachings of Silvanus* (VII, 4) (f); *The Three Steles of Seth* (VII, 5) (a); *Zostrianos* (VIII, 1) (a); *The Letter of Peter to Philip* (VIII, 2) (c); *Melchizedek* (IX, 1) (a); *The Thought of Norea* (IX, 2) (a); *The Testimony of Truth* (IX, 3) (c); *Marsanes* (X, 1) (a); *The Interpretation of Knowledge* (XI, 1) (b); *A Valentinian Exposition* (XI, 2) (b); *Allogenes* (XI, 3) (a); *Hypsiphrone* (XI, 4) (a?); *The Sentences of Sextus* (XII, 1) (f); *Unidentified Fragments* (XII, 3) (?); *Trimorphic Protennoia* (XIII, 1) (a); *The Gospel of Mary* (BG, 1) (c); and *The Act of Peter* (BG, 4) (f).

NAQLUN. *See* MONASTERY OF THE ARCHANGEL GABRIEL AT NAQLUN.

NAWRUZ. The first day of the Coptic year, which corresponds to the 11th of September in the Gregorian calendar. The main theme of this **feast** is renovation. The church beseeches the blessing of God for the new year. The church chants in joyful tunes (*faraihi*). It appears that this feast may have its origin in an ancient Egyptian tradition.

NEOCAESAREA, COUNCIL OF. This synod took place between 313 and 321, after the great persecution and before Constantine became the sole emperor of the Roman Empire. The council issued 15 canons, dealing with disciplinary measures for the clergy and moral questions. Other canons deal with the catechumenate, with the age for ordination to the priesthood (to not be below 30 years), and with the status of the *chorepiscopi* (country **bishops**).

NESTORIANS AND COPTS. Having been separate from Imperial Christianity since the first **Council of Ephesus** (431), the Syriac Church of the East reappeared in Egypt after the Arab conquest, in particular during the Abbasid period, and Nestorians were used as government employees. The Nestorians lived mainly in Cairo. Yahya ibn Sa'id of Antioch, the Melchite **patriarch** of the 11th century, gives the first mention of a Nestorian community. He quoted the sack of two Nestorian churches on 29 March 961. In 996, the house of their **bishop** was sacked. During the reign of al-Hakim, a Coptic Church in a suburb south of Old Cairo and a Nestorian church within its vicinity were destroyed. **Abu al-Makarim/Abu Salih** mentioned that a Muslim rented a property from a Nestorian **priest** who belonged to the Nestorian churches.

There was a monastery mentioned by the same author south of Old Cairo. It was restored during the reign of al-'Amir (1101–1130) and many monks came to dwell in it. By the year 1181, there were no more Nestorians in Egypt. The Copts bought this property during the patriarchate of Mark ibn Zur'ah and it was named after St. Philotheus of Antioch. In the year 1346, Nestorians were found in Damietta where they had a church named after the Virgin Mary located next to the church of the Franks. They are mentioned as new arrivals to this city. There was also a Nestorian church in **Alexandria** but no other information exists.

Regardless of the theological conflict between the Copts and the Nestorians, the Coptic scholars and the Coptic hierarchy read many Nestorian authors, and among them is Isaac of Nineveh, who wrote several mystical works and was very appreciated by Coptic monks. In his book *The Lamp of Darkness for the Explanation of the Service*, **Ibn Kabar** mentioned several Nestorian authors, among them Amr Matta al-Tayrhani, who was contemporary to Ibn Kabar, and Elijah, metropolitan of Nassibin. **Ibn al-Assal**, one of the great Coptic scholars of the Middle Ages, also referred several times to Nestorian authors.

NEW TESTAMENT, COPTIC. *See* COPTIC BIBLE.

NICAEA, COUNCIL OF. Nicaea was where the First Ecumenical Council was held in 325 A.D. The council assembled at the order of Emperor Constantine to discuss several dogmatic points, including the Arian heresy. The emperor allowed the **bishops** to use the imperial post to travel to the city of Nicaea. The council also discussed several disciplinary issues. The Coptic Church was represented by Patriarch **Alexander** of **Alexandria**, with his deacon **Athanasius** (who succeeded him as 20th **patriarch** of Alexandria).

In this council, **Arius** was excommunicated and his doctrine was condemned. The emperor did not take part in the discussion itself but initiated a tradition of theologian emperors, which developed in later centuries, such as during the reign of Justinian in the sixth century and during the time of the **iconoclastic** crisis. The Bishop of Ossius of Cordova was selected as an adviser to the emperor for religious affairs, and hence presided over the council. This council is regarded as the standard of orthodoxy. The **Council of Ephesus** and the **Council of Chalcedon** issued canons stating that no Creed would be accepted except the Creed defined in the Councils of Nicaea and **Constantinople**. The Bishop of Rome (that is, the pope) was too old to attend this council and so sent two delegates to represent him. This lack of attendance by the Pope of Rome became standard in councils to follow, until the Council of Vatican II.

The corpus of the Coptic canonical works has not survived, with the exception of only one Coptic manuscript that contains the canons of the councils and synods from Nicaea, Ancyra, Laodicia, Constantinople, and so on. This manuscript is scattered throughout the libraries of the Vatican, Naples, Paris, Michigan, and the French Institute in Cairo. Starting in the 12th century, the Copts used the Arabic versions of this canonical corpus. *See also* NICENE CREED.

NICENE CREED. This Creed was formulated at the **Council of Nicaea** (325 A.D.). It was inspired by the Syro-Palestinian and Eusebius' creeds. It mentioned for the first time the word *homoousios*, meaning "the same substance." This term was condemned during the crisis of Paul of Samosata, but **Alexander** of **Alexandria** and **Athanasius** gave the true meaning. The Creed is thus:

> We believe in one God, the Father, the ruler of all, the creator of all things visible and invisible, and in one Lord, Jesus Christ the Son of God, begotten as the only Son out of the Father, that is, out of the substance of the Father, God from God, light from Light, true God from true God, begotten not created, *homoousios* with the Father, the one through . . .

The Nicene Creed is recited prior to baptism; after the fifth century, Peter the Fuller introduced it into the **liturgy** after the gospel reading as a proclamation of Orthodox faith.

In the **Council of Constantinople** (381 A.D.), the following paragraph was added: "We believe in the Holy Spirit . . ." It became a standard declaration of faith for all Christians. The modification of one word—the *filioque*, in the 11th century—contributed to the final schism between the East and the West. This schism is known as the *filioque* crisis.

NITRIA. It is one of the earliest monastic habitations in Egypt. The site is called by Greek and Latin writers Nitria or the mountain of Nitria. It has been confused with **Kellia** and **Scetis** and was correctly identified by Hugh G. Evelyn White as Gabal al-Barnoug, where the present village of al-Barnoug stands at the edge of the Libyan Desert, about 15 kilometers south of Damanhur in the western part of the Delta. Close to al-Barnoug there are natron lakes from which natron was extracted. About 325–330, St. **Amoun** founded a colony of hermits there. One of his famous disciples, who lived with him in Nitria, is **Pambo**. Nitria prospered quickly and the number of the monks became very large so that St. Amoun and St. **Antony** established Kellia to provide more solitude for the monks. Around 386 St. **Jerome** reported 5,000 monks in Nitria; though the number may be exaggerated, it shows that it was an enormous colony of monks. **Palladius**, who lived for one year in Nitria, wrote the most detailed description of that monastic site at the end of the fourth century. He reported a church, a hostelry, shops, and seven bakeries. The monks lived independently in their cells during the weekdays and assembled to celebrate the weekly mass. Apparently, the number of the monks in Nitria decreased quickly and it was abandoned, probably before the end of the seventh century. When in 645 or 646, **Patriarch** Benjamin went from **Alexandria** to **Wadi al-Natrun**, he proceeded directly to Kellia without stopping at Nitria, implying that it was no longer an important monastic habitation. Unlike Kellia and Scetis, little remains at Nitria today.

NUBIA, CHRISTIANITY IN. The Nubian Church is unique among the Middle Eastern churches in that it started and prospered in an atmosphere of complete political independence. Some scholars believe that Queen Candace of the Ethiopians, who is mentioned in the Acts of the Apostles 8:27–39, was the Queen of Meroe (ca. 37). However, it was Patriarch **Athanasius** who ordained a **bishop** of Philae in Nubia in 362, the first historical evidence of the beginning of the spread of Christianity. According to the *Ecclesiastical History* of John of Ephesus, a Monophysite **priest** called Julian obtained a commission from Empress Theodora, wife of Emperor Justinian, to preach Christianity in Nubia. In 543, the Nobatian king and his subjects converted to Christianity. Theodore, Bishop of Philae, continued to work toward the spread of Christianity there until the year 551. Also, the Nubian kingdom of Makouria converted to Christianity before the end of the sixth century. Another sixth-century missionary in Nubia was Longinus, who succeeded in spreading the Jacobite faith southward to the southern kingdom of 'Alwa. Its capital Soba was about 18 kilometers south of the present-day Khartoum. Those Christian kingdoms did not lose their independence until the 13th century, and unlike most of the countries of the Middle East, Christianity continued to be the religion of the majority of the population there as late as the 14th century.

Despite the succession of Muslim rulers in Egypt since the **Arab conquest of Egypt**, the Coptic **patriarch** had a considerable spiritual influence in Nubia, where he used to consecrate bishops for Nubian bishoprics; the last one was Timotheos, who was consecrated Bishop of Faras and Qasr Ibrim in 1372. Nubian churches were decorated with wall paintings, the most significant of which were found in

Faras, Abdallah Nirqi, and Sonqi. The earliest paintings are from the seventh century, and by the beginning of the 13th century Nubian Christian art began to decline. Sanctuaries are decorated with Christ *Pantocrator* and by the Virgin and Child flanked by the Apostles. The Nativity is often depicted in the church's north aisle. The scene of the three Hebrews in the fiery furnace was popular, as well as many **saints**. The representation of Nubian kings reflects the political independence of Nubia and the royal association with the Church's rituals. *See also* NUBIAN LITURGY.

NUBIAN LITURGY. In 1960, the Egyptian government decided to build a high dam south of Aswan. Several archaeological missions unearthed many fragments of manuscripts in **Nubia** containing **liturgical** texts, such as the Holy Liturgy of St. Mark and a **lectionary**. The Nubian Church has remained true to its Eastern Orthodox origins throughout its history.

– O –

OLD TESTAMENT, COPTIC. *See* COPTIC BIBLE.

ON THE ORIGIN OF THE WORLD **(NHC II, 5; XII, 2).** A **Gnostic** compendium based on several sources dealing with Gnostic cosmogony, anthropogony, and **eschatology**. Anonymous and untitled, its current title has been editorially assigned on the basis of its content. It shares some material in common with the *Hypostasis of the Archons* (NHC II, 4), probably based on a common source. Extant only in Coptic, *On the Origin of the World* was originally composed in Greek, probably in third-century Egypt.

OPHITES. Gnostic heretics so designated by patristic heresiologists on the basis of the role played by the serpent of Genesis 3 (Greek *ophis*) in their mythology. In these accounts, the serpent is praised as the revealer of gnosis (knowledge) to Adam and Eve, and is equated by some with Jesus Christ. The pagan writer Celsus and **Origen** refer to certain "Ophians" who also venerated the serpent, and used in their ritual an elaborate diagram depicting the cosmos and the way of ascent for those in possession of gnosis. Epiphanius attributed to the Ophites a ritual involving the worship of a live snake.

ORATORY. (Latin, *oratorium*, place of prayer). The term *oratory* is used in Egypt to designate the small chapel adjoining the monk's cell for private worship. It is often equipped with a bench in front of the west wall. The most significant part of the oratory is the east wall, which usually features three niches; two of them are small and not decorated, and were used to keep the **liturgical** objects. The middle principal niches of the oratories are usually decorated with paintings of Christ in the Majesty or by the Virgin and Child flanked by angels and **saints** or Apostles. The most interesting oratory murals were found in **Kellia**, the **Monastery of St. Jeremiah**, and the **Monastery of St. Apollo**.

ORIENTATION TOWARD THE EAST. In Malachi, it is written that Christ is the Sun of Righteousness (Mal. 4:2). The Copts pray toward the East. The glorious Second Coming of Christ will appear in the East, in which He will come to judge the living and the dead. Christ described it as follows: "For as the lightning cometh out of the east and shineth even unto the west, so shall also the coming of the Son of Man be" (Matt. 24:27).

Hippolytus of Rome presented the Church as a ship sailing toward the east and toward heavenly paradise. In the third century **Origen**, in his book on *Prayer*, highlighted that prayer should be oriented toward the east. In the fourth century, according to Lactancius, in his poem *De ave Phoenice*, which was inspired from the book of the Physiologus, the phoenix (which is a representation of Christ) flies toward the east. Also in the same century, the **Didascalia**, written in Syria, mentioned that prayer should be oriented toward the east. During the martyrdom of Epima, it is stated that the Christians were praying toward east while the pagans were praying toward the west. Excavation of the necropolis site of Fag al-Gamous in Fayoum showed that the orientation of the corpses before the second century was eastward. A change to the opposite direction of orientation of the body was also noticed during the same era of Christianity. Consequently, in the baptismal rite during the renunciation of Satan, the person to be baptized is required to look toward the west, and stretch out his right hand and say,

"I renounce thee, Satan." Then he turns toward the east and stretching both hands says, "I join myself to Thee, Christ."

ORIGEN (185–ca. 254). Theologian. Origen is the most controversial person in Christian history. He is considered by the Fathers of the Church, such as **Eusebius of Caesarea** and Pamphile, as being a **saint**, while other Fathers such as Epiphanius, **Theophilus (Patriarch** of **Alexandria)**, and **Shenute** (or **Dioscorus**) considered him a heretic. In the sixth century, Emperor Justinian issued an edict (543 A.D.) condemning Origen, with the approval of Patriarch of Constantinople Mennas and Pope of Rome Vigilius (537–555), and this edict was confirmed by the **Second Council of Constantinople** in 553. It is worthy of mention that despite the opposition of three patriarchs of the Coptic Church—namely, Demetrius, Theophilus, and **Dioscorus** (and also **Shenute** to a certain extent)—no formal condemnation was issued against him. However, a warning was given regarding the reading of his books.

Origen was born at Alexandria. His father was martyred while Origen was young. He followed the lessons of Clement of Alexandria and became the head of the School of Alexandria after the departure of his master. After a visit to Caesarea, his former student ordained him a **priest**. This did not please **Bishop** Demetrius of Alexandria, who later excommunicated him. He left Alexandria and established a new Theological School in Caesarea. He suffered imprisonment during the reign of Decius and died soon after at the age of 70.

Origen was a prolific writer. He delivered homilies on the interpretation of the books of the Bible, both Old and New Testaments. He composed apologetic works to defend Christianity, such as *Against Celsus*. He issued a scientific edition and translation of the Old Testament. Origen was also the author of dogmatic treatises as well as spiritual treatises such as his books on *Prayer* and *Exhortation on Martyrdom*. In all his interpretations, he followed the allegorical method. However, he was accused of applying Matthew 19:12 literally and hence castrating himself. Under Justinian in the sixth century, Origen was condemned; because of this, most of his works were lost in the East and only Latin translation survived in the West. Despite his impressive list of publications, not a single work survives in Coptic or in Arabic.

– P –

PACHOMIUS (292–346). Saint, abbot. He is the founder of cenobitic or communal **monasticism**. He was born of pagan parents in a small village in Esna in Upper Egypt. As a soldier recruited in the Roman army, he had his first contact with Christianity where he experienced acts of charity from the Christian community at Thebes. In about 320, Pachomius established the first community of monks at Tabennisi in Upper Egypt. His form of monastic life was based on precise rules that governed almost every aspect of monks' lives, such as prayers, masses, work, meals, and sleep. The monks lived together in houses. Each house was inhabited by 40 monks, who were supervised by a steward. Some monasteries were composed of 30 or 40 houses. Pachomius left 11 monasteries, of which two were for **women**. The regulations of Pachomius grew up gradually to meet the requirements of a more complex monastic society that was influential and successful. The Pachomian monasticism proved popular especially in Middle and Upper Egypt. In 404, St. **Jerome** translated the Pachomian rules into Latin from an intermediate Greek translation from the Coptic text. Thus Western monasticism, in particular the Benedictine Order, owes much to the Coptic monastic traditions.

PALLADIUS (363–431). Monk, historian of early **monasticism**. He was born in Galatia and spent several years as a monk in Egypt. He stayed three years at **Alexandria** and then moved to **Nitria**. In 390, he went to **Kellia**, where he became a pupil of **Evagrius Ponticus**. It is not clear whether he was **Origenist** or not; however, both St. **Jerome** and St. Epiphanius accused him of Origenism. Around 400 he returned to Asia Minor, where he was consecrated **Bishop** of Helenopolis in Bithynia. He spoke in defense of St. John Chrysostom at the Synod of the Oak in 403, and was therefore forced into exile by Emperor Arcadius to Antinoe in Upper Egypt, where he visited the monasteries of that region. When Patriarch **Theophilus** died in 412, he returned to Galatia and then to the See of Aspona, where he composed the *Historia Lausiaca* in about 419. Its title derives from the dedication of the book to Lausiac, the chamberlain of Emperor Theodosius II. There are several recensions of this work with numerous translations in Latin, Syriac, Arabic, Armenian, and Ethiopic.

A number of fragments have been preserved in Coptic. It is an indispensable work for the study of Egyptian **monasticism**, and in particular in Nitria and **Scetis**.

PALM SUNDAY. *See* HOSANNA.

PAMBO (ca. 303–373). Ascetic and **priest**. He was one of the first ascetics and companions of St. **Amoun** in **Nitria**. St. **Macarius** took part in the celebration of the **liturgy** when he was ordained a priest in Nitria. Pambo possessed the gift of prophecy and was known for **fasting** until evening, silence, and humility. He despised gold and silver and did not trouble himself even to look how much silver was offered to him by Melania the elder. St. **Antony** praised Pambo highly. His name figures in the *Apophthegmata patrum*.

PARAMONE. This is the day that precedes the Feast of the Nativity and also the Epiphany. The **liturgy** is celebrated in annual tunes, but several *psalis* and hymns are added to the rite.

PARAPHRASE OF SHEM **(NHC VII, 1).** A **Gnostic** apocalypse in which Shem ascends to heaven and is given extensive revelations by a divine being called Derdekeas. Its title is given at the beginning of the tractate. The revelations consist of a cosmogony, an anthropology, and a Gnostic history of salvation. The cosmogonic myth reflects a system of three principles: Light, Darkness, and Spirit. There are no obvious Christian features in the text. A somewhat similar system, though in a Christian dress, is found in a treatise called *The Paraphrase of Seth*, discussed by Hippolytus in his account of the doctrine of certain **Sethians**. Extant only in Coptic, *Paraphrase of Shem* was originally composed in Greek, probably in late third-century Syria.

PATRIARCH. The term *patriarch* is a composition of the Greek *pater* meaning father and *archon* meaning leader, chief, or ruler. It has mainly taken on specific ecclesiastical meanings. The patriarch is the head of the entire Coptic Church. Throughout its long history, the church of **Alexandria** maintained the **apostolic succession** in an uninterrupted chain. Thus the Coptic patriarch is considered to be the successor of St. **Mark** the Evangelist. **Shenouda III** is the 117th

Pope of Alexandria and Patriarch of all Egypt, the Pentapolis, **Nubia**, the Sudan, Libya, and Ethiopia on the apostolic throne of St. Mark. The majority of the Coptic patriarchs had been chosen from among the monks, especially those of **Wadi al-Natrun**. A number of laymen were consecrated as patriarchs. Several methods were used in electing the Coptic patriarchs. The most common traditions are as follows: election by general consensus of bishops, presbyters, and lay leaders, election by the presbyters of Alexandria, and the apostolic practice of casting the lot. Some patriarchs were nominated by their predecessors and others by means of a vision, or a dream of a devout Copt. After the **Arab conquest of Egypt**, governmental intervention has influenced the election of a few patriarchs. Both **Cyril VI** and the present patriarch Pope Shenouda III have been chosen by means of casting an altar lot among final nominees. *See also* PATRIARCH'S CONSECRATION; PATRIARCHAL RESIDENCES; POPE; STRUCTURE OF THE COPTIC CHURCH; *HISTORY OF THE PATRIARCHS.*

PATRIARCHAL RESIDENCES. Alexandria became the residence of the **Bishop** of Alexandria during the beginnings of Christianity in Egypt. Alexandria continued to be the residence of the **patriarchs** of the See of St. **Mark** as late as the 11th century when Patriarch **Christodoulus** (1047–1077) definitively transferred his residence to the **Mo'allaqa** Church at Old Cairo to be closer to Egypt's ruler. However, Alexandria has remained in the official title of the Coptic patriarchs to the present-day: "Pope of Alexandria and Patriarch of the See of St. Mark." For them, the great city of **Alexandria** is a most holy site, where St. Mark the Evangelist began to preach the Gospel, founded the Church of Alexandria, and suffered martyrdom. We know a number of "temporary" papal residences other than Alexandria: the **Monastery of St. Macarius** in **Wadi al-Natrun**, the village of Mahallat Danyal near Kafr al-Sheikh, the town of Damru near al Mahalla al-Kubra, and the town of Tuch in the Delta. The **Church of St. Mercurius** at Old Cairo was the residence of Patriarch Michael (1145–1146). Patriarch John VIII (1300–1320) transferred the patriarchal seat to the Church of the Holy Virgin at Haret Zuwaila in Cairo, which remained the seat of the Coptic patriarchs until 1660. Matthew IV (1660–1675) resided at Haret al-Rum, Cairo. Patriarch Mark VIII (1796–1809) resided at the old Cathedral of St. Mark in

Azbakiyah, Cairo. The **Cathedral of St. Mark in Cairo**, which was inaugurated in 1968, is the **patriarchal residence** of the present patriarch, **Shenouda III.**

PATRIARCH'S CONSECRATION. The rite supposes that the **patriarch**-elect is a monk, although several times in Coptic history laymen were elected and consecrated as patriarchs, such as the patriarchs Afraham ibn Zur'ah and **Gabriel ibn Turayk.** If the candidate is a simple monk, then he should be raised to the second degree of **monasticism**, namely the Skema-bearers, and he would be ordained **priest** (if he had not previously been ordained). The rite comprises two distinct parts:

- the consecration of the patriarch-elect to the episcopate
- the enthronement as patriarch of **Alexandria**

There was an ancient tradition mentioned in the *History of the Patriarchs of the Coptic Church* that every new patriarch must go to the place where the head of St. **Mark** is buried and take its blessings. However, this tradition disappeared in the 15th century when the Venetians stole the relics.

The most complete manuscript of this rite is Ms 253 Lit. of the **Coptic Museum** in Old Cairo, dated 1364 A.D. The first publication of this rite was edited by R. **Tukhi** in Rome in 1761. No Coptic Orthodox edition of this rite has been printed to date.

PAUL OF THEBES (?–ca. 340 or 341). Saint, hermit. He is traditionally the first hermit. In addition to **Jerome**'s *Life of Paul*, written in Latin, there are Greek, Coptic, and Arabic texts on St. Paul, but he is mainly known from the Latin biography that Jerome composed, probably in 375 or 376. Paul was an Egyptian from the Lower Thebaid. Around 250 he fled into the Eastern Desert to escape the persecution of Emperor Decius, where he lived a life of prayer in a cave for almost 90 years. St. **Antony** visited him shortly before his death. It is said that a crow provided Paul with half a loaf of bread each day for his sustenance, but on the day Antony visited him the crow appeared with a whole loaf. After the death of Paul, two lions appeared and dug out the grave to help Antony bury him. Beginning with the medieval period, the two saints are often represented in wall paintings and **icons** standing together in prayer, while a crow is providing them with a loaf, and two lions stand at the feet of Paul.

PELAGIANISM. Pelagianism is not a doctrine about grace but an ascetic and reform movement. Pelagius was born in the early fourth century (ca. 350), perhaps in Britain. He came to Carthage in the late decades of the fourth century or the early decades of the fifth century. He adopted an ascetic life and gained a great reputation. He devoted his zeal for the reform of behavior at his time and was hence regarded as a great moralist and religious teacher. He wrote many books on the subject of reform, emphasizing the "will" and underestimating "grace." Pelagius sailed to Palestine where he met **Jerome**. His movement was adopted by many followers but was opposed by Augustine of Hippo. Pelagius returned to Carthage in 416.

Augustine wrote two letters to St. **Cyril** of **Alexandria**, wherein he explained the danger of this heresy. No reply from Cyril survived but one may assume that Augustine received a favorable answer, and so Pelagianism was condemned at the **Council of Ephesus** in 431 A.D. **Nestorius** in his conflict with St. Cyril took possession of some Pelegians.

PENANCE. The book of *The Shepherd* by Hermas (written in Rome in the mid-second century) mentioned baptism as the unique way for the remission of sins. But for Christians who committed a great sin after baptism, there is the *metanoia* or penance. Tertullian in the beginning of the third century published the first treatise *On Penance*, by adding theological depth. The ***Didascalia of the Apostles***, written in Syria in the beginning of the third century, exhorts the **bishop** to receive all penitents, whether rich or poor.

Clement and **Origen** are the first witnesses for the institution of penance in the Eastern Church. The Eastern tradition, following Clement and Origen's lead, emphasized the Church's ministers as healers and the importance of spiritual direction. Dionysius, **Patriarch** of **Alexandria**, was a leading figure in combating the Novatianists (who refused the rehabilitation of the *Lapsi*). During the persecution, the Church faced the problem of receiving the *Lapsi* after some bishops refused their penance, such as **Melitius** of Lycopolis (Egypt).

PETER I, SEAL OF THE MARTYRS. Peter was the 18th **Patriarch** of **Alexandria** (301–313 A.D.) and is commemorated on the 29th of Hathor. Peter was the son of a **priest**. His mother made a vow during the Feast of Peter and Paul to call him after the Apostle. He suffered martyrdom under Diocletian. There exists a Coptic homily on his life and martyrdom in addition to an encomium attributed to Flavian of Antioch narrating the life of Demetrius and Peter the patriarch. The *History of the Patriarchs* provides a detailed account of his activities as well as his biography, in Syriac, Latin, Armenian, and Georgian. Under Peter the Seal of the Martyrs, Bishop **Melitius** of Lycopolis began a schism by going about ordaining clergy while Peter was in exile. The debate was over what measures could be taken to avoid persecution and how to deal with penitent Christians who lapsed in order to avoid torture or death. The Coptic literary texts attribute to him several works such as a homily on the Archangel Michael, a homily on baptism, extracts of a homily on Passion Week, in addition to several letters and fragments.

PHYSIOLOGOS. This Greek text was begun around 200 B.C. by Paul of Mendes, who confused the scientific study of nature with magical traditions. Others continued the work after 200 B.C. In a Coptic text attributed to Eusthatius of Thrace, the book of the *Physiologos* is attributed to King Solomon. (This tradition survived also in Islamic tradition.) Coptic and other Oriental Christian literature drew upon the *Physiologos*, especially since it was composed in Egypt. Although the complete manuscript of the Coptic *Physiologos* did not survive, there are quotations and allusions to it in several writings. Most of these quotations are in religious texts relating to monks, **patriarchs**, and **saints**, meaning that the Christian **hierarchy** read this book. Though originally written in Greek in Egypt, the Coptic version of the *Physiologos* received a thorough study by A. van Lantschoot, who assembled 18 references to it.

PILGRIMAGE. The veneration of the **saints** at pilgrimage sites is one of the characteristics of the Coptic religious life, past and present. In the Late Antique period, the significant pilgrimage center of St. **Menas** (**Abu Mina**), which flourished from the fifth to the eighth century, attracted pilgrims from all over the world. Nowadays Copts flock annually to more than 60 pilgrimage centers all over Egypt. The pilgrimage sites associated with the Holy Virgin Mary and St. George (Mari Girgis) are the most famous among them. There are many pilgrimage sites believed to be blessed by the Holy Family in their **flight into Egypt** that are visited annually by hundreds of thousands of pious people. The pilgrimage site of St. George at Riziqat near Luxor is the most popular.

A visit to any one of them involves some customs and rituals that include special prayers in honor of the saints; offerings and donations of money, **incense**, or candles and the sacrifice of an animal such as a lamb; baptism of children; tattooing the cross on the children's right wrist; and often exorcisms. The pilgrimage is often described by the Egyptians as *mulid*, a colloquial Arabic term that designates a **feast** or a celebration in honor of a saint. Coptic *mulid* is an occasion for outdoor religious festivities combined with opportunities for commerce and entertainment. Some of its aspects have roots in the religious heritage of pharaonic Egypt and might be considered as "survivals." Beginning in the late 1970s, the Islamic fundamentalists' movements strove to affect the *mulid* practices of both Muslim and Copts. On the other hand, a "clericalization" of the activities of the Coptic *mulids* by the clerics is unmistakable.

PISTIS SOPHIA. A collection of **Gnostic** treatises contained in the **Askew Codex**, divided in the manuscript into four books. A title is found at the end of the second and the third books: "A Part of the Books of the Savior." Inscribed by a later hand at the beginning of the second book is the title, "The Second Book of the Pistis Sophia." All four books are now customarily referred to as *Pistis Sophia* ("Faith Wisdom") and divided into chapters numbered consecutively. In all four books, the risen Jesus is featured in dialogue with his disciples, including several women. Book 1 (chapters 1–62) is concerned with the repentance of the fallen Pistis Sophia, mother of the Gnostic race. Book 2 contains further material on the same subject (chapters 63–82), followed by discourses on various types of souls (chapters 83–101). In Book 3 (chapters 102–135), Jesus commissions his disciples, providing elaborate explanations of various mysteries. Book 4 (chapters 136–148) is a miscellany of ritual prayers, revelation discourses, and visions experienced by the disciples. The first two books contain extensive quotations from the Bible and apocryphal writings, including some of the Odes and Psalms of Solomon. *Pistis Sophia* is extant only in Coptic, but its various parts were originally composed in Greek, probably in Egypt during the third and early fourth centuries.

***PLATO, REPUBLIC 588A–589B* (NHC VI, 5).** A fractured and **Gnosticizing** Coptic translation of Socrates' parable on the human soul in Book 9 of Plato's *Republic*, a text quite popular in philosophical and religious circles. The translation was evidently produced in a Gnostic setting, probably in early fourth-century Egypt.

POPE. The Latin *papa* and the Greek *pappas* means simply "father." The title "pope" has been in use from the early third century for the **bishops** of **Alexandria**. The title of the **patriarch** of Alexandria is "Pope and patriarch of the great city of Alexandria and of all Egypt, the Pentapolis, **Nubia**, the Sudan, Libya, Ethiopia, and all Africa, and all countries of the preaching of St. Mark." The title "pope" belongs also to the Pope of Rome. In a council at Rome in1073, Pope Gregory VII prohibited the use of this title by any other bishop other than the Bishop of Rome.

PRAYER OF THANKSGIVING* (NHC VI, 7).** A Coptic translation of a prayer found in Greek in a magical papyrus (P. Mimaut) and in Latin at the end of the Hermetic tractate *Asclepius* (41b). Its incipit ("This is the prayer that they spoke") suggests that it has been excerpted from a larger work. The scribe of Codex VI probably inserted this prayer here on the assumption that it was a suitable conclusion to the preceding tractate, *The **Discourse on the Eighth and Ninth (NHC VI, 6). This prayer, composed in Greek in Egypt, probably in the second century, was presumably used in Hermetic conventicles.

***PRAYER OF THE APOSTLE PAUL* (NHC I, 1).** A prayer of praise and petition addressed to "The One who is" "through Jesus Christ," written into the front flyleaf of NH Codex I. A subscript title, "Prayer of Paul [the] Apostle," indicates that the prayer is attributable to St. Paul. Preserved only in Coptic, *Prayers of the Apostle Paul* is a **Valentinian Gnostic** text originally composed in Greek, probably in the late second or third century. Its provenience is unknown, but it could have been composed in Egypt.

PRIEST. The priest is mentioned several times in the New Testament. Christ chose a number of men and named them apostles (Luke 6:13; John 15:16). By the full authority that was committed to Him, He commanded them to go forth and baptize people everywhere and teach them to observe His commandments (Matt. 28:18-20). They alone were given the power of forgiving sins or withholding forgiveness (John 20:21-23). These apostles appointed bishops and priests in the same manner, according to the sacrament instituted by our Lord, and they, in turn, were succeeded by others in all the apostolic churches of Christendom. Paul set up Timothy as bishop at Ephesus, exhorting him not to neglect the spiritual gift that he was given under the guidance of prophecy, through the laying-on of hands of the presbytery (1 Tim.. 4:14), and prompted him to confide his own teaching into the hands of other competent and trustworthy men. Likewise, having named Titus **bishop** in Crete, Paul instructed him to carry out his intention in so doing, that is, to set up presbyters in each town (Titus 1:5).

In the writings of the early fathers there is ample evidence that ever since the apostolic age, the principle of an organized priesthood was closely followed. Ignatius, bishop of Antioch (c. 35–107), wrote to the Ephesians, "I exhort you to study to do all the things with a divine harmony, while your bishop presides . . . and your presbyters . . . along with your deacons, who are most dear to me, and are entrusted with the ministry of Jesus Christ." Candidates for the priesthood should have a genuine and unmistakable vocation for it, with no motive other than to participate fully and wholeheartedly in the sublime "service of the Spirit" (2 Cor. 3:8). It is because of this that St. Paul warned Timothy against hastily ordaining unfit persons (1 Tim. 5:22). Among the early fathers who dealt with the subject is **Jerome**, who grasped the essence of priesthood: "A clergyman . . . must first understand what his name means . . . and must endeavor to be that which he is called. Because the Greek word *cleros* means lot, or inheritance, the clergy are so called either because they are the lot of the Lord, or else because the Lord Himself is their lot and portion." Before ordination, the congregation testifies his good works, and he should know well the doctrines, be gentle, and charitable. His marriage must be lawful according to the canon. The bishop ordains him deacon, if he is not one. The priest is in charge of serving the altar, which includes all the liturgical service, **Eucharist**, Matrimony, Baptism, confession, and **unction of the sick**, etc. He is, by definition, one of the elders as Moses appointed elders to solve problems between the member of the congregation. The priest should instruct his people and educate them with humility and purity.

PSALIS. The *psalis* are hymns recited before the Odes and the Theotokia. The *psalis* could be sung with the Adam tune or with the Batos tune. There are several types of *psalis*. The first and most ancient type is the *psalis* "My Lord Jesus Christ" that could date prior to the eighth century. Some of the *psalis* are acrostic, meaning that the first letter of each stanza follows the alphabet. Some of these *psalis* end with the letter "O" (omega), the last letter in the Greek alphabet, while others end with "Ti," the last letter of the Coptic alphabet. Two Coptic *psalis* use the reverse order of the Coptic alphabet. At times, an author of a *psali* would put his name at the beginning of each stanza.

The most ancient *psalis* are anonymous, but later the authors of the *psalis* would insert their names in the last stanza. Sarkis is one of those authors of the *psalis*. He was a cantor in the Coptic Church in Jerusalem in the 14th century, where he learned Greek. He is the author of the *psali* of the three young men in the fiery furnace, as well as the Greek paraphrases that are recited on Sunday evening during the month of Kiahk. In his *psalis*, Sarkis used many Greek words, and at times, whole verses are given in Greek. In the 15th century, the **Bishop** of Assiut, Manfalut, and Abu Tig wrote a *psali* for the Sunday **Theotokia**. He borrowed several phrases from the Theotokia as well as from other *psalis*. Nicodemus is another author of *psalis* from the 18th century. He is of Upper Egyptian origin but lived in Cairo and wrote *psalis* commemorating **saints** who lived in the city. He visited the **Monastery of al-Baramous**, where he wrote a *psali* to Apollo and Abib. Nicodemus' style is totally Coptic, but at times he stereotypes expressions and idioms. Another monk, named Solomon the Hegomenus, from the **Monastery of the Syrians**, wrote two *psalis* in the early 19th century in honor of St. John Kame, but they are full of linguistic mistakes.

The *psalis* in the Coptic Church originated prior to the ninth century and are chanted to the present day. The earliest manuscript is from the library of the Monastery of the Archangel Michael at Hamuli preserved in the collection of Pierpont Morgan Library, dated 897 A.D. The first publication was edited by Qommos Philotaos al-Maqari, *Kitab al-absâliyat wal-Turûhât Watos wa Âdam* [The Book of *Psalis* and *Turuhat* Watos and Adam], in Cairo in 1913. It contains the *psalis* for the first part of the year according to the Coptic calendar. Bishop Matteos edited a reprint of this book, adding a second part. The reader will find also several *psalis* in the Book of the **Psalmodia** of the year and the Psalmodia of Kiahk. *See also* MUSIC, COPTIC.

PSALMODIA. The name is applied to (a) the book that contains the principal hymns for the ecclesiastical year; (b) the service that follows the offices of the Compline, midnight prayer, and morning prayer. This book contains the biblical odes (Exod. 15:1–21; Ps. 136; Dan. 3: 52–58; Ps. 148, 149, 150), the seven **Theotokia** (seven hymns to the Mother of God, each one for a day of the week), and the **doxologies**.

There are two types. The yearly Psalmody covers the whole year except the month of Kiahk. The Kiahk Psalmodia contains special psalmodies sung during the month of Kiahk, and Sunday vigils that last all night. It is commonly called "the seven and four" because seven Theotokias and four odes are thus sung. In addition to the odes and Theotokias, there are several *psalis* in Coptic and Arabic, the commentary, and *lobsh*.

The most ancient manuscript is among the collection of the Monastery of the Archangel Michael in Hamuli, discovered by peasants in 1910. It is now preserved in the collection of the Pierpont Morgan Library under number M 574. This manuscript is dated 892 or 893. An ostracon preserved in the **Coptic Museum** contains the third ode in Greek that could be dated to the seventh century. Some papyri were discovered by Flinder Petrie in the Monastery of al-Hamam and contain fragments of the third ode and a list of **saints**. The first publication of this text was edited by R. **Tukhi** in 1764. He did not adhere to the original manuscript and made some changes according to the Catholic faith. In 1908, a Coptic Orthodox monk, Mina al-Baramusi, published in **Alexandria** the Psalmodia with the help of **Bishop** Youannis of Munufia and Bishop Thomas of Ashmunin. In the same year, Claudius Labib published the Psalmodia according to the manuscripts of the **Patriarch** Cyril V and Bishop Isaac of Beni Suef. This edition was reprinted several times by the hegemon Attallah Arsenius al-Muharraqi, and the commission of the publication of Beni Suef. The Society of the Churches Renaissance published the same book for the first time in 1948. An Italian translation of Claudius Labib's edition was published by M. Borgi in 1962. *See also* MUSIC, COPTIC.

PSALMODY. *See* PSALMODIA.

– R –

RED MONASTERY. *See* MONASTERY OF ST. PSHOI AT SOHAG.

RESPONSORY. *See* WAHEM.

RUFAYLAH, YA'QUB NAKHLAH (1847–1908). Historian. He was one of the most active Copts who participated in the reform movement initiated by Patriarch **Cyril IV**. He was born in Cairo and joined a Coptic school where he learned English, Italian, and Coptic. He taught at the Coptic school of Harit al-Saqqayin that **Patriarch** Cyril IV established. He was appointed as a proofreader in the governmental press of Bulaq. Rufaylah established two schools in the city of Fayoum; one of them was for girls. He founded a number of welfare societies there. He compiled a number of books on the teaching of Arabic to English speakers and on teaching English to Egyptians. In one of the very first significant publications on the history of the Copts, *"Tarikh al-Ummah al-Qibtiyah: History of the Coptic Nation,"* which appeared in Arabic in 1899, Rufaylah exhorted intellectual Coptic laymen to preserve the surviving, unparalleled Coptic monuments, and he proposed a petition to the patriarch that they be protected, together with scattered manuscripts, in one place reserved for the purpose. His vision was fulfilled by **Marcus Simaika** and **Yassa 'Abd al-Masih**.

– S –

SABELLIANISM. Sabellianism is named after its originator, Sabellius from Cyrenaica. The followers of this heresy believed that God was one substance but three activities. He manifested Himself as the Father in the Old Testament, as the Son in the **New Testament**, and as the **Holy Spirit** in Church life. Dionysius of **Alexandria** condemned this heresy according to some quotations of **Eusebius** in the *Historia ecclesiastica* and by **Athanasius**. This became an accusation ascribed to every heretic such as **Arius** and **Melitius**. Basil the Great said that Sabellianism is a return to Judaism. Sabellianism was condemned in the **Council of Constantinople** in 381 A.D.

SAINT MARK FOUNDATION FOR COPTIC HISTORY STUDIES. It is a significant scientific institution of the Coptic Church. It was founded in 1998 by Fawzy Estafanous, former Chairman, Division of Anesthesiology and Critical Care Medicine, Cleveland Ohio, who is known for having built one of the foremost cardiac anesthesiology departments in the USA. The main task of the St. Mark Foundation is to write an up-to-date history of Christianity and monasticism in Egypt. It organizes every other year an international symposium on Christianity and monasticism in one region that is followed by a publication such as a volume on *"Christianity and Monasticism in the Fayoum Oasis,"* and another on *"Christianity and Monasticism in Upper Egypt. Volume 1: Akhmim and Sohag,"* Cairo: American University Press, 2005, 2008. One of the foundation's important goals is to promote an awareness of the Coptic heritage in Egypt and all over the world as well. A number of books in Arabic on the history of Christianity and its monuments in several Coptic dioceses appeared such as *"Christianity and Its Monuments in Aswan and Nubia,"* Cairo, 2003. Moreover, it plays an instrumental role in the ongoing project "The Coptic Cultural Center" of the Coptic Orthodox Patriarchate at **Anba Ruwais**. The foundation cooperates with **Shenouda the Archimandrite Coptic Society** in many cultural activities.

SAINTS. *See* HAGIOGRAPHY.

SAMUEL (1920–1981). Bishop. He was born Sa'd 'Aziz in Cairo. On 6 October 1981 he gave his life along with Egyptian President Anwar al-Sadat at the hands of Muslim extremist assassins. He graduated from the Faculty of Law at Fouad I University (now Cairo University) in 1941, and obtained a diploma in divinity from the **Clerical College** in 1944. He was a lecturer in the Theological Seminary at Addis Ababa in 1944, while helping in the establishment of the Sunday School there. In 1946, Emperor Haile Selassie decorated him with the order of the Star of Ethiopia. In 1948, he devoted his life as a monk under the name Makary. He was guided by Father Mina al-Baramousy (later Pope **Cyril VI**) at the Monastery of St. **Menas** in Old Cairo. In 1950, he joined the **Monastery of the Syrian** at **Wadi al-Natrun**. In 1954, Pope Yusab II commissioned him with Father Salib Suryal (1916–1994) and **Aziz S. Atiya** to participate in the second World Council of Churches Assembly, held in Evanston, Illinois. This was an important step toward the cooperation between the Coptic Church and other churches. He obtained a master's degree in religious education from Princeton Theological Seminary in 1955. From 1955 to 1962 he taught pastoral **theology** in the Clerical College and the **Higher Institute for Coptic Studies**. He established the St. Didymus Institute for the Blind. On 30 September 1962 he was ordained a bishop of public, social, and ecumenical services. Bishop Samuel was a vice-president of All Africa Conference of Churches (AACC), which he founded. He was instrumental in establishing Coptic churches in Europe, America, and Australia.

SAMUEL AL-SURIANY (1937–2003). Bishop. He was born Sameh Adli in Cairo. He obtained a bachelor of architecture degree from Cairo University in 1958. He participated in the excavations of some Coptic sites, assisting Peter Grossmann. On 5 February 1984 he joined the **Monastery of the Syrians** at **Wadi al-Natrun**. He was ordained **priest** on 27 November 1987 and Bishop of Toukh, Shebine al-Qanater, and Khanka on 6 June 1992. He established the Section of Coptic Architecture in the **Higher Institute of Coptic Studies** in 1984 in cooperation with Hishmat Misseha and Sami Sabri. He published numerous articles and books on Coptic history, architecture, and liturgy. His most important contributions are with Abûl Makarim Girgis Saadalah, *Churches and Monasteries in the XII Century*,

Cairo 1984; with Yusab of Fuwwah, *History of the Patriarchs*, Cairo 1992 (in Arabic); *Ancient Coptic Churches in Upper Egypt*, Cairo 1992; and *Ancient Coptic Churches in Lower Egypt*, Cairo 1996. Bishop Samuel reprinted many significant Arabic books, such as the **Synaxarion** of the Coptic Church and the *History of the Patriarchs of Alexandria*, and subsidized their prices.

SATURDAY OF JOY. *See* HOLY WEEK SATURDAY.

SAWIRUS IBN AL-MUQAFFA' (ca. 915–ca. 1000). Bishop, theologian. Despite Sawirus' great reputation as the first major Coptic Orthodox theologian to write in Arabic, we know surprisingly few details about his life. We do not know the exact date of his birth (or even his name at birth!), but before becoming a monk—where and when we do not know—he was known as Abu Bishr ibn al-Muqaffa' ("Son of Shriveled-Hand") and worked as a professional scribe, a position for which facility in Arabic was necessary. At some point he was consecrated Bishop of al-Ashmunayn, began to produce books (his *Commentary on the Creed* is dated to 950 and 955), became a theological counselor to at least two **patriarchs** (Abraham ibn Zur'ah, 975–978, and Philotheus, 979–1003), and gained renown as a theologian capable of debate, in Arabic, with representatives of any religious tradition.

The *History of the Patriarchs* records examples of Sawirus in debate, but these examples are anything but theologically subtle. One Friday, we are told, Sawirus turned the tables on some Muslims who challenged him to pronounce on whether a passing dog was Christian or Muslim by asking them to place meat (from which Copts abstained on Fridays) and wine (forbidden to Muslims) before the dog, to see which it would consume! Another time, we read, Sawirus defeated a Jewish scholar in debate at the court of the Fatimid, caliph al-Mu'izz, simply by quoting Isaiah 1:3: "The ox knows its owner, and the ass its master's crib; but Israel does not know. . . ." These stories may have delighted Christian readers; still, a better intimation of Sawirus' theological capacities is provided by the list of 20 titles recorded in *History of the Patriarchs*, a list expanded to 26 in Shams al-Ri'asa Abu al-Barakat **ibn Kabar**'s ecclesiastical encyclopedia *The Lamp of the Darkness*. Many of Sawirus' works have survived. They show us a theologian with a strong grounding in scripture and the Church Fathers (especially **Cyril** of **Alexandria**), a sophisticated command of the Arabic language, and a sense of fairness in debate that, if not precisely "ecumenical," presages the openness of spirit that would characterize the **Awlad al-'Assal** and other great theologians of the 13th century. Like them, he was prepared to learn from Arabophone theologians outside Egypt. In his *al-Bayan al-mukhtasar fi al-iman* (Concise Exposition of the Faith), he refers to and draws extensively from an Arabic work coming out of the Syrian Orthodox Church, *Kitab Ustath al-rahib* (The Book of Eustathius the Monk).

Such was Sawirus' reputation as the father of Coptic Orthodox ecclesial writing in Arabic that anonymous texts (or texts by suspect or insufficiently well-known authors) were regularly attributed to him in the manuscript tradition. In one notable case, credit for the collection and translation of what became the *History of the Patriarchs* (by Mawhub ibn Mansur ibn Mufarrij of Alexandria, who embarked upon this project in 1088) was assigned to Sawirus. Recent scholars have struggled to give credit where it is due, but this means assessing Sawirus as a theologian and apologist rather than as a historian.

SAYINGS OF THE FATHERS. The fourth and fifth centuries witnessed the spread of **monasticism** in the Egyptian desert. Monks strove to live according to certain ideals of conduct that were expressed by many early monks. The majority of these stories, memorable sayings, or anecdotes were provided in **Macarius'** settlements at **Nitria** and **Scetis**. These "words" were initially preserved only orally but were then put into writing, very probably in Coptic. They are preserved in two forms, one is alphabetically, and the other according to subject matter. The entire corpus is known as the ***Apophthegmata patrum*** or *Geronica*. It is a major source for the history of monastic spirituality, and it illustrates the cultural and social milieu of the monastic communities in Nitria, **Kellia**, and Scetis. By the sixth century, the Sayings of the Fathers were translated from Greek into Latin and soon thereafter into Syriac, Arabic, Georgian, and Armenian. Therefore it is not surprising that they influenced monasticism in the East and the West. The Arabic ***Bustan al-Ruhban*** or the *Garden of the Monks* is apparently based on the Sayings of the

Fathers. It is widely used by Egyptian monks and is highly appreciated by the Coptic laity.

SCETIS. *See* WADI AL-NATRUN.

SECOND TREATISE OF THE GREAT SETH **(NHC VII, 2).** A
Gnostic revelatory monologue given by Jesus Christ to a congregation of "perfect and incorruptible ones." The title, given in Greek at
the end, is curious because no mention is made in the text of **Seth.**
The text, containing polemics against Christians who are identifiably
orthodox, features a **docetic** interpretation of Jesus' Crucifixion that
has the spiritual Savior laughing above at the folly of those below
crucifying his fleshly body. The *Second Treatise of the Great Seth*,
extant only in Coptic, was originally composed in Greek, probably in
late second-century Egypt.

SEMI-ARIANS. Semi-Arian is the name given to those who believed
that Christ has a "like substance" of God (*homeosius*) but not the
same substance (*homoousius*). The key figure of this group is Basil
of Ancyra (356 A.D.). St. **Athanasius**, after his return from exile, was
able to convince them that Christ is "like" substance, meaning that
He is like in every aspect and hence *homoousius*. Many accepted his
point of view and were reconciled to the Orthodox Church.

SENTENCES OF SEXTUS **(NHC XII, 1).** Fragments of a Coptic
translation of a Christian collection of moral precepts composed in
Greek in second-century **Alexandria**. Latin, Syriac, Georgian, and
Armenian versions are also known.

SETHIANS. Gnostic heretics so designated by patristic heresiologists.
According to some accounts, they had an elaborate myth in which
Seth, son of Adam, played a prominent role as revealer of gnosis and
was equated by some with Jesus Christ. In this system, Gnostics are
referred to as the "seed" or "race" of Seth. Several of the treatises
preserved in Coptic in the **Nag Hammadi Codices** contain, or al-
lude to, a related mythological system. The most important of these
treatises is the *Apocryphon of John* (NHC II, 1; III, 1; IV, 1; BG,
2). Hippolytus attributes a completely different mythological system

to heretics he also refers to as "Sethians." This system posits three first principles: Light, Darkness, and Spirit. According to Hippolytus, this system is elaborated in a writing called "The Paraphrase of Seth," although Seth is not a prominent figure in the system. A similar doctrine based on the same first principles—Light, Darkness, and Spirit—is found in one of the Nag Hammadi Codices, *The Paraphrase of Shem* (NHC VII, 1). *See also* THREE STELES OF SETH; ZOSTRIANOS.

SEVERUS OF ANTIOCH (ca. 456–538). Saint and **patriarch**. The sources for the life of Severus, anti-Chalcedonian patriarch of Antioch from 512 to 518 A.D., are many and varied; among these sources are his letters and his cathedral homilies, which number 125. His friend Zechariah Scholasticus wrote the first biography of Severus from his early years to his ordination as patriarch. This biography survived only in Syriac. John, abbot of the Monastery of Beith Aphthonia, composed the second biography. It survived in a Syriac translation, and some fragments survived in Coptic. The third biography is ascribed to one of Severus' successors, Athanasius of Antioch (594–630 or 631), which has come down to us in Coptic, Arabic, and Ethiopic fragments. In addition, several apocryphal works ascribed to Severus reflect some traditions related to the life of Severus, especially in Egypt, such as the homily on Claudius of Antioch wherein the Pseudo-Severus narrated that he visited Upper Egypt up to the cataract and returned Via Assiut and Qossia.

Severus was born around 456 A.D. in Sozopolis (Pisidia) to a well-to-do family. His grandfather, according to Athanasius of Antioch, was a **bishop** who attended the **Council of Ephesus**. After the death of his father in 485, Severus and his two older brothers were sent by their mother to **Alexandria** to study grammar and rhetoric. He studied law in Beirut in 488. Severus was baptized in the Church of the Martyr Leontius at Tripolis. He became a monk in the area around Gaza in an anti-Chalcedonian monastery. Severus used the wealth of his parents to build a monastery around Gaza, which was consequently confiscated by the Chalcedonians. Severus was obliged to go to Constantinople to appeal to the emperor. While Severus was in Constantinople, he refuted a work of a Chalcedonian by his book the *Philalethes*, or "Friend of Truth." The *Philalethes* is a classic Christological work from the anti-Chalcedonian side. Because a florilegium is by its very nature selective, it was Severus's aim in this work to prove that by selectively citing the Patriarch **Cyril**, the Chalcedonians had made the great Alexandrian to be a proponent of the two-nature **Christology**: "The historical development of Cyril was in fact so ambivalent that his works could be a common arsenal for contrary Christologies depending upon what one sought in them." It was precisely this ambivalence that was to cause Severus from this point on to take up his pen repeatedly to defend Cyril's understanding of Christ. He played a pivotal role for the deposition of Macedonius, the patriarch of the city. Emperor Anastasius appointed him Patriarch of Antioch in 512. During his patriarchate, Severus delivered his 125 cathedral homilies. Among Severus's first official duties would have been the dispatch of *synodika* or a letter to other bishops containing the new patriarch's profession of faith and a list of anathemas. The addressees of this letter then replied with their own professions of faith and lists of anathemas, if they agreed to enter into communion with him. Severus sent his letters to John of Alexandria with the aim of reestablishing communion with Egypt. Extracts of the letters of the patriarchs of Alexandria, as well as those of Severus, survived only in Arabic translation in the book of the *Profession of the Fathers*.

After the death of Emperor Anastasius, Justin became emperor in 518. In the same year, Severus was exiled. On his arrival in Egypt, Severus was welcomed by Patriarch Timothy and went to the Monastery of Enaton outside Alexandria, where the deposed Bishop of Halicarnasus, Julian, also sought refuge. After his flight, some of the Antiochene clergy accused Severus of several crimes. However, he maintained excellent relations with other Antiochene clergy, as is demonstrated in his correspondence. Severus spent the next 20 years in exile. It was a difficult and dangerous period for him. Nobody knew where he was living except those who brought him the necessities of life; he was forever on the move, sometimes changing his abode when some disturbing news reached him. In the winter of 534–535, in response to repeated invitations from Justinian (that may have been prompted by Theodora), Severus finally went to Constantinople, accompanied by a large group of anti-Chalcedonians, and took up residence in one of the imperial palaces. He probably did not hold out much hope of a successful outcome, as he supposedly remarked before leaving Egypt. After Severus's death, **Theodosius** became the acknowledged leader of the anti-Chalcedonian party, directing it from Constantinople for the next 30 years.

Severus has a special place in the Coptic Church. His name is always mentioned after St. **Mark**, the founder of the Church, as a second founder. In the Coptic calendar, he has three **feasts**. He also wrote many liturgical hymns.

SHEFTISHI, YUHANNA. An 18th–19th-century **priest** and scholar. He was born in Cairo. He served as an interpreter, adjudicator for tax collection, and main recorder at the Tribunal of Commerce under the French administration following the Campaign of Napoleon Bonaparte in Egypt (1798–1801). He was appointed a colonel in the Coptic legion, which General **Ya'qub** had formed. He left Egypt for France after the withdrawal of the French from Egypt. In Paris, he instructed Jean François Champollion (1790–1832), who succeeded in deciphering the ancient Egyptian language, the pronunciation of the **Coptic language**, and Coptic names. He collaborated with the scholars who prepared the great work *Description de l'Egypte*; perhaps he was entrusted to provide "the principal passages from Arabic writers regarding the antiquities and geography of Egypt." He continued his ministry in Paris, where he used to celebrate the Coptic Mass as late as 1825, when he moved to Marseilles to live among the Egyptian refugees there.

SHENOUDA III (1923–). Monk, **bishop**, teacher, writer, politician, and 117th **patriarch** of the Coptic Church (1971–). He was born Nazir Gayed in Assiut. He played a great role in the renaissance of the Coptic Church. He studied history and graduated from Cairo University in 1947 and from the **Clerical College** in 1949. He served as an officer during his military service. He enjoyed postgraduate studies in archaeology and edited the *Sunday School Monthly Magazine*. In 1952, he was elected member of the Egyptian Journalists' Syndicate. In 1954, he joined the **Monastery of the Syrians**. As Father Antonius al-Suryani, he retired in a cave in **Wadi al-Natrun** for extended periods. In 1962, Pope **Cyril VI** ordained him as bishop for Christian education. The new Bishop Shenouda was also the dean of the Clerical College, which had been greatly developed under him.

He supervised the Sunday School movement that was instrumental in Coptic renewal and lay education.

In 1971, he was consecrated patriarch of the Coptic Church. Pope Shenouda III is convinced that when **monasticism** in the Egyptian deserts is strong, then Christianity and the Coptic Church are strong. Therefore, he repopulated many of the abandoned monasteries and encouraged the monasteries to be cultural centers and to receive visitors. The number of the monks and nuns is still growing. Coptic monasteries provided the Coptic Church with educated monks who were consecrated bishops in the new dioceses that Pope Shenouda established all over Egypt. Monks were sent also to serve in the monasteries that were founded in the United States, Australia, Europe, and Africa. In 1973, he visited Rome and with Pope Paul VI issued a joint statement on **Christology**. He visited the Archbishop of Canterbury in England in 1979. They both issued a joint statement based on the **Nicene Creed** in 1987 at the **Monastery of St. Pshoi in Wadi al-Natrun**. In the same year, he, the Greek Orthodox Patriarch of **Alexandria**, the Syrian Orthodox Patriarch of Antioch, the Greek Orthodox Patriarch of Antioch, and the Armenian Catholicon confessed the same faith in Christ "fundamentally and essentially." In 1988 there was a meeting between the Coptic Evangelical Community Council and Coptic Orthodox theologians upon the invitation of Pope Shenouda, which led to theological dialogue between the two churches. He ordained 180 deaconesses in 1981, and the Holy Synod issued the decree of the "consecrated women" in 1991.

Before the reign of Pope Shenouda, there were only a few Coptic churches in the Coptic **Diaspora**. Today, there are 125 churches in the United States, 27 churches in Canada, 37 churches in Australia, in addition to many churches in Europe and Africa. He traveled extensively for pastoral visits all over the world. Pope Shenouda is a great preacher who is admired by thousands of Copts attending his Wednesday lectures in the Cairo Cathedral. He is known as a poet of quality. He has written hundreds of books and articles on spirituality and **theology**. He is a writer for the most important newspaper in the Arab world, *Al-Ahram*. He has been editing his own weekly *al-Kiraza* for decades. Pope Shenouda reacted to the increasing attacks against the properties of Copts and their churches by Muslim extremists with only the minimum interference of the government to protect them. In 1981, he canceled all the Easter celebrations all over Egypt. Anwar al-Sadat issued a presidential decree that ordered the pope to leave to Wadi al-Natrun under what was effectively "monastery arrest." A committee of bishops had to perform the duties of the patriarchate until 1985 when President Hosny Mubarak revoked President Sadat's decree. Shenouda was received by thousands of Copts as a hero at the **Cathedral of St. Mark in Cairo**. Some of his opponents argued that the church became the main social outlet for the majority of the educated Copts, who were more excluded from the national and political life during his pontificate.

SHENOUDA THE ARCHIMANDRITE COPTIC SOCIETY. It was founded in December 1979 by Hany Takla and a small group of educated Copts in Los Angeles. The primary goal is to preserve, revive, and promote Coptic heritage. It was officially incorporated in the United States in 1983. Its membership base of over 200 members is spread all over the world with a concentration in the greater Los Angeles area. The society's activities emphasize the accumulation of study resources, education, and promotion of research in the field. Most of these activities are carried through the St. Shenouda Center for Coptic Studies in Los Angeles, established in 1992. The accumulation of study resources included establishment of a research library that covers all known aspects of Coptic studies. The libraries currently have about 4,300 volumes of monographs and periodicals. The Coptic Microform Library (CML), which started in 1980, contains copies of manuscripts and study material collected from all over the world, and is composed of over 335,000 frames. The manuscript collection, established in 2003, now has 33 items with about 3,900 folios. It is primarily a **liturgical** collection. The society also has a modest Coptic textile collection of about 10 items, established in 2002. The electronic sources are arranged under the Coptic Digital Library, which includes electronic Coptic texts and digital images of manuscripts and study material. It began as early as 1987 and now has about 300,000 images plus hundreds of electronic pages of Coptic biblical and literary texts. The society also has had a strong presence on the Internet since 1995. It has conducted multilevel classes, workshops, and public lectures in the **Coptic language** and other aspects of Coptic studies. It is currently organizing a comprehensive online study curriculum in the field to academically introduce students to the different aspects of the heritage of Coptic Christianity. In the area of promoting research in the field of Coptic studies, the society has published the *Bulletin of St. Shenouda the Archimandrite Coptic Society* (1984–2001), *St. Shenouda Coptic Newsletter* (1994–2004), *Coptica* (published in cooperation with **St. Mark Foundation for Coptic History Studies** [SMF], 2002–present), and *St. Shenouda Coptic Quarterly* (2004–present). In addition, it has awarded scholarships to graduate students pursuing Coptic studies, financed Coptic studies classes and visiting scholars, and cosponsored a Coptic lectures series at American universities. This was carried out in addition to organizing annual academic conferences, symposia in the field in Los Angeles since 1997, as well as cosponsoring with SMF four major symposia on Christianity and **monasticism** in Egypt.

SHENUTE OF ATRIPE (ca. 347–). Saint, abbot, He is an illustrious figure of Egyptian Christianity and a most significant Coptic writer. Around 370 Shenute became a monk under his uncle Pgol, who founded the **Monastery of St. Shenute,** also known as the White Monastery. After the death of the latter in about 385, Shenute became the monastery's abbot. The monastery grew considerably during his time. According to the Arabic version of his "Life" there were 2,200 monks and 1,800 nuns associated with the White Monastery. Shenute dealt strictly with his monks and nuns, and his rule was harsher than that of **Pachomius.** He strove against paganism in his region. In 431, he participated in the **Council of Ephesus** with Patriarch **Cyril.** The writings of Shenute are of great importance for the history of **Coptic literature.** His works are composed of about 1,870 extant leaves, which represent only a part of what may have been once 25,000 pages.

SIMAIKA, MARCUS (1864–1944). Founder of the **Coptic Museum.** He was born in Cairo to venerable and prosperous Coptic parents. From his youth he showed great interest in Egypt's Christian monuments. It is to his well-deserved credit that he founded the Coptic Museum in 1908. He succeeded in attracting the Coptic Church and the Egyptian public to support his efforts in establishing the museum. In 1906, Simaika became a member of the Commission for the Preservation of the Arab Monuments and later its chairman.

He was able to place the ancient Coptic churches and monasteries under the supervision of that committee. In collaboration with **Yassa 'Abd al-Masih**, he published the *Catalogue of the Coptic and Arabic Manuscripts in the Coptic Museum, the Patriarchate, the Principal Churches of Cairo and Alexandria and the Monasteries of Egypt*, in two volumes (Cairo, 1939–1942).

SIM'AN IBN KALIL (ca. 1145–ca. 1235). Monk, theologian. Like a number of other great figures in **Copto-Arabic literature** (including **Sawirus ibn al-Muqaffa'** and Shams al-Ri'asa Abu al-Barakat **ibn Kabar**), Sim'an ibn Kalil ibn Maqara began his career as a bureaucrat in government service. In 1173, he was (financial) secretary in the Department of the Army under none other than Salah al-Din al-Ayyubi, the famed Saladin. According to his great-nephew **al-Makin Jirjis ibn al-'Amid**, Sim'an remained in government service until sometime during the sultanate of Salah al-Din's younger brother al-Malik al-'Adil (1200–1218), but then withdrew and became a monk at the Monastery of St. **John the Little** in the **Wadi al-Natrun**, where he enclosed himself in a cell for more than 30 years. He wrote a number of books, including biblical commentaries and a philosophically informed apology of the Christian faith. His most beloved work, however, is *Rawdat al-farid wa-salwat al-wahid* (The Garden of the Hermit and Consolation of the Solitary), in which Sim'an explains the Christian faith and commends the life of virtue in 12 chapters of beautiful rhymed prose. Read throughout the Arabic-speaking Christian world, it was published in Egypt in 1873 and again in 1886, but awaits a modern edition.

SOBHY, GEORGY (1884–1964). Educator and physician. He was born into a family from al-Maymoun in the district of Wasta. He obtained his medical degree in 1904 and was appointed a resident in Kasr al-Aini Hospital. In 1909, he was sent on a scholarship to London. He was appointed a teacher of anatomy in the Faculty of Medicine, where he worked with Professor Elliot Smith, professor of genetics. With him, he examined approximately 3,000 corpses from different historical periods. He wrote a number of books and articles on the **Coptic language** and culture. In 1950, he published his most famous work, *Common Words in the Spoken Arabic of Egypt*, *of Greek or Coptic Origin.* He taught at Cairo University and the **Higher Institute of Coptic Studies.** He was a member of the board of the **Society of Coptic Archaeology.**

SOCIETY OF COPTIC ARCHAEOLOGY. It was founded in Cairo in 1934 by **Mirrit Boutros Ghali** as a scientific and scholarly institution. Its *Bulletin de la Société d'Archéologie Copte* is the first journal of **Coptology.** In addition to the *Bulletin*, the main publications of the society are the excavation reports and Coptic and Arabic source documents. With approximately 15,000 volumes in the society's library, it is the largest Coptological library in Egypt.

SOPHIA OF JESUS CHRIST **(NHC III, 4; BG, 3).** A **Gnostic** revelation discourse attributed to the risen Christ, seated on a mountain, presenting esoteric teaching to his "twelve disciples and seven women." "The Savior" presents his teaching in response to various questions put to him by the disciples, the final one posed by Mary Magdalene. *Sophia of Jesus Christ* is a "Christianized" expansion of another **Nag Hammadi** text, *Eugnostos the Blessed* (NHC III, 3; V, 1). The additional material deals with the human predicament and the saving work of Christ in imparting gnosis to his disciples. The title, "The Sophia [wisdom] of Jesus Christ," occurs at the beginning and the end of both copies. Extant completely only in Coptic, it was originally composed in Greek, probably in late second- or early third-century Egypt. Three fourth-century papyrus fragments of the Greek version were found at Oxyrhynchus.

STRUCTURE OF THE COPTIC CHURCH. Pope **Shenouda III** is the president of the Holy Synod, which is the highest ecclesiastical body in the Coptic Church. The Holy Synod is made up of all the Church's **bishops**. It assembles annually on the Saturday prior to the Pentecost Sunday. In 1985, Pope Shenouda established seven committees of the members of the Holy Synod and entrusted them with the tasks of the ecumenical relations, monastic affairs, pastoral affairs, faith and ethics, **liturgy**, and deacon affairs. Pope Shenouda divided the large dioceses into a number of small ones and founded many new dioceses to facilitate the work of the bishops in guiding their communities. He consecrated a number of extradiocesan bishops for several affairs such as public, social, and ecumenical services. Many bishops had been ordained to serve hundreds of thousands of Copts in the United States, Canada, Australia, and Europe, in addition to the Coptic Orthodox communities in Africa. Coptic monasteries provided the Church with the educated new bishops.

The following are the Coptic dioceses of

Lower Egypt: Dimyat and Kafr al-Sheikh and the Monastery of St. Demyana, Damanhur and Behira and Pentapolis, Minufiya, Benha and Qwisna, Tanta, Sharqyia, Zaqaziq and Minya al-Qamh, Mansura, Port Said, Isma'ilia, Suez, and Horgada.

Sinai: Al-Arish and North Sinai, al-Tur and South Sinai.

Upper Egypt: Giza, Fayoum, Beni Suef, Beni Mazar and al-Bahnasa, Biba and al-Fashn, Maghagha and Idwa, Samalout, Abu Qurqas, Minya, Dayr Mawwas, Matai, Malawi, Dayrut and Sanabu, Qusia and Mer, Assiut, Manfalout, Abnub, Abu Tig and Sidfa, Tima, Tahta, Sohag, Akhmim and Saqulta, Girga, Baliana, Nag' Hammadi, Dishna, Qena and Qift, Naqqada and Qus, Luxor and Armant and Esna, and Aswan

The **patriarch** of the Coptic Church is traditionally the Bishop of **Alexandria** and Cairo. However, Pope Shenouda also consecrated "general" bishops for some districts belonging to Greater Cairo in Halwan and Ma'sara, Ma'adi and Dar al-Salam, Shubra al-Khema, East Cairo, and Shebine al-Qanater and al-Khanka, and Old Cairo. There are also a number of general bishops, such as the bishop for youth affairs, and the bishop for African affairs. Outside of Egypt are the following: Jerusalem, Stevenage (U.K.), Scotland, Ireland, and East England (U.K.), Birmingham (U.K.), Glastonbury (U.K.), Hoxter-Brenkhausen (Germany), Vienna (Austria), Toulon (France), Marseilles (France), Rome (Italy), Milan (Italy), Melbourne (Australia), Sidney (Australia), Los Angeles (U.S.), Colleyville (U.S.), New Jersey (U.S.), Khartoum (Sudan), Atbara and Um-Durman (Sudan).

The abbots of the following monasteries are bishops residing in their monasteries: the Monastery of Patmus, the Monastery of St. Samuel (al-Qalamun), the **Monastery of al-Baramous**, the **Monastery of the Syrians**, **Abu Mina** (the Monastery of St. **Menas**), the **Monastery of St. Pschoi**, al-Muharraq (Monastery of the Holy Virgin Mary), the **Monastery of St. Antony**, and Dayr Mari Girgis at Khatatba. The following monasteries are also populated: the **Monastery of St. Macarius**, the **Monastery of St. Paul**, the **Monastery of the Archangel Gabriel at Naqlun**, the Monastery of St. George at Sedment, the **Monastery of St. Shenute**, the Monastery of St. Thomas, the Monastery of St. Michael (al-Malak), the Monastery of the Martyrs, the Monastery of the Holy Virgin, the Monastery of St. George, and the Monastery of St. Psote. The previous six monasteries are in the region of Akhmim the Monastery of St. Palamoun (**Nag Hammadi**), the Monastery of St. **Pachomius** (Luxor), the Monastery of St. George (al-Riziqat), the Monastery of the Potter (Esna), and the Monastery of St. Pachomius (Edfu).

Although the Coptic Church is a monastic organization as its patriarch and all its bishops are chosen from among the monks, the laymen play a considerable role in its activities in Egypt as well as in the **Diaspora**. The participation of **women** in these activities has remarkably improved in the past few decades.

SYNAXARION (*Kitab al-Sinaksar*). Collection of brief biographies of the **saints** and martyrs, arranged for daily reading according to their **feast** days. A characteristic feature of the Coptic Orthodox **liturgy** is that, in addition to appointed lections from the Pauline epistles, the Catholic epistles, the Acts of the Apostles, and the Gospels, there is a reading specific to every day in the calendar year, from a collection of very brief saints' lives called *Kitab al-Sinaksar* (from Greek, *synaxarion*). This collection gives much space to the martyrs of the pre-Constantinian persecutions of the Church, although it also includes notices for later martyrs, ascetics, and **patriarchs**, as well as biblical figures and a variety of other commemorations. Many questions about the history of this collection remain open. A model for it had existed (from about the 11th century) in the synaxaria of the Arabic-speaking Chalcedonian (or Melchite) community. The names conventionally associated with the production of a specifically Copto-Arabic synaxarion are those of **Butrus Sawirus al-Jamil** and especially **Mikha'il**, **Bishop** of Atrib and Malij, from the early and mid-13th century, respectively. Their specific contributions to the compilation are unknown, however, and internal manuscript evidence points to a 14th-century date of compilation. An additional complication in the study of the early Copto-Arabic synaxarion is the fact that two recensions exist in the manuscript tradition, one of Upper Egypt and one of Lower Egypt. The former may be older, but the latter has had the greater influence, not only in Egypt but also in Ethiopia, thanks to its translation into Ethiopic by one Sim'on at the **Monastery of St. Antony** around the year 1400. This Ethiopic version then underwent its own history of enrichment and later was translated *back* into Arabic. The volumes of the Synaxarion used in the Coptic Orthodox Church today, first published in 1935–1937, represent the tradition of the Lower Egyptian recension as enlarged and shaped by its modern editors, with contributions of material from the recension that passed through Ethiopia.

The regular commemoration of the saints and martyrs has undoubtedly played a role in the formation of the imaginations of the Coptic Orthodox faithful, reinforcing their identity as part of the "church of the martyrs," and inspiring them to imitate the saints' courage and steadfastness of faith, in spite of many difficulties and challenges throughout their community's history.

SYNCLETICA (4th century?). Saint and nun. Her "Life," which is wrongly attributed to St. **Athanasius**, dates probably from the fifth century. It is one of the oldest hagiographic writings depicting a **woman**. She originates from Macedonia, but her Christian parents settled in **Alexandria**. She withdrew to a tomb near the city and dedicated herself to asceticism. The *Apophthegmata patrum* preserves 18 apophthegms under her name. She is never described as having male features, and she enters the *Apophthegmata* as mother. Apparently she died after a long suffering from purulent osteitis at the age of 80.

– T –

TAFSIR. This word bears the meaning of "interpretation" or "commentary," depending on the text.

TEACHINGS OF SILVANUS **(NHC VII, 4).** A Christian collection of gnomic wisdom sayings addressed by an anonymous author to his "son." The title is given at the beginning of the tractate. "Silvanus" is probably meant to be the disciple of Peter and Paul named in the New Testament. The text represents a typically Alexandrian synthesis of biblical, Hellenistic, Jewish, early Christian, and philosophical religious and ethical teachings. It also contains some anti-**Gnostic** polemics. The tractate's inclusion in a codex in which all the others are Gnostic is therefore an anomaly. Extant only in Coptic, *Teachings of Silvanus* was originally composed in Greek, probably in late third-century **Alexandria**, though it contains much older traditional material.

TESTIMONY OF TRUTH (NHC IX, 3). A **Gnostic** homiletic tract written by an anonymous author addressed to a group of Christians with spiritual ears. It consists of a series of warnings against the false teachings of opponents clearly identifiable as Orthodox Christians. Advocating a strict encratic ethic, the author does not spare even other Gnostics, that is, those who, like **Valentinus** and **Basilides**, permit marriage. Extant only in Coptic, *Testimony of Truth* was originally composed in Greek, probably in late second-century **Alexandria**.

THEODOSIUS OF ALEXANDRIA. Saint and **patriarch**. He was the 33rd patriarch of **Alexandria** (535–566). He is commemorated on the 28th of Baounah. He was a devoted friend and disciple of **Severus of Antioch**. Riots of the Gaianites followed his consecration. He was able to exercise his authority only briefly but later was forced to go to Constantinople, where he became a symbol of anti-Chalcedonian orthodoxy. He acquired such an excellent reputation that the non-Chalcedonians Copts were called "Theodosians" after his name for a long time. Information concerning his life has survived in Coptic sources. Theodosius wrote a lengthy homily on John the Baptist, giving details on the life of the forerunner of Christ. He also wrote a homily on the Archangel Michael, and a third homily on the Virgin Mary that is currently in the Vatican Library. In this homily, he describes the virtues of the Virgin Mary, partially published by Robinson; there is a letter ascribed also to him.

THEODOTUS. A pupil of **Valentinus** the **Gnostic** who was active during the mid-second century. Some of his writings were excerpted by Clement of **Alexandria**, including an account of the

Valentinian myth close to that of another Valentinian teacher, Ptolemy. Nothing is known of his life, but it is likely that Theodotus taught in Alexandria.

THEOLOGY. *See* THEOLOGY IN THE COPTIC CHURCH.

THEOLOGY IN THE COPTIC CHURCH. It is hard to talk about a specifically Coptic theology, for the Coptic Church is part of the Eastern Christian Church. Thus, in order to define the development of Coptic theological thought, it is important to put it in the context of the historical development of the Coptic Church. Nothing is known about the beginning of the Coptic Church except that some pilgrims from Egypt heard the first preaching of St. Peter in Jerusalem (Acts 2:10). Apollos is another witness. He was a Jew born in **Alexandria** and learned in the scriptures who met Priscilla and Aquila in Ephesus (Acts 18:24). St. Mark is traditionally considered as the founder of the Coptic Church.

Some scholars, after the discovery of the **Nag Hammadi** manuscripts in 1945, developed the thesis of a heretical origin of Christianity in Egypt. It is possible that **Gnostics** were counted among the Christian groups of the time, but we do not have any information about their numbers or their activities, nor do we have any conclusive archaeological evidence relating to them. Other scholars have highlighted the role and activity of the Alexandrian Jews. However, archaeological material, such as the fragment of the Gospel of John discovered in Fayoum, shows clearly that Christianity was already widespread in Egypt by the beginning of the second century.

The second century is the age of the **"Apostolic Fathers."** This name is given to a circle of authors who enjoyed direct contact with the Apostles themselves. None of them had an actual or alleged relation with Egypt, but their works were copied and translated into the **Coptic language**. After the Apostolic Fathers came the apologetical and the antiheretical authors who strove to defend Christianity against pagans and heretics. None of their works survived in Coptic. By the end of the second and early in the third century, the School of Alexandria began its well-known activities. Among its key personalities were Pantaenus, Clement, and **Origen**. This school attained to its highest reputation under the direction of Origen. Many of the Church leaders during the three centuries that followed were either trained in it or even directed it. This school adopted the allegorical method of exegesis of the Bible. In the third century, another important pastoral event took place when **Bishop** Demetrius consecrated three bishops; after that time, the number of bishops began to increase. By the end of the third century, **Antony** had withdrawn from the world to become the first monk and hermit. Next to nothing of the output of the first masters of the School of Alexandria has survived in Coptic, except for the work of those who occupied the episcopal throne, such as **Athanasius** and **Cyril**. Monastic literature was written in Coptic or translated into that language.

A new era for the Christian Church began with the advent of Constantine and the edict of Milan in 313, where Christians gained freedom of worship. This century is characterized by theological debates. The Coptic Church played an important role in the ecumenical movement. Athanasius of Alexandria was a key person in combating the Arian heresy and defending the **Council of Nicaea. Monasticism** and monastic communities were instrumental in combating Christian heresies as well as pagan religions, especially in Upper Egypt. The theological literature of this century is characterized by the defense of the faith against heresies such as **Arianism** and **Apollinarianism**. In order to define the faith, the first ecumenical council was assembled in Nicaea to refute the Arian heresy, where Athanasius, the future **patriarch** of Alexandria, played a pivotal role. Apollinarianism was condemned in the second ecumenical **Council of Ephesus** in 380 A.D. We have also some exegetical works on the books of the Bible, in addition to homilies and collections of miracles related to the cult of martyrs (**Coptic literature** is rich of this area).

The fifth century is marked by **Christological** debates. These started with Nestorius, Bishop of Constantinople, and former student of the Theological School of Antioch, who preached that the Virgin Mary should not be called "**Theotokos**" (God-bearer) for she brought forth a man and should thus be called "Christotokos" (Christ-bearer). The first reaction came from Alexandria, when Cyril refuted his assertion through several theological treatises on the nature of Christ. Emperor Theodosius II summoned a council in Ephesus. This council ended in chaos; however, an exchange of letters after the council between Cyril of Alexandria and John of Antioch resulted in a sound theology of the nature of Christ that was accepted by both churches, the Alexandrian and the Antiochian.

The affair was reopened with a new definition by Eutyches, which required the assembly of a second council in Ephesus in 449 by the order of the Emperor Theodosius II. This council also ended in chaos. The emperor suddenly died shortly after this council, and the imperial authority (Pulcheria, sister of Theodosius II) convoked another council in Chalcedon in 451. This council promulgated a definition of faith that outlawed **Nestorianism** and Eutychianism, and exiled the Patriarch of Alexandria, **Dioscorus**. The council also recognized the *Tome* of Pope Leo I of Rome as orthodox, and in harmony with the views of the Church Fathers and Cyril of Alexandria. Only a few fragments related to these councils in the Coptic language survived in the biography of Dioscorus, and an apocryphal work by Dioscorus on Macarius of Tkow narrates the events of the **Council of Chalcedon**.

The definition of faith was problematical from the start because in the East it was seen as only an interpretation of the symbol or Creed of Nicaea. Also critical was the resolution of the council, later known as Canon 28, which gave to Constantinople (the "New Rome") equal privileges to those of Old Rome in ecclesiastical matters, and decreed that the eastern capital should hold second place after Rome. As a result of this canon, the traditional influence of Alexandria, the second-largest city of the empire, was diminished.

The reaction of the Bishop of Rome to the canon was also unfavorable, and he was reluctant to accept it explicitly. The issues of the formula "in two natures" and Canon 28, as well as the ratification of the *Tome* (considered by many in the East to be Nestorian), were to cause unrest and resentment among Christians in both East and West in the century that followed, and a lasting division in the churches of the eastern Roman Empire. Christians were polarized into "Dyophysites" and "Monophysites." With good reason, this could be called "the Great Schism" and contributed to the success of the Arab invasion.

In the 50 years after Chalcedon, there were repeated efforts by the imperial government in the East to restore ecclesiastical and political unity. The most famous example of this was the Henoticon of Emperor Zeno in 482, which emphasized the faith of Nicaea. Although it was a masterpiece of imperial diplomacy and nominally at least brought the eastern sees into communion, in the long run it was unsuccessful because for those opposed to the council, only an outright condemnation of the *Tome* of Leo and the Council of Chalcedon would suffice. However, Zeno left a lasting impression in the Coptic mentality; he is always mentioned as a God-fearing and pious emperor. His daughter Hilaria is considered one of the **saints** of the desert of **Scetis**.

The sixth century is marked by the continuous debate between "Monophysites" (or "Miaphysites") and "Dyophistes." After Emperor Zeno, emperors interfered in the elections of the patriarchs of Alexandria, imposing sometimes one of their followers who shared their faith. Miaphysite bishops and patriarchs were exiled. Among the great theologians of the sixth century, mention must be made of **Severus of Antioch** who wrote many theological treatises refuting the Dyophysite belief. Some of his works have survived in Coptic. **Theodosius of Alexandria** was also considered as one of the great figures of this century.

The sixth century saw the appearance of two new types of theological works. The first is the *Catenae* (chain of commentaries) on the Bible, arranging a collection of works of patristic exegesis verse by verse according to the book of the Bible. From this period we have a Coptic Catena on the four Gospels written in the Bohairic dialect, originally from the **Monastery of St. Macarius** and preserved now in the British Library. The second type are the florilegia, which are collections of patristic quotations on dogma drawn from the existing corpus, such as Athanasius, Cyril of Alexandria, Basil, **Gregory**, and so on. We do not have a florilegium in the Coptic language; only an Arabic translation of the Book of the *Philalethes* survives. Rufus of Shotep, an author of the sixth century, is one of the last representatives of the theological School of Alexandria.

The Coptic Church rejected the monothelite doctrine imposed by Emperor Heraclius in the seventh century. It was seen as a new version of the Chalcedonian faith. We have some indirect attestations reflecting the Coptic mentality, such as the "Life" of St. Samuel of Kalamon, or fragments from Patriarch Benjamin of Alexandria. Egypt was the target of several invasions in this century, first by the Persians and then by the Arabs. However, we have some Coptic theological books of this century, such as the *Questions of Theodore* and the answers of John the patriarch, and a discussion between a Jew and a Christian.

In the eighth and ninth centuries, the Coptic Church did not take part in the **iconoclastic** crisis. During this time only a few theological works were produced, including the translation of some patristic homilies. Starting from the 10th century, scholars and ecclesiastical authorities of the Coptic Church started to write in Arabic for the governors first and then for their congregations. *See also* NICENE CREED.

THEOPHILUS. Saint and **patriarch**. He was the 23rd Patriarch of **Alexandria** (385–412). He is commemorated on the 18th of Babeh. He was patriarch from 385 to 412 A.D. and played a significant role in increasing the prestige of the See of Alexandria. He was highly educated and an effective dean of the **Catechetical School of Alexandria**. However, when difficulties arose out of what is known as the **Origenist** controversy, he adopted the literal interpretation (anthropomorphic) rather than support the allegorical interpretation. His name is also linked to the deposition of John Chrysostom, Patriarch of Constantinople, who is considered a saint. It should be mentioned that most of our knowledge comes mainly from his enemies, especially **Palladius**. However, some of the Church Fathers considered him a great saint. He is remembered as an excellent example among the monks. Many **Sayings of the Fathers** show him as a good pastor. As for his literary works, most of his Greek works perished, with the exception of a few fragments. In the Coptic tradition, many works are attributed to him.

A. Homilies
- On the Cross and the confession of the thief, which have survived on papyrus and are preserved in the Museum of Turin as well as in the collection of Pierpont Morgan Library.
- On the **Assumption** of the Virgin Mary, several copies survived and are kept in the British Library, in the Freer Collection in Chicago, and in the Pierpont Morgan Library.
- On **penance** and chastity, which came to our knowledge through a unique manuscript in the British Library.

- On the building of the Church of John the Baptist, which is known from a manuscript from the **Monastery of St. Shenute**.
- On the three young men in the fiery furnace, which is included in a manuscript from the **Monastery of St. Macarius** and preserved in the Vatican Library.
- On the Archangel Raphael, which survives in a Coptic manuscript from the Monastery of St. Shenute as well as in an Arabic version.
- On the miracles of St. **Menas**, which is part of the collection of the Pierpont Morgan Library.

B. Letters
- A quotation from his festal letter of the year 401.
- Varia: Some fragments of his works.

C. Dialogue
- There exists an important dialogue with an anthropomorphetic monk in a manuscript in the Vatican Library that was originally from the Monastery of St. Macarius.

It is important to mention that the first homily on the visit of the Holy Family to Egypt is attributed to **Theophilus**. It is amazing that this homily survived in Syriac, Arabic, and Ethiopic versions and not a fragment survived in Coptic. There is also a homily on Peter and Paul, which is known only from Arabic versions.

THEOPISTUS OF ALEXANDRIA. Nothing is known about him. He is not commemorated in the **Synaxarion** or in any Coptic liturgical book. The name of **Alexandria** could be misleading by the connotation that he was a **patriarch** of that city, but no patriarch bore this name. It has been suggested that he could be identified as one of the followers of **Dioscorus** I to the **Council of Chalcedon**. He could be the one mentioned in the panegyric of Macarius of Tkow by Dioscorus of Alexandria.

THEOTOKIA. Part of the **Psalmodia** service. According to Abu al-Barakat **ibn Kabar**, in his encyclopedia *The Lamp of Darkness for* *the Explanation of the Service*, the compiler of the Theotokia was a virtuous potter who became a monk in Scetis. He adds that some people consider St. **Athanasius** to be the author of the Theotokia. Some modern scholars such as G. Giamberardini and J. Muyser identified several resemblances between the homilies of **Cyril** of **Alexandria** during the **Council of Ephesus** and the Coptic Theotokia. The Theotokia in fact contains not only extracts from the Cyrillian homilies but also from those of Proclus of Cizicus, Theodotus of Ancyra, and especially Homily 67 of **Severus of Antioch**. The Theotokia could be dated between the sixth and the eighth centuries.

The **Antiphonarion** of the Monastery of Hamuli preserved in the Pierpont Morgan Library contains extracts from the Theotokia for the consecration of the church at Qalamon. This Sahidic manuscript is dated 892–893 A.D. The fragments from the **Monastery of St. Macarius**, preserved in the collection of the State Library of Hamburg, contain the Theotokia, and can be dated to the 12th or 13th century. For editions, see the entry on Psalmodia.

THEOTOKION. A short hymn honoring the Virgin Mary.

THOUGHT OF NOREA **(NHC IX, 2).** A Sethian **Gnostic** text of only 52 lines introduced by a series of hymnic invocations of the **Sethian** Gnostic triad of Father, Mother, and Son, put into the mouth of Norea, sister-consort of Seth. No title is preserved; the current one is based on a phrase found toward the end of the tractate. In the text, Norea is a "saved savior" representing Gnostic humanity. The text shows some contact with another tractate in which Norea is prominent, the *Hypostasis of the Archons* (NHC II, 4). Extant only in Coptic, Norea was originally composed in Greek, probably in late second- or early third-century Egypt.

THREE STELES OF SETH **(NHC VII, 3).** A Sethian **Gnostic** writing consisting of three sets of prayers invoking and praising the three members of the **Sethian** divine triad in ascending order: the Son Adamas, the Mother Barbelo, and the transcendent Father. Each "stele" is demarcated in the text before and after ("The First Stele of Seth," etc.). At the end of the third stele is the title "The Three Steles of Seth." These prayers are associated with a Gnostic ascent ritual.

They are introduced as "The revelation of Dositheos about the three steles of Seth, the Father of the living and unshakable race." The title reflects a first-century Jewish legend according to which antediluvian lore transmitted from Adam to Seth was preserved on stone steles. The text, which shows no Christian influence, is heavily influenced by second- and early third-century Platonism. Extant only in Coptic, *Three Steles of Seth* was originally composed in Greek, probably in third-century Egypt.

THUNDER: PERFECT MIND (NHC VI, 2). A **Gnostic** revelation monologue pronounced by a feminine revealer figure, featuring self-predications and exhortations addressed to her listeners. The title occurs at the beginning of the tractate (Greek *bronte*, "thunder," is a feminine noun, probably here identifying the speaker as a voice of divine thunder). The speaker's self-predications are paradoxical ("I am the whore and the holy one; I am the wife and the virgin") and may originate in a Hellenistic Jewish riddle involving Eve, here expanded and interpreted with a Gnostic slant. *Thunder: Perfect Mind*, extant only in Coptic, was originally composed in Greek, possibly in second-century **Alexandria**.

TIMOTHY I. Saint and **patriarch**. He was the 22nd Patriarch of **Alexandria** (380–385). He is commemorated on the 26th of Abib. He was a disciple of **Athanasius** of Alexandria, and he attended the **Council of Constantinople** in 381. He left a collection of canonical law in Coptic that is a translation from the original Greek. A prayer on the **Fraction** is attributed to Timothy but it is by no means certain whether it belongs to Timothy I or his successor of the same name.

TIMOTHY II. Saint and **patriarch**. He was the 26th Patriarch of **Alexandria** (457–477). He is commemorated on the seventh of Misra. He was commonly known as Timothy Aelurus. He became patriarch after the murder of the Chalcedonian Patriarch Proterius (451–457). He was deposed and exiled several times. Even during his exile, he remained the secret patriarch and the spiritual leader of the anti-Chalcedonian party. He was ordained first as priest by **Cyril** of Alexandria. He attended the Synod of Ephesus in 449 with Patriarch **Dioscorus I**. He was then consecrated as patriarch by two of the great opponents of the **Council of Chalcedon**, Peter the Iberian and

Eusebius of Pelusium. From the anti-Chalcedonian part of the world, he is considered as a great champion of orthodoxy. His major theological work against the two natures survived only in an Armenian translation. An abridged version of this important book is conserved in Syriac. From this language we also have a collection of letters. The Coptic book of the *History of the Patriarchs* has a detailed chapter on him. There also exists a fragment of a Bohairic "Life" from the **Monastery of St. Macarius**. He is considered one of the great theologians of the anti-Chalcedonian Church of Egypt and the link between the theologians, especially Cyril of Alexandria and **Severus of Antioch**. Timothy played an important role in the reorganization of the Egyptian Church.

As mentioned, there are several works attributed to him in different languages, mainly Syriac, Armenian, and Greek; the Coptic tradition attributed several works to him. It is important to mention that it is hard to identify the author, for he is confused with his predecessor **Timothy I** of **Alexandria**. We have some fragments on the homily of the visit of the **Holy Family** to the site of Gebel al-Tayr. Another homily on the Archangel Michael is preserved in the British Museum and has a parallel in the collection of the Pierpont Morgan Library. A Coptic book on the Angel Murial is preserved in a Sahidic manuscript in the British Library. In the seventh century, John of Parallus refuted this homily. There exists a homily on the consecration of the Church of St. **Shenute**. This homily was preserved in a manuscript from the same monastery and there exists a complete Arabic version.

TREATISE ON THE RESURRECTION (NHC I, 4). A **Valentinian** Gnostic treatise in the form of a letter written by an unnamed Valentinian **Gnostic** teacher to his "son" Rheginos (otherwise unknown). Its title is given at the end of the treatise. The letter teaches that the resurrection is not physical but spiritual; those who are in possession of gnosis have already been "resurrected." Preserved only in Coptic, *Treatise on the Resurrection* was originally composed in Greek, probably late in the second century. Its provenience is unknown, but it could have been composed in Egypt.

TRIMORPHIC PROTENNOIA (NHC XIII, 1). A **Sethian Gnostic** revelatory monologue given in the first person by a feminine revealer called Protennoia ("First Thought"), who identifies herself in a series of self-predications and reveals her three appearances as Voice, Speech, and Logos. She reports that in her final appearance she "put on" Jesus. The tractate is divided into three separate discourses, each of them titled and numbered (a=1, b=2, g=3). The tractate title, in Greek, occurs at the end: *Protennoia Trimorphos* ("First Thought in Three Forms"). Extant only in Coptic, *Trimorphic Protennoia* was originally composed in Greek, probably in second-century Egypt.

TRIPARTITE TRACTATE (NHC I, 5). A lengthy **theological** treatise divided into three parts (divisions indicated by scribal decorations) for which no title is preserved in the manuscript. *Tripartite Tractate* contains a comparatively late, highly developed **Valentinian Gnostic** system, somewhat comparable in its arrangement to **Origen**'s treatise *On First Principles*. The first part deals with the transcendent Father and His principle emanations, the Son and the Church, and then describes the fall of the Logos, which results in the creation of the cosmos. The brief second part is an elaborate interpretation of Genesis 1–3 and the creation of Adam. The third part deals with the process of salvation and concludes with a trinitarian **doxology**. Preserved only in Coptic, *Tripartite Tractate* was originally composed in Greek, probably sometime in the third century. Its provenience is unknown, but it could have been composed in Egypt.

TRISAGION. "Holy God, Holy Mighty, Holy Immortal . . . have mercy upon us." The Trisagion was introduced into the Byzantine **liturgy** by Proclus of Cyzicus, who succeeded **Nestorius** as **Bishop** of Constantinople (431–446 A.D.). However, a papyrus from the fourth century preserved in the collection of the University of Strasbourg includes a Trisagion in the Liturgy of St. **Mark**. In the Coptic tradition, there is an insertion after the first phrase, "Holy God, Holy Mighty, Holy Immortal," and before the final phrase, "Have mercy upon us." In the first stanza, the insertion is "Who was born of a Virgin"; in the second stanza it is "Who was crucified for us"; and in the third stanza it is "Who rose from the dead and ascended into the heavens."

The phrase "Who was crucified for us" was introduced by the **Patriarch** of Antioch, Peter the Fuller (470, 485–489 A.D.). It became a slogan for those opposed to the **Council of Chalcedon** (i.e., Miaphysites). The interpretation of this hymn was meant to proclaim, by using an expression from the **Nicene Creed**, an essential aspect of Cyrillian **theology**. The Word as the only "subject" in Christ is also the subject of the death "in the flesh," which is "His own." Undoubtedly the *Trisagion* was interpreted as a hymn to the incarnate Word, and the interpolated form of it was formally orthodox. It would have been decidedly heretical had it been addressed to the Trinity, implying the passion of the three persons or the divine essence. The great theologian **Severus of Antioch** in his homily on the Annunciation, pronounced between 512 and 513 A.D. (i.e., the same year or few months later), explained clearly the meaning of the Trisagion. He delivered his last cathedral homily in Antioch on the same subject in 518.

It is important to mention that the Coptic Church addresses this hymn to Christ. The first stanza, "Who was born of the Virgin," and the last stanza, "Who rose from the dead and ascended into the Heavens," are accepted by Chalcedonians and anti-Chalcedonians alike. The Coptic Church is completely separate from the "heresy" of Theopaschiste. This addition was the cause of many riots, such as that which took place in November 512 A.D. This event was narrated by the Chalcedonian John Malalas and the anti-Chalcedon Pseudo-Dionysius of Tel Mahre.

TROPARIA OF SEXT AND NONE OF THE GOOD FRIDAY.
An examination of the text of the Troparia and the **Theotokia** of the Horologion and the **Good Friday** of the Coptic Church shows clearly that, with the exception of some minor additions and omissions, they are the same as the Troparia and the Theotokia of the **canonical hours** of the Greek Church. However, in some instances, the **Troparion** or the **Theotokion** of a Coptic canonical hour is not found in the corresponding Greek hour but in a different hour. The Coptic text has often marked difference from the actual text of the Greek Horologion. This divergence may possibly be explained by the fact that the Coptic text preserves the form of the Greek text, which was current in Egypt at the time when the translation was made. The case of "We worship Thine incorruptible form," which the actual Greek text changes "*Morphy*" (form) to "*icon*," may well

have been intentionally made by the iconodules at the time of the iconoclastic controversy. It is well known that the iconoclastic controversy started in the eighth century in Constantinople. Our text should be earlier than the eighth century (perhaps from the sixth or seventh centuries when the devotion and the prayer started to be addressed to Christ).

TROPARION "O ONLY BEGOTTEN"

O Only Begotten Son and the Word of God the immortal and everlasting, accepting everything for our salvation, was incarnated from the Theotokos the ever-Virgin Saint Mary, without change, Christ the God became Man, was crucified, through death trampled death, One of the Holy Trinity who is glorified with the Father and the Holy Spirit, Save us.

This familiar Monostrophic troparion of the Byzantine liturgy, which is found in the Greek **liturgies** of St. **Mark** and St. James, does not occur in any of the three liturgies of the Coptic Church. It is sung, however, in the Coptic Church on three occasions: namely, at the consecration of **bishops**, the consecration of the holy **chrism**, and the Canonical Hour of Sext on **Good Friday**.

The unique finite verb of this hymn is the last word "*save.*" It is true that the hymn-writer of this troparion selected almost all his vocabulary from various sources and combined them to form a pattern that became traditional from the earliest times. Yet this is not a combination of selections, but one in which a fine balance of phrases and sentences is created and in which a definite pattern of verbal repetition is cleverly constructed. This hymn is a compilation of the faith symbols of Nicaea-Constantinople and Chalcedon that could be accepted by both Chalcedonian and non-Chalcedonian churches alike. The text is attributed to either the **Patriarch** of Antioch, **Severus**, or to the Emperor Justinian (between 535 and 536).

TUBH. (Arabic, plural *Tubuhat*). This is a Coptic word meaning "pray for." The *Tubuhat* were introduced as deacon's responses in the liturgy or in the Holy Week (for the liturgies, see the Anaphora of St. Basil, St. Gregory, and St. Cyril).

The *Tubuhat* of the morning service of the Holy Week was composed before the 14th century and are mentioned by **ibn Kabar** in his book the *Lamp of Darkness for the Explanation of the Service.* The *Tubuhat* of the evening service were composed later. From an allusion in the *Tubuhat* of the evening service, "Save us from inflation, plagues, exiles and the sword of the enemies," one may be certain that this litany was written during the Mamluk period, perhaps during the reign of al-Zahir Beibars or later when Egypt was stricken by the Black Death and the governor wanted to banish Copts from Egypt, in addition to the failure of the Nile's inundation in those years.

The studies of Anton Baumstark show clearly that the author of this litany has an excellent knowledge of the early liturgies. He underlined many Arabic expressions in this text that occur in the Greek Liturgy of St. **Mark** attributed to St. Cyril. Baumstark also mentioned that the beginning of the Litany of Lent and the Holy Week, which states "Bend your knees, stand and bend your knees," is from the first century from the time of popes St. Cyprian and St. Cornelius.

TUKHI. *See* AL-TUKHI, RUFA'IL.

***TURUHAT* OF THE HOLY WEEK.** It is difficult to detect the history of a Coptic liturgical rite, for part of it had been written originally in Greek and translated after that to Coptic and then to Arabic, and another part had been directly written in Coptic and then translated to Arabic. A linguistic approach would be useless to determine the age of a Coptic liturgical book, for most of the vocabulary is taken from the scriptures.

Burmester published a description of the *Turuhat* [Expositions] in the Coptic Church. He also published the most ancient manuscript of the **lectionary** dated 1273 A.D., which contains many pericopes. We may notice that the *Turuhat* explain many pericopes of the Old Testament, such as the **Matins** of Holy Monday (concerning the first chapter of Genesis), the None or ninth hour of Monday of **Holy Week** (concerning the first chapters of the Genesis), Matins of the Tuesday of Holy Week concerning the Exodus, Sext or sixth hour of **Maundy Thursday**'s night concerning Isaiah, the Tierce or third hour, Sext, None of Maundy Thursday, and the Tierce of **Good Friday**.

The *Turuhat* always follows the actual reading even when there is divergence with the Manuscript Add. of the 5997 British Museum, as for the reading of the Sext, None, and eleventh hours of Wednesday evening.

It is quite clear that the *Turuhat* were compiled after the reforms of Peter of Behnasa in the 12th or 13th centuries. It seems that the **bishop** took some texts already known from Upper Egyptian manuscripts and included them in the *Book of Turuhat*; hence, we find some similarities between the commentary of **Palm Sunday** and the Ms. 575 fol. 106 from Pierpont Morgan Library in New York. By the 14th century, **Ibn Kabar** had noticed in his *Lamp of Darkness for the Explanation of the Service* that the commentary of the glorious Saturday does not correspond to the readings of this hour. This commentary still exists in the actual book, while Fr. Jacob Muyser discovered in a manuscript the commentary of this hour. This means that in the time of Ibn Kabar (early 14th century) the *Turuhat* book had assumed more or less the same reading as today. Some irregularities exist in the Coptic version.

The manuscripts are recent and do not reflect the time of composition. The *Book of Turuhat* was edited for the first time in 1914 by Philotheus al-Maqari and Michael Girgis. In 1948, Attalah Arsenius al-Muharaqqi reprinted this book, putting the Coptic text before the Arabic translation. This edition has been reprinted several times.

– U –

UNCTION OF THE SICK. Holy Sacrament. Apart from its use at home for a sick person, this service is performed publicly once a year on the last Friday of Lent, two days before Palm Sunday, using the tunes of Sundays during Lent. However, in Lower Egypt this sacrament was performed on the sixth Sunday of Lent. In Upper Egypt, it was performed on the morning of **Palm Sunday**. A compromise was reached between the two traditions after the 14th century. The order for the Unction of the Sick consists of an introduction and seven prayers or sections consisting of readings from the epistle, the gospel and prayer, and a conclusion. There are some similarities between the Coptic and Greek rites of the Unction of the Sick. However, the

Coptic rite is shorter than the Greek one. R. **Tukhi** edited the first Catholic publication in 1763 in Rome. Claudius Labib edited the first Orthodox edition of this rite in 1909. Hence, several editions have been published since then but unfortunately the Coptic text is not always mentioned. There are many manuscripts from the **Monastery of St. Macarius** dated to the 14th century.

– V –

***VALENTINIAN EXPOSITION* (NHC XI, 2).** A Valentinian **Gnostic** exposition of cosmogony, anthropogony, soteriology, and **eschatology** resembling that attributed to **Valentinian** teachers by the Church Fathers. No title is given in the manuscript, which is in fragmentary condition; the title currently used has been editorially assigned on the basis of content. The exposition is followed by five brief **liturgical** supplements on rituals used in a Valentinian community, one on the **Anointing**, two on Baptism, and two on the Eucharist. Extant only in Coptic, *Valentinian Exposition* was originally composed in Greek, probably sometime in the second century. Its provenience is unknown.

VALENTINUS. A Christian **Gnostic** teacher active in **Alexandria** in the early second century. Born in the Egyptian Delta, he was educated in Alexandria. He is reported by Irenaeus to have adapted the teachings of the Gnostic sect in creating his own system, which conformed to a greater degree to traditional Christian doctrine. Around 140 he moved to Rome, where he became active in ecclesiastical affairs. Irenaeus has a brief summary of a Gnostic myth taught by Valentinus. He was also a composer of epistles, homilies, and poetry, of which only small fragments are preserved in writings of Clement of Alexandria and Hippolytus of Rome. Some scholars also attribute to him the *Gospel of Truth* (NHC I, 3; XII, 2), extant in a Coptic translation of the original Greek. Valentinus had a number of prominent pupils who became active in Alexandria, Rome, and elsewhere, and his school spread into all areas of the Roman Empire and beyond, into Mesopotamia. Valentinian Christianity persisted in some areas into the seventh century.

VESPERS. *See* MATINS.

VESTMENTS. *See* MONASTIC AND LITURGICAL VESTMENTS.

VIRGIN MARY, APPARITION OF THE. The Desert Fathers only discreetly revealed any apparition of **saints** or angels. In the *Apophthegmata patrum*, it is mentioned that it is better to see our own sins than to see the angels. However, in the *History of the Patriarchs* of the Coptic Church, there are many references to apparitions of saints and the Virgin Mary. These apparitions took place usually in difficult times, such as times of persecutions or defeat. The French Dominican **priest** M. Vansleb listened to this phenomenon while visiting the Monastery of St. Damiana and did not believe it.

In the context of the defeat of the army in 1967, the Virgin Mary appeared at the Church of the Virgin Mary in the suburb of Zaytun in Cairo, on the evening of 2 April 1968. Many people, both Christians and non-Christians, saw her and many miracles took place. In the year 1986, the Virgin Mary appeared in the suburb of Shubra in a small church named after St. Damiana. This year is marked by the Islamist attacks against Coptic targets as well as tourists. Following the tensions between Copts and Muslims in Upper Egypt, in the year 2000, the Virgin Mary appeared in the Church of St. **Mark** in Assiut.

Mahmud Salah, a Muslim author, wrote a book about the apparition of the Virgin Mary in Egypt in which he documented carefully all the apparitions of the Virgin Mary, both in Egypt and elsewhere (*Haqiqat Dhuhur al-'Azra'* [The Truth about the Virgin Apparition] Cairo, 2001). He investigated the apparitions and concluded that they are real.

VIRTUES, THE TWELVE. The Twelve Virtues seem to be a monastic tradition from Upper Egypt and are illustrated in a niche of Bawit (chapel 6). Chapel 42 contains another inscription mentioning the twelve virtues of the Holy Spirit. The *Book of Ordinations* mentions that the **bishop** says inaudibly: " . . . Me, the poor sinner . . . , pour forth on me the twelve virtues of Your goodness."

A hymn for welcoming the **patriarchs** or the bishops details the Twelve Virtues of the Holy Spirit, praying that these virtues come upon the head of the patriarch or the bishop. A comparison between the different manuscripts of this hymn shows clearly that there is no fixed pattern of these virtues. Even the earlier manuscripts mention only 10 virtues.

– W –

WADI AL-NATRUN. It is the most significant **monastic** center in Egypt. Wadi al-Natrun is a desert depression extending about 50 kilometers long that runs southeast to northwest and lies in the Libyan Desert about 90 kilometers northwest of Cairo. The site has been known by many names: **Scetis**, Shiet, Shihat al-Isqit, and Wadi Habib. About 330 St. **Macarius** withdrew into that secluded region and followers settled around him. Within a few decades the region had been populated with hundreds of hermits, who were living in clusters around places where central facilities were available, such as a church and a refectory. Monks lived alone in independent cells and met on Saturdays and Sundays to celebrate mass and to take part in a common meal (*agape*). By the end of the fourth century, four monastic settlements existed in Wadi al-Natrun. They were the origin of the four monasteries of St. Macarius, St. Pshoi, St. **John the Little**, and Old Baramus. The **Monasteries of St. Pshoi** and of St. Macarius still exist. Remains of the monasteries of St. John the Little and of Old Baramus were recently discovered. In 407, 434, 444, and about 817, desert nomads sacked the monasteries of Wadi al-Natrun. Therefore, the monks built towers to live in and fortified their monasteries with walls. Thus, monastic life appeared to be more communal by the 14th century. The **theological** controversy between **Severus**, Bishop of Antioch and Julian, **Bishop** of Halicarnasus (?–518) on the corruptibility or incorruptibility of Christ before the Resurrection affected the monastic settlements of Scetis. The adherents of Bishop Severus established other monasteries: the present **Monastery of al-Baramous**, the Monastery of the Virgin of Anba Bishoi, which is known later as the **Monastery of the Syrians**, and a counterpart of the Monastery of John the Little that survived perhaps to the early 15th century. John of Petra, who probably had to flee from Scetis at the fourth sack around 570, tells us that 3,500 monks lived there around 550. The number of monks began to decline because of the poll tax, which was imposed on them after 705. According to the historian al-Maqrizi (1346–1442), only a few monks lived in the great **Monastery of St. Macarius** at that time. Many foreigners from almost the entire Mediterranean world spent a period of time in Scetis. In medieval times, Syrian, Armenian, and Ethiopian monks, and Franciscans lived there and endowed Scetis with a multiethnic character. Beginning in the eighth century the majority of the Coptic **patriarchs** and many bishops were chosen from among the monks of Wadi al-Natrun. Since the 1960s, these monasteries, which were nearly abandoned in the first half of the 20th century, have witnessed a considerable revival. The majority of the monks currently have received a degree in higher education. The monasteries of Wadi al-Natrun represent an important source for the history of the Coptic Church, and for **Coptic literature, art**, and architecture as well.

WAHEM. Coptic word meaning **liturgical** response.

WALL PAINTING. *See* ART, COPTIC.

WATANI. *Watani* is an Egyptian weekly Sunday newspaper published in Cairo, Egypt, and sold worldwide and is also available at website, www.wataninet.com. *Watani* provides complete coverage on national news and civil life, but distinguishes itself with a special focus on Coptic religious experience, culture, heritage, contributions to Egyptian society and world civilization, as well as contemporary social and political issues of special relevance to the Copts. Weekly columns include religious articles by His Holiness Pope **Shenouda III**, bishops, priests, and laity. *Watani*'s mission includes providing a forum for democracy, citizenship rights, and women's and minority issues.

The word *Watani* is Arabic for "My Homeland." The paper was founded in 1958 by the prominent Copt Antoun Sidhom (1915–1995). His weekly editorials in *Watani* from 1958–1995 were the strongest voice in defense of Coptic human rights in Egypt. Antoun Sidhom was a member of the Egyptian People's Assembly (Parliament) from 1984–1989 and a member of the Coptic Orthodox Church General Community Council from 1976–1995.

After Antoun Sidhom's death, his son Youssef Sidhom became editor-in-chief of *Watani* and took it to new heights. In 2001, *Watani*

International was born with intensive efforts by Magdi Khalil, who became its executive, and Saad Michael Saad, who became senior editor for religion and culture. *Watani* became the only newspaper in the Arab world that contains sections in Arabic, English, and French.

In 2000, *Watani* created a successful Youth Parliament experiment in which Muslim and Coptic youth emulate parliamentary life on a weekly basis. Graduates from this program, which continues today, become excellent participants in real-life politics.

Watani continues to be a national, not religious newspaper; however, with the increasing marginalization of Copts and their culture within the Egyptian society over the last decades, *Watani* has become increasingly significant in expressing and supporting Coptic existence and self-consciousness.

WATUS. This is the tune to which hymns are sung on Wednesdays, Thursdays, Fridays, and Saturdays. The name is taken from the first Coptic word of the first verse of the **Theotokia** of Thursday, "The bush which Moses saw in the wilderness."

WEDNESDAY OF JOB. The cycle of the **Holy Week**, although Job is not mentioned in this rite. There is an ancient oral tradition that links Job to Holy Wednesday and is called "The Wednesday of Job." This oral tradition is supported by a manuscript tradition. In fact, some manuscripts contain a collection of homilies for the Holy Week including four homilies attributed to John Chrysostom. Only a small allusion to this link survived in the excellent edition of the **Euchologion**, edited by Hegumen 'Abd al Masih Salib al-Mas'udi al-Baramousi, mentioned in the **Anaphora of St. Cyril**: "The priest shall sing with the melody of Job which is the melody of sorrow."

The melody of Job is not attested elsewhere, but the reference to "a melody of sorrow" makes one assume that this hymn, which has actually disappeared, was used for the recitation of the Book of Job for the Holy Week (for Holy Wednesday). It is important to mention that only the late manuscripts of the **lectionary of the Holy Week** dated in the 18th century contain a lesson from the Book of Job. It seems that earlier to that date the whole Book of Job was read during Holy Wednesday; hence, there was no need to have prophecies from this book. This tradition is dated back to the sixth century as attested by the homilies of Leontius of Constantinople.

WHITE MONASTERY. *See* MONASTERY OF ST. SHENUTE.

WOMEN IN THE COPTIC CHURCH. Egypt has known Christian women devoted to God since the early centuries of Christianity. St. **Antony** consigned his sister to women consecrated as virgins before he devoted his life to solitude and worship. Sources speak of female ascetics such as Amma Theodora, who lived toward the end of the fourth century in **Nitria** or **Scetis**. Her sayings were highly appreciated by many Church Fathers. The *Apophthegmata patrum* preserves 18 maxims attributed to Amma **Syncletica** and eight apophthegms under the name of Amma Sara. Mary, the sister of **Pachomius**, became the "mother" of a monastery. Some 1,800 nuns were associated with the **Monastery of St. Shenute** under **Shenute**. The **Monastery of St. Jeremiah** at Saqqara was in close contact with a monastery for women. Dayr al-Banat (the women's convent) existed in the region of al-Fayoum, probably until the beginning of the 11th century when it was destroyed, perhaps during the time of Caliph al-Hakim (996–1035). The Arab historian al-Maqrizi (1364–1442) mentioned four convents in Cairo. In the 19th century, there were five convents in Cairo.

Today, there are convents of St. Dimyanah at Bilqas near Damietta, St. George, St. Mercurius at Old Cairo, St. Theodore at Haret al Rum, the Holy Virgin, St. George at Haret Zuwaylah in Cairo, the Daughters of Mary in Beni Suef, St. Theodore at the west of Luxor, St. Pisentius near Naqqada, and St. Ammonius southwest of Esna. At present, Coptic religious women may be classified into three groups: contemplative nuns, active nuns and consecrated women, and deaconesses. In 1997, the contemplative nuns numbered 450, and there were 90 active nuns and 500 consecrated women. A considerable number of them are graduates of universities. The contemplative nuns strive to research their old Coptic heritage and try to reach the ideal ascetic life of the **saints** mentioned in **Coptic literature** and **Copto-Arabic literature**. During **fasting**, Copts can eat neither meat nor animal extracts; nuns eat only one meal daily, usually at noon. As a traditional monastic dress, the nuns wear the *qalansuwah*, which is a cap divided into two halves decorated with embroidered crosses. It is said that St. Antony used the *qalansuwah*. A number of convents claim that the Holy Family passed through their locations. They are decorated with **icons** and beautiful **wall paintings**. The production of icons is one of the convents' income sources. Mother Irini introduced anew the old Pachomian communal **monasticism** to her convent of Abu Sayfayn (**Church of St. Mercurius**). In addition to the Bible and the monastic traditional literature, such as the *Garden of the Monks* (**Bustan al-Ruhban**), contemplative nuns receive monastic education from the convents' superiors and **bishops**.

In 1965, **Athanasius**, Bishop of Beni Suef, established a female religious group called the Daughters of Mary. The aim of that group was to commit themselves as active nuns for their whole life. Its members render service in clinics, schools, centers for children with mental health problems, and in senior citizens' homes. This group was recognized by Patriarch **Cyril VI**, who declared that the community of the Daughters of Mary was special in its combination of ministry and the life of nuns. The success and the papal acknowledgment of this group led to the foundation of other groups of consecrated virgins and widows in many other dioceses in the last three decades of the 20th century. Some of the groups lived in nunneries within the towns, others with their own families or in communities. The services of the active nuns and consecrated women extended to education in slums and remote villages, to drug addicts, and to literacy lessons for adults.

Pope **Shenouda III** encouraged women to study in the **Clerical College** and ordained 180 deaconesses in 1981, whose community center became the Convent of St. Dimyanah. During his pontificate, the Holy Synod issued the decree of the "consecrated women" in 1991. The virgin or widow who desires to consecrate herself to the diaconal service serves three years as "consecrated." After five years, she could be promoted to "subdeaconess," and it requires five more years in the service to become a "deaconess." The Holy Synod confirmed that a "rite of consecration" should be performed in that official consecration. The expansion of the Church's activities in the **patriarchate** of Cyril VI, and his successor Shenouda III, means that more women are needed in the service of the Coptic community. Female volunteers, especially university students and graduates, are recruited in the Sunday Schools, social works, and charitable institutions. Anba Samuel, bishop of social and ecumenical affairs, established many training centers where women in the villages and the poor quarters of the cities could learn skills and crafts.

– Y –

YA'QUB, GENERAL (1745–1801). He was born at Mallawi in Middle Egypt in 1745. He was one of the powerful Coptic laymen who contributed to the renaissance of the Coptic Church in the 18th and 19th centuries. He was a financial commissioner of Asyut's Mamluk governor Sulayman Bey. Ya'qub concluded that neither the Turks nor the Mamluks were good for Egypt. He accompanied French General Louis Desaix to fight the fleeing Mamluk beys in Upper Egypt. He received permission from French General Kléber to form the Coptic Legion. In 1800, he defended the Coptic quarter, which was a target of Muslim mobs during a siege of three weeks. The Coptic Legion under the leadership of General Ya'qub clearly demonstrated that native Egyptians could learn how to fight, and many joined the army. General Ya'qub was the first Egyptian in modern times who spoke of an independent Egypt. He hoped that European powers might help to free Egypt from the rule of the Mamluks and Ottomans. He left Egypt for France not long after the withdrawal of the French from Egypt. In 1800, the old Coptic Cathedral at al-Azbakiah was built on land belonging to General Ya'qub, one year before his death.

YUHANNA, BISHOP OF SAMANNUD (?–after 1257). Bishop, scholar of Coptic. Yuhanna, who was consecrated Bishop of Samannud by Patriarch **Cyril III ibn Laqlaq** in 1235, is one of the pioneers of the scientific study of the **Coptic language**. He wrote a Bohairic-Arabic lexicon known as *al-Sullam al-kana'isi* (The Ecclesiastical Ladder), consisting of a list of words in the order in which they occur in biblical and other ecclesiastical works but without repetition (even in the event of different morphological cases of a word). The *Sullam* is preceded by a *Muqaddima* (Introduction) "which marks the absolute beginning of the study of Coptic grammar" (Sidarus, "Lexicography," 128). Yuhanna's work was soon surpassed, both by more sophisticated grammatical treatises and by more practical reference tools, but all later scholars of the Coptic language stand in his debt.

YUHANNA IBN ABI ZAKARIYYA IBN SABBA' (13th–14th c.). **Liturgical** encyclopedist. Yuhanna ibn Abi Zakariyya ibn Sabba' was the author of an encyclopedic compilation in 113 chapters with the rhymed title *al-Jawhara al-nafisa fi 'ulum al-kanisa* (The Precious Jewel in the Ecclesiastical Sciences). After a **theological**, biblical, and apologetic introduction (chapters 1–26), the work concentrates on ecclesial and ritual matters, frequently giving them typological and spiritual interpretations. For example, in chapter 113 we learn that the *naqus* is to be beaten to gather the faithful to prayer; this imitates Noah, who beat the *naqus* in order to gather the humans and animals who would be saved from God's wrath into the ark—which is a type of church. *The Precious Jewel* has been published a number of times, notably by the Franciscans in Cairo in 1966. It remains an important witness to the liturgical and spiritual life of the medieval Coptic Orthodox Church.

YUSAB, BISHOP OF FUWWAH (?–before 1271). Bishop, historian. Yusab, consecrated Bishop of Fuwwah in the western Delta by Patriarch **Cyril III ibn Laqlaq** sometime between 1237 and 1239, was a scholarly and active monk and church leader who was much involved in the ecclesiastical struggles of his day. He served, for example, as secretary of the synod held at the Citadel in 1240, which successfully brought Cyril's simoniacal practices under control. An understudied source for Coptic Church history is a work that was published in 1987 in Cairo under the title *Tarikh al-aba' al-batarika li-l-Anba Yusab usquf Fuwwah* (The History of the Fathers, the Patriarchs, by Anba Yusab, Bishop of Fuwwah). Preserved in a single manuscript (and modern copies made from it), this *History* has entries for the **patriarchs** of the Coptic Church from St. **Mark** the Evangelist through John XVI (103rd, 1676–1718). According to Samuel Moawad (see the bibliography), the work is best considered an anonymous compilation; it is largely but not entirely dependent on the better known *History of the Patriarchs*, and may have counted a history by Bishop Yusab among its sources. Further study of the work is necessary to establish the precise extent to which it is an independent witness to Coptic Church history.

YUSAB AL-ABAHH, BISHOP OF JIRJA AND AKHMIM (1735–1826). Saint, bishop, theologian. Yusab was a monk of the **Monastery of St. Antony** who, in 1791, was consecrated Bishop of Jirja and Akhmim. As bishop he was an educator and reformer who strove to counter Catholic preaching in his double diocese. Today he is venerated as a saint of the Coptic Orthodox Church (**feast** day: 17 Tuba); his remains are kept in the Monastery of St. Antony. Yusab's reputation as an author rests on the more than 30 treatises that he wrote and that are sometimes gathered together in the manuscript tradition under the title *Silah al-mu'munin* (The Believers' Weapon). These cover a wide range of topics, from the explanation of difficult verses of scripture (e.g., Matt. 18:9: "If your eye causes you to stumble, tear it out") to abuses in the church of his day (e.g., chatting in church or giving lavish private parties to celebrate saints' days), but they also reflect controversy with Catholics, Muslims, and others.

YUSUF AL-QIBTI (17th c.). A Copt and one of the few Egyptians who had cultural contacts with Europe in modern times before Napoleon Bonaparte's expedition and the reign of Mohammed Ali (1805–1848). He expressed his wish to Pope Urban III (1623–1644) to join the Vatican Library as a *scriptor* to correct the proofs printed in Greek and Arabic. In 1624–1625, Yusuf al-Qibti copied a number of Arabic manuscripts that are now preserved in the Vatican.

– Z –

ZOSTRIANOS **(NHC VIII, 1).** A lengthy **Sethian Gnostic** apocalypse (132 pages of the manuscript) reported in the first person in the name of the prophet, Zostrianos, associated in antiquity with Zarathustra (Zoroaster). The title occurs at the end, to which is added: "Oracles of Truth of Zostrianos, God of truth, Teachings of Zoroaster." Unfortunately, Codex VIII is very fragmentary, so much of the text is lost in lacunae. Zostrianos reports his ascent through the very levels of the universe and his encounter with various heavenly beings. Lacking obvious Christian influences, the text is heavily influenced by second- and early third-century Platonism. Zostrianos was one of the apocalypses read by members of Plotinus' School in Rome in the mid-third century (VP 16). Extant only in Coptic, *Zostrianos* was originally composed in Greek, probably in the early third century, possibly in Egypt.

Bibliography

CONTENTS

INTRODUCTION

This bibliography is selective; there can be, in fact, no exhaustive, "complete" Coptic bibliography because research in Coptic studies is very complex and differentiated. The history of the Coptic Church, for example, requires research in original Greek, Latin, Coptic, Syriac, Ethiopian, and Arabic sources, by scholars specializing in such diverse disciplines as history, classics, papyrology, theology, patristics, Coptology per se, and Arabic studies. They publish monographs and articles with their findings in French, German, and other modern languages as well as English. However, a major segment of the titles listed below are in English.

The *Coptic Encyclopedia*, edited by Aziz S. Atiya (New York: Macmillan, 1991), is highly recommended to readers of this dictionary, and especially to beginners. This monumental eight-volume work comprises approximately 2,800 entries written by 215 scholars. It is undoubtedly the most important reference tool for Coptic studies, covering almost every aspect of Christianity in Egypt. As such, the *Coptic Encyclopedia* represents an essential reference tool for anyone interested in the history, art, and archaeology of Christian Egypt, the Coptic language, and Coptic literature, as well as Copto-Arabic literature. Each entry includes a bibliography for those who want to pursue a given topic in depth. The School of Religion of Claremont Graduate University, Claremont, California, is currently embarking on projects to prepare a supplement to the *Coptic Encyclopedia* and to expand its accessibility by developing an online version.

Beginning in 1976, the International Association for Coptic Studies has organized a congress every four years. The proceedings of these important gatherings of scholars from many countries are published with up-to-date bibliographies on the discoveries of the intervening years in each field of Coptic studies, such as Coptic literature, Coptic art, and monasticism (http://rmcisadu .let.uniroma1.it/~iacs/).

Many monographs and articles incorporating new research and additional bibliographical information that appeared after the publication of the *Coptic Encyclopedia* are mentioned in this bibliography.

Note: In the following bibliography, *CE* refers to *The Coptic Encyclopedia*, edited by Aziz S. Atiya, 8 volumes, New York: Macmillan, 1991.

I. GENERAL

Atiya, Aziz Suryal (ed.). *The Coptic Encyclopedia*, 8 vols., New York: Macmillan, 1991.

International Association for Coptic Studies (IACS), http://rmcisadu.let .uniroma1.it/~iacs/ (accessed 4 February 2008).

Kammerer, W. *A Coptic Bibliography*. University of Michigan Press: Ann Arbor, 1950.

Orlandi, Tito. "Coptic Bibliography." International Association for Coptic Studies (IACS), http://rmcisadu.let.uniroma1.it/cmcl. (subscription required)

Simon, Jean. "Bibliographie copte." *Orientalia* 18 (1949)–36 (1967).

II. ARCHAEOLOGY, ART, AND ARCHITECTURE

Badawy, Alexander. *Coptic Art and Archaeology. The Arts of the Christian Egyptians from the Late Antique to the Middle Ages*. Cambridge, Mass.: M.I.T. Press, 1978.

Bagnall, Roger S., and Dominic W. Rathbone. *Egypt from Alexander to the Early Christians: An Archaeological and Historical Guide*. Los Angeles: J. Paul Getty Museum, 2004.

Bénazeth, Dominique. "Actualité des musées et expositions (2000–2004)." In *Huitième congrès international d'études coptes (Paris 2004) I. Bilans et perspectives 2000–2004*, ed. Anne Boud'hors and Denyse Vaillancourt, 69–93. Cahiers de la Bibliothèque copte, 15. Paris: De Boccard, 2006.

Bolman, Elizabeth, ed. *Monastic Visions: Wall Paintings in the Monastery of St. Antony at the Red Sea*. New Haven, Conn.: Yale University Press, 2002.

Drewer, Louis, and Hourihane Colum. "Coptic Art in the Index of Christian Art: A Research Source." In *Actes du Huitième congrès international d'études coptes, Paris, 28 juin–3 juillet 2004*, vol. 1, ed. Nathalie Bosson and Anne Boud'hors, 197–98. Orientalia Lovaniensia Analecta, 163. Louvain: E. Peeters, 2007.

Gabra, Gawdat, and Marianne Eaton Kraus. *The Treasures of Coptic Art in the Coptic Museum and Churches of Old Cairo*. Cairo: American University in Cairo Press, 2007.

Gabra, Gawdat, and Gertrud M. J. van Loon, with Darkene L. Brooks Hedstrom. *The Churches of Egypt*. Cairo: American University in Cairo Press, 2007.

Gabra, Gawdat, with Tim Vivian. *Coptic Monasteries. Egypt's Monastic Art and Architecture*. Cairo: American University in Cairo Press, 2002.

Grossman, Peter. "Architectural Elements of Churches: Khurus." In *CE*, vol. 1, 212ff.

———. *Christliche Architektur in Ägypten*. Leiden: E. J. Brill, 2002.

Innemée, Karel C. "Coptic Art, Progress in Research and Conservation Projects 2000–2004." In *Huitième congrès international d'études coptes (Paris 2004) I. Bilans et perspectives 2000–2004*, ed. Anne Boud'hors and Denyse Vaillancourt, 251–59. Cahiers de la Bibliothèque copte, 15. Paris: De Boccard, 2006.

Langen, Linda, and Hans Hondelink. "Icons, Coptic." In *CE*, vol. 4, 1278–80.

Meinardus, Otto. *The Historic Coptic Churches of Cairo*, 72–75. Cairo: Philopatron, 1994.

Sadek, Ashraf, and Bernadette Sadek. *L'incarnation de la lumière: Le renouveau iconographique copte à travers l'œuvre de Isaac Fanous*, 29–31. Limoges: Le Monde Copte, 2000.

Skalova, Zuzana, and Gawdat Gabra. *Icons of the Nile Valley*. Cairo: Longman, 2003.

III. BIBLE

Krause, Martin. "Koptische Literatur." In *Lexikon der Ägyptologie*, vol. 3, ed. Wolfgang Helck and Wolfart Westendorf, cols. 694–728. Wiesbaden: Otto Harrassowitz, 1980.

Metzger, Bruce M. *The Early Versions of the New Testament: Their Origin, Transmission, and Limitations*. Oxford: Clarendon Press: 1977.

———. "New Testament, Coptic Versions of the." In *CE*, vol. 6, 1787–89.

Nagel, Peter. "Die Arbeiten an den koptischen Bibeltexten 1992–1996." In *Ägypten und Nubien in spätantiker und christlicher Zeit. Akten des 6. Internationalen Koptologenkongress*, ed. Stephen Emmel, Martin Krause, Siegfried G. Richter, and Sofia Schaten, 38–48. Sprachen und Kulturen des Christlichen Orients, Band 6, 2. Wiesbaden: Reichert Verlag, 1999.

———. "Old Testament, Coptic Translations of." In *CE*, vol. 6, 1836–40.

———. "The Present State of Work in the Edition of the Sahidic Version of the Old Testament." In *Acts of the Third International Congress of Coptic Studies, Warsaw, 20–25 August, 1984*, ed. Wlodzimierz Godlewski, 281–83. Warsaw: International Association of Coptic Studies, 1990.

Orlandi, Tito. "The Future of Studies in Coptic Biblical and Ecclesiastical Literature." In *The Future of Coptic Studies*, ed. R. McL. Wilson, 143–63. Leiden: E. J. Brill, 1978.

Schmitz, Franz-Josef, and Gerd Mink. *Liste der koptischen Handschriften des Neuen Testaments, I. Die sahidischen Handschriften der Evangelien*, I/1, I, 2/1, I, 2/2. Berlin: Walter de Gruyter, 1986, 1989, 1991.

Schüssler, Karlheinz. *Biblia Coptica. Die koptischen Bibeltexte. Das sahidische Alte und Neue Testament. Vollständiges Verzeichnis mit Standorten*, vols.1, 3. Wiesbaden: Harrassowitz, 1995–2004.

———. "Zum Stand der koptischen Bibeltexte." In *Coptic Studies on the Threshold of a New Millennium: Proceedings of the Seventh International Congress of Coptic Studies, Leiden, 27 August-2 September 2000*, vol. 1, ed. Mat Immerzeel and Jacques van der Vliet, 221–35. Louvain: E. Peeters, 2004.

Till, Walter. "Coptic and Its Value." *Bulletin of the John Rylands Library* 40, no. 1 (1957): 229–58.

IV. COPTIC LANGUAGE AND LITERATURE

Biedenkopf-Ziehner, Anne. "Koptologische Literaturübersicht, 1967/68." *Enchoria* 2 (1972): 103–136; 6 (1976): 93–119; 10 (1980): 151–183.

Emmel, Stephen. "A Report on Progress in the Study of Coptic Literature, 1996–2004." In *Huitième congrès international d'études coptes (Paris 2004) I. Bilans et perspectives 2000–2004*, ed. Anne Boud'hors and Denyse Vaillancourt, 173–204. Cahiers de la Bibliothèque copte, 15. Paris: De Boccard, 2006.

———. *Shenoute's Literary Corpus*. 2 vols. Corpus Scriptorum Christianorum Orientalium 599, 600 (Subsidia 111, 112). Louvain: Peeters, 2004.

Funk, Wolf-Peter. "Research in Coptic Linguistics 1996–2004." In *Huitième congrès international d'études coptes (Paris 2004) I. Bilans et perspectives 2000–2004*, ed. Anne Boud'hors and Denyse Vaillancourt, 206–16. Cahiers de la Bibliothèque copte 15. Paris: De Boccard, 2006.

Kasser, Rodolphe. "Dialects." In *CE*, vol. 8, 87–101.

Krause, Martin. "Refarat der koptischen literarischen Texte und Urkunden von 1992–1995." *Archiv für Papyrusforschung und verwandte Gebiete* 44, no. 1 (1998): 140–71.

———. "Refarat der koptischen literarischen Texte und Urkunden von 1996–1997." *Archiv für Papyrusforschung und verwandte Gebiete* 45, no. 2 (1999): 281–301.

Layton, Bentley. *A Coptic Grammar: Sahidic Dialect*. Wiesbaden: Harrassowitz, 2000.

———. *Coptic in 20 Lessons. Introduction to Sahidic Coptic with Exercises and Vocabularies*. Louvain: E. Peeters, 2007.

Orlandi, Tito. "Coptic Literature." In *CE*, vol. 5, 1450–60.

———. "Coptic Literature." In *The Roots of Egyptian Christianity*, ed. Birger A. Pearson and James E. Goehring, 51–81. Philadelphia: Fortress Press, 1986.

———. *Elementi di lingua e litteratura copta*. Milan: La Goliardica, 1970.

———. "Koptische Literatur." In *Ägypten in spätantik-christlicher Zeit. Einführung in die koptische Kultur*, ed. Martin Krause, 117–47. Sprachen und Kulturen des christlichen Orients, 4. Wiesbaden: Reichert, 1998.

Reintges, Chris H. *Coptic Egyptian (Sahidic Dialect): A Learner's Grammar*. Cologne: Rüdiger Köppe Verlag, 2004.

Richter, Siegfried G., and Gregor Wurst. "Koptische literarische Texte." *Archiv für Papyrusforschung und verwandte Gebiete* 47, no. 1 (2001): 196–228.

———. "Refarat über der Edition koptischer literarischer Texte und Urkunden von 2000 bis 2002." *Archiv für Papyrusforschung und verwandte Gebiete* 49, no. 1 (2003): 127–61.

Wilfong, Terry G. "Coptic Literature." In *The Oxford Encyclopedia of Ancient Egypt*, ed. Donald B. Bedford, vol. 1, 295–302. Oxford: Oxford University Press, 2001.

V. COPTO-ARABIC STUDIES

General References (Referred to Below in Abbreviated Fashion)

Atiya, Aziz Suryal, ed. *The Coptic Encyclopedia*, 8 vols. New York: Macmillan, 1991. A standard tool in English. (*CE*)

Gibb, H. A. R. et al., eds. *The Encyclopaedia of Islam*, new ed., 11 vols. Leiden: Brill, 1954–. Some articles are of importance to Copto-Arabic studies. (*EI*)

Graf, Georg. *Geschichte der christlichen arabischen Literatur*. 5 vols. Studi e Testi 118, 133, 146, 147, 172. Vatican City: Biblioteca Apostolica Vaticana, 1944–1953.
Still the fundamental tool for the study of Arabic Christian literature. Graf was consulted for every article. (*GCAL*)

Wadi, Abullif. "Introduzione alla letteratura arabo-cristiana dei Copti." *Studia Orientalia Christiana Collectanea* 29–30 (1996–1997): 441–492 [in Arabic].
An introduction that the author of these articles found a very helpful starting point for his own work. ("Introduzione")

Frequently Cited Surveys (of Canon Law, History, Lexicography, Grammar)

Cöln, Franz Joseph. "The Nomocanonical Literature of the Copto-Arabic Church of Alexandria." *Ecclesiastical Review* 56 (1917): 113–41. ("Nomocanonical Literature")

Den Heijer, Johannes. "Coptic Historiography in the Faṭimid, Ayyubid and Early Mamluk Periods." *Medieval Encounters* 2 (1996): 67–98. ("Coptic Historiography")

Sidarus, Adel Y. "Coptic Lexicography in the Middle Ages: The Coptic Arabic Scalae." In *The Future of Coptic Studies*, ed. R. McL. Wilson, 125–42. Leiden: E. J. Brill, 1978. ("Coptic Lexicography")

——. "Medieval Coptic Grammars in Arabic: The Coptic *muqaddimāt*." *Journal of Coptic Studies* 3 (2001): 63–79. ("Medieval Coptic Grammars")

'Abd al-Masih al-Isra'ili

Graf. *GCAL*, vol. 2: 319–20.

Samir, Khalil. "'Abd al-Masih al-Isra'ili al-Raqqi." In *CE*, vol. 1, 5–7.

——. "Mansur ibn Sahlan ibn Muqashshir." In *CE*, vol. 5, 1524–25.

Wadi. "Introduzione," 480 (#17).

Abu al-Majd ibn Yu'annis

Graf. *GCAL*, vol. 2, 449–50.

Masri, Pierre. "Les anciens explications arabes du Credo." *al-Mashriq* 74 (2000): 453–85, esp. 474–79.

Samir, Khalil. "Abu al-Majd ibn Yu'annis." In *CE*, vol. 1, 21–23.
Wadi. "Introduzione," 480 (#17).
Wadi. "Introduzione," 458 (#66).

Abu Salih Yu'annis

Cöln. "Nomocanonical Literature," 116–19.
Graf. *GCAL*, vol. 2, 320–21.
Wadi. "Introduzione," 479 (#21).

al-As'ad ibn al-'Assal

Atiya, Aziz S. "As'ad Abu al-Faraj Hibat Allah ibn al-'Assal." In *CE*, vol. 1, 282–83.
Bailey, Kenneth E. "Hibat Allah ibn al-'Assal and His Arabic Thirteenth Century Critical Edition of the Gospels (with special attention to Luke 16:16 and 17:10)." *NEST Theological Review* 1 (1978): 11–26.
Graf. *GCAL*, vol. 2, 403–7.
Samir, Samir Khalil. "La version arabe des évangiles d'al-As'ad Ibn al-Assal." *Parole de l'Orient* 19 (1994): 441–551.
Sidarus, Adel Y. "Medieval Coptic Grammars," 68–69.
Wadi. "Introduzione," 466–465 (#49). "Introduzione," is published "back to front."
Wadi, Abullif. *Studio su al-Mu'taman Ibn al-'Assal*. Studia Orientalia Christiana Monographiae, 5, 89–96. Cairo: Franciscan Centre of Christian Oriental Studies; Jerusalem: Franciscan Printing Press, 1997.
———. "La traduction des Quatres Évangiles d'al-As'ad Ibn al-'Assal (XIIIe s.)." *Studia Orientalia Christiana Collectanea* 24 (1991): 217–24.

Athanasius, Bishop of Qus

Bauer, Gertrud. *Athanasius von Qus: Qiladat al-Tahrir fi 'Ilm al-Tafsir; eine koptische Grammatik in arabischer Sprache aus dem 13./14. Jahrhundert*. Islamkundliche Untersuchungen, 17. Freiburg/Br.: K. Schwarz, 1972.
Frederick, Vincent. "Athanasius, bishop of Qus." In *CE*, vol. 1, 303–4.
Graf. *GCAL*, vol. 2, 445.
Sidarus, Adel. "Athanasius von Qus und die arabisch-koptische Sprachwissenschaft des Mittelalters." *Bibliotheca Orientalis* 34 (1977): 22a–35b.
———. "Medieval Coptic Grammars," 70–74.

——. "La tradition sahidique de philologie gréco-copto-arabe (manuscrits des XIIIᵉ-XVᵉ siècles). In *Etudes Coptes VII: neuvième Journée d'études, Montpellier, juin 1999*, ed. N. Bosson, 265–304. Cahiers de la Bibliothèque Copte, 12. Louvain: E. Peeters, 2000.

Vycichl, Werner. "Muqaddimah." In *CE*, vol. 8, 166–69.

Wadi. "Introduzione," 459 (#63).

Awlad al-'Assal

Note: See also the individual articles for al-As'ad, al-Safi, and al-Mu'taman.

Atiya, Aziz S. "Awlad al-'Assal." In *CE*, vol. 1, 309–11.

Graf. *GCAL*, vol. 2, 387–414.

Wadi. "Introduzione," 466–463 (#48–52). "Introduzione" is published "back to front."

Wadi, A. *Studio su al-Mu'taman Ibn al-'Assal*. Studia Orientalia Christiana Monographiae, 5. Cairo: Franciscan Centre of Christian Oriental Studies, 1997.

Bulus al-Bushi

Atiya, Aziz S. "Bulus al-Bushi." In *CE*, vol. 2, 423–24.

Davis, Stephen J. *Coptic Christology in Practice: Incarnation and Divine Participation in Late Antique and Medieval Egypt*. Oxford: Oxford University Press, 2008.

Graf. *GCAL*, vol. 2, 356–60.

Samir, Khalil, ed. *Traité de Paul de Bus, sur l'Unité et la Trinité, l'Incarnation, et la vérité du christianisme*. Patrimoine Arabe Chrétien, 4. Zouk Mikhael, Lebanon: Patrimoine Arabe Chrétien, 1983.

Sellew, Philip. "A Blessing for Reading the Apocalypse in the Paschal Liturgy." In *Coptic Studies on the Threshold of a New Millennium: Proceedings of the Seventh International Congress of Coptic Studies, Leiden, 27 August-2 September 2000*, vol. 1, ed. Mat Immerzeel and Jacques van der Vliet. Louvain: E. Peeters, 2004.

Skalova, Zuzana, and Stephen Davis. "A Medieval Icon with Scenes from the Life of Christ and the Virgin in the Church of Abu Seifein, Cairo: An Interdisciplinary Approach." *Bulletin de la Société d'Archéologie Copte* 39 (2000): 211–38.

Wadi. "Introduzione," 470–69 (#41). "Introduzione" is published "back to front."

Butrus al-Sadamanti

Atiya, Aziz S. "Butrus al-Sidmanti." In *CE*, vol. 2, 431–32.

Graf. *GCAL*, vol. 2, 351–56.

Van den Akker. *Butrus al-Sadamanti: Introduction sur l'Herméneutique.* Recherches ILOB, Nouvelle Série, B. Orient Chrétien, 1. Beirut: Dar el-Machreq, 1972.

Wadi. "Introduzione." 471–470 (#39). "Introduzione" is published "back to front."

Butrus Sawirus al-Jamil, Bishop of Malij

Frederic, Vincent. "Butrus Sawirus al-Jamil." In *CE*, vol. 2, 431.

Graf. *GCAL*, vol. 2, 340–44.

Wadi. "Introduzione," 473 (#35).

Christodoulos

Atiya, Aziz Suryal, Yassa 'Abd al-Masih, and O. H. E. Burmester. *History of the Patriarchs of the Egyptian Church, Known as the History of the Holy Church by Sawirus ibn al-Mukaffa'*, vol. 2, part 3, *Christodoulos-Michael (A.D. 1046–1102)*. Cairo: Société d'Archéologie Copte, 1959.

Burmester, O. H. E. "The Canons of Christodoulos, Patriarch of Alexandria (A.D. 1047–1077)." *Le Muséon* 45 (1932): 51–84.

Den Heijer, Johannes. "Le patriarcat copte d'Alexandrie à l'époque fatimide." In *Alexandrie médiévale 2*, ed. Christian Décobert, 83–97. Études alexandrines, 8. Cairo: Institut Français d'Archéologie Orientale, 2002.

Graf. *GCAL*, vol. 2, 321.

Labib, Subhi Y. "Christodoulos." In *CE*, vol. 2, 544–47.

Wadi, "Introduzione," 479–78 (#22). "Introduzione" is published "back to front."

The Confession of the Fathers

Davis, Stephen J. *Coptic Christology in Practice: Incarnation and Divine Participation in Late Antique and Medieval Egypt.* Oxford: Oxford University Press, 2008.

Graf. *GCAL*, vol. 2, 321–23.

Graf, Georg. "Zwei dogmatische Florilegien der Kopten." *Orientalia Christiana Periodica* 3 (1937): 345–402.

Wadi. "Introduzione," 478 (#24).

Copto-Arabic Literature: Apocalyptic

Graf. *GCAL*, vol. 1, 273–97.

Grypeou, Emmanouela. "'The Visions of Apa Shenute of Atripe': An Analysis in the History of Traditions of Eastern Christian Apocalyptic Motifs." In *Christian Crossroads: Essays on the Medieval Christian Legacy*, ed. Juan Pedro Monferrer-Sala, 157–67. Gorgias Eastern Christianity Studies, 1. Piscataway, N.J.: Gorgias Press, 2007.

Hoyland, Robert G. *Seeing Islam as Others Saw It: A Survey and Evaluation of Christian, Jewish and Zoroastrian Writings on Early Islam*, 278–94. Studies in Late Antiquity and Early Islam, 13. Princeton, N.J.: Darwin Press, 1997.

Papaconstantinou, Arietta. "'They Shall Speak the Arabic Language and Take Pride in It': Reconsidering the Fate of Coptic after the Arab Conquest." *Le Muséon*, 120 (2007) 273–299.

Van Lent, Jos. "Coptic Apocalyptic Prophecies from the Islamic Period." PhD diss., Leiden University, forthcoming.

———. "The Nineteen Muslim Kings in Coptic Apocalypses." *Parole de l'Orient* 25 (2000): 643–93.

Copto-Arabic Literature: Catechetical Literature

Davis, Stephen J. *Coptic Christology in Practice: Incarnation and Divine Participation in Late Antique and Medieval Egypt*. Oxford: Oxford University Press, 2008.

Swanson, Mark N. "A Copto-Arabic Catechism of the Later Fatimid Period: 'Ten Questions That One of the Disciples Asked of His Master.'" *Parole de l'Orient* 22 (1997): 474–501.

———. "The Specifically Egyptian Context of a Coptic Arabic Text: Chapter Nine of the *Kitab al-Idah* of Sawirus ibn al-Muqaffa'." *Medieval Encounters* 2 (1996): 214–27.

———. "Telling (and Disputing) the Old, Old Story: A Soteriological Exchange in Late Twelfth-Century Egypt." *Coptica* 5 (2006): 67–80.

———. "'These Three Words Will Suffice': The 'Jesus Prayer' in Coptic Tradition." *Parole de l'Orient* 25 (2000): 619–55.

———. "Two Vatican Manuscripts of 'The Book of the Master and the Disciple' (Eight Chapters) of Mark ibn al-Qunbar." *Orientalia Christiana Periodica* 66 (2000): 185–93.

Zanetti, Ugo. "Le livre de Marc Ibn Qanbar sur la confession retrouvée." *Orientalia Christiana Periodica* 49 (1983): 426–33.

Copto-Arabic Literature: Hagiography

Armanios, Febe, and Bogaç Ergene. "A Christian Martyr under Mamluk Justice: The Trials of Salib (d. 1512) According to Coptic and Muslim Sources." *Muslim World* 96 (2006): 115–44.

Atiya, Aziz S. "Martyrs, Coptic." In *CE*, vol. 5, 1550–59.

———. "Saints, Coptic." In *CE*, vol. 7, 2081–87.

Baumeister, Theolfried. "Martyrology." In *CE*, vol. 5, 1549–50.

Crum, W. E. "Barsaumâ the Naked." *Proceedings of the Society of Biblical Archaeology* 29 (1907): 135–49, 187–206.

Den Heijer, Johannes. "Apologetic Elements in Coptic-Arabic Historiography: The Life of Afraham ibn Zur'ah, 62nd Patriarch of Alexandria." In *Christian Arabic Apologetics during the Abbasid Period (750–1258)*, ed. Samir Khalil Samir and Jørgen S. Nielsen, 192–202. Studies in the History of Religions (*Numen* Bookseries), 63. Leiden: E. J. Brill, 1994.

Frankfurter, David, ed. *Pilgrimage and Holy Space in Late Antique Egypt*. Religions in the Graeco-Roman World, 134. Leiden: E. J. Brill, 1998.

Graf. *GCAL*, vol. 1, 487–555, esp. 531–40.

Raineri, Osvaldo. *Gli atti etiopici del martire egiziano Giorgio il Nuovo (+978)*. Studi e Testi, 392. Vatican City: Biblioteca Apostolica Vaticana, 1999.

Swanson, Mark N. "'Our Father Abba Mark': Marqus al-Antuni and the Construction of Sainthood in Fourteenth-Century Egypt." In *Christian Crossroads: Essays on the Medieval Christian Legacy*, ed. Juan Pedro Monferrer-Sala, 217–28. Gorgias Eastern Christianity Studies, 1. Piscataway, N.J.: Gorgias Press, 2007.

Voile, Brigitte. "Barsum le Nu: Un saint copte au Caire à l'époque mamelouke." In *Saints Orientaux*, ed. Denise Aigle, 151–68. Hagiographies médiévales compares, 1. Paris: De Boccard, 1995.

Copto-Arabic Literature: Origins and Development

Rubenson, Samuel. "Translating the Tradition: Some Remarks on the Arabization of the Patristic Heritage in Egypt." *Medieval Encounters* 2 (1996): 4–14.

Sidarus, Adel. "The Copto-Arabic Renaissance in the Middle Ages: Characteristics and Socio-Political Context." *Coptica* 1 (2002): 141–60.

Swanson, Mark N. "Recent Developments in Copto-Arabic Studies, 1996–2000." In *Coptic Studies on the Threshold of a New Millennium: Proceedings of the Seventh International Congress of Coptic Studies, Leiden, 27 August–2 September 2000*, vol. 1, ed. Mat Immerzeel and Jacques van der Vliet. E. Peeters: Luvain, 2004.

———. "St. Shenoute in Seventeenth-Century Dress: Arabic Christian Preaching in *Paris, B.N. ar. 4761*." *Coptica* 4 (2005): 27–42.

Cyril II

Atiya, Aziz Suryal, Yassa 'Abd al-Masih, and O. H. E. Burmester. *History of the Patriarchs of the Egyptian Church, Known as the History of the Holy Church by Sawirus ibn al-Mukaffa'*, vol. 2, part 3, *Christodoulos-Michael (A.D. 1046–1102)*. Cairo: Société d'Archéologie Copte, 1959.

Burmester, O. H. E. "The Canons of Cyril II, LXVII Patriarch of Alexandria." *Le Muséon* 49 (1936): 245–88.

Den Heijer, Johannes. "Considérations sur les communautés chrétiennes en Égypte fatimide: l'État et l'Église sous le vizirat de Badr al-Jamali (1074–1094)." In *L'Égypte fatimide, son art et son histoire*, ed. Marianne Barrucand, 569–578. Paris: Presses de l'Université de Paris-Sorbonne, 1999.

Graf. *GCAL*, vol. 2, 323–24.

Labib, Subhi Y. "Cyril II." In *CE*, vol. 3, 675–77.

Wadi. "Introduzione," 478 (#23).

Cyril III ibn Laqlaq

Graf. *GCAL*, vol. 2, 360–67.

Khater, Antoine, and O. H. E. Burmester. *History of the Patriarchs of the Egyptian Church, Known as the History of the Holy Church by Sawirus ibn al-Mukaffa'*, vol. 4, 1–2. Cairo: Société d'Archéologie Copte, 1974.

Labib, Subhi Y. "Cyril III ibn Laqlaq." In *CE*, vol. 3, 677.

Wadi. "Introduzione," 469–68 (#42). "Introduzione" is published "back to front."

Wadi, A. *Studio su al-Mu'taman Ibn al-'Assal*, 42–65. Studia Orientalia Christiana Monographiae, 5. Cairo: Franciscan Centre of Christian Oriental Studie, 1997.

Farajallah al-Akhmimi

Cöln. "Nomocanonical Literature," 129–36.

Frederick, Vincent. "Farajallah al-Akhmimi." In *CE*, vol. 4, 1089.

Graf. *GCAL*, vol. 2, 427.

Wadi. "Introduzione," 460–59 (#62). "Introduzione" is published "back to front."

Gabriel II ibn Turayk

Antonios Aziz Mina. *Le Nomocanon du patriarche copte Gabriel II ibn Turayk (1131–1145)*, with an introduction by Khalil Samir. Patrimoine Arabe Chrétien, 12–13. Beirut: CEDRAC, 1993.

Burmester, O. H. E. "The Canons of Gabriel Ibn Turaik, LXX Patriarch of Alexandria." *Le Muséon* 46 (1933): 43–54.

———. "The Canons of Gabriel ibn Turaik, LXX Patriarch of Alexandria (First Series)." *Orientalia Christiana Periodica* 1 (1935): 5–45.

———. "The Laws of Inheritance of Gabriel ibn Turaik." *Orientalia Christiana Periodica* 1 (1935): 315–27.

Graf. *GCAL*, vol. 2, 324–27.

Labib, Subhi Y. "Gabriel II." In *CE*, vol. 4, 1127–29.

Samir Khalil. "Gabriel II, patriarche copte d'Alexandrie (1131–1145)." In *Dictionnaire d'histoire et de géographie ecclésiastiques*, ed. Alfred Baudrillart et al., vol. 19 (1981), 528–39. Paris: Letouzey et Ané, 1912–.

Wadi. "Introduzione," 477–76 (#27). "Introduzione" is published "back to front."

Gabriel III

Graf. *GCAL*, vol. 2, 414.

MacCoull, Leslie S.B. "A Note on the Career of Gabriel III, Scribe and Patriarch of Alexandria." *Arabica* 43 (1996): 357–60.

Samir, Khalil. *Al-Safi ibn al-'Assal: Brefs chapitres dur la Trinité et l'Incarnation*. Patrologia Orientalis 42.3 (no. 192). Turnhout, Belgium: Brepols, 1985. 624–31([12]–[19]).

Swanson, Mark N. "The Monastery of St. Paul in Historical Context." In *The Cave Church of Paul the Hermit at the Monastery of St. Paul in the Eastern Desert of Egypt*, ed. William Lyster, chap. 2. New Haven, Conn.: Yale University Press, forthcoming.

Gabriel V

'Abdallah, Alfonso. *L'Ordinamento liturgico di Gabriele V—880 patriarca copto, 1409–1427*. Cairo: Franciscan Centre for Oriental Christian Studies, 1962.

Graf. *GCAL*, vol. 2, 456.

Samir, Khalil. "Gabriel V." In *CE*, vol. 4, 1130–33.

Wadi. "Introduzione," 455 (#75).

The History of the Churches and Monasteries of Egypt

Atiya, Aziz S. "Abu al-Makarim." In *CE*, vol. 1, 23.

Den Heijer, Johannes. "The Composition of the History of the Churches and Monasteries of Egypt: Some Preliminary Remarks." In *Acts of the Fifth International Congress of Coptic Studies*, ed. D. W. Johnson and T. Orlandi, vol. 2, 209–19. Rome: C.I.M., 1993.

———. "Coptic Historiography," 77–81.

Evetts, Basil Thomas Alfred, ed. *The Churches and Monasteries of Egypt and Some Neighbouring Countries Attributed to Abû Sâlih, the Armenian.* Gorgias Reprint Series, 17. Oxford: The Clarendon Press, 1895. Reprint, Piscataway, N.J.: Gorgias Press, 2001.

Graf. *GCAL*, vol. 2, 338–40.

Martin, Maurice. "La Delta chrétien à la fin du XIIᵉ siècle." *Orientalia Christiana Periodica* 63 (1997): 181–99.

Wadi. "Introduzione," 474 (#33).

The History of the Patriarchs

Atiya, Aziz Suryal, Yassa 'Abd al-Masih, and O. H. E. Burmester, eds. *History of the Patriarchs of the Egyptian Church, Known as the History of the Holy Church by Sawirus ibn al-Mukaffa'*, vol. 2, 1–3. Cairo: Société d'Archéologie Copte, 1943–1959.

Den Heijer, Johannes. "Coptic Historiography." 69–77.

———. "History of the Patriarchs of Alexandria." In *CE*, vol. 4, 1238–42.

———. *Mawhub ibn Mansur ibn Mufarrig et l'historiographie copto-arabe: Étude sur la composition de l'Histoire des Patriarches d'Alexandrie.* Corpus Scriptorum Christianorum Orientalium 513 (subs. 83). Louvain: E. Peeters, 1989.

Evetts, Basil Thomas Alfred, ed. *History of the Patriarchs of the Coptic Church of Alexandria.* Patrologia Orientalis 1 (1907): 99–214, 381–519; 5 (1910): 1–215; 10 (1915): 357–551. Paris: Firmin-Didot, 1907–1915.

Graf. *GCAL*, vol. 2, 301–6.

Johnson, David W. "Further Remarks on the Arabic History of the Patriarchs of Alexandria." *Oriens Christianus* 61 (1977): 103–16.

Khater, Antoine, and O. H. E. Burmester, eds. *History of the Patriarchs of the Egyptian Church, Known as the History of the Holy Church by Sawirus ibn al-Mukaffa'*, III.1–3, IV.1–2. Cairo: Société d'Archéologie Copte, 1968–1974.

Swanson, Mark N. *The Coptic Papacy in Islamic Egypt.* The Popes of Egypt, 2. Cairo: American University in Cairo Press, forthcoming.

Wadi. "Introduzione," 480–479 (#18, 20); 477 (#25–26); 473 (#34). "Introduzione" is published "back to front."

Ibn Kabar, Shams al-Ri'asa Abu al-Barakat

Ashtor, E. "Baybars al-Mansuri." In *EI*, vol. 1, 1127–28.

Atiya, Aziz S. "Ibn Kabar." In *CE*, vol. 4, 1267–68.

Graf. *GCAL*, vol. 2, 438–45.

Samir, Samir Khalil. "L'Encyclopédie liturgique d'Ibn Kabar (+1324) et son apologie d'usages coptes." In *Crossroads of Cultures: Studies in Liturgy and Patristics in Honor of Gabriele Winkler*, ed. H.-J. Feulner, Elena Velkovska, and R. F. Taft, 619–55. Orientalia Christiana Analecta, 260. Rome: PIO, 2000.

Sidarus, Adel Y. "Coptic Lexicography," 132–34.

———. "Sullam." In *EI*, vol. 9, 848–49.

Wadi. "Introduzione," 461–60 (#60). "Introduzione" is published "back to front."

Wadi, Abullif. "Abu al-Barakat Ibn Kabar, Misbah al-Zulmah (cap. 18: il digiuno e la settimana santa)." *Studia Orientalia Christiana Collectanea* 34 (2001): 233–322, esp. 239–43.

Ibn Katib Qaysar

Davis, Stephen"Introducing an Arabic Commentary on the Apocalypse: Ibn Kâtib Qaysar on Revelation." In *Harvard Theological Review* 101.1 (2008), 77–96.

Frederic, Vincent. "Ibn Katib Qaysar." In *CE*, vol. 4, 1268.

Graf. *GCAL*, vol. 2, 379–87.

Sidarus, Adel. "L'influence arabe sur la linguistique copte." In *History of the Language Sciences/Geschichte der Sprachwissenschaften/Histoire des sciences du langage*, ed. Sylvain Auroux et al., vol. 1, 321–25. Handbücher zur Sprach- und Kommunikationswissenschaft, 18.1. Berlin: Walter de Gruyter, 2000.

———. "Medieval Coptic Grammars," 67.

Wadi. "Introduzione," 467–66 (#47). "Introduzione" is published "back to front."

Ibn al-Rahib, al-Nushu' Abu Shakir

Atiya, Aziz S. "Abu Shakir ibn al-Rahib." In *CE*, vol. 1, 33–34.

Den Heijer, "Coptic Historiography," 83–88.

Graf. *GCAL*, vol. 2, 428–34.

Sidarus, Adel. "Coptic Lexicography," 132–34.

———. "Ibn al-Rahib." In *EI*, Supplement, 396.

———. *Ibn ar-Rahibs Leben und Werk: Ein Koptisch-arabischer Enzyklopädist des 7./13. Jahrhunderts*. Freiburg: Klaus Schwarz Verlag, 1975.

———. "Medieval Coptic Grammars," 70.

———. "L'oeuvre philologique copte d'Abu Shakir Ibn al-Rahib (XIIIᵉ s)." In *Studies on the Christian Arabic Heritage*, ed. Rifaat Ebied and Herman Teule, 1–23. Eastern Christian Studies, 5. Louvain: E. Peeters, 2004.

Wadi. "Introduzione," 462 (#55).

Jirjis ibn al-'Amid al-Makin

Al-Mawsu'a al-lahutiyya al-shahira bi-l-Hawi l-Ibn al-Makin, 4 vols. Cairo: Dayr al-Muharraq, 1999–2001.
Graf. *GCAL*, vol. 2, 450–53.
Wadi, "Introduzione," 458–457 (#68). "Introduzione" is published "back to front."

John XI

Bilaniak, Petro B. T. "Coptic Relations with Rome." In *CE*, vol. 2, 609–11.
Coquin, René-Georges. "Dayr al-Maghtis." In *CE*, vol. 3, 818–19.
Graf. *GCAL*, vol. 4, 118–19.
Labib, Subhi Y. "John XI." In *CE*, vol. 4, 1344–46.
Luisier, Philippe. "Jean XI, 89ème patriarche copte: Commentaire de sa lettre au pape Eugène IV, suivi d'une esquisse historique sur son patriarcat." *Orientalia Christiana Periodica* 60 (1994): 519–62.
———. "La lettre du patriarche copte Jean XI au pape Eugène IV: Nouvelle edition." *Orientalia Christiana Periodica* 60 (1994): 87–129.
Swanson, Mark N. *The Coptic Papacy in Islamic Egypt*. The Popes of Egypt, 2. Cairo: American University in Cairo Press, 2007.
Wadi. "Introduzione," 455–454 (#77). "Introduzione" is published "back to front."

al-Makin Jirjis ibn al-'Amid

Atiya, Aziz S. "Makin, Ibn al-'Amid al-." In *CE*, vol. 5, 1513.
Cohen, Cl., and R.-G. Coquin. "al-Makin b. al-'Amid." In *EI*, vol. 6, 143–44.
Den Heijer. "Coptic Historiography," 88–95.
Graf. *GCAL*, vol. 2, 348–51.
Wadi. "Introduzione," 471 (#38).
Wadi, A. "Al-Makin Jirjis Ibn al-'Amid wa-tarikhuhu." In *Actes de la septième rencontre des Amis du patrimoine arabe-chrétien*, 5–24. Cairo: Franciscan Centre for Oriental Christian Studies, 1999.

Maqara

Coquin, René-Georges. "Macarius the Canonist." In *CE*, vol. 5, 1490–91.
Graf. *GCAL*, vol. I, 560–63; vol. 2, 437.

Troupeau, Gérard. *Catalogue des manuscripts arabes. Première partie: Manuscrits chrétiens*. Vol. I. Paris: Bibliothèque Nationale, 1972. (See the description of mss. 251 and 252 for the contents of the compilation.)
Wadi. "Introduzione," 460 (#61).

Marqus ibn al-Qunbar

Cöln. "Nomocanonical Literature," 125–27.
Evetts, Basil Thomas Alfred, ed. *The Churches and Monasteries of Egypt and Some Neighbouring Countries Attributed to Abû Sâlih, the Armenian*, 20–43. Gorgias Reprint Series, 17. Oxford: Clarendon Press, 1895. Reprint, Piscataway, N.J.: Gorgias Press, 2001.
Graf. *GCAL*, vol. 2, 327–32.
Samir, Samir Khalil. "Vie et Oeuvre de Marc ibn al-Qunbar." In *Christianisme d'Égypte: Hommages à René-Georges Coquin*, 123–58. Cahiers de la Bibliothèque Copte, 9. Louvain: E. Peeters, 1995.
Swanson, Mark N. "Telling (and Disputing) the Old, Old Story: A Soteriological Exchange in Late Twelfth-Century Egypt." *Coptica* 5 (2006): 69–82.
———. "Two Vatican Manuscripts of 'The Book of the Master and the Disciple' (Eight Chapters) of Mark ibn al-Qunbar." *Orientalia Christiana Periodica* 66 (2000): 185–93.
Wadi. "Introduzione," 476–475 (#30). "Introduzione" is published "back to front."
Zanetti, Ugo. "Le livre de Marc Ibn Qanbar sur la confession retrouvé." *Orientalia Christiana Periodica* 49 (1983): 426–33.

Matthew I

Graf. *GCAL*, vol. 2, 455–56.
Khater, Antoine, and O. H. E. Burmester. *History of the Patriarchs of the Egyptian Church, Known as the History of the Holy Church by Sawirus ibn al-Mukaffa'*, vol. 3, part 3, *Cyril II–Cyril V (A.D. 1235–1894)*, 235–71. Cairo: Société d'Archéologie Copte, 1970.
Labib, Subhi Y. "Matthew I." In *CE*, vol. 5, 1569–70.
Swanson, Mark N. *The Coptic Papacy in Islamic Egypt*. The Popes of Egypt, 2. Cairo: American University in Cairo Press, 2007.
———. "'Our Father Abba Mark': Marqus al-Antuni and the Construction of Sainthood in Fourteenth-Century Egypt." In *Christian Crossroads: Essays on*

the Medieval Christian Legacy , ed. Juan Pedro Monferrer-Sala, 217–28. Gorgias Eastern Christianity Studies, 1. Piscataway, NJ: Gorgias Press, 2007.
Wadi. "Introduzione," 456 (#72–74).

Mawhub ibn Mansur ibn Mufarrij

Atiya, Aziz Suryal, Yassa 'Abd al-Masih, and O. H. E. Burmester. *History of the Patriarchs of the Egyptian Church, Known as the History of the Holy Church by Sawirus ibn al-Mukaffa'*, vol. 2, part 3, *Christodoulos-Michael (A.D. 1046–1102)*. Cairo: Société d'Archéologie Copte, 1959.

Den Heijer, Johannes. "Coptic Historiography," 69–77.

――. *Mawhub ibn Mansur ibn Mufarrig et l'historiographie copto-arabe: Étude sur la composition de l'Histoire des Patriarches d'Alexandrie*. Corpus Scriptorum Christianorum Orientalium, 513 (subs. 83). Louvain: E. Peeters, 1989.

――. "Mawhub ibn Mansur ibn Mufarrij al-Iskandarani." In *CE*, vol. 5, 1573–74.

Wadi. "Introduzione," 480–479 (#20). "Introduzione" is published "back to front."

Mikha'il, Bishop of Atrib and Malij

Cöln. "Nomocanonical Literature," 127–29 (where *al-Tibb al-Ruhani* is tentatively but incorrectly attributed to Marqus ibn al-Qunbar).

Coquin, René-Georges. "Mikha'il." In *CE*, vol. 5, 1625–27.

Graf. *GCAL*, vol. 2, 414–27.

Teule, Herman, and Lucas van Rompay. "Newsletters Christian Arabic Studies II & III." *Parole de l'Orient* 25 (2000): 776–77 (on Michael Kleiner's dissertation on the Ethiopic translation of *The Book of Spiritual Medicine*).

Wadi. "Introduzione," 463–62 (#54). "Introduzione" is published "back to front."

Mikha'il, Metropolitan of Damietta

Burmester, O. H. E. "The Sayings of Michael, Metropolitan of Damietta." *Orientalia Christiana Periodica* 2 (1936): 101–28.

Coquin, René-Georges. "Mikha'il." In *CE*, vol. 5, 1624–25.

Cöln. "Nomocanonical Literature," 119–124.

Evetts, Basil Thomas Alfred, ed. *The Churches and Monasteries of Egypt and Some Neighbouring Countries Attributed to Abû Sâlih, the Armenian*, 20–43.

Gorgias Reprint Series, 17. Oxford: Clarendon Press, 1895. Reprint, Piscataway, N.J.: Gorgias Press, 2001.

Graf. *GCAL*, vol. 2, 333–35.

Graf, Georg. *Ein Reformversuch innerhalb der koptischen Kirche im zwölften Jahrhundert.* Collectanea Hierosolymitana, 2. Paderborn: Ferdinand Schöningh, 1923.

Wadi. "Introduzione," 475 (#31).

al-Mufaddal ibn Abi al-Fada'il

Graf. *GCAL*, vol. 2, 450.

Den Heijer, J. "al-Mufaddal b. Abi 'l-Fada'il." In *EI*, vol. 7, 305.

———. "Coptic Historiography," 88–95.

Wadi. "Introduzione," 458 (#67).

al-Mu'taman ibn al-'Assal

Atiya, Aziz S. "Mu'taman Abu Ishaq Ibrahim ibn al-'Assal, al-." In *CE*, vol. 6, 1748–49.

Graf. *GCAL*, vol. 2, 407–14.

Sidarus. "Coptic Lexicography," 129–30.

Wadi. "Introduzione," 464–463 (#51). "Introduzione" is published "back to front."

Wadi, A. *Studio su al-Mu'taman Ibn al-'Assal.* Studia Orientalia Christiana Monographiae, 5. Cairo: Franciscan Centre of Christian Oriental Studies, 1997.

———, ed. *Al-Mu'taman Ibn al-'Assal: Summa dei principi della Religione.* 4 vols. Studia Orientalia Christiana Monographiae, 6a-b, 7a-b. Cairo: Franciscan Centre of Christian Oriental Studies, 1998–1999.

al-Rashid Abu al-Khayr ibn al-Tayyib

Frederic, Vincent. "Abu al-Khayr al-Rashid ibn al-Tayyib." In *CE*, vol. 1, 20–21.

Graf. *GCAL*, vol. 2, 344–48.

Wadi. "Introduzione," 472 (#37).

Wadi, A. "Al-Rasid Ibn al-Tayyib et son *Tiryaq*." *Studia Orientalia Christiana Collectanea* 28 (1995): 19–40.

Zanetti, Ugo. "Abu l-Hayr ibn al-Tayyib: Sur les icons et la croix." *Parole de l'Orient* 28 (2003): 667–701.

al-Safi ibn al-'Assal

Cöln. "Nomocanonical Literature," 136–41.

Graf. *GCAL*, vol. 2, 388–403.

Samir, Khalil. "Safi ibn al-'Assal, al-." In *CE*, vol. 7, 2075–79.

———. *Al-Safi ibn al-'Assal: Brefs chapitres dur la Trinité et l'Incarnation*. Patrologia Orientalis 42.3 (no. 192). Turnhout, Belgium: Brepols, 1985.

Wadi. "Introduzione," 465–464 (#50). "Introduzione" is published "back to front."

Wadi, A. *Studio su al-Mu'taman Ibn al-'Assal*. Studia Orientalia Christiana Monographiae, 5, 97–116. Cairo: The Franciscan Centre of Christian Oriental Studies, 1997.

Sawirus ibn al-Muqaffa'

Atiya, Aziz S. "Sawirus ibn al-Muqaffa'." In *CE*, vol. 7, 2100–2102.

Atiya, Aziz S., Yassa 'Abd al-Masih, and O. H. E. Burmester. *History of the Patriarchs of the Egyptian Church, Known as the History of the Holy Church by Sawirus ibn al-Mukaffa'*, vol. 2, part 2, *Khaël III—Senouti II (A.D. 880–1066)*, 137–39, 164–65. Cairo: Société d'Archéologie Copte, 1948.

Davis, Stephen J. *Coptic Christology in Practice: Incarnation and Divine Participation in Late Antique and Medieval Egypt*. Oxford: Oxford University Press, 2008.

Graf. *GCAL*, vol. 2, 300–318.

Griffith, Sidney. "The *Kitab Misbah al-'Aql* of Severus ibn al-Muqaffa': A Profile of the Christian Creed in Arabic in Tenth Century Egypt." *Medieval Encounters* 2 (1996): 15–42.

Samir, Khalil. *Sawirus ibn al-Muqaffa': The Lamp of Understanding*. Arabic Christian Tradition, 1. Cairo: Dar al-'Alam al-'Arabi, 1978.

Swanson, Mark N. "'Our Brother, the Monk Eustathius': A Ninth-Century Syrian Orthodox Theologian Known to Medieval Arabophone Copts." *Coptica* 1 (2002): 119–40.

Wadi. "Introduzione," 483–481 (#12–13). "Introduzione" is published "back to front."

Sim'an ibn Kalil

Graf. *GCAL*, vol. 2, 336–38.

Sidarus, Adel. "La pré-renaissance copte arabe du Moyen Âge (deuxième moitié du XIIe / début du XIIIe siècle)." In *Eastern Crossroads: Essays on*

Medieval Christian Legacy, ed. Juan Pedro Monferrer-Sala, 201–4. Gorgias Eastern Christianity Studies, 1. Piscataway, N. J.: Gorgias Press, 2007. Wadi. "Introduzione," 474 (#32).

The Synaxarion

'Abd al-Masih, Mikha'il, and Armaniyus Habashi Shihata al-Birmawi. *Al-Sinaksar*. 2 vols. Cairo: 1935–1937.

Atiya, Aziz S. "Synaxarion, Copto-Arabic: The List of Saints." In *CE*, vol. 7, 2173–90.

Budge, E. A.Wallis. *The Book of the Saints of the Ethiopian Church: A Translation of the Ethiopic Synaxarium . . . Made from the Manuscripts Oriental 660 and 661 in the British Museum*. 4 vols. Cambridge: University Press, 1928.

Colin, Gérard. "Le synaxaire éthiopien: État actuel de la question." *Analecta Bollandiana* 106 (1988): 274–317, esp. 277–83.

Coquin, René-Georges. "Mikha'il." In *CE*, vol. 5, 1625–27, esp. 1626b–1627a.

———. "Synaxarion, Copto-Arabic: Editions of the Synaxarion." In *CE*, vol. 7, 2171–73.

———. "Synaxarion, Ethiopian." In *CE*, vol. 7, 2190–92.

———. "Quelle est la date possible de la recension de Basse-Égypte du Synaxaire des coptes?" In *Études coptes IV: quatrième Journée d'études, Strasbourg 26–27 mai 1988*, 75–84. Cahiers de la Bibliothèque Copte, 8. Louvain: E. Peeters, 1995.

Graf. *GCAL*, vol. 2, 343, 416–20.

al-Thiqa ibn al-Duhayri

Frederick, Vincent. "Ibn al-Dahiri." In *CE*, vol. 4, 1266.

Graf. *GCAL*, vol. 2, 378–79.

Sidarus. "Medieval Coptic Grammars," 68.

Wadi. "Introduzione," 467 (#45).

al-Wadih ibn Raja'

Atiya, Aziz Suryal, Yassa 'Abd al-Masih, and O. H. E. Burmester. *History of the Patriarchs of the Egyptian Church, Known as the History of the Holy Church by Sawirus ibn al-Mukaffa'*, vol. 2., part 2, *Khaël III–Senouti II (A.D. 880–1066)*, 151–70. Cairo: Société d'Archéologie Copte, 1948.

Frederick, Vincent. "Wadih ibn Raja,' al-." In *CE*, vol. 7, 2311.
Graf. *GCAL*, vol. 2, 318–19.
Wadi. "Introduzione," 481–480 (#16). "Introduzione" is published "back to front."

al-Wajih Yuhanna al-Qalyubi

Graf. *GCAL*, vol. 2, 375–77.
Sidarus. "Medieval Coptic Grammars," 67–68.
Wadi. "Introduzione," 467 (#46).

Yuhanna, Bishop of Samannud

Frederick, Vincent. "Yuhanna, Bishop of Samannud." In *CE*, vol. 7, 2355–56.
Graf. *GCAL*, vol. 2, 371–75.
Sidarus. "Coptic Lexicography," 127–28.
———. "Medieval Coptic Grammars," 65–66.
Vycichl, Werner. "Muqaddimah." In *CE*, vol. 8, 166–69.
———. "Sullam." In *CE*, vol. 8, 204–7.
Wadi. "Introduzione," 468–467 (#44). "Introduzione" is published "back to front."

Yusab al-Abahh, Bishop of Jirja and Akhmim

Graf. *GCAL*, vol. 4, 138–42.
Samir, Khalil. "Yusab." In *CE*, vol. 7, 2360–62.
Wadi. "Introduzione," 447–446 (#112). "Introduzione" is published "back to front."

Yusab, Bishop of Fuwwah

Graf. *GCAL*, vol. 2, 369–71.
den Heijer. "Coptic Historiography," 81–83.
Moawad, Samuel. "Zur Originalität der Yusab von Fuwah zugeschriebenen Patriarchengeschichte." *Le Muséon* 199 (2006): 255–70. English abstract, 269–70.
Samu'il al-Suryani and Nabih Kamil, eds. *Tarikh al-aba' al-batarika li-l-Anba Yusab usquf Fuwwah*. Cairo: Institute of Coptic Studies, 1987.
Wadi. "Introduzione," 469–468 (#42–43). "Introduzione" is published "back to front."

Yuhanna ibn Abi Zakariyya ibn Sabba'

Atiya, Aziz S. "Ibn Siba', Yuhanna ibn Abi Zakariyya." In *CE*, vol. 4, 1272.

Graf. *GCAL*, vol. 2, 448–49.

Mistrih, V., ed. *Jûhannâ ibn Abî Zakarîâ ibn Sibâ': Pretiosa margarita de scientiis ecclesiasticis*. Cairo: Franciscan Centre for Oriental Christian Studies, 1966.

Wadi. "Introduzione," 459–458 (#65). "Introduzione" is published "back to front."

VI. COPTOLOGY IN EGYPT

Atiya, Aziz Suryal. "Higher Institute of Coptic Studies." In *CE*, vol. 4, 1230.

———. "Ya'qub Nakhlah Rufaylah." In *CE*, vol. 7, p. 2353.

Basta, Munir. "Iqladiyus Labib." In *CE*, vol. 4, 1302.

Bierbrier, M. L. *Who Is Who in Egyptology*, 3rd ed. London: Egypt Exploration Society, 1995.

Ghali, Mirrit Boutros. "Clerical College." In *CE*, vol. 2, 563ff.

———. "Georgy Sobhy: 1884–1964." *Bulletin de la Société d'Archéologie Copte* 19 (1967–1968): 315ff.

———. "Murad Kamil." In *CE*, vol. 6, 1968ff.

———. " Sami Gabra." In *CE*, vol. 7, 2090.

———. "Society of Coptic Archaeology." In *CE*, vol. 7, 2142.

———. "Yassa 'Abd al-Masih." In *CE*, vol. 7, 2353ff.

Ghali, Wassef Boutros. "In Memoriam, Mirrit Boutros-Ghali (1908–1992)." *Bulletin de la Société d'Archéologie Copte* 32 (1993): 1–10.

Krause, Martin. "Coptological Studies"; "Coptology." In CE, vol. 2, 613–18.

Moftah, Laurence. "A Musical Resurrection." *al-Ahram Weekly Online*, no. 791, http://weekly.ahram.org.eg/2006/791/cu4.htm 20-26 April 2006 (accessed 25 March 25, 2008).

Nasim, Sulayman. "Habib Jirjis." In *CE*, vol. 4, 1189.

Saad, Michael, "Habib Girgis." *Bulletin of Saint Shenouda the Archimandrite Coptic Society* 4 (1998): 29–33.

Samir, Khalil. "Yusuf al-Qibti." In *CE*, vol. 7, 2365.

VII. GNOSTICISM

Attridge, Harold W., ed. *Nag Hammadi Codex I (The Jung Codex)*. Nag Hammadi Studies 22–23. Leiden: E. J. Brill, 1985.

Böhlig, Alexander, and Frederik Wisse, eds. *Nag Hammadi Codices III, 2 and IV, 2: The Gospel of the Egyptians (The Holy Book of the Great Invisible Spirit)*. Nag Hammadi Studie, 4. Leiden: E. J. Brill, 1975.

Dubois, Jean-Daniel. "Études gnostiques 2000–2004." In *Huitième congrès international d'études coptes (Paris 2004) I. Bilans et perspectives 2000–2004*, ed. Anne Boud'hors and Denyse Vaillancourt, 151–71. Cahiers de la Bibliothèque copte, 15. Paris: De Boccard, 2006.

Emmel, Stephen, ed. *Nag Hammadi Codex III, 5: The Dialogue of the Savior*. Nag Hammadi Studies, 26. Leiden: E. J. Brill, 1984.

Filoramo, Giovanni. *A History of Gnosticism*, trans. Anthony Alcock. Oxford: Basil Blackwell, 1990.

Foerster, Werner. *Gnosis: A Selection of Gnostic Texts*, trans. R. McL. Wilson. Vol. 1: *Patristic Evidence*, vol. 2: *Coptic and Mandaean Sources*. Oxford: Clarendon Press, 1972, 1974.

Hedrick, Charles W., ed. *Nag Hammadi Codices XI, XII, XIII*. Nag Hammadi Studies, 28. Leiden: E. J. Brill, 1990.

Jonas, Hans. *The Gnostic Religion: The Message of the Alien God and the Beginnings of Christianity*, 2nd ed. Boston: Beacon Press, 1963.

Kasser, Rodolophe, Marvin Meyer, and Gregor Wurst (eds.). *The Gospel of Judas*. Washington, D.C.: National Geographic Society, 2006.

Layton, Bentley, ed. *The Gnostic Scriptures*. Garden City, N.Y.: Doubleday, 1987.

———. *Nag Hammadi Codex II, 2–7, Together with XIII, 2, Brit. Lib. Or. 4926(1), and P. Oxy. 1, 654, 655*. Nag Hammadi Studies, 20–21. Leiden: E. J. Brill, 1989.

———. *The Rediscovery of Gnosticism: Proceedings of the International Conference on Gnosticism at Yale, New Haven, Connecticut, March 28–31, 1978*. Studies in the History of Religions (Supplements to *Numen*), 41. Vol. 1: *The School of Valentinus*, vol. 2: *Sethian Gnosticism*. Leiden: E. J. Brill, 1980, 1981.

Parrott, Douglas M., ed. *Nag Hammadi Codices V, 2–5 and VI, with Papyrus Berolinensis 8502, 1 and 4*. Nag Hammadi Studies, 11. Leiden: E. J. Brill, 1979.

———, ed. *Nag Hammadi Codices III, 3–4 and V, 1, with Papyrus Berolinensis 8502,3 and Oxyrhynchus Papyrus 1081: Eugnostos and The Sophia of Jesus Christ*. Nag Hammadi Studies, 27. Leiden: E. J. Brill, 1991.

Pearson, Birger A., ed. *Gnosticism and Christianity in Roman and Coptic Egypt*. New York: T. & T. Clark International, 2004.

———. *Gnosticism, Judaism, and Egyptian Christianity*. Minneapolis, Minn.: Fortress Press, 1990.

———. *Nag Hammadi Codices IX and X.* Nag Hammadi Studies, 15. Leiden: E. J. Brill, 1981.

———, ed. *Nag Hammadi Codex VII.* Nag Hammadi and Manichaean Studies, 30. Leiden: E. J. Brill, 1996.

Robinson, James M., and Richard Smith, ed. *The Nag Hammadi Library in English,* 3rd ed. San Francisco: Harper & Row, 1988.

Rudolph, Kurt. *Gnosis: The Nature and History of Gnosticism,* trans. Robert McL. Wilson. San Francisco: Harper & Row, 1983.

Schmidt, Carl, ed. *The Books of Jeu and the Untitled Text in the Bruce Codex.* Nag Hammadi Studies, 13. Leiden: E. J. Brill, 1978.

———. *Pistis Sophia,* trans. Violet MacDermot. Nag Hammadi Studies, 9. Leiden: E. J. Brill, 1978.

Scholer, David M., "Bibliographia Gnostica: Supplementum." *Novum Testamentum* (1998).

———. *Nag Hammadi Bibliography 1948–1969.* Nag Hammadi Studies, 1. Leiden: E. J. Brill, 1971.

———. *Nag Hammadi Bibliography 1970–1994.* Nag Hammadi and Manichaean Studies, 32. Leiden: E. J. Brill, 1997.

Sieber, John H. *Nag Hammadi Codex VIII.* Nag Hammadi Studies, 31. Leiden: E. J. Brill, 1991.

Stroumsa, Gedalyahu G. *Another Seed: Studies in Gnostic Mythology.* Nag Hammadi Studies, 24. Leiden: E. J. Brill, 1984.

Turner, John D. *Sethian Gnosticism and the Platonic Tradition.* Bibliothèque copte de Nag Hammadi, "Études" 6. Québec: Les Presses de l'Université Laval, 2001.

Turner, John D., and Anne McGuire. *The Nag Hammadi Library after Fifty Years: Proceedings of the 1995 Society of Biblical Literature Commemoration.* Nag Hammadi and Manichaean Studies, 44. Leiden: E. J. Brill, 1997.

van den Broek, Roelof. *Studies in Gnosticism and Alexandrian Christianity.* Nag Hammadi and Manichaean Studies, 39. Leiden: E. J. Brill, 1996.

Waldstein, Michael, and Frederik Wisse, ed. *The Apocryphon of John: Synopsis of Nag Hammadi Codices II,1; III,1; and IV,1 with BG 8502,2.* Nag Hammadi and Manichaean Studies, 33. Leiden: E. J. Brill, 1995.

VIII. HAGIOGRAPHY

Abd -al-Masih, Yassa. "Doxologies in the Coptic Church. Edited Bohairic Doxologies." *Bulletin de la Société d'Archéologie Copte* 6 (1940): 19–76.

———. "Doxologies in the Coptic Church: The Use of Doxologies." *Bulletin de la Société d'Archéologie Copte* 4 (1938): 97–113.

———. "Doxologies in the Coptic Church. Unedited Sa'idic Doxologies Volumes XIII and XIV of the Pierpont Morgan Collection of Coptic MSS." *Bulletin de la Société d'Archéologie Copte* 5 (1939): 175–91.

———. "Doxologies in the Coptic Church. Unedited Bohairic Doxologies. I (Tût-Kyahk)." *Bulletin de la Société d'Archéologie Copte* 8 (1942): 31–61.

———. "Doxologies in the Coptic Church. Unedited Bohairic Doxologies. II (Tûbah-An-Nâsi)" *Bulletin de la Société d'Archéologie Copte* 11 (1945): 95–158.

———. "Remarks on the Psalis of the Coptic Church." *Bulletin de l'institut des Etudes Coptes* 1 (1958): 85–100.

Amélineau, Emile. "Histoire des Monastères de la Basse Egypte." *Annales du Musée Guimet 25*. Paris: n.p., 1894.

———. *Monuments pour servir à l'histoire de l'Egypte chrétienne au IV et V siècles, Mémoires des membres de la Mission Archéologique Française au Caire*, 4. Paris: n.p., 1888.

Baumeister, Theofried. *Martyr invictus. Der Martyrer als Sinnbild der Erlösung in der Legende und im Kult der frühen koptischen Kirche, zur Kontinuität des ägyptischen Denkens*. Münster: Regensberg, 1972.

Bibliotheca Hagiographica Orientalis (BHO), Subsidia Hagiographica X. Brussels: n.p. 1910; reprint 1954.

Colin, Gérard. "Le Synaxaire Ethiopien: Etat actuel de la question." *Analecta Bollandiana* 106 (1988): 273–317.

Coquin, René-Georges. "Un Complément aux 'Vies sahidiques de Pachôme': le manuscrit IFAO, Copte 3." *Bulletin de l'Institut Français d'Arcéologie Orientale* 79 (1979): 209–47.

———. "Compte-Rendu Recherches sur Jules d'Akfahs." *Bulletin de la Société d'Archéologie Copte* 37 (1998): 149–55.

———. "Un demi-feuillet retrouvé des vies Coptes de Pachôme (*BHO* 824–1161). *Analecta Bollandiana* 102 (1984): 315–19.

———. "Le synaxaire des Coptes, un nouveau témoin de la récension de la Haute Egypte." *Analecta Bollandiana* 96 (1977): 351–65.

Delehaye, Hippolyte. "Les martyrs d'Egypte." *Analecta Bollandiana* 40 (1922): 5–154, 299–364.

———. *Les Origines du culte des Martyrs, Subsidia Hagiographica 20*. Bruxelles: n.p., 1933.

Devos, Paul. "De Jean Chrysostome à Jean de Lycopolis." *Analecta Bollandiana* 96 (1978): 389–403.

———. "Fragments coptes de l'"Historia monachorum"" Vie de S Jean de Lycopolis (BHO 515)." *Analecta Bollandiana* 87 (1969): 417–40.

———. "Saint Jean de Lycopolis et l'empereur Marcien. A propos de Chalcedoine." *Analecta Bollandiana* 94 (1976): 303–16.

———. "La servante de Dieu Poemenia d'après Pallade." *Analecta Bollandiana* 87 (1969): 189–212.

Fenoyl, De Maurice. *Le sanctoral Copte, Recherches de l'Institut de lettres Orientales de Beyrouth XV.* Beyrouth: Imprimerie Orientale, 1960.

Gabra, Gawdat. "Untersuchungen zum Difnar der koptischen Kirche. I Quellenlage, Forschungsgeschichte und künftige Aufgaben." *Bulletin de la Société d'Archéologie Copte* 35 (1996): 37–52.

———. "Untersuchungen zum Difnar der koptischen Kirche. II zur Kompilation." *Bulletin de la Société d'Archéologie Copte* 37 (1998): 49–68.

Garitte, Gérard. *Vita Antonii versio Sahidica, CSCO,* 117–18. Louvain: E. Peeters, 1949.

Horn, Jürgen. *Untersuchungen zur Frömmigkeit und Literatur der christlichen Ägypter- das Martyrium des Viktor, Sohnes des Romanos.* Göttingen: n.p., 1988.

Lanne, Emmanue. "La prière de Jésus dans la tradition égyptienne. Témoignagne des psalies et des inscriptions." *Irénikon* 50 (1977): 163–203. Reprinted in *Tradition et Communion des Eglises—Bibliotheca Ephemeridum Theologicarum Lovaniensium 129,* 307–38. Leuven: n.p., 1997.

Lefort, Louis Théophile. *Pachomii Vitae Sahidice scriptae, CSCO,* 99–100. Louvain: E. Peeters, 1933.

Leipoldt, Johannes. *Shenute von Atripe.* Leipzig: n.p., 1903.

Malak, Hanna. "Les Livres Liturgiques de l'Eglise Copte." *Mélanges Eugène Tisserant, III (Studi e Testi, 233),* 1–35. Vatican: Biblioteca apostolica vaticana, 1964.

Meinardus, Otto Frericn August. *Christian Egypt, Ancient and Modern.* Cairo: American University Press, 1977.

———. "The Twenty-four Elders of the Apocalypse in the Iconography of the Coptic Church." *Studia Oorientalia Christiana Collectanea* 13 (1968–1969): 141–58.

Moftah, Ragheb, and Martha Roy. "Music, Coptic description of the Corpus." In *CE,* vol. 6, 1715–29.

Müller, Detlef G. *Die Engellehre der koptischen Kirche- Untersuchengen zur Geschichte der Christlichen Frömmigkeit in Ägypten.* Wiesbaden: Harrassowitz, 1959.

O'Leary, De Lacy. *The Saints of Egypt.* London: n.p., 1927. Reprint: Amsterdam: n.p., 1974.

Pietersma, A. The Acts of Phileas, Bishop of Thmuis. *Cahiers d'Orientalisme VII*. Genève: Patrick Cramer, 1990.

Till, Walter. "Johannes der Taufer in der Koptischen Literatur." *Mitteilung des Deutschen Archäologichen Instituts Kairo* 16 (1958): 310–32.

———. "Koptische Heiligen und Martyrerlegenden." *Orientalia Christiana Analecta* (Rome) 102 (1935): 138–54.

Timm, Walter. *Christliche Stätten in Ägypten*. Beihefte zum Tubinger Atlas des Vorderen Orients, 36. Wiesbaden: Reichert, 1979.

van Esbroeck, Michel. "La dormition chez les Coptes." *Actes du IV° Congrès Copte—Louvain-la Neuve, PIOL* 41, 436–45. Louvain: E. Peeters, 1992.

Viaud, Gérard. "Les 24 presbytres de l'Apocalypse dans la tradition Copte." *Bulletin de la Société d'Archéologie Copte* 29 (1990): 123–45.

Winstedt, Eric O. *Coptic Texts on Saint Theodore*. London: n.p., 1910. Reprint Amsterdam: Philo, 1984.

Youhanna, Nessim Youssef. "De nouveau, la christianisation des dates des fêtes de l'ancienne religion égyptienne." *Bulletin de la Société d'Archéologie Copte* 31 (1992): 109–11.

———. "Nicodème auteur des psalies." *Orientalia Christiana Periodica* 60 (1994): 625–33.

———. *Recherches sur Jules d'Akfahs*. PhD diss., l'Université de Montpellier III, 1993.

———. "Recherches d'hymnographie copte: Nicodème et Sarkis." *Orientalia Christiana Periodica* 64 (1998): 383–402.

———. "Une relecture des glorifications coptes." *Bulletin de la Société d'Archéologie Copte* 34 (1995): 77–83.

———. "Une relecture des Théotokies Coptes." *Bulletin de la Société d'Archéologie Copte* 36 (1997): 157–70.

———. "Un témoin méconnu de la littérature copte." *Bulletin de la Société d'Archéologie Copte* 32 (1993): 139–47.

Zanetti, Ugo. "Bohairic Liturgical Manuscripts." *Orientalia Chirsitiana Periodica* 60 (1995): 65–94.

IX. HISTORY

Adams, William Y. *Nubia, Corridor to Africa*. Princeton, N.J.: Allen Lane, 1977.

Atiya, Aziz Suryal. "Ahl al-Dhimmah." In *CE*, vol. 1, 72ff.

———. "Alexandria, Historic Churches in." In *CE*, vol. 1, 92–95.

———. "Ayyubid Dynasty and the Copts." In *CE*, vol. 1, 314ff.

———. "Eusebius of Caesarea." In *CE*, vol. 4, 1070ff.

———. *A History of Eastern Christianity*. London: Methuen, 1968.

———. "Kharaj." In *CE*, vol. 5, 1413ff.

———. "Mamluks and the Copts." In *CE*, vol. 5, 1517ff.

———. "Ottomans, Copts under the." In *CE*, vol. 6, 1856ff.

———. "Tulunids and Ikhshids, Copts under the." In *CE*, vol. 7, 2280ff.

Bagnall, Rogers S. *Egypt in Late Antiquity*. Chichester, West Sussex: Princeton University Press, 1993.

Bahr, Samira. "Modern Egypt, Copts in." In *CE*, vol. 5, 1663ff.

Baumeister, Theofried. "Geschichte und Historiographie des Ägyptischen Christentums: Studien und Darstellungen der letzten Jahre." In *Huitième congrès international d'études coptes (Paris 2004) I. Bilans et perspectives 2000–2004*, ed. Anne Boud'hors and Denyse Vaillancourt, 37–67. Cahiers de la Bibliothèque copte, 15. Paris: De Boccard, 2006.

Boud'hours, Anne. "Manuscrits coptes 'chypriotes' à la bibliothèque nationale." *Etudes coptes III. Cahiers de la Bibliothèque Copte* 4 (1989): 11–20

Bowman, Alan K. *Egypt after the Pharaohs: 332BC–AD 642 from Alexander to the Arab Conquest*. London: British Museum Publications, 1986.

Butler, Alfred. *The Arab Conquest of Egypt*. Oxford, 1902. 2nd, amplified ed. Oxford: P. M. Fraser, 1977.

Daly, M. W. *The Cambridge History of Egypt*. Vol. 2: *Modern Egypt, from 1517 to the end of the Twentieth Century*. Cambridge: Cambridge University Press, 1998.

Davis, Stephen J. *The Early Coptic Papacy: The Egyptian Church and Its Leadership in Late Antiquity*. Cairo: American University in Cairo Press, 2004.

Décobert, Christian. "Sur l'arabisation et l'islamisation de l'Égypte médiévale." In *Itinéraires d'Égypte: Mélanges offerts au père Maurice Martin S. J.*, ed. Christian Décobert. Bibliothèque d'Étude, 106. Cairo: n.p., 1992.

Edwards, David N. "The Christianization of Nubia: Some Archaeological Pointers." *Sudan & Nubia* 5 (2001): 89–96.

Ferré, André. "Fatimids and the Copts." In *CE*, vol. 4, 1097–1100.

Frantz-Murphy, Gladys. "Conversion in Early Islamic Egypt: The Economic Factor." In *Documents de l'Islam médiéval: Nouvelles Prespectives de Recherche*, ed. Yusuf Ragib, 11–17. Textes arabes et études islamiques, 29. Cairo: n.p., 1991.

———. "Umayyads, Copts under the." In *CE*, vol. 7, 2286–89.

Fraser, P. M. "Alexandria, Christian and Medieval." In *CE*, vol. 1, 88–92.

Gabra, Gawdat, ed. *Be Thou There. The Holy Family's Journey in Egypt*. Cairo: American University in Cairo Press, 2001.

Gellens, Sam I. "Egypt, Islamization of." In *CE*, vol. 3, 939–42.

Godlewski, Wlodzimierz. "Nubian Studies 2000–2004." In *Huitième congrès international d'études coptes (Paris 2004) I. Bilans et perspectives 2000–2004*, ed. Anne Boud'hors and Denyse Vaillancourt, 217–30. Cahiers de la Bibliothèque copte, 15. Paris: De Boccard, 2006.

Haas, Christopher. *Alexandria in Late Antiquity: Topography and Social Conflict.* Baltimore, Md.: Johns Hopkins University Press, 1997.

Hamilton, Alastair. *The Copts and the West, 1439–1822. The European Discovery of the Egyptian Church.* Oxford: Oxford University Press, 2006.

Hanna, Sami A. *Medieval and Middle Eastern Studies in Honor of Aziz Suryal Atiya.* Leiden: E. J. Brill, 1972.

Heinen, Heinz. "Alexandria in Late Antiquity." In *CE*, vol. 1, 95–103.

———. "Provincial Organization of Egypt." In *CE*, vol. 6, 2022–24.

Khalil, Magdy. *Aqbat al-Mahgar* (The Copts in the Diaspora). Cairo: Dar al-Khayyal, 1999.

Lapidus, I. M. "The Conversion of Egypt to Islam." *Israel Oriental Studies* 2 (1972): 248–62.

Louca, Anwar. "Chiftichi, Yuhanna." In *CE*, vol. 2, 519ff.

Mayeur-Jaouen, Catherine. "The Coptic Mouleds: Evolution of the Traditional Pilgrims." In *Between Desert and City: The Coptic Orthodox Church Today*, ed. Nelly van Doorn-Harder and Kari Vogt, 212–29. Institute for Comparative Research in Human Culture. Oslo: Novus forlag, 1997.

Megally, Mounir. "Bashmuric Revolts." In *CE*, vol. 2, 349–51.

Meinardus, Otto. *Christians in Egypt.* Cairo: American University in Cairo Press, 2006.

Naguib, Sélim. *Les Coptes dans l'Égypte d'aujourd'hui.* Brussels: Solidarité-Orient, 1996.

Partrick, Theodore Hall. *Traditional Egyptian Christianity: A History of the Coptic Orthodox Church.* Greensboro, N.C.: Fisher Park Press, 1996.

Petry, Carl F. "Copts in the Late Medieval Egypt." In *CE*, vol. 2, 618–635.

———, ed. *The Cambridge History of Egypt.* Vol. 1: *Islamic Egypt, 640–1517.* Cambridge: Cambridge University Press, 1998.

Reid, Donald M. *Whose Pharaohs? Archaeology, Museums and Egyptian National Identity from Napoleon to World War.* Cairo: American University in Cairo Press, 2002.

Shoucri, Munir. "Cyril IV." In *CE*, vol. 3, 677–679.

Tagher, Jacques. *Christians in Muslim Egypt: An Historical Study of the Relations between Copts and Muslims from 640 to 1922.* Arbeiten zum spätantiken und koptischen Ägypten, 10. Altenberg: Oros Verlag, 1998.

Timm, Stefan. *Das christlich-koptische Ägypten in arabischer Zeit.* 6 vols. Wiesbaden: Reichert, 1984–1992.

Van Doorn-Harder, Nelly. "Kyrillos VI (1902–1971): Planner, Patriarch and Saint." In *Between Desert and City: The Coptic Orthodox Church Today*, ed.

Nelly van Doorn-Harder and Kari Vogt, 230–42. Institute for Comparative Research in Human Culture. Oslo: Novus forlag, 1997.

Watson, John. "Signposts to Biography—Pope Shenouda III." In *Between Desert and City: The Coptic Orthodox Church Today*, ed. Nelly van Doorn-Harder and Kari Vogt, 243–53. Institute for Comparative Research in Human Culture. Oslo: Novus forlag, 1997.

X. MONASTICISM

Atiya, Aziz S. "Jerome." In *CE*, vol. 4, 1323ff.

Behlmer, Heike. "Women and the Holy in Coptic Hagiography." In *Actes du Huitième congrès international d'études coptes, Paris, 28 juin–3 juillet 2004*, vol. 2, ed. Nathalie Bosson and Anne Boud'hors, 405–16. Orientalia Lovaniensia Analecta, 163. Louvain: E. Peeters, 2007.

Boutros, Ramez. "Une question de méthode pour l'etude des pèlerinages et lieux saints chrétiens en Égypte." In *Actes du Huitième Congrès International d'Études Coptes, Paris, 28 juin–3 juillet 2004*, vol. 1, ed. Nathalie Bosson and Anne Boud'hors, 25–40. Orientalia Lovaniensia Analecta, 163. Louvain: E. Peeters, 2007.

Brakke, David. "Research and Publications in Egyptian Monasticism, 2000–2004." In *Huitième congrès international d'études coptes (Paris 2004) I. Bilans et perspectives 2000–2004*, ed. Anne Boud'hors and Denyse Vaillancourt, 111–26. Cahiers de la Bibliothèque copte, 15. Paris: De Boccard, 2006.

Capuani, Massimo. *Christian Egypt: Coptic Art and Monuments through Two Millennia*. Cairo: American University in Cairo Press, 2002.

Coquin, René- Georges. "Patriarchal Residences." In *CE*, vol. 6, 1912ff.

Coquin, René-Georges, and Maurice Martin. "Dayr al-Muharraq." In *CE*, vol. 3, 840ff.

Gabra, Gawdat, with Tim Vivian. *Coptic Monasteries: Egypt's Monastic Art and Architecture*. Cairo: American University in Cairo Press, 2002.

Godlewski, Wlodzimierz. "Excavating the Ancient Monastery of Naqlun." In *Christianity and Monasticism in the Fayoum Oasis*, ed. Gawdat Gabra, 155–71. Cairo: American University in Cairo Press, 2005.

Goehring, James E. *Ascetics, Society and the Desert: Studies in Early Egyptian Monasticism*. Harrisburg, Penn.: Trinity Press, 1999.

Grossmann, Peter. "The Pilgrimage Center of Abu Mina." In *Pilgrimage and Holy Space in Late Antique Egypt*, ed. David Frankfurter, 281–302. Leiden: E. J. Brill, 1998.

Guillaumont, Antoine. "Antony, Saint." In *CE*, vol. 1, 149–51.

——. "Evagrius Ponticus." In *CE*, vol. 4, 1076ff.

——. "Kellia: History of the Site." In *CE*, vol. 5, 1396–8.

——. "Macarius the Egyptian, Saint." In *CE*, vol. 5, 1491ff.

——. "Mary the Egyptian, Saint." In *CE*, vol. 5, 1560ff.

——. "Monasticism, Egyptian." In *CE*, vol. 5, 1661–64.

——. "Nitria." In *CE*, vol. 6, 1794–96.

——. "Palladius." In *CE*, vol. 6, 18.

——. "Syncletica." In *CE*, vol. 7, 2192.

Guiliaumont, Antoine, and K. H. Kuhn. "Paul of Thebes, Saint." In *CE*, vol. 6, 1925ff.

Innemée, Karel C. "Deir al-Surian (Egypt): Conservation Work of Autumn 2000." *Hugoye: Journal of Syriac Studies* 4, no. 2, 2001, http://syrcom.cua.edu//Hugoye (accessed 10 February 2008).

——. Deir al-Surian (Egypt): New Discoveries of 2001–2002." *Hugoye: Journal of Syriac Studies* 5, no. 2." 2002, http://syrcom.cua.edu//Hugoye (accessed 10 February 2008).

——. "Excavation at the Site of Deir el-Baramus 2002–2005." *Bulletin de la Société d'archéologie copte* 44 (2005): 55–68.

——. "Recent Discoveries of Wall-Painting in Deir Al-Surian." *Hugoye: Journal of Syriac Studies* 1, no. 2, 1998, http://syrcom.cua.edu//Hugoye (accessed 10 February 2008).

——. "The Wall Paintings of Deir al-Surian: New Discoveries of 1999." *Hugoye: Journal of Syriac Studies* 2, no. 2, 1999, http://syrcom.cua.edu//Hugoye (accessed 10 February 2008).

Innemée, Karel C., and L. van Rompay. "La presence des Syriens dans le Wadi al-Natrun (Egypte)." *Parole de l'Orient* 23 (1998): 167–202.

Innemée, Karel C., L. Van Rompay, and E. Sobczynski. "Deir al-Surian (Egypt): Its Wall-paintings, Wall-texts and Manuscripts." *Hugoye: Journal of Syriac Studies* 2, no. 2 (1999), http://syrcom.cua.edu/Hugoye (accessed 10 February 2008).

Krause, Martin. "Das Mönchtum in Ägpten." In *Ägypten in spätantik-christlicher Zeit. Einführung in die koptischeKulture*, ed. Martin Krause, 149–74. Wiesbaden: Reichert Velag, 1998.

Lyster, William, ed. *The Cave Church of Paul the Hermit at the Monastery of St. Paul, Egypt.* New Haven, Conn.: Yale University Press, in press.

Martin, Maurice. "Monasteries in Cyprus." In *CE*, vol. 5, 1647ff.

Mikhail, Maged, and Tim Vivian. "The Life of Saint John the Little: An Encomium by Zacharias of Sakha." *Coptic Church Review* 18, no. 1&2 (1997): 1–46.

Papaconstantinou, Arietta. *Les culte du saints en Ègypte des Byzantines aux Abbassides. L'apport des inscriptions et des papyrus grecs et coptes.* Paris: n.p., 2001.

Regnault, Lucien. "Amun, Saint." In *CE*, vol. 1, 119.

———. "Apophthegmata Patrum." In *CE*, vol. 1, 177ff.

———. "Pambo." In *CE*, vol. 6, 1877ff.

Russel, Norman. *The Lives of the Desert Fathers. The Historia Monarchum in Aegypto.* Kalamazoo, Mich.: n.p., 1980.

Vielleux, Armand. "Pachomian Monasticism." In *CE*, vol. 5, 1664–66.

———. "Pachomius, Saint." In *CE*, vol. 6, 1859–64.

Watson, John. "Abouna Matta El Meskeen: 'Contemporary Desert Mystic.'" *Coptic Church Review* 27, no. 3& 4 (2006): 66–92.

Wilfong, Terry G. "Coptic Papyrology 2000–2004." In *Huitième congrès international d'études coptes (Paris 2004) I. Bilans et perspectives 2000–2004*, ed. Anne Boud'hors and Denyse Vaillancourt, 321–36. Cahiers de la Bibliothèque copte, 15. Paris: De Boccard, 2006.

XI. THEOLOGY AND LITURGY

Abdallah, Alfonso. *L'ordinamento Liturgico di Gabriele V–88 Patriarca Copto.* Cairo: Ain Shams Press, 1962.

'Abd al-Masih Salib al-Mas'udi. *Al-Khuulaji al-Muqaddas.* Cairo: n.p., 1902.

Alcock, Antony. *The Life of Saint Samuel of Kalamun by Isaac the Presbyter.* London: Aris & Philips, 1983.

Allen, Pauline, and C. Datema. "Leontius presbyter of Constantinople." *Byzantina Australiensia* 9 (1991): 67–95.

Alliot, Maurice. *Le Culte d'Horus à Edfou au temps des Ptolémées.* Bibliothèque d' Etudes, 20. Cairo: Institut Français d'Archéologie Orientale, 1949, 1954.

Amacker, Rene, and Junod Eric Pamphile. *Eusèbe de Césarée, Apologie pour Origène.* Sources Chrétiennes, 464. Paris: Cerf, 2002.

Amélineau, Emile. *Monuments pour servir à l'histoire de l'Egypte chrétienne au IV et V siècles.* Mémoires des membres de la Mission Archéologique Française au Caire, 4. Cairo: n.p., 1888.

———. *Oeuvres de Schenoudi: Texte Copte et traduction française*, vol. 2, 3. Paris: n.p., 1914.

Anonymous. "Apparition miraculeuse de la Sainte Vierge a Zeitoun." *Le Monde copte* 1 (1977): 23–32.

Arras, Victor. "De Transitu Mariae Apocrypha Aethiopice 1." *Corpus Scriptorum Christianorum Orientalium* 342. Scriptores Aethiopici, 66. Louvain: E. Peeters, 1973.

———.Transitu Mariae Apocrypha Aethiopice 2." *Corpus Scriptorum Christianorum Orientalium* 352. Scriptores Aethiopici, 69. Louvain: E. Peeters, 1974.

Assemani, Giuseppe. *Bibliotheca Orientalis Clemento-Vaticana II, avec postface par Joseph-Marie Sauget (Rome 1721)*. Hildesheim: Georg Olms Verlag, 1975.

Assfalg, Julis. *Die Ordnung des Priestertums, Ein altes liturgisches Handbuch der koptischen Kirche*. Cairo: Centre of Oriental Studies of the Franciscain Custody of the Holy Land, 1955.

Atanassova, Diliana. "Zu den Sahidischen Pascha-Lektionaren." In *Coptic Studies on the Threshold of a New Millennium: Proceedings of the Seventh International Congress of Coptic Studies, Leiden, 27 August–2 September 2000*, vol. 1, ed. Mat Immerzeel and Jacques van der Vliet, 607–20. Louvain: E. Peeters, 2004.

Atiya, Aziz S. "Ibn Kabar." In *CE*, vol. 4, 1267–68.

Atiya, Aziz S., Yassa Abd Al-Masih, and Oswald Hugh E. Khs-Burmester. *History of the Patriarchs of the Egyptian Church*, vol 2, no. 3. Cairo: n.p., 1959.

Audet, J.-P. *La Didachè: Instructions des apôtres*. Paris: J. Gabalda, 1958.

Bagnall, Rogers S. *Egypt in Late Antiquity*. Princeton, N.J.: Princeton University Press, 1993.

Bardy, Gustave. "Aux Origines de l'Ecole d'Alexandrie." *Recherches de science religieuse* 27 (1937): 65–90.

———. "Monarchianism." In *Dictionnaire de théologie catholique*, vol. 10, part 2, cols. 2193–2209. Paris: n.p., 1929.

———. "Pour l'histoire de l'Ecole d'Alexandrie." *Vivre et penser* 2 (1942): 80–109.

Barkhuizen, J. H. "Justinian's Hymn O monogenh 'uio' tou Qeou." *Byzantinische Zeitschrift* 77 (1984): 3–5.

Barnes, Timothy David. *Constantine and Eusebius*. Cambridge, Mass.: Harvard University Press 1981.

Barns, C. "A Letter Ascribed to Peter of Alexandria." *Journal of Theological Studies* 24 (1973): 443–55.

Baumstark, Anton. *Comparative Liturgy*, rev. ed. B. Botte, English ed. F. L. Cross. London: Mowbray, 1958.

———. "Drei griechische Passionsgesänge ägyptischer Liturgie." *Oriens Christianus* 3 (1929): 69–78.

Baumstark, Anton, and W. Heffening. "Zwei altertümliche Litaneien aus dem Pashabuch der koptischen Kirche." *Oriens Christianus* 36 (1941): 74–100.

Bell, Harold Idris. *Jews and Christians in Egypt*. London: Oxford University Press, 1924.

Bernardin, A. "A Coptic Sermon Attributed to St. Athanasius." *Journal of Theological Studies* 38 (1937): 113–29.

———. "The Resurrection of Lazarus." *American Journal of Semitic Language* 57 (1940): 262–90.

Bethune-Baker, James Franklin. *An Introduction to the Early History of Christian Doctrine to the Time of the Council of Chalcedon*, 9th ed. London: Methuen, 1951.

Bindley, Thomas Herbert. *St. Cyprian, On the Lord's Prayer*. London: Society for Promoting Christian Knowledge, 1898.

Bishop, E. *Liturgica historical*. Oxford: Clarendon Press, 1962.

Blaudeau, Philippe. "Timothée Aelure et la direction ecclésiale de l'Empire post-Chalcédonien." *Revue des Etudes Byzantines* 54 (1996): 107–33.

Bonner, C. "A Coptic Fragment of Melito's Homily on the Passion." *Harvard Theological Review* 32 (1939): 141–42.

Bonner, Gerald. *St. Augustine of Hippo. Life and Controversies*, 2nd ed. London: Canterbury Press, 1986.

Borgehammar, Stephan. *How the Holy Cross Was Found: From Event to Medieval Legend*. Stockholm: Almqvist and Wiksell International, 1991.

Boud'hors, Anne, and Ramez Boutros. *L'homélie sur l'église du rocher attribuée à Timothée Aelure*. Patrologia Orientalis, 49, Fasc. 1/N217. Turnhout: Brepols, 2001.

Boularand, E. *L'Hérésie d'Arius et la "foi" de Nicéa*. Paris: n.p., 1972.

Botte, Bernard. *La tradition Apostolique*, 2nd ed. Paris: Cerf, 1984.

Bradshaw, Philip F. *Ordination Rites of the Ancient Churches of East and West*. New York: Pueblo, 1990.

Brakke, David. "The Authenticity of Then Ascetic Athanasiana." *Orientalia* 63 (1994): 17–57.

Brakmann, Heinzgerd. "Nueue Funde und Forschungen zur Liturgie der Kopten." In *Ägypten und Nubien in spätantiker und christlicher Zeit. Akten des 6. Internationalen Koptologenkongress*, ed. S. Emmel, M. Krause, S. Richter, and S. Schaten, 451–64. Sprachen, und Kulturen des Christlichen Orients, Band 6, 1. Wiesbaden: Reichert Verlag, 1999.

———. "Nueue Funde und Forschungen zur Liturgie der Kopten (2000–2004)." In *Huitième congrès international d'études coptes (Paris 2004) I. Bilans et perspectives 2000–2004*, ed. Anne Boud'hors and Denyse Vaillancourt, 127–49. Cahiers de la Bibliothèque copte, 15. Paris: De Boccard, 2006.

Brent, Allen. *Hippolytus and the Roman Church in the Third Century: Communities in Tension before the Emergence of a Monarch Bishop*. Leiden: E. J. Brill, 1995.

Brière, Maurice, and Francois Graffin. *Les Homiliae Cathédrales de Sévère d'Antioche*. Patrologia Orientalis, 38 Fasc. 2, No. 175. Turnhout: Brepols, 1976.

Brightman, Frank Edward. *Liturgies Eastern and Western*, vol. 1. Oxford: Clarendon Press, 1896.

Brogi, Marco. "La santa Salmodia Annuale della Chiesa Copta." *Studia Orientalia Christiana Aegyptiaca.* Cairo: n.p., 1962.

Brooks, Ernest Walter. *Hymns of Severus of Antioch and Others in the Syriac Version of Paul of Edessa as Revised by James of Edessa.* Patrologia Orientalis, 6, Fasc 1, and 7 fasc. 3. Paris: n.p., 1911–1912.

Brown, P. *Augustine of Hippo.* Berkeley: University of California Press, 1967.

Browne, Gerald. "Gregory of Nazianzus. Encomium of Basil of Caesarea." *Michigan Coptic Texts—Papyrologica Castroctaviana*, 28–34. Studia et Textus, 7. Barcelona: n.p., 1979.

Budde, Achim. *Die ägyptische Basilios-Anaphora. Text–Kommentar-Geschichte.* Jerusalemer Theologisches Forum, 7. Münster: n.p., 2004.

Budge, Ernest Alfred Wallis. *Coptic Homilies in the Dialect of Upper Egypt.* London: British Museum, 1915.

——. *Coptic Martyrdoms in the Dialect of Upper Egypt.* London: British Museum, 1914.

——. *Miscellaneous Coptic Texts in the Dialect of Upper Egypt.* London: British Museum, 1915.

——. *Palladius, the Paradise or the Garden of the Holy Fathers.* 2 vols. London: Chatto and Windus, 1907.

——. *Saint Michael the Archangel: Three Encomiums by Theodosius, Archbishop of Alexandria, Severus, Patriarch of Antioch, and Eustathius of Trake.* London: British Museum, 1894.

Burmester, Oswald Hugh E. "Baptismal Rite of the Coptic Church." *Bulletin de la Société d'Archéologie Copte* 11 (1945): 27–86.

——. "The Canons of Christodulos, Patriarch of Alexandria (A.D. 1047–1077)." *Le Muséon* 45 (1932): 71–84.

——. "The Canon of Cyril II." *Le Muséon* 49 (1936): 254–83.

——. "The Canons of Gabriel Ibn Turaik." *Orientalia Christiana Periodica* 1 (1934): 5–45.

——. "The Canonical Hours of the Coptic Church." *Orientalia Christiana Periodica* 2 (1936): 78–100.

——. "The Consecration of the Patriarch of Alexandria." *Eastern Churches Quarterly* 11, no. 4 (1953): 179–90.

——. *The Egyptian or Coptic Church Detailed Description of Her Liturgical Services and Rites.* Cairo: n.p., 1967.

——. "Homilies of the Holy Week lectionary." *Le Muséon* 45 (1934): 21–70.

——. *The Horologion of the Egyptian Church.* Studia Orientalia Christiana Aegyptiaca. Cairo: n.p., 1973.

——. *Koptische Handschrift, 1.* Wiesbaden: F. Steiner, 1975.

——. *Le Lectionnaire de la semaine sainte.* Patrologia Orientalis, 24 fasc 2, 25 fasc 2. Paris: n.p., 1933, 1943.

——. "The Office of Genuflection on Whitsunday." *Le Muséon* 47 (1934): 205–57.

——. *The Ordination Rites of the Coptic Church.* Cairo: n.p., 1985.

——. *The Rite of Consecration of the Patriarch of Alexandria.* Cairo: n.p., 1960.

——. "The Sayings of Michael, Metropolitan of Damietta." *Orientalia Christiana Periodica* 2 (1936): 101–28.

——. "Tûrûhat of the Coptic Church." *Orientalia Christiana Periodica* 3 (1937): 78–109.

——. "Tûrûhat of the Coptic Year." *Orientalia Christiana Periodica* 3 (1937): 505–49.

——. "Two Services of the Coptic Church Attributed to Peter, Bishop of Behnesa." *Le Muséon* 45 (1937): 235–54.

Burns, Arthur. E. *Introduction to the Creed.* London: n.p., 1899.

Butcher, Edith Louise. *The Story of the Church of Egypt.* London: n.p., 1897.

Bute, John. *The Coptic Morning Service for the Lord's Day.* London: Cope and Fenwick, 1908.

Butler, Alfred Joshua. *The Ancient Coptic Churches of Egypt.* 2 vols. Oxford: Clarendon Press, 1884.

Cabrol, Francois. "Absolution." In *Dictionnaire d'archéologie chrétienne et de liturgie*, vol. 1. Paris: n.p., 1907.

Canatalamessa, Francois. *Easter in the Early Church*, trans. J. Quigley and J. Lienhard. Collegeville, Minn.: Liturgical Press, 1993.

Casurellam, A. *The Johanine Paraclete in the Church Fathers (Beiträge zur Geschichte der Biblischen Exege).* Tubingen: Mohr, 1983.

Chadwick, Henry. "Faith and Order at the Council of Nicaea." *Harvard Theological Review* 53 (1960): 171–96.

Chaîne, Marius. "Une Homélie de Saint Grégoire de Nysse traduite en Copte, et attribuée à Saint Grégoire de Nazianze." *Revue de l'Orient Chrétien* 17 (1912): 395–409; 18 (1913): 36–41.

——. "Une lettre de Sévère d'Antioche à la diaconesse Anastasie." *Oriens Christianus* 3, (1913): 32–58.

——. "Sermon sur la pénitence attribué à Saint Cyrille d'Alexandrie." *Mélanges de l'Université Saint Joseph* 6 (1913): 493–528.

Charles, N. "Le 'Thesaurus de Trinitate' de saint Cyrille d'Alexandrie." *Revue d'Histoire Ecclésiastique* 45 (1950): 34–35.

Chase, Fredric Henry. *Confirmation in the Apostolic Age.* London: McMillan, 1909.

——. "The Lord's Prayers in the Early Church," vol. 1, 3. Cambridge: Cambridge University Press, 1891; Reprint: Nendeln, Liechtenstein: Kraus Reprint, 1967.

Chestnut, Roberta C. *Three Monophysite Christologies, Severus of Antioch, Philoxenus of Mabbug and Jacob of Sarug.* Oxford: Oxford University Press, 1976.

Clédat, Jean, et al. *Le monastère et la nécrople de Baouit.* Mémoires de l'Institut Français d'Archéologie Orientale, 111. Cairo: n.p., 1999.

Colin, Gérard. "Le Synaxaire Ethiopien, Etat actuel de la question." *Analecta Bollandiana* 106 (1988): 273–317.

Complani, Alberto. "Epifanio (Ancoratus) e Gregorio di Nazianzo (Epistolae in Copto: identificazione e status quaestiones." *Augustianum* 35 (1995): 321–27.

——. *Le lettere festali di Atanasi di Alessandria.* Studio storico critico Corpus Manoscritti Copti Letterari. Roma: n.p., 1989.

——. "La prima lettera festale di Cirillo di Alessandria e la testimonianza di P. Vindob K. 10157." *Augustinianum* 39 (1999): 129–38.

Connolly, Richard Hugh. *Diaclasia apostolorum: The Syriac Version Translated and Accompanied by the Verona Latin Fragments.* Oxford: Clarendon Press, 1929.

Coquin, René-Georges "La consécration des églises dans le rite copte, ses relations avec les rites syrien et byzantin." *L'Orient Syrien* 9 (1964): 149–89.

——. "Le corpus canonum copte. Un nouveau complement le ms I.F.A.O. Copte 6." *Orientalia* 50 (1981): 40–86.

——. "Un discours attribué au patriarche Cyrille sur la dédicace de l'église de Raphaël rapportant les propos de son oncle, le patriarche Théophile." *Bulletin de la Société d'Archéologie Copte* 33 (1994): 25–56.

——. "Un discours attribué au patriarche Cyrille sur la dédicace de l'Eglise de Raphaël rapportant les propos de son oncle, le patriarche Théophile." *Bulletin de la Société d'Archéologie Copte* 36 (1997): 9–58.

——. "Fragments d'une chronique relatifs à un patriarche d'Alexandrie probablement Théodose (535–566 A.D.)." *Bulletin de la Société d'Archéologie Copte* 30 (1991): 1–24.

——. "Les lettres festales d'Athanase (CPG 2102) un nouveau complément le Ms IFAO Copte 25." *Orientalia Lovansiana Periodica* 15 (1984): 133–58.

——. *Le livre de la consécration du Sanctuaire de Benjamin.* Bibliothèque des d'Etudes Coptes, 13. Cairo: n.p., 1975.

——. *Les vertus (APETAI) de l'Esprit en Egypte.* Mélanges H.-Ch. Puech. 447–57. Paris: Presse universitaires de France, 1974.

Coquin, René-Georges, and Enzo Lucchesi. "Un complément au corpus Copte des lettres festales d'Athanase (Paris B.N. Copte 176)." *Orientalia Lovansiana Periodica* 13 (1982): 137–42.

Cowell, B. "Alexander (St.)." In *Dictionary of Christian Biographies*, 1, cols. 79–82. ed. Michael Walsh, Vendor: Liturgical Press, 2001.

Cramer, Maria. "Studien zu koptischen Pascha-Büchern." *Oriens Christianus* 49 (1965): 90–115.

Crum, Walter Ewing. *Catalogue of the Coptic Manuscripts in the British Museum*. London: British Museum, 1905.

———. *Catalogue of the Coptic Manuscripts in the Collection of the John Rylands Library Manchester*. Manchester: n.p., 1909.

———. *Coptic Dictionary*. Oxford: Clarendon Press, 1936.

———. *Coptic Manuscripts Brought from the Fayyum by W. M. Petrie Together with a Papyrus in the Bodleian Library*. London: D. Nutt, 1893.

———. *Der Papyruscodex saec VI–VII der Phillipsbibliothek in Cheltenham*. Strassburg: n.p., 1915.

———. "Sévère d'Antioche en Egypte." *Revue de l'Orient Chrétien* 23 (1923): 97–100.

———. "Texts Attributed to Peter of Alexandria." *Journal of Theological Studies* 4 (1902–1903): 387–97.

———. *Theological Texts from Coptic Papyri*. Oxford: n.p., 1913.

Crum, Walter Ewing, and H. G. Evelyn White. *The Monastery of Epihanius at Thebes: The Metropolitan Museum of Art Egyptian Expedition*, 2 vols. New York, 1926; Reprint, New York: Arno Press, 1973.

Cuming, Geoffrey J. "The Anaphora of St. Mark: A Study of Development." In *Essays on Early Eastern Eucharistic Prayers*, ed. P. Bradshaw, 57–72. Collegeville, Minn.: Pueblo Books, 1997.

———. *The Liturgy of St Mark*. Orientalia Christiana Analecta, 234. Rome: n.p., 1990.

Dallen, James. *The Reconciling Community, the Rite of Penance*. New York: Pueblo, 1986.

Daniélou, Jean. *The Bible and the Liturgy*. London: Longman and Todd, 1956.

Daoud, Marcus. *The Liturgy of the Ethiopian Church*. Cairo: n.p., 1959.

David, J. "Les éclaircissements de Saint Athanase sur les Psaumes, Fragments d'une traduction Copte." *Revue de l'Orient Chrétien* 24 (1924): 3–57.

De Lagarde, Marcus. *Cantenae in Evangelia aegyptiacae quaie spersunt*. Göttingen: n.p., 1886.

Delehaye, Hippolyte. "Le Calendrier d'Oxyrhynque pour l'année 535–536." *Analecta Bollandiana* 53 (1924): 83–99.

Depuydt, Leo. *Catalogue of the Coptic Manuscripts in the Pierpont Morgan Library*. Corpus of Illuminated Manuscripts, 4, 5. Louvain: E. Peeters, 1993.

Derda, Tomazs, and Katarzyna Urbaniak-Walczak. "P. Naqlun Inv. 10/95; Greek Excerpts from a Liturgy with Their Coptic Translation." *Journal of the Juristic Papyrology* 26 (1996): 7–21.

De Vis, Henri. *Homélies Coptes de la Vaticane*. 2 vols. Copenhagen: Hauniae, 1922, 1929.

Devos, Paul. "Les cinq premières lettres festales de Saint Athanase d'Alexandrie." *Analecta Bollandiana* 110 (1992): 5–20.

Dix, Gregory. *The Treatise on the Apostolic Tradition of St. Hippolytus of Rome*. Reissued with corrections, preface, and bibliography by H. Chadwick. London: Alban Press, 1992.

Doresse, Jean, and Emmanuel Lanne. *Un témoin archaique de la liturgie copte de S Basile*. Bibliothèque du Muséon, 47. Louvain: E. Peeters, 1960.

Dragas, G. D. "The Homoousion in Athanasius Contra Apollinarem." In *Arianism, Historical and Theological Reassessments*, 233–42. Philadelphia: Philadelphia Patristic Foundation, 1985.

Drake, Harold Allen, et al. *Eudoxia and the Holy Sepulchre. A Constantinian Legend in Coptic*. Studio dell'Antichità, 67. Milan: Cisalpino-Goliardica, 1980.

Drescher, James. *Coptic Texts Relating to Saint Menas*. Cairo: n.p., 1946.

———. *Three Coptic Legends*. Suppl Annales du Services des Antiquités de l'Egypte, 4. Cairo: n.p., 1947.

Drijvers, Han. J. W., and J. Willem Drijvers. *The Finding of the True Cross, the Judas Kyriakos Legend in Syriac*. Corpus Scriptorum Christianorum Orientalium, 565, Subs 93. Louvain: E. Peeters, 1997.

Drioton, Etienne. "La discussion d'un moine anthropomorphite Audien avec le patriarche Théophile d'Alexandrie en l'année 399." *Revue de l'Orient Chrétien* 20 (1915–1917): 92–100, 113–128.

Du Bose, William. *The Ecumenical Councils*, 4th ed. Edinburgh: T. & T. Clark, 1926.

Duchesne, Lucien. *Early History of the Christian Church*. London: J. Murray, 1924.

———. *L'Eglise au VIe siècle*. Paris: Fontemoing, E. de Boccard, 1925.

Ebeid, Rifaat Y., and M. J. Young. *The Lamp of the Intellect of Severus Ibn Al-Muqaffa' Bishop of Al-Ashmunain*. Corpus Scriptorum Christianorum Orientalium, 365. Louvain: E. Peeters, 1975.

Ehrardt, Albert. *The Apostolic Succession in the First Two Centuries of the Church*. London: n.p., 1953.

Elanskaya, Alla. *The Literary Coptic Manuscripts in the A. S. Pushkin State Fine Arts Museum in Moscow*. Leiden: E. J. Brill, 1994.

Emmel, Stephen. "Theophilus's Festal Letter of 401 as Quoted by Shenute." In *Divitiae Aegypti: Koptologsche und verwandte Studien zu Ehren von Martin Kraus*, ed. C. Flück, 93–98. Wiesbaden: Reichert Verlag, 1995.

Evelyn White, Hugh G. *The Monasteries of Wadi N'Natrun*. 3 vols. New York: Metropolitan Museum of Art Egyptian Expedition, 1928–1933.

Evetts, Basil Thomas Alfred. *History of the Patriarchs of the Egyptian Church.* Patrologia Orientalis, 1, Fasc 4. Paris: n.p., 1941.

Fehrenbach, E. "Bénir (manière de)." In *Dictionnaire d'archéologie chrétienne et liturgie,* vol. 2, 1:746–58. Paris: n.p., 1910.

Fenwick, John. *The Significance of Similarities in the Anaphoral Intercession Sequence in Coptic Anaphora of Saint Basil and Other Ancient Liturgies,* ed. E. Livingstone, 355–62. Studia Patristica 18, no. 2. Louvain: E. Peeters, 1989.

———. *The Anaphoras of St Basil and St James.* Orientalia Christiana Analecta, 240. Rome: n.p., 1992.

Fiey, Jean-Maurice. "Coptes et Syriaques, Contacts et échanges." *Studia Orientalia Chirsitiana Collectanea* 15 (1972–1973): 295–366.

Fleish. "Une homélie de Théophile d'Alexandrie en l'honneur de St Pierre et St. Paul-texte arabe." *Revue de l'Orient Chrétien* 28 (1938–46): 371–419.

Florovsky, G. *Eschatology in the Patristic Age: An Introduction,* vol. 2, ed. Kurt Aland and F. L. Cross, 235–50. Studia Patristica, Texte und Untersuchungen zur Geschichte der Altchristlichen Literatur, 64. Berlin: n.p., 1957.

Frend, William Hugh Clifford. "An Eucharistic Sequence from Qasr Ibrim." *Jahrbuch für Antike und Christentum* 30 (1987): 90–98.

———. "Nationalism as Factor in Anti-Chalcedonian Feeling in Egypt." *Studies in Church History* 18 (1982): 39–46.

———. *The Rise of Christianity.* Philadelphia, Penn.: Fortress Press, 1984.

———. *The Rise of the Monophysite Movement.* Cambridge: Cambridge University Press, 1979.

Frend, William Hugh Clifford, and I. A. Muirhead. "Greek Manuscript from the Cathedral of Qasr Ibrim." *Le Muséon* 89 (1976): 43–49.

Garitte, Gérard. "Fragments Coptes d'une lettre de Sévère d'Antioche à Sotérichos de Césarée." *Le Muséon* 65 (1952): 185–98.

———. "Textes Hagiographiques Orientaux relatifs à Saint Léonce de Tripoli II, L'homélie de Sévère d'Antioche." *Le Muséon* 79 (1966): 335–86.

———. *Vita Antonii versio Sahidica.* Corpus Scriptorum Christianorum Orientalium, 117–118. Louvain: E. Peeters, 1949.

Gascou, Jean. *Un nouveau document sur les confréries chrétiennes P. Stras Copte inv. 644,* ed. A. Boud'hors, J. Gascou, and D. Vaillancourt, 167–78. Etudes Coptes 9, Cahiers de la Bibliothèque Copte, 14. Paris: De Boccard, 2006.

Gawdat, Gabra, "Untersuchungen zum Difnar der Koptischen Kirche." *Bulletin de la Société d'Archéologie Copte* 35 (1996) 37–52; 37 (1998): 48–69.

Geerard, Maurice. *Clavis Patrum Graecorum.* 5 vols. Turnhout: Brepols, 1973–1998.

Gero, S. "The So-called Ointment Prayer in the Coptic Version of the Didache: A Re-evaluation." *Harvard Theological Review* 70 (1977): 67–84.

Giamberardini, Gabriele. *Il culto mariano in Egitto*. 3 vols. Cairo-Jerusalem: n.p., 1975–1984.

———. *La sorte dei defunti nella tradizione Copta*. Studia Orientalia Christiana Aegyptiaca. Cairo: n.p., 1965.

Gibson, M. *The Disdascalia Apostolorum in English*. London: n.p., 1903.

Gill, Joseph. *The Council of Florence*. Cambridge: n.p., 1959.

Gingras, G. Egeria. *Diary of a Pilgrimage, Ancient Christian Writers*. New York: Newman Press, 1970.

Goehring, James E. "A New Coptic Fragment of Melito's Homily on the Passion." *Le Muséon* 97 (1984): 255–60.

Goehring, James E., and W. H. Willis. "Melito of Sardis on Passover—Coptic Text Translation; Notes and Variant Reading Fragments Transcription and Placement." In *The Crosby-Schoeyen Codex Manuscript 193 in Schoyen Colection*, ed. by James E. Goehring, 1–79. Corpus Scriptorum Christianorum Orientalium, 521, Subs 85. Louvain: E. Peeters, 1990.

Godron, Gérard. *Textes relatifs à Saint Claude d'Antioche*. Patrologia Orientalis, 35, fasc. 4. Turnhout: Brepols, 1971.

Gordillo, M. *Theologia orientalium cum Latinorum comparata. Commentatio historica*. Orientalia Christiana Analecta, 158. Rome: n.p., 1960.

Graf, Georg. *Ein Reformversuch innerhalb der koptischen Kirche im zwölften Jahrhundert*. Paderborn: n.p., 1923.

———. "Zwei dogmatische Florilegien der Kopten." *Orientalia Christiana Periodica* 3 (1937): 380–402.

Gregg, Robert, ed. *Arianism Historical and Theological Reassessments, Papers from the Ninth International Conference on Patristic Studies*. Philadelphia: Philadelphia Patristic Foundation, 1985.

Grillmeier, Aloys. *Christ in Christian Tradition, from the Apostolic Age to Chalcedon*, trans. J. Bowden, vol. 1. London: Mowbrays, 1975.

———. *Christ in Christian Tradition*, vol. 2, part 1, trans. P. Allen and John Cawte. London: Mowbray, 1985.

———. *Christ in Christian tradition*, trans. O. C. Dean, vol. 2 part 4. London: Mowbray, 1996.

———. "La peste d'Origène. Soucis du patriarche d'Alexandrie à l'apparition d'origenistes en Haute Egypte." In *Alexandrina, Mélanges offerts au P. C. Mondésert*, 221–24. Paris: Cerf, 1987.

Griggs, Wilfred. "Early Christian Burials in the Fayoum." In *Christianity and Monasticism in the Fayoum Oasis*, ed. Gawdat Gabra, 185–96. Cairo: American University in Cairo Press, 2005.

Griveau, Robert. *Les fêtes Coptes par Maqrizi*. Patrologia Orientalis, 10, fasc. 4. Paris: n.p., 1915.

Guidi, Ignazio. "Il testamento di Isaaco e il testamento di Giacobbe." *Rendiconti del Accademia de Lincei ser* 5, no. 9 (1900): 157–80, 223–64.

Guillaumont, Antoine. *Aux origines du monachisme chrétien.* Spiritualité Orientale, 30. Bellefontaine: n.p., 1979.

———. "Les visions mystiques dans le monachisme oriental ancien." In *Les Visions mystiques (Colloque organisé par le Secrétariat d'Etat à la Culture 1976)*, 116–27. Paris: Nouvelles de l'Institut Catholique de Paris, 1977.

Hainthaler, Teresa. "John Philoponus, philosopher, theologian in Alexandria." In *Christ in Christian Tradition*, ed. Aloys Grillmeier, vol. 2, part 4, trans. O. C. Dean. London: Mowbray, 1996.

Hammerschmidt, Ernest. *Die Koptische Gregoriosanaphora.* Syrische und Griechische Einflusse auf Eine Ägyptische Liturgie. Berlin: n.p., 1957.

———. "Some Remarks on the History of, and Present State of Investigation into, the Coptic Liturgy." *Bulletin de la Société d'Archéologie Copte* 19 (1968): 89–113.

———. *Studies in the Ethiopic Anaphoras.* Berlin: n.p., 1961.

Hanson, Richard Patrick Crosland. *The Search for Christian Doctrine of God, the Arian Controversy 318–381.* Edinburgh: T. & T. Clark, 1988.

Hatch, P. "A Fragment of a Lost Work on Dioscorus." *Harvard Theological Review* 19 (1926): 377–81.

Hauben, H. "On the Melitians in P. London VI (P. Jews) 1914: The Problem of the Papas Heriascus." In *Proceedings of the 16th International Congress of Papyrology, New York 24–31 July 1980*, ed. Rogers S. Bagnall, 454–55. American Studies in Papyrology, 23. Chico, CA: Scholars Press, 1981.

Haugh, R. *Photius and the Carolingians: The Trinitarian Controversy.* Belmont, Mass.: Nordland, 1975.

Hefele, Karl Joseph. *A History of the Council of the Church from the Original Documents*, trans. W. Robinson Clark. Reprint, New York: AMS Press, 1972.

Henner, Jutta. *Fragmenta Liturgica Coptica.* Antike und Christentum, 5. Tübingen: Mohr Siebek, 2000.

Hespel, Robert. *Sévère d'Antioche, Le Philalethe.* Corpus Scriptorum Christianorum Orientalium, 133–134. Louvain: E. Peeters, 1952.

Holl, K. *Enthusiasmus und Bussgewalt.* Leipzig: n.p., 1898.

Horner, George. *The Service for the Consecration of a Church and Altar According to the Coptic Rite.* London: n.p., 1902.

Hubai, Paul. "The Legend of St Mark. Coptic Fragments." *Studia in Honorem L. Foti*, 165–89. Studia Aegyptiaca, 12. Budapest: n.p., 1989.

Hyvernat, Henri. *Les Actes des martyrs de l'Egypte.* Paris, 1886–1887; Reprint, New York: Hildesheim, 1977.

Ihm, C. *Die Programme der christlichen Apsismalerei vom vierten Jahrhundert bis zur Mitte des achten Jahrhunderts.* Wiesbaden: Harrassowitz, 1960.

Jakobielski, Stefan. *A History of the Bishopric of Pachoras on the Basis of Coptic Inscriptions,* vol. 3, Faras. Warsaw: Éditions scientifiques de Pologne, 1972.

Jeffreys, Elisabeth, M. Jeffreys, and Roger Scott. *The Chronicle of John Malalas.* Byzantina Australiensa, 4. Canberra: Humanities Research Centre, Australian National University, 1986.

Johnson, David W. *A Panegyric on Macarius Bishop of Tkow Attributed to Dioscorus of Alexandria.* Corpus Scriptorum Christianorum Orientalium, 415, 416. Louvain: E. Peeters, 1983.

Johnson, M. "The Baptsimal Rite and Anaphora in the Prayers of Serapion of Thmuis: An Assessment of a Recent 'Judicious Reassessment.'" *Worship* 73 (1999): 140–68.

Kahle, Paul. *Bala'iza Coptic Texts from Deir El-Bala'izah in Upper-Egypt.* 2 vols. London: Oxford University Press, 1954.

Kamil, Jill. *Christianity in the Land of the Pharaohs, the Coptic Orthodox Church.* London: Routledge, 2002.

Kammerer, Winifred. *A Coptic Bibliography.* Ann Arbor: University of Michigan Press, 1951.

Kannengiesser, C. *Arius and Athanasius, Collected Studies Series CS 353.* Variorum, Hampshire: Brookfield, 1991.

Karpozilos Apostolos, D. "A Coptic Trisagion from Egypt. P. Yale inv. 2119 19.0 X 18.5 cm. IX cent. A.D." *Orientalia Christiana Periodica* 39 (1973): 454–60.

Kelly, John Norman Davidson. *Early Christian Creeds,* 3rd ed. London: Longman Group, 1972.

Kemp, Eric Waldram. *Canonization and Authority in the Western Church.* London: Oxford University Press, 1948; Reprint, New York: AMS Press, 1980.

Khater, Antoine, and Oswald Hugh E. Burmester. *Catalogue of the Coptic and Christian Arabic Mss Preserved in the Cloister of Saint Menas at Cairo.* Cairo: n.p., 1967

——. *Catalogue of the Coptic and Christian Arabic Mss Preserved in the Library of the Church of the All-Holy Virgin Mary Known as Qasriat Ar-Rihan at Old Cairo.* Cairo: n.p., 1973.

——. *Catalogue of the Coptic and Christian Arabic Mss Preserved in the Library of the Church of Saints Sergius and Bacchus Known as Abu Sargah at Old Cairo.* Cairo: n.p., 1977.

——. *History of the Patriarchs of the Egyptian Church,* vol. 3, part 1. Textes et Documents, 11. Cairo: n.p., 1968.

Kidd, Beresford James. *A History of the Church to A.D. 461*, vol. 1. Oxford: n.p., 1922.

Kim, K. W. "Origen's Text of John in His on Prayer, Commentary on Matthew and against Celsus." *Journal of Theological Studies* 1 (1950): 74–84.

Krause, Martin. "Das koptische Antiphonar aus dem Handschriften von Hamuli." In *Ägypten–Münster, Kulturwissenschaftliche Studien zu Ägypten, dem Vorderen Orient und verwandeten Gebieten (Festschrift E. Graefe)*, ed. Anke Ilona Blöbaum et al., 167–85. Wiesbaden: Harrassowitz, 2003.

Kugener, Marc-Antoine. *Vie de Sévère, by Zacharias Scholasticus*. Patrologia Orientalis, 2. Paris: n.p., 1904.

Kuhn, K. H. "Four Additional Sahidic Fragments of a Panegyric on John the Baptist Attributed to Theodosius." *Le Muséon* 96 (1983): 251–65.

———. *A Panegyric on John the Baptist Attributed to Theodosius Archbishop of Alexandria*. Corpus Scriptorum Christianorum Orientalium, 268–269. Louvain: E. Peeters, 1966.

———. "A Panegyric on John the Baptist Attributed to Theodosius Archbishop of Alexandria." *Le Muséon* 76 (1963): 55–77.

———. *A Panegyric on John the Baptist Attributed to Theodosius Archbishop of Alexandria*. Corpus Scriptorum Christianorum Orientalium, 268–269. Louvain: E. Peeters, 1966.

———. "Three Further Fragments of a Panegyric on John the Baptist Attributed to Theodosius." *Le Muséon* 88 (1975): 103–12.

———. "Two Leaves from a Codex from Qasr Ibrim." *Journal of Egyptian Archaeology* 77 (1991): 145–49.

Kuhn, K. H., and H. J. Tait. *Thirteen Coptic Acrostic Hymns from Manuscript M574 of the Pierpont Morgan Library*. Oxford: Griffith Institute, 1996.

Kuhner, R. "Physiologus." In *Acts of the Second International Congress of Coptic Studies*, ed. Tito Orlandi and F. Wisse, 135–47. Rome: C.I.M, 1985.

Kwok-kit, Ng. M. *The Spirituality of Athanasius, A Key for Proper Understanding of This Important Church Father*. European University Studies. Bern: Peter Lang, 2001.

Labib, Iqladios. *Kitab al-Absalmodia al-Kiyahkiah* (The Book of the Psalmodia of Kihak). Cairo: Ain Shams Press, 1911–1922.

Lafontaine, Guy. "Une Homélie Copte sur le diable et sur Michel attribuée à Grégoire le théologien." *Le Muséon* 92 (1979): 37–60.

———. "La version Copte Bohaïrique du Discours 'Sur l'amour des pauvres' de Grégoire de Nazianze." *Le Muséon* 93 (1980): 199–236.

———. "La Version Copte des discours de Grégoire de Nazianze." *Le Muséon* 94 (1981): 37–45.

———. "La Version Copte Sahidique du discours 'Sur la Pâques' de Grégoire de Nazianze." *Le Muséon* 93, no. 2 (1980): 37–52.

Laga, C., J. A. Munitiz, and L. van Rompay, eds. *After Chalcedon, Studies in Theology and Church History Offered to Professor Albert Van Roey for His Seventieth Birthday.* Louvain: E. Peeters, 1985.

Lake, Kirsopp. *Eusebius, the Ecclesiatical History with an English Translation.* Loeb Classical Library. London, 1926; Reprint, Cambridge, Mass.: Harvard University Press, 1980.

Lanne, Emmanuel. *Le grand Euchologue du Monastère Blanc.* Patrologia Orientalis, 28, fasc 2. Paris: n.p., 1958.

Lash, E. *Les Homélies Cathédrales de Sévère d'Antioche, Homélies I-XVII.* Patrologia Orientalis, 38, fasc. 2. Turnhout: Brepols, 1976.

Layton, Bentley. *Catalogue of Coptic Literary Manuscripts in the British Library Acquired since the Year 1906.* London: British Library, 1987.

Lebon, Joseph. *Le Monophysisme Sévèrien- étude Historique, Littéraire et Théologique.* Louvain, 1909; Reprint, New York: AMS, 1978.

Lefort, Theophile. "Athanase auteur Copt." *Le Muséon* 69 (1956): 233–41.

———. "Une citation copte de la pseudo-clémentine 'de virginité." *Bulletin de l'Institut Français d'Archéologie Orientale* 30 (1931): 509–11.

———. "La 'de virginitate' de S. Clément ou de S Athanase." *Le Muséon* 40 (1927): 249–64.

———. "L'homélie de S Athanase des papyrus de Turin." *Le Muséon* 71 (1958): 5–50, 209–39.

———. *Lettres festales et pastorales en Copte.* Corpus Scriptorum Christianorum Orientalium, 150–151. Louvain: E. Peeters, 1955.

———. *Les Pères Apostoliques en Copte.* Corpus Scriptorum Christianorum Orientalium, 135. Louvain: E. Peeters, 1952.

———. "S. Athanase sur la virginité." *Le Muséon* 42 (1929): 197–274.

Leijssen, Lambert. *Confirmation: Its Origins, History and Pastoral Situation Today.* Louvain: E. Peeters, 1989.

Leith, John H., ed. *Creeds of the Churches: A Reader in Christian Doctrine from the Bible to the Present.* Garden City, N.Y.: Anchor Books, 1963.

Leloir, Lucien. *L'accompagnement spirituel selon la tradition monastique ancienne, principalement arménienne,* 83–96. Mélanges Antoine Guillaumont, Cahiers d'Orientalisme, 20. Geneva: Patrick Cramer, 1988.

Lightfoot, Joseph Barber. *The Apostolic Fathers.* 2 vols. New York: n.p., 1890.

Lilla, Salvatore. *Clement of Alexandri. A Study in Christian Platonism and Gnosticism.* Oxford: Oxford University Press, 1971.

Lucchesi, Enzo. *Chénouté a-t-il écrit en grec?* 201–10. Mélanges Antoine Guillaumont, Cahiers d'Orientalisme, 20. Genève: Patrick Cramer, 1987.

———. "Compléments aux Pères Apostoliques en Copte." *Analecta Bollandiana* 99 (1981): 396–408.

———. "Deux nouveaux témoins coptes du 'Peri Pscha' de Meliton de Sardes." *Analecta Bollandiana* 102 (1984): 383–93.

———. "Encore un témoin Copte du 'Peri Pascha' de Meliton de Sardes." *Vigileae Christianae* 41 (1987): 290–92.

———. "Un fragment copte inédit de l'homélie CIII sur l'épiphanie de Sévère d'Antioche." *Journal of Theological Studies* 30 (1979): 197–201.

———. "Les homélies sur l'Ecclésiaste de Grégoire de Nysse." *Vigileae Christianeae* 36 (1982): 292–93.

———. "Notice touchant l'homélie XIV de Sévère d'Antioche." *Vigilea Christianae* 33 (1979): 291–93.

———. "Un nouveau complément aux lettres festales d'Athanase." *Analecta Bollandiana* 119 (2001): 255–60.

———. "Le Pasteur d'Hermes en Copte." *Vigillae Christianae* 43 (1989): 393–96.

———. "Une (pseudo-) Apocalypse d'Athanase en Copte." *Analecta Bollandiana* 115 (1997).

———. "Le Recueil des lettres d'Ignace d'Antioche." *Vigilea Christianae* 42 (1988): 313–17.

———. "Le sort d'un feuillet copte relatif à une homélie inédite attribuée à Pierre d'Alexandrie." *Analecta Bollandiana* 103 (1985): 94.

Lucchesi, Enzo, and P. Devos. "Un Corpus Basilien en Copte." *Analecta Bollandiana* 99 (1981); 93–94.

Luibheid, Colm. "The Alleged Second Session of the Council of Nicaea." *Journal of Theological Studies* 34 (1983): 165–74.

———. *The Council of Nicea.* Galway, Ire.: n.p., 1982.

Luibhied, Colm, Jaroslav Pelikan, Jean Leclercq, and Karlfried Froehlich. *Pseudo Dionysius: The Complete Works, Classics of Western Spirituality.* New York: Paulist Press, 1987.

MacCoull, Leslie S. B. "The Coptic Verso of P. Berlo. Sarisch. 7." *Bulletin of the American Journal of the Papyrologists* 38 (2001): 39–50.

———. "Holy Family Pilgrimage in Late Antiquity Egypt, the Case of Qosqam." In *Akten des XII Internationalen Kongresses für Christliche Archäologie: Jahrbuch für Antike und Christentum* 20 (1995): 987–93.

———. "The Rite of the Jar: Apostasy and Reconciliation in the Medieval Coptic Orthodox Church." In *Peace and Negociation: Strategies for Coexistence in the Middle Ages and the Renaissance*, ed. D. Wolfthal, 145–62. Turnhout: Brepols, 2000.

———. "Three Coptic Papyri in the Duke University Collection." *Bulletin of the American Society of Papyrologist* 20 (1983): 139–41.

Mahmud, Salah. *Haqiqat Dhuhur al-'Athra'* (The Truth about the Virgin Apparition). Cairo: Egyptian Organization Authority, 2001.

Maspero, Jean. *Fouilles exécutées à Baouit.* Mémoires de l'Institut Français d'Archéologie Orientale, 35. Cairo: Institut Français d'Archéologie Orientale, 1931.

McEnerney, John I. *Cyril of Alexandria, Letters 1–50, 50–102, The Fathers of the Church 76, 77.* Washington, D.C.: Catholic University of America Press, 1987.

McGukin, John Anthony. *St Cyril of Alexandria: The Christological Controversy, Its History, Theology and Texts.* Supplements to Vigiliae Christianae, 23. Leiden: E. J. Brill, 1994.

Meinardus, Otto Fredriech August. *Christian Egypt Ancient and Modern.* 2nd ed. Cairo: American University in Cairo Press, 1977.

———. *Christian Egypt, Faith and Life.* Cairo: American University in Cairo Press, 1970.

———. *Coptic Saints and Pilgrimages.* Cairo: American University in Cairo Press, 2002.

———. "The Nestorians in Egypt: A Note on the Nestorians in Jerusalem." *Oriens Christianus* 51 (1967): 112–29.

———. "Der Segensgestus Christi im koptischen Altarziborium." *Archiv für Liturgiewissenschaft* 19 (1978): 106–13.

———. "A Study on the Canon Law of the Coptic Church." *Bulletin de la Société d'Archéologie Copte* 16 (1962): 231–42.

———. *Two Thousand Years of Coptic Christianity.* Cairo: American University in Cairo Press, 1999.

Merras, M. *The Origin of the Celebration of the Christian Feast of Epiphany, an Ideological, Cultural and Historical Study.* University of Joensuu Publications in the Humanities, 16. Joensuu, Finland: University of Joensuu, 1995.

Meyendorff, John. *Christ in Eastern Christian Thought.* New York: St. Vladimir's Seminary Press, 1975.

Migne, Jaques-Paul. *Patrologia Graeca.* Turnhout: Brepols, n.d.

Mimouni, Simon Claude. *Dormition et Assomption de Marie, Histoire des traditions anciennes, Théologie Historique.* Paris: Beauchesne, 1995.

Mina, Togo. *Le martyre d'Apa Epima.* Suppl Annales du Services des Antiquités de l'Egypte. Cairo: n.p., 1936.

Mingana, Alphonse. *Commentary of Theodore of Mopsuestia on the Lord's Prayer and on the Sacraments of Baptism and the Eucharist.* Woodbrooke Studies, 6. Cambridge: W. Heffer, 1933.

Mistrih, Vincent. *Pretiosa margarita de Scientiis Ecclesiasticis.* Studia Orientalia Christiana Aegyptiaca. Cairo: n.p., 1966.

Mossay, Justin. *Les fêtes de Noel et d'Epiphanie, d'après les sources cappadociennes du IV siècle.* Louvain: E. Peeters, 1965.

Mourant, John, and William Collinge. *Saint Augustine, Four Antipelagian Writings*. The Fathers of the Church, 86. Washington, D.C.: Catholic University of America, 1992.

Müller, Detlef G. *Die Engellehre der koptischen Kirche- Untersuchungen zur Geschichte der christlichen Frömmigkeit in Ägypten*. Wiesbaden: Harrassowitz, 1959.

Munier, Henri. *Catalogue Général du Musée du Caire*. Cairo: n.p., 1912.

Muyser, Jacob. "Le Psali copte pour la première heure du Samedi de la joie." *Le Muséon* 60 (1952): 175–84.

Nau, Francois. *Un Martyrologe et douze Ménologes Syriaques*. Patrologia Orientalis, 2, fasc.1. Paris: n.p., 1905.

Naz, Raoul. "Causes de béatification et de canonisation." In *Dictionnaire de droit canonique*, vol. 3, cols. 10–37. Paris: n.p., 1942.

Neale, John Mason. *The Patriarchate of Alexandria*. London: n.p., 1947.

O'Leary, De Lacy. *The Daily Office and Theotokia of the Coptic Church*. London: n.p., 1911.

———. *The Difnar (Antiphonarium) of the Coptic Church*. 3 vols. London: n.p., 1926–1928.

———. *Primary Guide to Coptic Literary Material*. London: n.p., 1938.

Opitz, H. G. *Urkunden zur Geschichte des arianischen Streites:318–328*. Berlin, 1934.

Orlandi, Tito. "Un codice Copto del 'Monastero bianco -Encomii di Severo di Antiochia, Marco Evangelista, Atanasio di Alessandria." *Le Muséon* 81 (1968): 351–405.

———. "Due fogli papiracei da Medinet Madi Fayum l'Historia Horsiesi." *Egitto e Vicino Oriente* 13 (1990): 109–26.

———. "Un encomio copto di Raffaele arcangelo 'Relatio Theophili.'" *Rivista del Studi Orientali* 47 (1974): 211–33.

———. "Un frammento copto di Teofilo di Alessandria." *Rivista degli Studi Orientali* 44 (1970): 23–26.

———. "Gregorio di Nisso nella letteratura Copte." *Vetera Christiana* 18 (1981): 334–37.

———. *Omelie Copte, Corona Patrum*. Turin: n.p., 1981.

———. *Shenute contra Origenistas*. Rome: Unione Accademica Nazionale, 1985.

———. *Storia della Chiesa di Alessandria*. Studio dell'Antichità, 27. Milan: n.p., 1968.

———. *Storia della Chiesa di Alessandria*. Studio dell'Antichità, 31. Milan: n.p., 1970.

———. "Teodosio di Alessandria nella letteratura copta." *Giornale italiano di filologia* 23 (1971): 175–85.

――― . *Testi Copti, Encomio di Atanasio, Vita di Atanasio*. Studio dell'Antichita, 21. Milan: n.p., 1968.

――― . "Theophilus of Alexandria in Coptic Literature." In *Studia Patristica*, vol. 16, ed. E. Livingstone, 100–104. Louvain: E. Peeters, 1975.

――― . "La tradizione Copta dell'Encomio di Atanasio di Gregorio Nazianzeno." *Le Muséon* 83 (1970): 351–66.

――― . "La versione copta (saidica) dell'Encomio di Pietro alessandrino." *Rivista degli Studi Orientali* 45 (1970): 151–75.

Orlandi, Tito, and Alberto Compagnano. *Vite dei monachi Phif e Longino.* Studio dell Antichita, 51. Milan: n.p., 1975.

Osborn, Eric. *The Philosophy of Clement of Alexandria*. Cambridge: University Press, 1957.

Palmieri, A. "La Procession du Saint-Esprit du Père et du Fils." In *Dictionnaire de théologie catholique*, vol. 5, cols. 762–829. Paris: n.p., 1913.

Partrick, Theodore H. *Traditional Egyptian Christianity: A History of the Coptic Orthodox Church.* Greensboro, N.C.: Fisher Park Press, 1996.

Pearson, Birger, and Tim Vivian, with D. B. Spanel. *Two Coptic Homilies Attributed to Saint Peter of Alexandria.* Rome: C.I.M., 1993.

Pelikan, Jaroslav. *The Christian Tradition*, vol. 2: *The Spirit of Eastern Christendom 600–1700.* Chicago: University of Chicago Press, 1974.

Pelikan, Jaroslav, and V. Hotchkiss. *Creeds and Confessions of Faith in the Christian Tradition.* New Haven, Conn.: Yale University Press, 2003.

Pernigotti, S., and D. Amaldi. *Pagine di un codice Copto-Arabo nel Museo Nazionale di S. Matteo a Pisa.* Supplemen, Egitto et Vicino Oriente 4 (1981). Studi e Ricerche, 3. Pisa: n.p., 1982.

Piankoff, Alexander. "La descente aux enfers dans les textes égyptiens et dans les apocryphes coptes." *Bulletin de la Société d'archéologie copte* 7 (1941): 33–46.

Pietersma, A., and S. Comstock. " A Sahidic Lectionary of the New Testament and the Psalm." *Bulletin of the American Society of Papyrologists* 29 (1992): 57–66.

Pleyte, W., and P. Boeser. *Manuscrits Coptes du Musée d'Antiquité des Pays-Bays à Leide publiés d'après des ordres du gouvernement.* Leiden: E. J. Brill, 1897.

Porcher, E. "La première homélie cathédrale de Sévère d'Antioche." *Revue de l'Orient Chrétien* 19 (1914) 69–78, 135–42.

――― . "Sévère d'Antioche dans la littérature Copte." *Revue de l'Orient Chrétien* 12 (1907): 119–24.

Poschmann, Bernhard. *Penance and the Anointing of the Sick.* New York: Herder & Herder, 1964.

Proverbio, D. V. "Le recensioni del Miracoli di Doroteo e Teopista." *Orientalia* 61 (1992): 78–91.

Quasten, Johannes. *Patrology, Spectrum.* 3 vols. Utrecht: n.p., 1956.

Quecke, Hans. "Ein Koptisch-Arabisches Horologion in der Bibliotheca des Katharinenklosters auf den Sinai." *Le Muséon* 78 (1965): 99–117.

——. "Neue Greichishe Parallelen zum koptischen Horologion." *Le Muséon* 78 (1964): 285–94.

——. *Untersuchungen zum Koptischen Stundengebet.* l'Institut Orientaliste de Louvain, 3. Louvain: n.p., 1970.

Quibell, James Edward. *Excavations in Saqqara.* Cairo: n.p., 1910–1912.

Rees, R., and B. Pelagius. *A Reluctant Heretic.* Woodbridge, Suffolk: Boydell Press, 1988.

Renoux, Arnold. *Le Codex Arménien Jérusalem 121.* Patrologia Orientalis, 35, Fascicule 1. Turnhout: Brepols, 1975.

Riedel, Wilhem. *Die Kirchenrechtsquellen des Patriarchats Alexandrien.* Leipzig: n.p., 1908.

Riedel, Wilhem, and Walter Ewing Crum. *The Canons of Athanasius of Alexandria.* London: n.p., 1904.

Richard, Marcel. "Les écrits de Théophile d'Alexandrie." *Le Muséon* 52 (1939): 33–50.

——. "L'introduction du mot 'Hypostase' dans la Théologie de l'incarnation." *Mélanges de Science Religieuse* 2 (1945): 5–32, 243–70.

Robertson, Maria. "A Coptic Melody Sung Interchangeably in Different Languages: Comparisons Thereof and Proposed Dating Therefore." In *Coptic Studies Acts of the Third International Congress of Coptic Studies,* ed. W. Godlewsiki, 365–71. Warsaw: PWN-Editions scientifiques de Pologne, 1990.

Rock, D. *The Church of Our Fathers.* 3 vols. London: n.p., 1849–1853.

Roll, Susan. *Towards the Origins of Christmas.* Louvain: E. Peeters, 1995.

Rordorf, Willy, and André Tuilier. *La Doctrine des douze apôtres (Didachè).* Sources chrétiennes, 248. Paris: Cerf, 1998.

Rorem, Paul. *Pseudo Dionysius, A Commentary on the Texts and an Introduction to Their Influence.* New York: Oxford University Press, 1993.

Rossi, I. *I papyri copti del Museo Egizio di Torin.* Turin: n.p., 1884, 1887.

Rouillard, P. *Histoire de la pénitence des origines à nos jours.* Paris: n.p., 1996.

Russel, N. *Cyril of Alexandria, The Early Church Fathers.* London: Routledge, 2000.

Samir, Khalil. "Le Saint Esprit dans la liturgie Copte." *Proche Orient Chrétien* 53 (2003): 1–24.

——. "Vie et oeuvres de Marc Ibn al-Qunbar." *Christianisme d'Egypte,* 123–58. Mélanges René-Georges Coquin, Cahiers de la Bibliothèque Copte, 9. Louvain: E. Peeters, 1995.

Sauget, Joseph-Marie. *Premières recherches sur l'origine et les caractéristiques des Synaxaires Melkites.* Subsidia Hagiographica, 45. Bruxelles: n.p., 1969.

Sauneron, Serge. "Les Hermitages d'Esna." In *Mémoires de l'Institut Français d'Archéologie Orientale*. 4 vols. Cairo: Institut Français d'Archéologie Orientale, 1974.

Schaff, Philip, and Henry Mace. *Nicene and Post Nicene Fathers of the Christian Church*. 14 vols., 2nd ed. Grand Rapids, Mich.: n.p., 1985.

Schmidt, Carl. *Der Erste Clemensbrief in altkoptischer Übersetzung, TU32/1*. Leipzig: n.p., 1908.

Sellew, Philip. "An Early Coptic Witness of the Dormitio Maria at Yale P. CT. YBR inv. 1788 revisited." *Bulletin of the American Society of Papyrologists* 37 (2000): 37–69.

Shoemaker, Stephen. *Ancient Traditions of the Virgin Mary's Dormition and Assumption*. Oxford Early Christian Studies. Oxford: Oxford University Press, 2004.

Simaika, Marcus, and Yassa 'Abd. Al-Masih. *Catalogue of the Coptic and Arabic Manuscripts in the Coptic Museum, the Patriarchate, the Principal Churches of Cairo and Alexandria and the Monasteries of Egypt*, vol 2, Fasc. I. Cairo: n.p., 1942.

Skalova, Zuzana, and Gawdat Gabra. *Icons of the Nile Valley*. Cairo: Longman, 2003.

Skalova, Zuzana, and Youhanna Nessim Youssef. "St. Mark the Evangelist with Severed Head, Unique Iconography in Egypt." *Byzantino-Slavica* 56 (1995): 721–34.

Sorabji, Richard. *Philoponus and the Rejection of Aristotelian Science*. London: Duckwork, 1987.

Souter, A. *An Unpublished Latin Fragment against the Apollinarists*, 39–49. Miscellanea F. Ehrle, Studi e testi, 37. Rome: n.p., 1924.

Spanel, David. "Two Fragmentary Saidic Coptic Texts Pertaining to Peter, Patriarch of Alexandria." *Bulletin de la Socété d'Archéologie Copte* 24 (1979–1982): 85–102.

Spicq, Ceslas. *Theological Lexicon of the New Testament*. Peabody, Mass.: Hendrickson, 1994.

Stead, Christopher. "Eusebius and the Council of Nicaea." *Journal of Theological Studies*, n.s. 24 (1974): 85–100.

Sterry, C. *The Fraction in the Eastern Eucharistic Liturgies*, ed. E. Livingstone, 81–87. Studia Patristica, 26. Louvain: E. Peeters, 1993.

Störk, Lothar. *Koptische Handschriten 4, Die Handschriften der Staatbibliothek zu Hamburg- Teil 1: Liturgische Handschriften*. Verzeichnis der Orientalischen Handschriften in Deutschland, Band XXI, 2. Stuttgart: Franz Steiner Verlag, 1996.

Stuckwisch, D. R. "The Basilian Anaphoras." In *Essays on Early Eastern Eucharistic Prayer*, ed. P. Bradshawp, 109–30. Collegeville, Minn.: Liturgical Press.

Taft, Robert. *The Liturgy of the Hours in East and West*. Collegeville, Minn.: Liturgical Press, 1986.

Tanner, Norman. *Decrees of the Ecumenical Councils*. London: Sheed & Ward, 1990.

Taylor, David. *The Syriac versions of the DE SPIRITU SANCTO by Basil of Caesarea*. Corpus Scriptorum Christianorum Orientalium, 577. Louvain: E. Peeters, 1999.

Teule, Herman G. B. *Gregory Barhebraeus Ethicon—Mêmrâ I*. Corpus Scriptorum Christianorum Orientalium, 535, Syr 219. Louvain: E. Peeters, 1993.

Till, Walter, and Johannes Leipold. *Der Koptische Text der Kirchenordnung Hippolytus (TU 58)*. Berlin: n.p., 1954.

Treu, U. "Amos VII, 14, Schenute und der Physiologus." *Novum Testamentum* 10 (1969): 234–40.

Tukhi, Ruphail. *The Book of the Three Anaphoras which Are Those of Saint Basil, Saint Gregory the Theologian and Saint Cyril with Other Holy Prayers*. Rome: n.p., 1736.

Turner, P. *The Meaning and Practice of Confirmation Perspectives from a Sixteenth Century Controversy*. New York: Peter Lang, 1987.

Urbaniak-Walczak, Katarzyna. "Zwei verschiedene Rezensionen der Homilie über die Auferstehung der jungfrau Maria von Theophilus von Alexandrien." *Göttinger Mizsellen* 101 (1988): 73–74.

van der Vliet, Jacques. "S Pachome et S Athanase un entretien apocryphe." *Analecta Bollandiana* 110 (1992): 21–27.

Van Esbroeck, Michel. "La dormition chez les Coptes." In *Actes du IV Congrès Copte-Louvain-la-Neuve, 5–10 septembre 1988*, ed. M. H. Rassart-Debergh and J. Ries, 436–45. l'Institut Orientaliste de Louvain, 40–41. Leuven: n.p., 1992.

———. "Fragments sahidiques du Panégyrique de Grégoire le Thaumaturge par Grégoire de Nysse." *Orientalia Lovansiensa Periodica* 6, no. 7 (1975–1976): 555–68.

Van Lantschoot, Arnold. "L'Assomption de la sainte vierge chez les Coptes." *Gregorianum* 27 (1946): 439–526.

———. "Une lettre de Sévère d'Antioche à Théognoste." *Le Muséon* 69 (1946) 469–77.

———. "Lettre de St. Athanase au sujet de l'amour et de la tempérance." *Le Muséon* 40 (1927): 265–92.

———. "A propos du Physiologus." In *Coptic Studies in Honor of Walter Ewing Crum*, 339–63. Bulletin of the Byzantine Institute, 2. Boston: Byzantine Institute, 1950.

———. *Les questions de Théodore*. Studi e Testi, 192. Vatican: n.p., 1957.

van Oort, Johannes, and Johannes Roldnaus, eds. *Chalkedon: Geschichtre und Aktualität. Studien zur Rezeption der Christologischen Formel von Chalkedon.* Louvain: E. Peeters, 1998.

Vansleb, Jean Michel. *Nouvelle relation en forme de journal d'un voyage fait en Egypte en 1672.* Paris: n.p., 1677.

Veilleux, Armand. *Pachomian Koinonia.* Cistercien Studies Series, 45. Kalamazoo, Mich.: Cistercian Publications, 1980.

Viaud, Gérard. "La Procession des deux Fêtes de la Croix et du Dimanche des Rameaux dans l'Eglise Copte." *Bulletin de la Socété d'Archéologie Copte* 19 (1967–1968): 211–26.

———. "Le quidra dans la tradition Egyptienne." *Bulletin de la Société d'Archéologie Copte* 37 (1998): 117–20.

Villecourt, Lucien. "Les Observances liturgiques et la discipline du jeûne dans l'église copte." *Le Muséon* 36–38 (1923–1925).

Vivian, Tim. *St. Peter of Alexandria, Bishop and Martyr.* Studies in Antiquity and Christianity. Philadelphia: Fortress Press, 1988.

von Harnack Adolf. *History of Dogma.* 3 vols. London: Williams and Norgate, 1897–1912.

Wadi, Awad. "Abu al-Barakat Ibn Kabar, Misbah al-Zulmah (cap. 18: il diginuno e la settimanta santa)." *Studia Oorientalia Christiana Collectanea* 34 (2001): 233–322.

Wegman, Herman. *Christian Worship in East and West—A Study Guide to Liturgical History,* trans. Gordon W. Lathrop. New York: Pueblo, 1985.

Weinandy, Thomas G., and Daniel Keating (eds.). *The Theology of Saint Cyril of Alexandria: A Critical Appreciation.* London: T. & T. Clark, 2003.

Williams, R. "Arius." *Heresy and Tradition.* London: Darton, 1987.

Winkler, D. "Miaphysitism: A New Term for Use in the History of Dogma and in Ecumenical Theology." *Harp* 3 (1997): 33–40.

Wipszycka, Ewa. "Les Confréries dans la vie religieuse de l'Egypte chrétienne." In *Proceedings of the XII International Congress of Papyrology,* Toronto, 1970, 511–25.

———. *Etudes sur le Christianisme dans l'Egypte de l'antiquité tardive.* Studia Ephemeridis Augustinianum, 52. Rome: n.p., 1996.

———. "Les ordres mineurs dans l'Eglise d'Egypte au IV-VIII siècle." *Journal of the Juristic Papyrology* 23 (1993): 181–215.

———. *Les Resources et les activités économiques des églises en Egypte du IVe au VIIe siècle.* Brussels: Fondation Egyptologique de la reine Elisabeth 1972.

Witakowswki, Wolfgang. *Pseudo-Dionysius of Tel-Mahre, Chronicle Part III.* Translated Texts for Historians, 22. Liverpool: University Press, 1996.

Woolley, Reginald Maxwell. *Coptic Offices: Society for Promoting Christian Knowledge*. London: McMillan, 1930.

Worrell, William. *The Coptic Manuscripts in the Freer Collection*. University of Michigan Studies, Humanistics Series Vol. 10. New York: n.p., 1923; Reprint, 1972.

Yassa 'Abd Al-Masih. "Doxologies in the Coptic Church." *Bulletin de la Société d'Archéologie Copte* 4 (1938): 97–113; 8 (1942): 31–61; 11 (1946): 95–158.

———. "The Hymn of the Three Children in the Furnace." *Bulletin de la Société d'Archéologie Copte* 12 (1946–1947): 1–15.

———. "Remarks on the Psalis of the Coptic Church." *Bulletin de l'Institut des Etudes Coptes* 1 (1958): 85–100.

Youhanna Nessim Youssef. "Ancient and Modern Legends Concerning the Holy Family in Egypt." *Coptic Church Review* 22, no. 3 (2001): 71–76.

———. "The Arabic Life of Severus of Antioch attributed to Athanasius." *Patrologia Orientalis 49 Fascicule 4 N 220*. Preface by Pauline Allen. Pontificio Istituto Orientale Roma. Turnhout: Brepols, 2004.

———. "Arabic Manuscripts of the Philalethes of Severus of Antioch." *Proche Orient Chrétien* 51 (2001): 261–66.

———. "An Arabic Text Attributed to Severus of Antioch on the Robber." *Bulletin de la Société d'Archéologie Copte* 41 (2002): 53–69.

———. "La christianisation des fêtes osiriaques." *Bulletin de la Société d'Archéologie Copte* 29 (1990): 147–53.

———. "Consecration of the Myron at Saint Macarius Monastery (MS. 106Lit.)." *Coptica* 2 (2003): 106–21.

———. "A Contribution to the Coptic Biography of Severus of Antioch" In *Coptic Studies on the Threshold of a New Millennium: Proceedings of the Seventh International Congress of Coptic Studies, Leiden, 27 August–2 September 2000*, vol. 1, ed. Mat Immerzeel and Jacques van der Vliet, 413–26. Louvain: E. Peeters, 2004.

———. "Coptic Fragment of a Letter of Severus of Antioch." *Oriens Christianus* 42 (2003): 116–22.

———. "Coptic Monastic Sites in the Seventh and Eighth Centuries According to a Homily Ascribed to Severus of Antioch." *Coptic Church Review* 23, no. 4 (2002): 103–7.

———. "De nouveau, la christianisation des dates des fêtes de l'ancienne religion égyptienne." *Bulletin de la Société d'Archéologie Copte* 31 (1992): 109–13.

———. "The Encomium of St. Philotheus Ascribed to Severus of Antioch." *Coptica* 1 (2002): 169–221.

———. "Les fêtes d'été et les fêtes d'hiver dans le calendrier copte." *Aula Orientalis* 11 (1993): 173–78.

———. "Un fragment d'un lectionnaire sur parchemin." *Göttinger Miszellen* 149 (1995): 105–9.

———. "A Homily on Severus of Antioch by a Bishop of Assiut." *Patrologia Orientalis 50 Fascicule 1 N 222*. Pontificio Istituto Orientale Roma. Turnhout: Brepols, 2006.

———. "The Homily on the Archangel Michael Attributed to Severus of Antioch Revisited." *Bulletin de la Société d'Archéologie Copte* 42 (2003): 103–17.

———. *Jean évêque d'Assiut, de Manfalut et d'Abu Tig et ses activités littéraires*, ed. C. Cannuyer, 311–18. Etudes Coptes 8, Cahiers de la Bibliothèque Copte, 13. Paris: Lille, 2003.

———. "Letter of Severus of Antioch to Anastasia the Deaconess." *Bulletin de la Société d'Archéologie Copte* 40 (2001): 126–36.

———. "Nicodème auteur des psalies." *Orientalia Christiana Periodica* 60 (1994): 625–33.

———. "Note sur la date de la traduction d'une doxologie Copte." *Göttinger Miszellen* 166, (1998): 91–93.

———. "Notes on the Cult of Severus of Antioch in Egypt." *Ephemerides Liturgicae* 115 (2001): 101–7.

———. "Notes on the Traditions Concerning the Trisagion." *Parole de l'Orient* 29 (2004): 147–59.

———. "A propos du nombre des icônes dans quelques Eglises Coptes." *Bulletin de la Société d'Archéologie Copte* 39 (2000): 251–56.

———. "Quelques allusions au physiologus." *Göttinger Miszellen* 135 (1993): 53–58.

———. "The Quotations of Severus of Antioch in the Book of the Confessions of the Fathers." *Ancient Near Eastern Studies* 40 (2003): 178–229.

———. "Recherches d'hymnographie copte: Nicodème et Sarkis." *Orientalia Christiana Periodica* 64 (1998): 383–402.

———. "Recommendations to the Priests Severus of Antioch or Severus of Ashmunain." *Journal of Coptic Studies* 4 (2002): 187–95.

———. "Une relecture des glorifications coptes." *Bulletin de la Société d'Archéologie Copte* 34 (1995): 77–83.

———. "Une relecture des Theotokies Copte." *Bulletin de la Société d'Archéologie Copte* 36 (1997): 153–70.

———. "Les rituels de la reconsécration." In *Ägypten und Nubien in spätantiker und christlicher Zeit, Akten des 6. Internationalen Koptologenkongresses*, ed. Stephen Emmel, M. Krause, S.G. Richter, and S. Schaten, 511–15. Sprachen und Kulturen des Christlichen Orients, Band 6. Wiesbaden: Reichert, 1999.

——. "Severus of Antioch in Scetis." *Ancient Near Eastern Studies* 43 (2006): 141–62.

——. "Severus of Antioch in the Coptic Liturgical Book." *Journal of Coptic Studies* 6 (2004): 141–50.

——. "Severus of Antioch in the Coptic Theotokia." In *Prayer and Spirituality in the Early Church: Liturgy and Life*, vol. 3, ed. G. Dunn Neil and L. Cross, 93–108. Sydney: n.p., 2003.

——. "Severus of Antioch in the History of the Patriarchs of the Coptic Church." *Parole de l'Orient* 28 (2003): 435–58.

——. "Severus of Antioch Seen by Modern Coptic Historians." *Coptic Church Review* 23, no. 4 (2003): 98–106.

——. "Some Patristic Quotations from Severus of Antioch in Coptic and Arabic Texts." *Ancient Near Eastern Studies* 40 (2003): 238–47.

——.Un témoin méconnu de la littérature copte." *Bulletin de la Société d'Archéologie Copte* 32 (1993): 139–47.

——. "Two Liturgical Quotations from Coptic Hagiographical Texts." *Abr Nahrain* 35 (1998): 145–49.

——. "Two Folios of the Marriage Rite in Sahidic Dialect." *Göttinger Miszellen* 202 (2004): 103–8.

Youhanna, Nessim Youssef, and Martyrus al-Suriani. "The Psalis of Saint John Kame." *Bulletin de la Société d'Archéologie Copte* 39 (2000): 257–65.

Zanetti, Ugo. "Bohairic Liturgical Manuscript." *Orientalia Christiana Periodica* 61 (1995): 65–94.

——. "La distribution des psaumes dans l'horologion copte." *Orientalia Christiana Periodica* 56 (1990): 323–69.

——. "Esquisse d'une typologie des Euchologes Coptes Bohaïriques." *Le Muséon* 100 (1987): 407–18.

——. "Horologion Copte et vêpres byzantines." *Le Muséon* 102 (1989): 237–54.

——. *Les lectionnaires coptes annuels: Basse-Egypte.* l'Institut Orientaliste de Louvain, 33. Louvain: n.p., 1985.

——. "La vie de saint Jean Higoumène de Scété au VIIe siècle." *Analecta Bollandiana* 114 (1996): 273–405.

XII. WOMEN

Behlmer, Heike. "Women and the Holy in Coptic Hagiography." In *Actes du Huitième Congrès International d'Études Coptes, Paris, 28 juin–3 juillet 2004*, vol. 1, ed. Nathalie Bosson and Anne Boud'hors, 405–16. Orientalia Lovaniensia Analecta, 163. Louvain: E. Peeters, 2007.

Chaillot, Christine. "The Diaconate of Women in the Coptic Orthodox Church." *Orthodox Outlook* 3 (1990): 15ff.

Elm, Susana. *"Virgin of God." The Making of Asceticism in Late Antiquity.* Oxford: Clarendon Press, 1994.

Van Doorn-Harder, Nelly. "Discovering New Roles: Coptic Nuns and Church Revival." In *Between Desert and City: The Coptic Orthodox Church Today*, ed. Nelly van Doorn-Harder and Kari Vogt, 83–98. Institute for Comparative Research in Human Culture. Oslo: Novus forlag, 1997.

Wilfong, Terry G. *Women of Jeme. Lives in a Coptic Town in Late Antique Egypt.* Ann Arbor: University of Michigan Press, 2002.

About the Author and Contributors

ABOUT THE AUTHOR

Gawdat Gabra is the former director of the Coptic Museum, Cairo, a member of the board of the Society of Coptic Archaeology, and chief editor of the St. Mark Foundation for Coptic History Studies. He is the author, coauthor, and editor of numerous books related to the literary and material culture of Egyptian Christianity, including *Be Thou There: The Holy Family's Journey in Egypt* (2001), *Coptic Monasteries: Egypt's Monastic Art and Architecture* (2002), *Christianity and Monasticism in the Fayoum Oasis* (2005), *The Treasures of Coptic Art in the Coptic Museum and Churches of Old Cairo* (2007), and *The Churches of Egypt* (2007). Gabra taught at American and Egyptian universities. He is currently a visiting professor of Coptic studies at Claremont Graduate University, California.

ABOUT THE CONTRIBUTORS

Birger A. Pearson is emeritus professor of religious studies at the University of California, Santa Barbara. He is the author or editor of numerous books on Gnosticism and Egyptian Christianity, including *The Roots of Egyptian Christianity* (1986) and *Gnosticism, Judaism, and Egyptian Christianity* (1990).

Mark N. Swanson is the Harold S. Vogelaar Professor of Christian-Muslim Studies and Interfaith Relations at the Lutheran School of Theology at Chicago. He has also taught at Luther Seminary in St. Paul, Minnesota (1998–2006) and at the Evangelical Theological Seminary in Cairo, Egypt (1984–1998). His scholarly interests include the study of Arabic Christian literature and early Christian-Muslim encounter, as well as the history of the Egyptian Christian community in the Middle Ages. He recently coedited *The Encounter of Eastern Christianity with Early Islam* (2006) with Emmanouela Grypeou and David Thomas, and is now finishing a book entitled *The Coptic Papacy in Islamic Egypt.*

Youhanna Nessim Youssef is a senior research associate at the Center for Early Christian Studies at the Australian Catholic University. He is also senior research fellow of the Centre for Classics and Archaeology at the University of Melbourne. He taught at the High Institute of Coptic Studies in Cairo (1993–1996). His scholarly interests include the study of patristic texts, especially of Severus of Antioch, the Coptic liturgy, as well as Coptic hagiography. He recently edited *A Homily on Severus of Antioch by a Bishop of Assiut* (2006), *The Arabic life of Severus of Antioch Attributed to Athanasius* (2004), and is now finishing a book entitled *Le manuscrit 106 Liturgie* with Ugo Zanetti.